NOVELL'S

NetWare® 6 Administrator's Handbook

NOVELL'S

NetWare® 6 Administrator's Handbook

KELLEY J. P. LINDBERG AND JEFFREY L. HARRIS

Novell.

Novell Press, Provo, UT

Novell's NetWare® 6 Administrator's Handbook

Published by
Wiley Publishing, Inc.
909 Third Avenue
New York, NY 10022
www.wiley.com

Copyright © 2002 by Novell, Inc., Indianapolis, Indiana

Published by Wiley Publishing, Inc., Indianapolis, Indiana
Published simultaneously in Canada

For general information on our other products and services or to obtain technical support, please contact our Customer Care Department within the U.S. at 800-762-2974, outside the U.S. at 317-572-3993, or fax 317-572-4002.

Wiley also publishes its books in a variety of electronic formats. Some content that appears in print may not be available in electronic books.

Library of Congress Cataloging-in-Publication Data:
Library of Congress Control Number: 2001099736
ISBN: 0-7645-4882-4
Manufactured in the United States of America
10 9 8 7 6 5 4 3 2

Welcome to Novell Press

Novell Press, the world's leading provider of networking books, is the premier source for the most timely and useful information in the networking industry. Novell Press books cover fundamental networking issues as they emerge — from today's Novell and third-party products to the concepts and strategies that will guide the industry's future. The result is a broad spectrum of titles for the benefit of those involved in networking at any level: end user, department administrator, developer, systems manager, or network architect.

Novell Press books are written by experts with the full participation of Novell's technical, managerial, and marketing staff. The books are exhaustively reviewed by Novell's own technicians and are published only on the basis of final released software, never on prereleased versions.

Novell Press is an exciting partnership between two companies at the forefront of the knowledge and communications revolution. The Press is implementing an ambitious publishing program to develop new networking titles centered on the current versions of NetWare, GroupWise, BorderManager, ManageWise, and networking integration products.

Novell Press books are translated into several languages and sold throughout the world.

Ryan Johnson
Publisher
Novell Press, Novell, Inc.

Novell Press

Publisher
Ryan Johnson

Wiley Publishing

Acquisitions Editor
Katie Feltman

Project Editor
Alex Miloradovich

Technical Editor
Warren Wyrostek

Copy Editor
Alex Miloradovich

Editorial Managers
Ami Frank Sullivan and
Kyle Looper

Project Coordinator
Maridee Ennis

Graphics and Production Specialists
Beth Brooks, Joyce Haughey,
Jacqueline Schneider,
Betty Schulte, Rashell Smith,
Erin Zeltner

Quality Control Technicians
Dave Faust, John Greenough,
Marianne Santy, Charles Spencer

Proofreading and Indexing
TECHBOOKS Production
Services

About the Authors

Kelly J. P. Lindberg, an award winning author, worked at Novell for more than eleven years before leaving to become a full-time writer. While at Novell, she was the senior program manager for NetWare 3.12, NetWare 4.1, intraNetWare, and other Novell products. Ms. Lindberg, a CNE, has written numerous articles and many other Novell Press books about NetWare products, including all the books in the NetWare Administrator's Handbook series and Novell's Introduction to intraNetWare. She makes her home in Utah, and can be reached at lindberg@inconnect.com.

Jeffrey L. Harris, a seven-year veteran of Novell, has worked throughout the Novell organization, including stints in Novell Technical Services, Major Market Sales Operations, Technical/Product Marketing and Contract Management. Mr. Harris has written books, articles, marketing collateral, and technical white papers on several products and technologies, including: directories, network and Internet security, network protocols, and proxy caching. Mr. Harris has a B.S. in Computer Science and a Masters of Business Administration (MBA).

For my mom and dad, who continually show me that with a sense of humor and a sense of adventure, you can accomplish nearly anything.

— Kelley J. P. Lindberg

For my family — Susan, Tyler, Rylee, Austin, and Joshua — without whom none of this would matter: May I one day be capable of living up to the examples that they set every day.

— Jeffery L. Harris

Preface

As the administrator of a NetWare 6 network, you are faced with a host of new features and technologies that extend the business value of NetWare like never before. You not only have to understand these technologies, but you need to know how to make them work together so your network runs smoothly. To do this, you can arm yourself with information from many different resources: architecture manuals, online documentation, magazines, books, technical Web sites, and even the phone numbers of your most knowledgeable acquaintances. With all the powerful features and flexibility built into NetWare 6, you may need to tap all these resources — at one time or another — to properly manage your network.

When you are administering a network, however, there are three principal tasks, based on a more limited body of information, that occupy most of your time:

▶ Installation

▶ Configuration

▶ Maintenance

As a result, you usually don't want to wade through periodicals, Web sites, or product docs searching for that one detail you can't quite remember. Instead, you just need quick access to information about the technology, concept, or utility that will help you get the job done. Novell's NetWare 6 Administrator's Handbook has been written with those needs in mind.

Filled with concept overviews, installation procedures, configuration options, reference material and maintenance tips, this handbook can be your quick reference to the daily tasks associated with NetWare 6. The Instant Access pages at the beginning of each chapter help you immediately identify the information, utilities, and commands necessary to perform common tasks. So keep this book handy. It will help you spend less time looking for information and more time managing your network.

What's New in NetWare 6

Even if you have been working with NetWare 5 or NetWare 5.1 you are going to see a lot of new features in NetWare 6. That's because NetWare 6 is finishing the journey that began with NetWare 5 — to redefine NetWare as a comprehensive platform for delivering a single view of all your networks and data sources, One Net. All the new features in NetWare 6 are designed to meet three user requirements:

- *My personal Net experience should go where I go.*
- *Data location and storage medium are completely transparent to me.*
- *The data important to me is always available, regardless of location, time, or access method.*

Here are just a few examples of new NetWare 6 features that help accomplish these three goals:

- **Novell Storage Service (NSS) 3.0.** Extends the storage management features of NetWare to support disk pools that span servers, user and directory space quotas, secure data removal with data shredding, and volume sizes up to 8TB (Terabytes).

- **iFolder.** Lets today's networks escape the restrictions of LAN architecture and deliver simple, location-independent access to a user's data.

- **The Novell Native File Access Pack.** Clients can now access NetWare volumes using their native file systems, such as Windows CIFS, Macintosh AFP, and Linux/UNIX NFS.

- **Novell NetDrive.** Gives Windows workstations a "thin client" method for accessing NetWare 6 files and directories without the need for the entire Novell client.

- **Apache Web server.** NetWare 6 includes a port of the industry-leading Apache Web server, which provides the foundation for all the new Web-based services in NetWare 6. It can be loaded side-by-side with the NetWare Enterprise Web server so as not to burden your eCommerce server.

- **NetWare Web access.** Provides secure access to file, print, and email services via any modern Web browser. Special client software or VPN connections are not required!

- **NetStorage.** NetWare 6 includes a fully functional WebDAV server that allows you to access and collaborate on files using only Internet standards.

- **Clustering technology.** NetWare 6 offers the ultimate in high availability computing with clustering technology that supports clusters of up to 32 different servers.

- **Multi-processor support.** Greatly increase the performance of your NetWare services with the multi-processor support in NetWare 6.

- **Advanced user authentication services.** Now available in NetWare 6, with the inclusion of Novell Modular Authentication Services (NMAS). Administrators can choose password-based authentication, certificate-based authentication, or multi-factor authentication that requires both a password and a certificate.

- **Expanded printing capabilities.** Now users can easily print from any location to any printer, even across the Internet, using the new Internet Printing Protocol (IPP) support in Novell Distributed Print Services (NDPS).

- **NetWare Remote Manager.** Provides a new level of administrator access. Use any NetWare utility, safely and securely, from any location, to keep your network in top shape.

You will also note that some legacy NetWare features are no longer offered in NetWare 6. Some of these include:

- Queue-based printing is no longer offered. It has been replaced by NDPS and iPrint.

- The ZEN for Clients Starter Pack has been removed from NetWare 6.

- Support for DOS and Windows 3.x clients has been removed from NetWare 6. This includes such DOS configuration files as NET.CFG.

- Support for many legacy client command line utilities, such as NPRINT, have been removed from the NetWare 6 client.

What's Covered in This Book

The major components and features of NetWare 6 are explained in the chapters and appendices of this book. To help better organize the chapters for a logical flow, they have been organized into parts consistent with Novell's stated design goals for the release of NetWare 6. Chapters within each section will present the features that help achieve these goals.

Section I: Getting Started

▶ **Chapter 1** details the various installation options available with NetWare 6, including new Server Installation, Server Upgrade, and Server Migration Wizards. It also covers the installation of on-line documentation.

▶ **Chapter 2** takes you through the install and upgrade procedures for the various NetWare clients that ship with NetWare 6. It also introduces Native File Access Pack as a new way to access files without using the traditional Novell client.

▶ **Chapter 3** introduces the suite of management tools used in Novell networks. This includes ConsoleOne as the standard management interface, along with a new set of Web-based management tools. These include Web Manager, NetWare Remote Manager, iMonitor, and iManage.

Section II: Delivering One Net

▶ **Chapter 4** describes the console-based utilities and commands available with NetWare 6. It also presents valuable information for optimizing and maintaining your NetWare servers.

▶ **Chapter 5** gives you an overview of Novell eDirectory architecture and major components. It also introduces basic eDirectory administrative tasks and the regular maintenance operations that will keep the directory running smoothly.

▶ **Chapter 6** explains how eDirectory is used to effectively manage network users and groups. It also presents the fundamentals of network security and presents the options available to you for making your network safe from attack — both intentional and accidental.

▶ **Chapter 7** presents the powerful printing services available on NetWare 6, including both Novell Distributed Print Services (NDPS) and the new iPrint services that leverage the Internet Printing Protocol (IPP) to deliver true "print from anywhere to anywhere" capability.

Section III: Providing Transparent Storage and Access

▶ **Chapter 8** introduces the powerful new release of Novell storage services, which makes it possible to create your own storage area network without spending vast amounts of money on a secondary architecture. It presents the new NetStorage technology that permits Web-based access of NetWare files. Finally, it describes Storage Management Services (SMS) as the foundation for NetWare 6 backup/restore operations.

▶ **Chapter 9** explores the foundations for NetWare 6 Web servers, including the new Apache Web server for NetWare and Novell Enterprise Web server.

▶ **Chapter 10** covers NetWare file access capabilities — specifically, the new NetWare Web services suite, including NetStorage, NetDrive, iFolder, NetWare Web access, NetWare Web Search server, and FTP server.

Section IV: Enabling Constant Availability

▶ **Chapter 11** explains the ins and outs of multiprocessor support in NetWare 6, including installation, configuration, and available multiprocessor services.

▶ **Chapter 12** introduces the newly expanded NetWare clustering services with support for up to 32-way clustering.

Appendices

▶ **Appendix A** lists all supported DSTRACE commands used to manage eDirectory. It also describes the most common eDirectory error codes and provides information on how to troubleshoot these errors.

- **Appendix B** provides a brief overview of NetWare basics and a comprehensive set of planning worksheets.
- **Appendix C** provides information on a variety of additional resources you can turn to for more help or information — user groups, Novell's Web site, other books, publications, etc.

What This Book Is Not

Novell's NetWare 6 Administrator's Handbook is not designed to introduce you to the world of data networking. In order to cover the broad feature set in NetWare 6, it is assumed that you, as an IT professional, are familiar with the underlying concepts, technologies, and protocols upon which today's networks are built. In order to keep the size of this book manageable and to optimize its usefulness as a quick-reference handbook, the authors provide only brief introductions to basic concepts, as necessary to introduce features, but they have not written the book to be a complete reference work.

You most likely have an existing network of some sort into which you are, or will soon be, introducing NetWare 6. You know the network architectures, topologies, protocols, and clients with which you will be working. *Novell's NetWare 6 Administrator's Handbook* shows you how to integrate the benefits of NetWare 6 into your existing environment quickly and efficiently.

Acknowledgments

As is usually the case, this book wouldn't have been possible without the willing collaboration of many who provided information, support, and encouragement. Here is where we get to shine a light on their contributions.

First and foremost, many thanks to Robyn Openshaw-Pay, for managing our relationship with Hungry Minds and running interference. Without her, this book would have had a hard time getting off the ground.

Thanks to the folks at Hungry Minds: our editor, Alex Miloradovich, who has been the definition of responsive and professional, even when we were throwing curves at him; Warren Wyrostek, who kept us honest with an excellent technical review; Maridee Ennis, for coordinating the book's production; Katie Feltman, who had to deal with sometimes irrational writers to get this project out the door; and Ami Sullivan, who expertly managed the editorial staff.

There are many people at Novell who have contributed to the success of this book:

Thanks to David Rowley, Jeff Fischer, and Tom Christensen for giving us access to the hardware and support we needed to create a working NetWare 6 environment.

Thanks to David Chenworth, for his insights into Apache Web server for NetWare and Enterprise Web server.

Thanks to Corby Morris, for taking the time to show us the power of NetStorage.

Thanks to Darcy Partridge and Earle Wells, for sharing their knowledge of NFAP and Novell clients.

Thanks to several of the instructional designers in Novell Education, Jason Corry, Dave Coughanour, Chris Grayson, Diana Nelson, and Robb Tracy. They broke the path we followed to understand the many new features and technologies of NetWare 6.

And last but not least, thanks for Stephanie Galt, in Novell System Test, for keeping us up on the latest builds and issues as NetWare 6 progressed toward its release.

Contents at a Glance

Contents

Part II   Delivering One Net   135

Chapter 4   NetWare 6 Server Management   137

Chapter 5   Novell eDirectory Management   177

Chapter 10   NetWare File Access   413

Part IV   Enabling Constant Availability   471

Chapter 11   NetWare Multiprocessor Support   473

PART I

Getting Started

In This Part

For some of you this is where your NetWare journey begins. Others have most likely been working with NetWare for many years, and this is another upgrade of the industry's premier net operating system. Yet others lie somewhere in between these two extremes.

One of the first things you will recognize is that NetWare is not a typical, flashy application server. NetWare was designed for the specific tasks of network storage, file sharing, and print sharing. It operates as part of the network "plumbing," and it is performing at its best when people don't even realize it's there. Basic design decisions were made to make NetWare the best at performing these tasks, and nearly 20 years later it is still the best operating system on the market for performing critical net operations. The capabilities of a specialized net operating system such as NetWare continue to prove their worth in the face of ever-mounting evidence that a general-purpose operating system is incapable of delivering the necessary levels of performance and security required by today's mission-critical net environments.

Global business networks and the Internet now require distributed net storage, transparent access to net data, and a consistent net experience, regardless of location or access method. These are all requirements that are well within the original design vision for NetWare, so Novell has effectively extended that design to deliver these capabilities in the form of NetWare 6.

The three chapters comprising Part I of this book begin by taking you through the NetWare 6 installation process. They introduce the major components of a NetWare net — namely the NetWare server and the NetWare client — and describe the common administrative tasks necessary to keep them on an even keel.

CHAPTER I

NetWare 6 Installation

Instant Access

Preparing to install

There are four recommended tasks to prepare your network for NetWare 6:

- ► Back up your data
- ► Update eDirectory (if necessary)
- ► Update eDirectory schema (if necessary)
- ► Update Certificate Authority object in eDirectory

Installing

- ► To install a new server, run INSTALL from the root of the NetWare 6 Operating System CD-ROM.

Upgrading

- ► *NetWare 4.x or 5.x* — To upgrade to NetWare 6 choose one of these options:
  - • Perform an Accelerated Upgrade by running ACCUPG.exe from the root of the NetWare 6 Operating System CD-ROM. This requires that you first copy the entire NetWare 6 Operating System CD-ROM to a NetWare server that will function as the Staging server.
  - • Perform an In-Place upgrade by running INSTALL from the root of the NetWare 6 Operating System CD-ROM.
  - • Perform a server migration by installing and running NetWare Migration Wizard from a client workstation. This utility is available on the NetWare 6 Operating System CD-ROM (\PRODUCTS\MIGRTWZD.EXE).

- ► *NetWare 3* — To upgrade to NetWare 6, perform a server migration by installing and running NetWare Migration Wizard from a client workstation. This utility is available on the NetWare 6 Operating System CD-ROM (\PRODUCTS\MIGRTWZD.EXE).

- ► *NT v3.51 or v4* — To upgrade to NetWare 6, perform a server migration by installing and running NetWare Migration Wizard from a client workstation. This utility is available on the NetWare 6 Operating System CD-ROM (\PRODUCTS\MIGRTWZD.EXE).

Getting Ready for NetWare 6

Whether you are building a new network with NetWare 6 or installing it into an existing network, there are certain preparations you should make so the installation goes as smoothly as possible.

For those of you creating a new network from the ground up, you have the opportunity to do all the little things that will make that network easier to manage down the road. Carefully consider your choices of cabling, protocols, addressing, naming schemes, and access methods, because these are the network building blocks that are very difficult to change once they have been implemented. Factor in issues such as potential company growth, mergers or acquisitions, reorganizations, and all the other business considerations of the twenty-first century. If you don't, your network may lack the flexibility necessary to adapt to changes at the organizational level.

All of these factors will then have to be weighed against the realities of your budget. There will be inevitable compromises, but this type of advanced planning will make sure those compromises don't come back to haunt you once the network is running.

TIP

As a network administrator, you may already be familiar with the network planning process. However, if you are interested in learning more about good network design techniques, see Appendix B for some additional reference materials.

Server Hardware Planning

You will need to consider the following as you prepare the server hardware for the NetWare 6 installation:

- *Processor speed*: The server must have a Pentium II processor or higher. Novell also recommends Pentium III 700 MHz processors for multi-processor servers.

- *CD-ROM drive*: The server must have a CD-ROM drive that can read ISO9660 CD-ROMs. Novell also recommends using a CD-ROM drive that is compatible with the El Torito specification so that you can boot the server directly from the CD.

- *Server memory*: A NetWare 6 server should have a minimum of 256MB of system memory (RAM). Novell recommends 512MB memory for best operation.

▶ *Types of storage adapters and devices*: Know the name of the server's storage controllers (SCSI board, IDE controller, etc.) and the types of devices (hard disks, CD-ROM/DVD drives, tape drive, etc.) attached to those controllers.

▶ *Size of hard disks*: There are two considerations when determining the appropriate size of your server hard disk(s): The DOS partition and the NetWare partition. The DOS partition is a portion of the hard disk reserved for DOS system files, server startup files, and any other DOS utilities you want to store on the server. The server should have a DOS partition of at least 200MB, but a good rule of thumb is to start with the minimum and then add 1MB for every MB of server RAM installed. That way you will be able to do a core dump to the DOS partition if necessary.

TIP

The remainder of the disk is used for NetWare partition(s), which will store network data and applications. You should plan on a minimum of 2GB for your NetWare partition — for the SYS volume. Novell recommends 4GB to give additional room for network data and other applications. Your best bet is to over-estimate wherever possible so you don't have to worry about adding disk space shortly after installing the server.

▶ *Network adapters*: Know the type of network adapters installed in the server and have a copy of the latest LAN drivers available. Also, you should note the adapter's settings and the frame type(s) associated with each board. The default frame type for TCP/IP is Ethernet II and the default frame type for IPX is Ethernet 802.2.

▶ *Display and input devices*: For working on the console, there should be a SVGA or better video adapter and monitor along with a standard keyboard and mouse (USB, PS/2, or Serial). However, for physical security reasons it's not a bad idea to remove the keyboard and mouse when not in use, thus removing one potential area for mischief.

▶ *Server name*: Determine the appropriate name for this server within the conventions of your overall network naming scheme. The server name can be between 2 and 47 characters in length and can incorporate alphanumeric characters, hyphens, and underscores.

▶ *Special hardware configuration*: If your server supports any special hardware configurations, such as PCI HotPlug or multiple processors, make sure to note any applicable drivers that will need to be loaded once NetWare 6 has been installed.

Volume Planning

You will need to consider the following as you determine the size and type of volumes to create within your NetWare partition(s):

- *Type of volume to create*: NetWare 6 now uses NSS volumes as its default volume type. NSS volumes offer a large number of advantages over traditional NetWare volumes, and now support most of the traditional file system features. However, there are still a few features that are not available with NSS volumes, such as block suballocation, auditing, file name locks and data migration. Unless you need one of these features, it will make sense to leverage the many advantages of NSS volumes.

For more information on NSS features see Chapter 8.

X-REF

- *Size of SYS volume*: The SYS volume is the storage location for all NetWare system files and products. As such, it is absolutely critical that your SYS volume not run out of space. NetWare 6 requires a minimum of 2GB for its SYS volume. Novell recommends 4GB to leave room for the installation of additional products.

- *Size of additional volumes*: It is usually a good idea to reserve the SYS volume for NetWare files and create additional volumes for network applications and data. NSS provides disk pools that can span physical drives. Multiple volumes can reside inside each disk pool. Once created, these additional volumes can be used in any way you see fit. You can organize data in volumes based on who needs access, on the type of name space required for the files, or on how you want the data distributed across the network. Remember to keep volume names consistent with your global naming strategy.

- *File compression*: File compression is now available on both NSS and traditional NetWare volumes. You can choose to implement File Compression at any time, but once installed it cannot be removed without recreating the Volume.

- *Block suballocation and block size*: These are only applicable to traditional NetWare volumes. A block is a unit of space set aside for file storage. Block size is determined by the overall size of the volume, as shown in the following table.

VOLUME SIZE	BLOCK SIZE
0 to 31MB	4KB
32 to 149MB	8KB
150 to 499MB	16KB
500MB to 1999MB	32KB
2000MB and greater	64KB

NOTE

Block suballocation permits you to subdivide a storage block so that multiple small files can share a single block. To conserve disk space on traditional volumes, block suballocation is enabled by default. However, if your server will store primarily large files, you can disable block suballocation to eliminate the additional management overhead.

Protocol Planning

Your biggest considerations as you decide which protocols to run on the NetWare 6 server will be:

► What is already out there?

► How will network usage evolve in the future?

The world has already decided that its primary network protocol is IP, due to its exclusive use on the Internet. However, NetWare's original IPX protocol is still in wide use and is easier to configure and manage than IP. Beyond that, there are some additional protocols and protocol configurations that should be considered prior to implementation.

► *Internet Protocol (IP)*: Novell made the move to IP as its default protocol with the release of NetWare 5, and if your network is connected with any external network or the Internet you will be using IP to make that connection. An IP network requires some advanced planning in order to be sure that all devices will be able to communicate, particularly if you are connecting your network to the outside world, as demonstrated in the following table.

Server IP address	Each device on an IP network must have a unique address. If you are connecting to the Internet, you can reserve a unique address, or block of addresses, through the Internet Network Information Center (InterNIC).

Server subnet mask	The subnet mask identifies a portion of the network. Subnet masks allow you to divide your network into more manageable segments.
Default router address	This entry determines where packets with an unknown network address will be sent. The default router is often that which connects your network to the Internet. If you want to specify a specific default router, make sure you have that information prior to the NetWare 6 installation.
DNS information	If you want to use Domain Name services on your network, you need to know your network's domain name as well as the addresses of any name servers you want to use. Configuring DNS on NetWare 6 is covered in Chapter 4.

▶ *Internet Packet Exchange (IPX)*: IPX is a Novell proprietary protocol that became a de facto standard due to NetWare's market acceptance. It is a very easy protocol to install and configure, but with the advent of the Internet, business realities have pushed it into the category of legacy protocol at this point. However, if you have a small or isolated network, IPX may still be a viable option for you.

Server internal IPX network number	Each server on an IPX network must have a unique internal net number. This number can be randomly generated during installation or you can specify it manually.

WARNING

You can choose to install both IP and IPX protocol stacks on your NetWare 6 server in order to support both legacy applications and external connectivity. However, this solution adds significant administrative overhead since both environments have to be managed separately. Furthermore, since IP and IPX services cannot interact, you may run into trouble accessing IPX services from an IP segment and vice versa.

▶ *Compatibility Mode*: Novell created Compatibility Mode (CM) to assist network administrators in making the transition from IPX networks to IP networks, since many legacy network applications were dependent on IPX. CM makes it possible to run IPX-dependent applications to receive the information they need in an IPX format, even though the network is running IP.

Compatibility Mode (CM) driver	The CM driver acts as a virtual network adapter, to which IPX can be bound. The CM driver can then internally route IPX packets and deliver IPX-based information to IPX applications running on the server. IPX services reach IPX clients by being encapsulated within the equivalent IP packets.
SLP	In order to properly handle IPX-based routing and service advertisement, CM relies on the IP-equivalent Service Location Protocol (SLP). Make sure SLP is configured on your network if you want to use CM.
Migration agent	The migration agent makes it possible for external systems to interact with the internal IPX network created by the CM driver. The migration agent tunnels IPX packets through the IP network so IP and IPX systems can interact, or IPX segments can communicate across an IP backbone.

NOTE

NetWare 6 no longer installs Compatibility Mode by default. If you need to configure Compatibility Mode on your network, see the NetWare 6 on-line documentation for more information.

▶ *Simple Network Management Protocol (SNMP):* If you plan on using SNMP-based network management utilities, you can configure some SNMP event information during installation. Know the type of information about this server that you want to be sent whenever an event occurs. This might include the server's hardware description, its location, and the name of the responsible administrator. Also know the IPX or IP address of the SNMP management console that should be notified when the event occurs.

eDirectory Planning

There are some basic pieces of eDirectory information you have to supply in order to complete the NetWare 6 installation.

X-REF

Some general eDirectory design concepts are presented in Chapter 5. For more information on eDirectory design see Appendix A for additional reference material.

▶ *eDirectory tree name:* You will need to know the name of the eDirectory tree into which the NetWare 6 server will be installed.

▶ *Server location within the eDirectory tree*: Prior to installing the server, make sure you are familiar with the organization of your eDirectory tree. You will need to specify the context within which the server will reside. This consists of the name of the Organization or Organizational Unit to which this server will belong.

▶ *Administrator name and password*: If you are installing the first server in a new tree, an admin account will be created and you will specify the admin password. If you are installing the server into an existing eDirectory tree, you will need to provide the name, including context, and password of the existing admin user.

▶ *Server's time zone*: You will need to specify the server's time zone and whether or not that time zone supports daylight saving time.

▶ *Time synchronization*: NetWare provides its own proprietary time synchronization service that is largely self-configuring. The first NetWare server in a network will be created as a Single Reference timeserver. Subsequent servers, even if they are installed in a new eDirectory tree, will default to Secondary timeservers. If your eDirectory tree will span geographic locations or manages a heterogeneous server environment — including UNIX, Linux, or Windows servers — you will probably want to implement a time synchronization scheme based on the standard Network Time Protocol (NTP).

More information on time synchronization is provided in Chapter 4.

X-REF

Print Planning

Novell Distributed Print Services (NDPS) is a revolutionary network print architecture introduced with the release of NetWare 5. NDPS has been strengthened in NetWare 6 with the release of iPrint, which leverages NDPS to deliver standards-based print support based on the Internet Printing Protocol (IPP).

Most importantly, NetWare 6 no longer offers legacy queue-based printing support. So if you haven't started making the transition to NDPS, now is the time. To plan for an NDPS printing environment you will want to consider the following:

▶ *Install NDPS on this server*: You need to determine whether or not this server will need to function as part of the NDPS environment. If not, you can skip the NDPS installation that is offered as part of the NetWare 6 installation.

▶ *Install an NDPS broker on this server*: The NDPS broker provides the management framework within which all print activities will occur. The NDPS installation routine will install an NDPS broker on a server only if there is no other broker within 3 hops of the server. If desired, you can override this setting and specify whether or not to install a broker on this server.

▶ *Disable any broker services*: The NDPS broker provides three principal services: Service Registry, Event Notification and Resource Management. Depending on how you choose to configure your NDPS environment, one or more of these services may not be needed on the server.

▶ *Understand your current print environment*: If you are migrating from a queue-based printing system or a non-NetWare printing environment, it is important that you map your current printing resources and determine where to locate brokers to best serve the needs of your organization.

Network Preparation

Prior to any type of NetWare 6 installation there are certain tasks that should be performed to prepare an existing network and other NetWare servers for the introduction of NetWare 6. Novell includes Deployment Manager (see Figure 1.1) to help identify and automate these tasks. You can run Deployment Manager from any Windows workstation by executing NWDEPLOY.EXE from the root of the NetWare 6 Operating System CD.

Deployment Manager features are organized into three main categories: Network Preparation, Installation/Upgrade Options, and Post-Installation Tasks. To view the various installation and upgrade options available with NetWare 6, select Installation/Upgrade Options in the left pane. This section of Deployment Manager provides brief overviews and checklists for NetWare 6 installations and upgrades. All of this material will be presented in more detail throughout this chapter. You should review the information offered in Deployment Manager to be familiar with it.

NOTE

You can run Deployment Manager and review its overviews and checklists from any workstation. However, to actually perform the network checks and updates necessary to prepare your network for the NetWare 6 installation you will need to have the NetWare client installed. See Chapter 2 for information on installing the NetWare client.

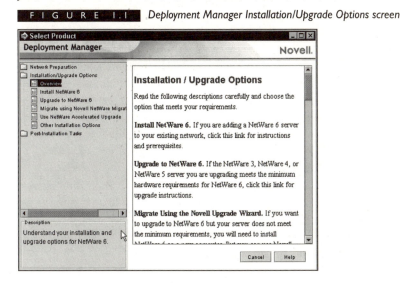

FIGURE 1.1 *Deployment Manager Installation/Upgrade Options screen*

Installing a New Server

After you have gathered all the information you need and made the necessary decisions with regards to installation and configuration, you are ready to perform the NetWare 6 installation. This section explains how to install a new server. If you are upgrading from a previous version of NetWare or from a different network operating system, skip to "Upgrading an Existing Server to NetWare 6" later in this chapter.

There are four distinct steps to the NetWare 6 installation:

- ▸ Preliminary hardware configuration
- ▸ (Conditional) configure the DOS partition
- ▸ Install startup files and create SYS volume
- ▸ NetWare 6 Installation Wizard

The first two steps prepare the server for the installation of the NetWare 6 operating system.

The third step takes you through the hardware setup and creates the SYS volume on which the NetWare 6 system files will be stored. This portion of the installation is text-based and runs under DOS on the server. This is the "blue screen" installation for which NetWare has become famous over the years.

Throughout this portion of the installation you will be prompted to review the default configuration and Modify or Continue at each screen. Choose Modify to make changes to the default values that the installation routine offers. Choose Continue to accept values and proceed with the installation. In some cases you will need to press F10 to save your changes before continuing.

The final step sets up the server's environment and switches to a graphical format called the NetWare 6 Installation Wizard. The Installation Wizard is a Java-based application that allows you to use a mouse during the rest of the installation.

Preliminary Hardware Configuration

Before you start the NetWare 6 installation there are a couple of things you should review to make sure your server hardware is ready to go.

▶ Since it is best to recreate disk partitions from scratch to prevent any potential conflicts, make a backup of your AUTOEXEC.BAT, CONFIG.SYS and any necessary device drivers, such as that for your CD-ROM. Make sure you have everything you need to boot the machine to DOS and access the CD-ROM drive.

▶ In order to ensure that the DOS environment can allocate sufficient resources for running the NetWare installation, include the following two lines in your CONFIG.SYS. You will have to reboot the server for these changes to take effect.

```
Files=50
Buffers=30
```

▶ Install and configure network adapters in the server as necessary. Refer to the manufacturer's documentation for configuration instructions.

▶ Install and configure a CD-ROM drive in the server as necessary. Refer to the manufacturer's documentation for configuration instructions.

▶ Boot the server and enter the CMOS setup. Check the date and time settings on the hardware clock, and adjust as needed so that they are accurate. Also, confirm that your CD-ROM drive is listed as a boot device if you want to boot from the NetWare 6 installation CD.

Configuring a DOS Partition

Insert the NetWare 6 Operating System CD in your CD-ROM drive and reboot the system. If the system does not automatically launch into the NetWare 6 installation procedure, complete the following steps to create the DOS partition for your server.

1. If there is an existing operating system, make sure that all data to be saved has been backed up.

2. Boot the server. The NetWare 6 License/Cryptography is a bootable disk that has all the utilities you need to setup the DOS partition. It includes a version of DR-DOS, but you may also use MS-DOS v3.3 or later for the partition operation.

3. Use the FDISK command to delete any existing partitions on your server's hard disk(s). Then create a Primary DOS partition of at least 200MB + 1MB for each MB of RAM in your server. Make sure the DOS partition is marked as Active in FDISK.

4. Reboot the system from floppy one more time. Use the FORMAT command to format the partition you have created and transfer DOS system files.

```
Format C: /S
```

5. Transfer any required device drivers, CONFIG.SYS, and AUTOEXEC. BAT to your newly formatted C: drive. This should enable you to boot directly from the C: drive and access the CD-ROM as drive D:

Install Startup Files and Create SYS Volume

Complete the following steps to install NetWare 6 startup files and create the SYS volume. If you boot from CD-ROM you will start directly from Step 2.

1. Insert the NetWare 6 Operating System CD in your CD-ROM drive.

2. From the DOS prompt change to the CD-ROM's drive letter (usually D), and type **INSTALL**.

3. Review the NetWare license agreement and press F10 to accept.

4. Review the JInfonet license agreement and press F10 to accept.

5. At the Installation Type screen, make your desired selections — choose New Server and either Express install or Custom install — and select Continue. If you chose Express install you can skip ahead to Step 1 in the "NetWare 6 Installation Wizard" section, which follows. The Express install detects drivers and installs the NetWare server with default settings and default software programs. The Custom installation will walk you through each step of the server installation and allow you to customize and explore your selections more closely. The settings include:

- 4GB SYS volume (with remaining disk space left as free space)

- LAN and disk drivers auto-discovered and loaded

- The three default products installed: Novell Distributed Print Services (NDPS), NetWare Administration server, and Novell Advanced Audit Services
- Country code: 1
- Code page: 437
- Video mode: VGA Plug N Play
- Keyboard: United States
- Mouse: Auto-discovered and loaded

IMPORTANT

If you want to automate the installation with a response file, select F3 and specify the path to the appropriate file. The NetWare 6 installation automatically creates a response file during any NetWare 6 installation and saves it to SYS:NI\DATA\RESPONSE.NI. By making minor modifications to this file, such as changing the server name, IP address, etc, you can use the response file from one server to automatically create another with the same characteristics. For more information on using response files, refer to the NetWare 6 Installation guide under "Other Installation Options."

6. At the Server Settings screen, make your desired selections, as follows, and select Continue.

- *Server ID number*: This is a random number for identifying the server on the network. It only needs to be changed if you are filtering addresses or if you have a pre-defined addressing scheme for your servers.

- *Load server at reboot*: Specify whether or not you want NetWare to restart automatically when the server is rebooted. This adds a line to your AUTOEXEC.BAT to load SERVER.EXE.

- *Server SET parameters*: If your server devices, such as network or storage adapters, require any special load parameters, they can be entered here and stored in the STARTUP.NCF file, which is located in the NWSERVER directory on your DOS partition.

7. At the Regional Settings screen make your desired selections and select Continue. These three settings: Country, Code Page, and Keyboard make sure NetWare correctly processes keyboard input and extended characters.

8. At the Mouse and Video mode screen make your desired selections and select Continue. At this point, the installation program copies startup files and drivers to the DOS partition.

9. At the Adapters screen make your desired selections and select Continue.

   - NetWare 6 will auto detect the appropriate Host Adapter Module (HAM) for your storage adapters. If it is not detected, you can choose the appropriate HAM from the dropdown menu or install one that has been supplied by the hardware vendor.

   - NetWare 6 will auto detect whether or not you need Platform Support Modules (for improved multiprocessor support) or HotPlug Support Modules (for HotPlug PCI support). If it doesn't list any, then you shouldn't need them.

10. In the Device screen make your desired selections and select Continue.

   - NetWare 6 will auto detect the appropriate Custom Device Module (CDM) for your attached storage devices (HDD, CD-ROM, etc.). If it is not detected, you can choose the appropriate CDM from the dropdown menu or install one that has been supplied by the hardware vendor.

   - NetWare 6 will auto detect the appropriate driver for your network board. If it is not detected you can choose the appropriate network board driver from the dropdown menu or install one that has been supplied by the hardware vendor.

   - Some server and network configurations require you to load special NetWare Loadable Modules (NLM) before completing the server installation. One example is ROUTE.NLM, which is necessary for installing a server into a Token Ring network.

11. At the Volume SYS and Partition Properties screen, make your desired selections and select Continue. Make sure you press F10 to save any changes you might make before continuing.

   - *File system type*: NetWare 6 now uses NSS for the SYS volume.

   - *NetWare partition size (MB)*: Specify the size of the NetWare partition for the SYS volume — and thereby the size of the SYS volume. Novell recommends 4GB for SYS in case you want to install all the optional products.

   - *File compression*: Specify whether or not to implement file compression to conserve disk space. This is probably not necessary for SYS as long as you restrict SYS usage to only NetWare products and services.

- *Unpartitioned disk space (MB):* This line identifies the free space available for creating additional partitions and volumes later in the installation process. Additional partitions and volumes can also be created after the installation is complete by using ConsoleOne.

At this point, the installation program mounts the SYS volume and copies all the necessary system files to it. Then the installation program launches the NetWare 6 Installation Wizard, a graphical program that will take you through the rest of the installation.

NetWare 6 Installation Wizard

Continue with the following steps to set up the NetWare 6 server environment.

1. Enter a name for this server and then select Next.

2. At the Encryption screen make your desired selections and select Next. Insert the NetWare 6 License/Cryptography diskette, or browse to the path where your NetWare Crypto License file (.NFK) is located.

3. At the Configure File System screen make your desired selections and select Next. This screen shows you a list of currently defined partitions. If you have free space available and would like to create new partition(s) now, complete the following. Otherwise skip to Step 4.

   a. Highlight Free Space in the partitions list and select Create.

   b. Enter a volume name.

   c. Select the volume type, either NSS or Traditional.

   d. Enter the desired size of the new volume in the Space to Use field and select Apply to Volume.

   e. Select OK to create the volume and return to the Volume Information screen.

   f. Repeat this process for any other volumes you want to create.

4. At the Mount Volumes screen make your desired selections and select Next. If you want to install additional Novell products to volumes other than SYS during the installation, choose to mount the volumes now. Otherwise you can choose to mount the volumes later.

5. At the Protocols screen make your desired selections and select Next. Highlight a listed network board and choose the protocols that will be bound to that board. You can choose IP, IPX, or both. If you choose IP, specify the server's IP address and subnet mask. You may also specify a default router/gateway. (Leave this field blank to have the network

locate it automatically.) If you have multiple network boards installed, repeat this process for each board. Similarly, you can select the IPX frame type and specify appropriate network numbers if you are using the IPX protocol on your network.

NOTE

If you are still using Compatibility Mode (CM) to permit legacy IPX applications to run on your IP network, click Advanced and select the IPX Compatibility tab to configure CM settings. For more information see the Novell on-line documentation.

6. At the Domain Name Service screen make your desired selections and select Next. If you are using DNS on your network, specify a host name for the server, your organization's domain, and then enter the address(es) of the nearest DNS name servers.

X-REF

For more information on installing DNS/DHCP in a NetWare environment see Chapter 5.

7. At the Time Zone screen make your desired selections and select Next. Select the time zone in which the server will reside. If this time zone uses daylight saving time, make sure the daylight saving time box is checked.

8. At the NDS Install screen make your desired selections and select Next. Choose whether this server is being installed into a new eDirectory tree or an existing eDirectory tree.

   a. Enter the appropriate directory tree name.

   b. Enter the appropriate context for the server. If the context does not exist, you can define it here by clicking Add. If it does exist you can select the Browse button and navigate to the appropriate location.

   c. Enter a name, context and password for the admin user. If this is a new admin, a new User object will be created with the password you specify. If you are installing the server into an existing tree, specify a valid user with sufficient rights to install the server into the context you have specified.

X-REF

For more information on eDirectory rights see Chapter 5.

9. At the NDS Summary screen, review your selections and select Next.

10. At the Licenses screen make your desired selections and select Next. Insert the NetWare 6 License/Cryptography diskette, or specify the path to your NetWare license files (.NLF). You may also select the Install Without Licenses checkbox. This option allows you only two user connections to the server. Licenses can be installed after the server installation, if desired. More information on NetWare licensing is provided later in this chapter.

11. At the UAL Connection License Certificate Context screen, make your selection and select Next. NetWare 6 uses a new User Access License (UAL) licensing scheme that links a license unit directly to a user object so they can login from any workstation at any location without fear of not having a licensed connection available. License certificates should be installed at or above the Users' context in the eDirectory so they are readily available.

12. At the Components screen make your desired selections and select Next. Choose any additional products you want to install on the server at this time. Regardless of the component selections you make, the NetWare 6 installation will install certain core services, required for basic operation and management, including the following:

- NetWare 6 Core Operating System
- Certificate server 2.21
- iMonitor 1.5
- NetWare Remote Manager
- iManage 1.0
- Web Manager
- ConsoleOne 1.3.2
- Novell Modular Authentication Service
- Storage Management Services
- NetWare Port Resolver

13. At the Novell Certificate Server 2.21 screen make your desired selections and select Next. If no Organizational CA object exists, one will be created here automatically. Select Export the Trusted Root Certificate if you would like to be able to install the server certificate on a client, such as a Web browser, to enable secure communications using SSL or other cryptographic operations between the client and the server.

14. At the LDAP Configuration screen make your desired selections and select Next. Select the Allow Clear Text Passwords checkbox if you would like LDAP clients to be able to login with unencrypted passwords. This option is not recommended if you believe there is any chance of on-the-wire packet snooping.

15. At the eDirectory iManage Install Options screen make your desired selections and select Next. iManage is a role-based management tool. It creates Role objects that can be assigned to user objects to grant rights to perform specific management tasks. The iManage role objects will be stored in the context that you specify.

X-REF

For more information on iManage see Chapter 3.

16. At the Summary screen make your desired selections and select Finish to complete the installation. To customize settings for the NetWare 6 OS or any of the additional products you are installing, select Customize.

   a. At the Product Customization screen, navigate to the operating system component or NetWare service that you want to customize in the left pane.

   b. If any configuration information is available, the Configure button in the right pane will be active. Select Configure to view the current configuration and make any desired changes, if applicable.

17. At this point, NetWare system and service files will be copied to the SYS volume of the server. When the file copy completes, select Yes to reboot the server. Remove the installation CD-ROM prior to rebooting the server.

When the computer reboots, the server will automatically restart if you made this selection during the installation. Otherwise, change to the NWSERVER directory in DOS and run SERVER.EXE to start NetWare 6.

Once the server is running you will see a graphical screen within which NetWare utilities can be displayed. To bring up ConsoleOne, the primary NetWare management utility, select the Novell button at the bottom of the screen and select ConsoleOne. You may toggle out of the graphical environment to the various text-based server screens by pressing Alt+Esc.

Upgrading an Existing Server to NetWare 6

There are multiple upgrade options with NetWare 6 depending on your current version of NetWare and your goals for the upgrade. There are three types of upgrades available with NetWare 6: Accelerated Upgrade, In-Place Upgrade, and Server Migration. Not every upgrade option is available for every Network Operating System (NOS). Table 1.1 outlines the upgrade options and NOS versions on which they can be used.

TABLE 1.1	Upgrade Options and NOS Versions	
UPGRADE TYPE	**SUPPORTED NOS**	**DESCRIPTION**
Accelerated	NetWare 5.x NetWare 4.x	Uses an intermediary Staging server that hosts a copy of the NetWare 6 Operating System CD-ROM. Permits remote upgrades managed from a workstation running the Accelerated Upgrade utility.
In-Place	NetWare 5.x NetWare 4.x	Traditional upgrade method in which the server is upgraded directly from the server console.
Server Migration	NetWare 5.x NetWare 4.x NetWare 3.x Windows NT v3.51 or v4	Uses the NetWare Migration Wizard from a workstation to move server data from an existing Source server to a new Destination server. Most flexible installation option, but NetWare 6 must be previously installed on the Destination server.

Network Preparation

Prior to any upgrade, use Deployment Manager to prepare an existing network and NetWare servers for the introduction of NetWare 6 (see Figure 1.2).

Run Deployment Manager from any Windows workstation by executing NWDEPLOY.EXE from the root of the NetWare 6 Operating System CD. Deployment Manager features are organized into three main categories: Network Preparation, Installation/Upgrade Options, and Post-Installation Tasks. This section will focus on the Network Preparation tasks. Other Deployment Manager features are discussed throughout this chapter.

F I G U R E   1 . 2 *Deployment Manager Network Preparation screen*

Select Product

Deployment Manager   Novell.

Network Preparation
   Overview
   Step 1: Back up data
   Step 2: View and update NDS versio
   Step 3: Prepare for NDS eDirectory 8
   Prepare a Novell Cluster for Upgrade
   Prepare a server with NDS7 & NSS.
   Step 4: Update the Certificate Autho
Installation/Upgrade Options
Post-Installation Tasks

Network Preparation

Before you install or upgrade any server on your network to NetWare* 6, you should complete these steps.

Step 1: Back Up Data

If you are upgrading a server on your network to a new version of NetWare, you should back up the server data and the NDS* data. Follow the instructions in this step to back up your NetWare 3, NetWare 4, or NetWare 5 server.

Step 2: View and Update NDS Version

You must update NDS before you upgrade or install your

Description
Installation or upgrade options for NetWare 6.

               Cancel   Help

NOTE

You can run Deployment Manager and review its overviews and checklists from any workstation. However, to actually perform the network checks and updates necessary to prepare your network for the NetWare 6 installation you will need to have the NetWare client installed. See Chapter 2 for information on installing the NetWare client.

To examine network preparation tasks, select the Network Preparation folder in the left pane. Select Overview to see an outline of the four tasks recommended for preparing your network for NetWare 6. To perform those tasks complete the following steps:

NOTE

To complete some of these tasks you will need to be logged in as a user with administrative rights at the root of the tree.

I. *Step One: Back up data:* Use your preferred data archive utility, such as NetWare's own Storage Management Services (SMS), to back up all eDirectory and server data on any server that will be upgraded to NetWare 6.

For more information on backing up your net data see Chapter 8.

X-REF

2. *Step Two: View and update NDS versions*: NetWare 6 requires eDirectory v7.47 or newer on existing servers in order to upgrade them to NetWare 6. To review the current eDirectory configuration on your network with Deployment Manager, complete the following:

    a. Select Step 2: View and Update NDS versions in the left pane of Deployment Manager.

    b. Browse to the eDirectory tree or container you want to search for NetWare servers and select Next. Select Include Subordinate containers to search the entire tree or tree branch.

    c. Deployment Manager will show you the version of eDirectory installed on each server it finds and whether or not it needs to be updated. If no server needs to be updated, select Exit to return to the Deployment Manager main menu.

    d. Select Next to perform the eDirectory update on those servers that require it.

    e. Select Next to restart eDirectory on that server.

    f. Select Exit to return to the Deployment Manager main menu.

3. *Step Three: Prepare for NDS eDirectory 8.6*: If you are installing NetWare 6 into an existing eDirectory environment, Deployment Manager will review the existing eDirectory schema and prepare it for the installation of eDirectory v8.6. To review the current schema configuration on your network with Deployment Manager complete the following steps:

For more information on eDirectory schema see Chapter 5.

X-REF

    a. Select Step 3: Prepare for NDS eDirectory 8.6 in the left pane of Deployment Manager.

    b. Browse to the eDirectory tree you want to review and select Next.

    c. Select a server that holds a replica of the Root partition and select Next.

    d. Select Exit to return to the Deployment Manager main menu.

4. *Update Certificate Authority object in eDirectory*: NetWare 6 requires Novell Certificate server 2.0 or later. If you are installing NetWare 6 into an existing eDirectory environment, open Step 4: Update the Certificate Authority object in Deployment Manager and follow the steps to check your installed version of Novell Certificate server and update if necessary.

NetWare 4.x and 5.x

Regardless of the upgrade option you choose for your Netware 4 and/or NetWare 5 servers, you should review and complete the minimum requirements described in this section prior to performing the upgrade.

The server to be upgraded must be running one of the following versions of NetWare:

NetWare support packs are available on-line at `support.novell.com/filefinder/6385`.

▶ NetWare 5.1 Support Pack 2 or later

▶ NetWare 5.0 Support Pack 6 or later

▶ NetWare 4.2 with Support Pack 8 or later

▶ NetWare 4.0 with Support Pack 8 or later

The server hardware must meet the minimum requirements for NetWare 6 as described in the "Server Hardware Planning" section earlier in this chapter.

NetWare maintains deleted files in a salvageable state. Make sure there are no deleted files you want to salvage prior to the upgrade. All deleted files will be purged as part of the upgrade.

Make diskette copies of LAN drivers and the AUTOEXEC.NCF from the server's SYS volume.

If necessary, review the "Preliminary Hardware Configuration" section earlier in this chapter to make sure your server hardware is ready for the upgrade.

Deployment Manager also includes two options for further preparing a NetWare 5 server for the NetWare 6 installation:

I. (Conditional) *Preparation for server with NDS7 and NSS*: During the upgrade from eDirectory 7, which shipped originally with NetWare 5, to eDirectory 8, which is used with NetWare 6, NSS volumes will lose all their trustee assignments. To prevent this, complete the following:

   a. Select Preparation for server with NDS7 and NSS in the left pane of Deployment Manager.

b. Browse to the eDirectory tree or container you want to search for NetWare servers and select Next. Select Include Subordinate containers to search the entire tree or tree branch.

c. Select the Update NDS checkbox for those servers that host NSS volumes and select Next.

WARNING

Only complete this step immediately before a NetWare 6 upgrade because the update makes eDirectory unusable until NetWare 6 is installed. Make sure the NW 5 server has been updated to the appropriate service pack prior to doing the eDirectory update.

d. eDirectory files for those servers will be updated and the servers will restart.

2. (Conditional) *Pre-upgrade a NetWare cluster*: NetWare 6 provides greatly improved clustering features. This option prepares an existing NetWare 5 cluster to be upgraded to a NetWare 6 cluster. This involves the following tasks:

- Saves all trustee assignments so they will not be lost during the upgrade.
- Identifies shared partitions so the new NetWare 6 safety features can be installed.
- Deactivates the NetWare 5 cluster preparatory to the upgrade.

X-REF

For more information on preparing your existing NetWare 5 cluster for NetWare 6 NCS see Chapter 12.

NetWare 3.x

Migration Wizard copies the NetWare 3 file system and bindery objects to a destination Novell eDirectory tree. When the bindery objects are copied to the destination eDirectory tree, they are automatically converted to eDirectory objects.

Windows NT

Migration Wizard migrates NT domain users and local and global groups from a Windows NT v3.51 or v4 server to a destination eDirectory tree. During the migration, the NT users and groups are converted to eDirectory objects and placed in the destination eDirectory tree. Novell NetWare Migration Wizard 6 also migrates NT shared folders to a NetWare file system while migrating and converting Windows NT permissions to NetWare trustee rights.

Accelerated Upgrade

The NetWare Accelerated Upgrade utility is an advanced utility designed for network administrators that have a lot of experience troubleshooting and installing NetWare products.

Accelerated Upgrade lets you manage this installation of NetWare 6 from any Windows workstation so you don't have to physically visit every server that needs to be upgraded. It also offers a script file option that lets you customize the NetWare 6 installation for automated installation. Because of this, Accelerated Upgrade can be significantly faster than the standard installation process. However, it does not let you install any additional network products or licensing certificates. Remote installation of NetWare products can be done with Deployment Manager and will be discussed later in this chapter.

To perform an Accelerated Upgrade complete the following steps:

1. Choose an existing NetWare server, perhaps one that has already been upgraded to NetWare 6, which will function as a staging server for the Accelerated Upgrade.

   a. Copy the entire NetWare 6 Operating System CD-ROM to a folder on that server.

   b. (Conditional) Copy the NetWare 6 Cryptography License (NICIFK) from the NetWare 6 License/Cryptography diskette to the LICENSE directory in that same folder. This is required if you will be upgrading NetWare 4.x servers that don't yet have cryptographic services installed.

2. Launch the Accelerated Upgrade utility from a Windows workstation by executing ACCUPG.EXE from the Root of the NetWare 6 Operating System CD-ROM. Make sure you are logged in as a user with administrative rights to the root of the eDirectory tree.

3. At the Accelerated Upgrade welcome screen, select Next.

4. Browse to the NetWare server and folder on the network where you copied the NetWare 6 CD files and select Next.

5. Enter the password for the user account with which you are currently logged in and select OK. This password will be used to create a server-to-server connection between the staging server and the target server.

6. Select the name of the server to be upgraded and select Next. This server will be known as the target server.

7. Review the summary of the target server's current configuration and select Next. Configuration parameters that do not meet Novell recommendations will be highlighted in red.

8. At the Select Settings for Target server screen, make your selections and select Next.

   a. *Reboot server after upgrade*: Select this checkbox to have the server automatically reboot after the upgrade is finished. If this option is not selected, the server will have to be rebooted manually after the upgrade is complete.

   b. *Update drives to latest NetWare 6 LAN and disk drivers*: Select this checkbox to have the NetWare 6 upgrade attempt to update your current drivers to the most recent versions. If you choose this option, make sure you have copies of your current drivers handy in case the update doesn't work.

   c. *Remove unsupported DOS utilities*: Leave this checkbox unselected. This option is for use with NetWare 4 servers only.

9. At the Summary screen, select Finish to start copying files to the target server.

When the file copy process is finished, the target server will need to reboot. This will happen automatically if you selected that option in Step 8. If not, restart the server by typing **RESTART SERVER** at the server console.

In-Place Upgrade

This is the simplest and most straightforward way to upgrade to NetWare 6. However, it does require that your existing NetWare server have a DOS partition large enough to support NetWare 6. If your DOS partition is smaller than 200MB you need to create a new DOS partition and perform a new server installation as described previously, or consider a server migration, which will be discussed later in this chapter.

Similar to installing a new server, there are two parts to the NetWare 6 in-place upgrade after the hardware and DOS partition has been configured. The first part takes your through the hardware setup and creates volume SYS, is text-based, and runs under DOS on the server. This is the "blue screen" installation for which NetWare has become famous over the years. Throughout this portion of the installation you will be prompted to review the default configuration and Modify or Continue at each screen. Choose Modify to make changes to the default values that the installation routine offers. Choose Continue to accept values and proceed with the installation. In some cases you will need to press F10 to save your changes before continuing. The bottom portion of each screen will present the options.

The second part of the upgrade switches to a graphical format called the NetWare 6 Installation Wizard. The Installation Wizard is a Java-based application that allows you to use a mouse during the rest of the installation.

To perform an in-place upgrade complete the following steps:

1. Bring down the server by typing **DOWN** at the server's command line. A NetWare 4.x server also requires you to type **EXIT**.

2. Insert the NetWare 6 Operating System CD in your CD-ROM drive.

3. From the DOS prompt change to the CD-ROM's drive letter (usually D), and type **INSTALL**.

4. Review the NetWare license agreement and press F10 to accept.

5. Review the JInfonet license agreement and press F10 to accept.

6. At the Welcome screen make your desired selections — choose Upgrade and either Express or Custom — and select Continue. The Express upgrade retains all your server data such as files, directory structures, partitions and volumes. It also installs default NetWare 6 products, including NDPS, NetWare Administration server, and Novell Advanced Audit service. If you chose Express install you can skip ahead to Step 13, which begins step-by-step coverage of the NetWare 6 Installation Wizard. The Custom installation will walk you through each step of the upgrade process and allow you to customize and explore your selections more closely.

IMPORTANT If you want to automate the installation with a response file, press F3 and specify the path to the appropriate file. The NetWare 6 installation automatically creates a response file during any NetWare 6 installation and saves it to SYS:NI\DATA\RESPONSE.NI. By making minor modifications to this file — such as changing server name, IP address, etc. — you can use the response file from one server to automatically create another with the same characteristics. For more information on using response files refer to the NetWare 6 Installation guide under Other Installation Options.

7. At the Server Settings screen make your desired selections and select Continue.

   a. *Load server at reboot*: Specify whether or not you want NetWare to restart automatically when the server is rebooted. This adds a line to your AUTOEXEC.BAT to load SERVER.EXE.

b. *Server SET parameters*: If your server devices, such as network or storage adapters, require any special load parameters they can be entered here and stored in the STARTUP.NCF file, which is located in the NWSERVER directory on your DOS partition.

c. *Backup Startup Directory (optional)*: If you would like to keep a copy of the current NWSERVER folder on the DOS partition, specify the new folder name here.

8. At the Regional Settings screen, make your desired selections and select Continue. These three settings: Country, Code Page, and Keyboard, make sure that NetWare correctly processes keyboard input and extended characters.

9. At the Mouse and Video screen make your desired selections and select Continue. At this point, the installation program copies startup files to the DOS partition and prepares to configure the server environment.

10. At the Storage Adapters screen make your desired selections and select Continue.

a. NetWare 6 will auto detect the appropriate Host Adapter Module (HAM) for your storage adapters. If it is not detected you can choose the appropriate HAM from the dropdown menu or install one that has been supplied by the hardware vendor.

b. NetWare 6 will auto detect whether or not you need Platform Support Modules (for improved multiprocessor support) or HotPlug Support Modules (for HotPlug PCI support). If it doesn't list any, then you shouldn't need them.

11. In the Storage Devices screen make your desired selections and select Continue.

NOTE

NetWare 6 will auto detect the appropriate Custom Device Module (CDM) for your attached storage devices (HDD, CD-ROM, etc.). If it is not detected you can choose the appropriate CDM from the dropdown menu or install one that has been supplied by the hardware vendor.

12. In the Network Adapters screen make your desired selections and select Continue.

a. NetWare 6 will auto detect the appropriate driver for your network board. If it is not detected, choose the appropriate network board driver from the dropdown menu or install one that has been supplied by the hardware vendor. You can also view the current load line if you don't remember the name of the LAN driver that needs to be installed.

b. Some server and network configurations require you to load special NetWare Loadable Modules (NLM) before completing the server installation. One example is ROUTE.NLM, which is necessary for installing a server into a Token Ring network.

13. At this point, the installation program mounts the SYS volume and copies all the necessary system files to it. Then the installation program launches the NetWare 6 Installation Wizard, which begins at the Encryption screen, where you enter the path to your cryptography license, and then select Next.

TIP

The cryptography license has an extension of NFK and can be found on the NetWare 6 Cryptography/License diskette.

14. At the Configure File System screen make your desired selections and select Next. This screen shows the currently defined volumes. If you have free space available and would like to create new partition(s) now, complete the following steps.

a. Highlight Free Space in the partitions list and select Create.

b. Enter a volume name.

c. Select the volume type, either NSS or Traditional.

d. Enter the desired size of the new volume in the Space to Use field and select Apply to Volume.

e. Select OK to create the volume and return to the Volume Information screen.

f. Repeat this process for any other volumes you want to create.

15. (Conditional) At the Mount Volumes screen make your desired selections and select Next. If you have created new volumes and want to install additional Novell products to volumes other than SYS during the installation, choose to mount the volumes now. Otherwise you can choose to mount the volumes later.

16. At the Protocols screen make your desired selections and select Next. You may not change your currently installed protocols at this time. However, if you want to add a protocol that is not currently loaded, either IP or IPX, you may do so by selecting the appropriate checkbox.

If you choose IP, specify the server's IP address and subnet mask. You may also specify a default router/gateway (leave this field blank to have the network locate it automatically). If the server has multiple network adapters, repeat this process for each board. Similarly, you can select the IPX frame type and specify appropriate network numbers if you are using the IPX protocol on your network.

17. At the Domain Name Service screen make your desired selections and select Next. If you are using DNS on your network, specify a host name for the server, your organization's domain, and then enter the address(es) of the nearest DNS name server(s).

X-REF

> **For more information on installing DNS/DHCP in a NetWare environment see Chapter 4.**

18. Enter a valid eDirectory Username/Password and select OK. This user must have admin rights at the root of the tree.

19. At the NDS Summary screen, review your selections and select Next.

20. At the Licenses screen make your desired selections and select Next. Insert the NetWare 6 License/Cryptography diskette, or specify the path to your NetWare license files (.NLF). You may also select the Install without licenses checkbox. This option allows you only two user connections to the server. Licenses can be installed after the server installation, if desired. More information on NetWare licensing is provided later in this chapter.

21. At the UAL Connection License Certificate Context screen, make your selection and select Next. NetWare 6 uses a new User Access License (UAL) licensing scheme that links a license unit directly to a user object so they can login from any workstation at any location without fear of not having a licensed connection available. License certificates should be installed at or above the users' context in the eDirectory so they are readily available.

22. At the Components screen make your desired selections and select Next. Choose any additional products you want to install on the server at this time. Information about the installation and configuration of all NetWare 6 additional products will be discussed in other chapters throughout this book.

23. At the Novell Certificate server 2.21 screen make your desired selections and select Next.

    a. (Conditional) Novell eDirectory requires an Organizational Certificate Authority for its cryptographic services. If you are upgrading from NetWare 5 one will already exist and this option will not be available. Otherwise, select Create Organizational Certificate Authority.

    b. Select Export the Trusted Root Certificate if you would like to be able to install the server certificate on a client, such as a Web browser, to enable secure communications using SSL or other cryptographic operations between the client and the server.

24. At the LDAP Configuration screen make your desired selections and select Next. Select the Allow Clear Text Passwords checkbox if you would like LDAP clients to be able to login over unsecured connections. This is not recommended for security reasons.

25. At the eDirectory iManage Install Options screen make your desired selections and select Next. iManage is a role-based management tool. It creates role objects that can be assigned to user objects to grant rights to perform specific management tasks. The iManage role objects will be stored in the context that you specify.

For more information on iManage see Chapter 3.

X-REF

26. At the Summary screen make your desired selections and select Finish to complete the installation. To customize settings for the NetWare 6 OS or any of the additional products you are installing, select Customize.

    a. At the Product Customization screen, navigate to the operating system component or NetWare service that you want to customize in the left pane.

    b. If any configuration information is available, the Configure button in the right pane will be active. Select Configure to view the current configuration and make any desired changes, if applicable.

At this point, NetWare system and service files will be copied to the SYS volume of the server. When the file copy completes, select Yes to reboot the server. Remove the installation CD-ROM and any license diskettes prior to rebooting the server.

Server Migration

Migration Wizard migrates a server's file system and all network data—such as NetWare 4.x or 5.x eDirectory database, NetWare 3.x Bindery database, or Windows NT Domain—from a source server to a new NetWare 6 destination server. There are several steps to the migration process:

- ► Prepare the Migration Wizard workstation
- ► Prepare the destination server
- ► Prepare the source server
- ► Copy files and data from the source server to the destination server
- ► Transfer all network data from the source server to the destination server and convert to eDirectory format
- ► Down the source server and allow the destination server to insert itself into the network and take over the operations of the source server

Complete the tasks described in the following sections to prepare for the server migration.

Install NetWare Migration Wizard

Migration Wizard requires a Windows workstation with the following characteristics:

- ► Windows 98, Windows NT 4, or Windows 2000 workstation with at least 50MB available disk space.

TIP

If you are migrating from Windows NT, you can run Migration Wizard from either a Windows NT 4 or Windows 2000 workstation, or directly from the Windows NT 4 server from which you are migrating data. However, the migration will be faster if you run Migration Wizard from the server rather than from the workstation because files are copied directly from server-to-server rather than via the client workstation.

- ► Install the Novell client that ships with NetWare 6 or run a minimum of Novell client v3.3 for Windows 98, or Novell client for Windows NT/2000 version 4.8 or later.
- ► If the source server is running NetWare 4.x, configure the Novell client for IPX or IPX and IP protocols.
- ► For best performance, the source server, destination server, and client workstation should be located on a common network segment.

To install the Migration Wizard software, insert the NetWare 6 Operating System CD-ROM into your workstation CD-ROM and complete the following steps:

1. Browse to PRODUCTS\MIGRTWZD and run MIGRTWZD.EXE.

2. At the Welcome screen select Next.

3. At the Software License Agreement screen select Yes.

4. At the Choose Destination Location screen select Next. Browse to an alternative installation location if desired. The default is C:\PROGRAM FILES\NOVELL\NETWARE MIGRATION WIZARD.

5. At the Setup Complete screen, select Finish to close the Migration Wizard installation.

Prepare the destination server

The destination server is the new computer that will receive the data from the source server. This server must be installed into a temporary tree. After data is migrated from the source server to the destination server, Migration Wizard automatically modifies the destination server's AUTOEXEC.NCF file to include the source server's name and internal IPX number/server ID. Then, when the Destination server reboots, it takes the place of the source server in the network.

Prepare the server hardware and install NetWare 6 on the new server. For information on doing this, see "Getting Ready for NetWare 6" and "Installing a New Server" earlier in this chapter. To make sure the destination server is ready for the migration process, complete the following tasks:

▶ Make sure you select the pre-migration server option during the NetWare 6 installation. And then select the Custom option to verify that you have enough room on your destination server to accommodate your source server data.

WARNING

When you install a NetWare 6 server as a pre-migration server, it does not configure the core management services as it does during a regular NetWare 6 installation. Make sure you install the following services after the installation is complete: iManage, iMonitor, NetWare Remote Manager, Web Manager, and Novell Modular Authentication Services (NMAS).

▶ Make sure the destination server is installed into a temporary eDirectory tree with a different server name from that of the source server. If this is not done, the destination server will not assume the identity of the source server after the migration.

► Create volumes on the destination server that are the same size as, or larger than, volumes on the source server. Volume names on the destination server must be the same as the volume names on the source server.

► Migration Wizard migrates compressed volumes. If you are migrating compressed volumes to uncompressed volumes, Migration Wizard decompresses the volumes during the migration. Make sure you have enough room on the uncompressed volume(s) of the destination server to accommodate the source volumes once they are decompressed.

► (Conditional) If migrating from NetWare 3 or NetWare 4, install and configure the IPX protocol on the destination server. If desired, you can remove IPX after completing the migration.

► (Conditional) If you are migrating from NetWare 3 or Windows NT, determine whether you want to use a Template object to migrate your users to the destination eDirectory tree. A Template object is used to define additional eDirectory user attributes for bindery or domain users during the migration. Template objects are especially useful for defining additional attributes that are not found in the binderies or domains.

IMPORTANT

In order to migrate home directories, you *must* use a Template object. If there is a conflict between the properties of a Template object and legacy user properties or policy settings, the properties of the Template object will, in most cases, take priority. The last name, full name, and description of every Legacy object is always migrated and these corresponding properties from the Template object are overwritten. If you decide to use a Template object, you can create one in ConsoleOne by selecting File ➪ New ➪ Object ➪ Template. IP addresses for the source server will not be migrated.

Prepare the source server

The source server contains the files, volumes, and network data and objects that will be copied to the new NetWare 6 server during the migration. To make sure the source server is ready for the migration process, complete the tasks described in the following sections.

NetWare 4.x and 5.x   Complete the following tasks to prepare your NetWare 4.x or 5.x servers for migration to NetWare 6.

▶ Update the source server with its latest, appropriate Support Pack.

 NetWare support packs are available on-line at `support.novell.com/filefinder/6385`.

▶ (Conditional) If you are migrating data from NetWare 4, make sure the source server's volumes are running long name space support on all volumes to be copied. To add long name space support to a NetWare 4.11 or NetWare 4.2 volume, enter the following at the server console: **LOAD LONG** and then **ADD NAME SPACE LONG TO** *volumename*.

▶ Load DSREPAIR and run the Unattended Full Repair, Time Synchronization, and Report Synchronization Status options to make sure the eDirectory environment is healthy prior to the migration. See the "Post-Installation Tasks with Deployment Manager" section, later in this chapter, for more information on these three operations.

▶ Use your preferred data archive utility, such as NetWare's own Storage Management Services (SMS), to back up all eDirectory and server data on the source server, so you can recover should a problem occur during the migration.

▶ Use ConsoleOne to verify that you are authenticated as a User with Supervisor Rights to the both the NetWare 4.x or 5.x server.

NetWare 3.x   Complete the following tasks to prepare your NetWare 3.x servers for migration to NetWare 6.

▶ The source server must be running NetWare 3.11 or later.

▶ Update the source server with its latest, appropriate Support Pack or system file updates.

 NetWare support packs are available on-line at `support.novell.com/filefinder/6385`.

▶ Load one of the following NLM programs at the server console of each NetWare 3 source server that you are planning to migrate:

• NetWare 3.11: load TSA311.nlm

• NetWare 3.12 and 3.2: load TSA312.nlm

▶ Use your preferred data archive utility to back up all bindery and server data on the source server, so you can recover should a problem occur during the migration.

▶ Use SYSCON to verify that you are authenticated as a User with Console Operator rights to the NetWare 3.x server.

Windows NT   Complete the following tasks to prepare your NetWare 3.x servers for migration to NetWare 6.

▶ Make sure you have the following NT permissions:

  • Write/Modify permission to the NT Domain and the Registry of the PDC

  • Read permission to all folders and files you are migrating

▶ Make sure you have the Supervisor Right to the NetWare destination server.

▶ If you are running Migration Wizard directly from the source server, install the Novell client that ships with NetWare 6, or a minimum of Novell client for Windows NT/2000 version 4.8 or later.

▶ Install the latest Microsoft Service Pack on the source server.

▶ If you are running Migration Wizard from a workstation, make sure the workstation is registered within the domain to which you want to migrate. If you want to change the domain your workstation is registered in, complete the following instructions for Windows NT or Windows 2000.

  • *Windows NT workstations*: At the workstation, right-click Network Neighborhood and then select Properties. Select the Identification tab and then select Change ⇨ Domain. Specify the appropriate domain, enter your Administrator name and password, and then select OK. Reboot the workstation and launch Migration Wizard again.

  • *Windows 2000 workstations*: At the workstation, right-click My Computer, and then select Properties. Select the Network Identification tab and click Properties. Enter the computer name and appropriate domain, and then select OK. Reboot the workstation and launch Migration Wizard again.

Running Migration Wizard

Once the migration workstation, destination server, and source server are prepared, you are ready to start the actual migration process. This process varies, as described in the following sections, with the type of source server with which you are working.

WARNING

Migration Wizard should only be used during network off hours due to the bandwidth it will consume during the actual data migration.

NetWare 4.x and 5.x   Run Migration Wizard from the location where you installed it, and then complete the following steps:

1. Select Create a New Project and then OK.

2. Select NetWare 4 or NetWare 5 and select OK.

3. Enter a name for the project and specify a place to save it, then select Next. By default, Migration Wizard saves all projects to C:\Program Files\Novell\NetWare Migration Wizard.

4. Select the eDirectory tree that contains your source server and select Next.

5. Select your source server from the eDirectory tree and select Next.

6. Select the eDirectory tree that contains your destination server and select Next.

7. Select your destination server from the destination eDirectory tree and select Next.

8. To save your project and access the Project window, select Create.

9. In the Project window, select Copy Volumes. Before Migration Wizard starts copying files, it backs up your directory and file trustees, and saves them in files located on the source and the destination server. Once the eDirectory migration is complete, Migration Wizard restores the trustees from the files it stored on the destination server.

10. Select each volume name from the text field, and then select Yes. You do not need to copy all volumes at once. You can select volumes to copy now, and then copy other volumes later by reopening the project file.

WARNING

If you copy your volumes in phases, there is an additional step to make sure that all trustee assignments are restored properly. When you are ready to copy the final volume, make sure you select all previously-copied volumes and click Cancel. If you don't do this, Migration Wizard will restore trustee assignments only to the last volume(s) that was (or were) copied.

11. Highlight each volume name from the text field, and then select Yes or No. If you have very large volumes, or if you want to reconfigure your data by putting existing directories into different folders on the destination server, you should consider using a backup tape to copy your volumes. If you choose to do this, DO NOT restore the source server's standard SYS: directories to the destination server. These were created during the NetWare 6 installation on the destination server.

12. Decide if you want to copy the source server's SYS: directories to the destination server's SYS:MIG directory, and then select Next. If there are files in the source server's SYS: directories that you want to utilize on the destination server, you can copy the files from the SYS:SYS.MIG directory into the appropriate SYS: directory on the destination server.

NOTE

Remember, any applications that have NLM installed on the source server's SYS: volume will have to be reinstalled after the migration.

13. Choose the method for handling duplicate filenames between the source server and the destination eDirectory tree, and then select Next. You can choose from three options:
    - Don't copy over existing files
    - Copy the source file if it is newer
    - Always copy the source file

14. Choose how you would like to copy your volumes and then select Next. You can choose from two options:
    - Copy volumes with users logged in
    - Disable login

TIP

Migration Wizard does not copy open files. If you disable user login during the migration, you can be sure that no other users will login to the network and open files during the file copy.

15. Enter the passwords for the source and destination trees and select Next.

16. If prompted, resolve any critical errors or warnings and select Next.

17. To copy the file system to the destination eDirectory tree, select Migrate.

18. Review the error and success logs and select Done.

NetWare 3.x   Run Migration Wizard from the location where you installed it — by default: Start ➪ Programs ➪ Novell ➪ NetWare Migration Wizard ➪ NetWare Migration Wizard — and then complete the following steps:

1. Select Create a New Project and then OK.

2. Select NetWare 3 and select OK.

3. Enter a name for the project and specify a place to save it, then select Next. By default, Migration Wizard saves all projects to C:\Program Files\Novell\NetWare Migration Wizard.

4. Select the source server, or servers, from the list of available NetWare 3 servers and select Next.

5. Select the eDirectory tree into which the NetWare 3 bindery objects will be installed and select Next.

6. Have Migration Wizard find any NetWare 3 and eDirectory User objects that have the same name by selecting Yes, and then Next. During the migration, Migration Wizard will look for duplicate usernames in the destination eDirectory tree and on the NetWare 3 source server. Migration Wizard will then display its findings and you can determine whether or not to merge the matching user names.

7. To save your project and access the Project window, select Create. Migration Wizard will create success and error logs to document the migration process. You will be able to view these logs at the end of the migration process.

8. To initiate the object comparison, browse the tree and select an eDirectory container, and then click OK. Migration Wizard will search this container and all subordinate containers for matching eDirectory usernames.

9. To continue the object comparison, click Next to begin searching for duplicate usernames.

10. Then determine how you want to handle each of the matching usernames and select Finish. You have the following three merge options for each duplicate NetWare 3 user. If no selection is made, Migration Wizard will automatically merge the NetWare 3 user with the displayed eDirectory user.

    • *Merge the NetWare 3 user with the displayed eDirectory user*: To select this option do nothing.

    • *Merge with an eDirectory user other than that currently displayed*: Select the arrow by the eDirectory username to view a drop-down list containing all the eDirectory users that have the same username (including context) as the adjacent NetWare 3 user. Select one of the eDirectory names and continue with the next NetWare 3 user.

- *Do not merge the NetWare 3 user with any eDirectory user:* If you know that none of the listed eDirectory users represents the same person as the adjacent NetWare 3 user, click the arrow by the eDirectory username and then click Don't Merge.

11. The Project window now appears. Review the three steps in the Using the Project Window screen and select Close.

NOTE

The NetWare 3 users that you chose to merge with eDirectory User objects appear automatically in the destination eDirectory tree. Here you can plan the migration process prior to actually performing it. All object modeling is done offline, meaning that none of the changes actually take place until the migration project is actually run.

12. Use the Project window to plan the migration, as follows. The source server's objects and data are shown in the left side of the Project window, and the destination eDirectory tree is displayed in the right side of the Project window.

a. Determine which NetWare 3 bindery objects and volume data will be copied to which containers in the destination server's eDirectory tree.

b. Create new containers and folders, as needed, for the NetWare 3 bindery objects in the eDirectory tree.

X-REF

For more information on creating containers and folders in eDirectory, see Chapter 5.

c. Drag and drop NetWare 3 bindery objects, folders, and volumes into eDirectory containers.

13. From the Migration Wizard toolbar, select Project ⇨ Verify and Migrate Project. The verification will review the proposed locations for the new NetWare 3 objects to make sure they do not conflict with existing names in the destination eDirectory tree.

IMPORTANT

You may be notified during the verification that certain NLM files are outdated on your NetWare 3 source server. Those files MUST be updated. The proper versions of these NLMs are supplied with Migration Wizard. They are available in the Products\NW3X directory that the Migration Wizard installation routine creates. By default this is C:\PROGRAM FILES\NOVELL\NETWARE MIGRATION WIZARD\Products\NW3X. Copy *only* the NLM files that Migration Wizard prompts you to. After copying the NLM files, reboot the NetWare 3 source server and re-launch Migration Wizard.

14. Read the Welcome screen and select Next.

15. (Conditional) If you are migrating more than one server, choose the order that you want your servers migrated in and select Next. This matters only if you have duplicate User objects among your source servers.

16. If prompted, specify the volume to which you want to migrate your NetWare 3 print queue and select Next.

17. (Conditional) If you want to apply a Template object to newly created users, browse the tree, select the Template object from the tree view, and then select Next. Home directories are not automatically migrated. To migrate them, you must drag and drop the NetWare 3 directory that lists the home directories into the destination eDirectory tree. Then use a Template object when migrating your NetWare 3 users to the destination eDirectory tree and make sure that the specified home directory path in the Template object points to the location where you dropped the NetWare 3 directory in the destination eDirectory tree.

NOTE

If you have not created a Template object but you want to use one now, save the project and exit Migration Wizard. Use ConsoleOne to create the Template object, then restart Migration Wizard and select Open Last Project. Pick up the migration project starting with Step 12 above.

18. Choose an option for handling duplicate files between the NetWare 3 source server(s) and the destination eDirectory tree and select Next. You have three options:

- Don't copy over existing files
- Copy the source file if it is newer
- Always copy the source file

19. If you are migrating this NetWare 3 server for the first time, select Yes and then Next. If you are continuing with a previous migration, select No and then Next.

NOTE

> When you migrate users and groups from NetWare 3, Migration Wizard stores a table in the bindery of each source server of the eDirectory names that it associates with the migrated NetWare 3 users as they are migrated to the destination eDirectory tree. This way, you can migrate NetWare 3 objects in phases and Migration Wizard will remember where they were migrated. This also lets Migration Wizard assign the correct file permissions to the appropriate users.

20. Enter the password for the destination eDirectory tree and select Next.

21. Enter the password for the source server that you are migrating and select Next. If you are migrating multiple servers at one time, you will see this screen for every source server that you migrate.

22. Verify that you have enough disk space on the destination volume to accommodate the NetWare 3 file system and select Next. Migration Wizard will also scan the contents of all dropped folders and verify that you have sufficient rights to migrate them.

23. (Conditional) Resolve any naming conflicts between objects of different types and select Next. You can choose to rename them or not migrate them. If you are migrating multiple servers at one time, you will see this screen for every source server that you are migrating.

24. (Conditional) Resolve any naming conflicts between objects of the same type and select Next. You can choose to merge them or not migrate them. If you are migrating multiple servers at one time, you will see this screen for every source server that you are migrating.

25. Verify that you do not want to migrate the NetWare 3 users listed, and select Next. You will see this screen for every source server that you are not migrating. If you see a user, or users, that should be migrated, select Cancel to return to the Project Window and drag and drop those users that should be migrated.

26. Verify that you do not want to migrate the NetWare 3 groups listed, and select Next. You will see this screen for every source server that you are not migrating. If you see a group, or groups, that should be migrated, select Cancel to return to the Project Window and drag and drop those users that should be migrated.

27. Resolve any critical errors and select Next. Warnings, or non-critical errors, can be resolved after the migration. To resolve a critical error or warning, read the description in the text field located beneath it. This description should give you a good idea of what could be the possible cause of the error and a suggestion for fixing it.

28. Read the Verification Summary and click Proceed to start the actual migration.

29. View the Error Log and the Success Log.

This completes the NetWare 3 migration process. Complete the following post-migration tasks to make sure the new server is ready to function in your NetWare 6 environment.

▶ Modify the print configuration if you want to convert your queue-based printing to NDPS.

X-REF

> **For more information on converting from queue-based printing to NDPS, see Chapter 7.**

▶ Confirm that all migrated applications are functioning properly.

▶ Install any additional NetWare 6 products and services. This can be done from the server console by selecting Novell ➪ Install from the graphical management interface, or remotely from a workstation using Deployment Manager.

▶ Confirm that each migrated user has the correct Novell client properties so they can successfully log into the destination eDirectory tree.

▶ Modify user login scripts as needed to accommodate the new data location in the eDirectory tree.

▶ Reassign home directories if they were not migrated.

Windows NT Run Migration Wizard from the location where you installed it — by default: Start ➪ Programs ➪ Novell ➪ NetWare Migration Wizard ➪ NetWare Migration Wizard — and then complete the following steps:

1. Select Create a New Project and then OK.

2. Select Microsoft Windows NT 3.51/4 server and select OK.

3. Verify that the NT domain that appears in the grayed-out text field is the domain that you want to migrate. Migration Wizard automatically displays the NT domain of which your workstation or server is a member.

4. Enter a name for the project and specify a place to save it, then select Next. By default, Migration Wizard saves all projects to C:\Program Files\Novell\NetWare Migration Wizard.

5. Select the eDirectory tree into which the NT domain data will be installed and select Next. If you are not logged into the appropriate eDirectory tree, its name will not appear in the drop-down list. To remedy this, select the Browse button to log into the eDirectory tree.

6. Select Yes to have Migration Wizard find any NT Domain and eDirectory User objects that have the same name, and select Next. During the migration, Migration Wizard will look for duplicate usernames in the destination eDirectory tree and on the NT source server. Migration Wizard will then display its findings and you can determine whether or not to merge the matching user names.

7. To save your project and access the Project Window, select Create. Migration Wizard will create success and error logs to document the migration process.

8. To initiate the object comparison, browse the tree, select an eDirectory container, and then click OK. Migration Wizard will search this container and all subordinate containers for matching eDirectory usernames.

9. Continue the object comparison by clicking Next to begin searching for duplicate usernames.

10. Then, determine how you want to handle each of the matching usernames and select Finish. You have the following three merge options for each NT user. If no selection is made, Migration Wizard will automatically merge the NT user with the displayed eDirectory user.

   - *Merge the NT user with the displayed eDirectory user*: To select this option do nothing.

   - *Merge the NT user with a different eDirectory user*: Select the arrow by the eDirectory username to view a drop-down list containing all the eDirectory users that have the same username (including context) as the adjacent NT user. Select one of the eDirectory names and continue with the next NTuser.

- *Do not merge any of the eDirectory users with the NT user*: If you know that none of the listed eDirectory users represents the same person as the adjacent NT user, click the arrow by the eDirectory username and then click Don't Merge.

11. The Project window now appears. Review the three steps in the Using the Project Window screen and select Close.

NOTE

The NT users that you chose to merge with eDirectory User objects appear automatically in the destination eDirectory tree. Here you can plan the migration process prior to actually performing it. All object modeling is done offline, meaning that none of the changes actually take place until the migration project is actually run.

12. Use the Project window to plan the migration. The source server's objects and data are shown in the left side of the Project window, and the destination eDirectory tree is displayed in the right side of the Project window. Perform the following:

a. Determine which NT objects and data will be copied to which containers in the destination server's eDirectory tree.

b. Create new containers and folders, as needed, for the NT bindery objects in the eDirectory tree.

X-REF

For more information on creating containers and folders in eDirectory, see Chapter 5.

c. Drag and drop NT domain objects, folders, and volumes into eDirectory containers.

13. From the Migration Wizard toolbar, select Project ⇨ Verify and Migrate Project. The verification will review the proposed locations for the new NT objects to make sure they do not conflict with existing names in the destination eDirectory tree.

14. Read the Welcome screen and select Next.

15. (Conditional) If you want to apply a Template object to newly created users, browse to the Template object and select Next. To migrate NT home directories you MUST use a template. Make sure the Home Directory property is defined for the Template object you are using.

NOTE

If you have not created a Template object but you want to use one now, save the project and exit Migration Wizard. Use ConsoleOne to create the Template object, then restart Migration Wizard and select Open Last Project. Pick up the migration project starting with Step 12 above.

16. Choose an option for handling duplicate files between the NT source server(s) and the destination eDirectory tree and select Next. You have three options:

- Don't copy over existing files
- Copy the source file if it is newer
- Always copy the source file

17. Choose an option for handling NT user passwords and select Next. You have three options:

- *Assign the same password to all users*: Migration Wizard will assign the same password to all migrated users.

- *Assign a randomly generated password to all users*: Migration Wizard will randomly generate passwords, assign them, and then store the passwords it assigns in a file that it creates, named *project_name*_OUT.TXT. This file is saved in the same directory where your migration project is located.

- *Read passwords from a file*: Migration Wizard will migrate the current NT passwords to the destination eDirectory tree by reading them from a text file. You must create the text file containing the NT passwords before you begin the migration. For more information on how to create this file, click the Help button.

18. At the NT Migration Options screen, make your desired selections and select Next. You have three options:

- *Migrate file permissions*: Normally, Migration Wizard migrates file and directory permissions. If, for some reason, you want to reassign file and directory permissions, you can choose to not copy the file and directory permissions here and then assign them later with ConsoleOne.

- *Migrate Everyone permissions*: The eDirectory container that you drop the NT Domain Info object into will be assigned the permissions that were associated with group Everyone. If you are migrating the Everyone permissions, be sure to drop the NT

Domain Info object high enough in the eDirectory tree so that all NT users will inherit those permissions.

NOTE

Every new folder that is created in the NT domain automatically receives the Everyone permissions by default.

- *Restart option*: Normally, this information is not needed; however, if you have previously run a migration and deleted the eDirectory objects from the destination tree, and you are planning to start over and migrate the same domain again, check this checkbox.

NOTE

When you migrate users and groups from NT, Migration Wizard stores a table of NT names and associated eDirectory usernames in the registry of the Primary Domain Controller (PDC). Migration Wizard then uses this information when migrating the file system so that it can remember where each user and group has been migrated to in the destination eDirectory tree. By storing this information, Migration Wizard can assign the correct file permissions to the appropriate users.

19. In the Verify NT to NetWare Project window, select Next to begin the verification.

20. (Conditional) Resolve any naming conflicts between objects of different types and select Next. You can choose to rename them or not migrate them. If you are migrating multiple servers at one time, you will see this screen for every source server that you are migrating.

21. (Conditional) Resolve any naming conflicts between objects of the same type and select Next. You can choose to merge them or not migrate them. If you are migrating multiple servers at one time, you will see this screen for every source server that you are migrating.

22. (Conditional) Verify that you do not want to migrate the NT users and groups listed and select Next. This procedure will be repeated three times — for NT local groups, NT global groups, and NT users that were not dragged and dropped into the destination eDirectory tree.

23. If you see a user, or users, that should be migrated, select Cancel to return to the Project Window and drag and drop those users that should be migrated. Then select Project ➪ Start Migration, and restart the migration with Step 12 above.

24. Resolve any critical errors. Warnings or non-critical errors can be resolved after the migration. To resolve a critical error or warning, read the description in the text field located beneath it. This description should give you a good idea of what could be the possible cause and a suggestion for fixing it.

25. Select Proceed to start the actual migration.

26. Enter the password for the destination eDirectory tree and select Next.

27. View the Error Log and the Success Log.

This completes the Windows NT migration process. Complete the following post-migration tasks to make sure the new server is ready to function in your NetWare 6 environment.

▶ Install the latest Novell client software on any workstations that were used exclusively for NT domain access. Alternatively, you can use Native File Access Pack to allow workstations to access NetWare files without any client software.

For more information on the Novell client and the Native File Access Pack see Chapter 2.

X-REF

▶ Use ConsoleOne to make sure that your NT users and groups have been migrated to the correct place in the destination eDirectory tree and have the correct file and shared permissions. If you don't see the permissions you were expecting, go to a DOS prompt and type **CACLS/?**, then follow the on-screen instructions. NT permissions are sometimes hidden in Microsoft utilities. This command will let you see all permissions associated with your NT objects, even the hidden ones.

▶ At the destination NetWare server, use ConsoleOne to view the volume you migrated your data to and verify that it was done correctly.

▶ Configure printer mappings in NDPS.

For more information on NDPS, see Chapter 7.

X-REF

▶ Check the migrated users' home directories to make sure they were migrated the way you expected them to be.

▶ Distribute the new eDirectory passwords to all of your users. The passwords are located in a password file that Migration Wizard created for you named *project_name*_OUT.TXT. This file is located in the same directory where you saved your migration project.

Post-Installation Tasks with Deployment Manager

Once you have installed a NetWare 6 server, or servers, into your network you can add additional products remotely through Deployment Manager. There are three post-installation tasks with which you should be familiar.

▸ *Use DSREPAIR to check eDirectory and schema status*: Almost invariably, when you make significant changes to an eDirectory-managed network, such as the introduction of NetWare 6, you need to make sure everything gets back to an even keel. Deployment Manager recommends using DSREPAIR to accomplish this (see Figure 1.3). DSREPAIR lets you review and repair eDirectory databases and communications. To review and repair your eDirectory environment, perform the following:

WARNING

Full Unattended Repair can take a while on a large network. It also locks the eDirectory database during some of its tasks. Do not run this option when the network is busy.

FIGURE 1.3 *Post-installation tasks on Deployment Manager*

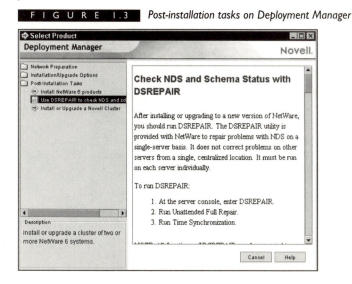

a. Type DSREPAIR to load the DSREPAIR utility at the console of the server you recently installed or upgraded (see Figure 1.4).

▶ · ◀

FIGURE 1.4   *DSREPAIR main menu*

b. Select Time synchronization. Look at the Time is in sync column to see if all servers report as being in Sync (see Figure 1.5). Press the Esc key to go back to the main menu.

▶ · ◀

FIGURE 1.5   *Time synchronization report*

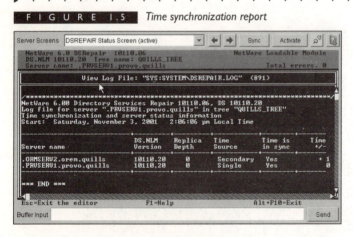

c. Select Report synchronization status. The last line of the report should tell you that all servers are synchronized (see Figure 1.6). Press the Esc key to go back to the main menu.

FIGURE 1.6 *Replica synchronization report*

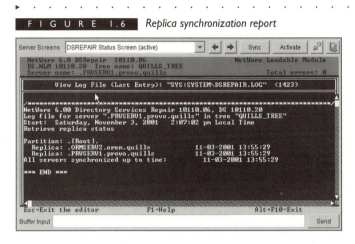

d. Select Unattended full repair. This option will perform the most common set of eDirectory repair features and automatically correct any errors it finds (see Figure 1.7). If you get errors reported, run Unattended full repair again to make sure they are properly fixed. Press the Esc key to go back to the main menu.

FIGURE 1.7 *Unattended full repair report*

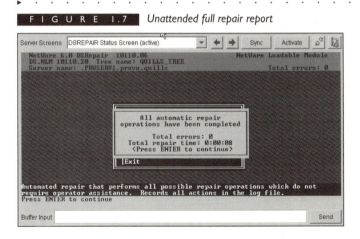

e. Exit DSREPAIR by selecting Exit and Yes.

TIP

These same tasks can be run remotely by using RConsoleJ from ConsoleOne. For more information on using RConsoleJ see Chapter 3. For more information on managing eDirectory databases and communications see Chapter 5.

▶ *Install or upgrade a Novell cluster*: If you are ready to implement Novell Cluster Services (NCS), or if you prepared an existing NetWare 5 cluster for upgrade as part of your network preparation for NetWare 6, you can use this option in Deployment Manager to create a NetWare 6 cluster.

X-REF

The installation and configuration of NCS is covered in Chapter 12.

▶ *Install NetWare 6 products*: This option lets you install products on your NetWare 6 servers remotely, instead of having to visit the server directly. It also provides a much nicer interface than the text-based NWCONFIG utility. To install a new product on the NetWare 6 server, complete the following:

NOTE

The installation of NetWare 6 products with Deployment Manager also requires the NICI client. For more information on the NICI client and how it is installed see Chapter 2.

a. Select Install NetWare 6 Products in the left pane of Deployment Manager.

b. Select the Target server from the list of available servers and then select Next.

c. Provide authentication information to connect to the target server and select OK. If you have any problem connecting, select Details and Connect by Address. Then supply the IP address of the server to which you want to attach.

d. At the Components screen, select the products you want to install and select Next. You may also deselect any products that have already been installed, or that do not need to be installed at this time.

e. (Conditional) Depending on the products you choose to install, you may be prompted to provide additional information.

f. At the Summary screen make your desired selections. To customize any product settings for the products you are installing, select Customize, and at the Product Customization screen, navigate to the operating system component or NetWare service that you want to customize in the left pane. If any configuration information is available, the Configure button in the right pane will be active. Select Configure to view the current configuration and make any desired changes, if applicable.

g. Select Finish to complete the product installation.

The selected NetWare 6 products will be copied to the target server. When the file copy is complete, you will return to the Deployment Manager main menu. You may want to review and note any changes to the target server's AUTOEXEC.NCF for future reference.

Novell Licensing Services

Novell Licensing Services (NLS) has been updated for NetWare 6 to support a new licensing model known as User Access License (UAL). In this model, users gain access to network services by connecting to the network instead of a specific server. The eDirectory User object for each user on the network receives a license unit, reserved for their User object, which provides them access to network services at any time and from any network workstation, regardless of location.

The UAL model replaces the Server Connection License model used with NetWare 5 and previous versions of NetWare. The UAL model is much easier to manage since you no longer have to track connections on individual servers, just connections to the network as a whole.

When you install or upgrade to NetWare 6, NLS is automatically installed. Actual license certificates may be installed either during the installation or post-installation. NetWare 6 uses iManage to install and manage license certificates. You can't do it from ConsoleOne. License certificates enable users to access network resources, including NetWare servers and NLS-enabled applications and services.

For more information on iManage, see Chapter 3.

X-REF

Introduction to NLS

There are three main components to NLS:

▶ *License Service Provider (LSP)*: This is the licensing software that runs on NetWare 6 servers. When you install NetWare 6 and its license certificates, the LSP software is copied to the server and an LSP object is created in the eDirectory tree. An LSP provides the actual licensing service. It handles requests from NLS clients and maintains the license certificates, which are stored in eDirectory.

TIP

> Any eDirectory partition that will contain License Certificate objects should have at least one of its replicas stored on a server operating as an LSP.

▶ *NLS client*: This is software that requests licensing services from an LSP. The NLS client will locate and communicate with LSPs as needed to request license information on behalf of NLS-enabled applications. NLS clients are used on both client workstations and NetWare servers. Nothing needs to be done to load an NLS client. The necessary components are installed with the Novell client for workstations and as part of the NetWare installation for servers.

▶ *NLS eDirectory objects*: There are two main licensing objects used by NLS, in addition to the LSP object mentioned above.

  • *License Certificate object*: When an NLS license is installed, a License Certificate object is created that corresponds to the printed license statement that is typically included in the packaging for software products. The name of the License Certificate object typically corresponds to a serial number or name specified by the software vendor.

  • *License Container object*: The License Container object is a special container object in eDirectory that is used to store License Certificate objects. When you install a license certificate, NLS creates a new License Container object unless a license container already exists. Each license container holds one or more license certificates. License Container objects are named using publisher, product, and version.

NLS requests are handled through the following process:

I. An application, either from a server or a workstation, issues a request to the NLS client.

2. The NLS client library packages the request from the application and submits it to an LSP.

3. The LSP examines the request and determines whether it can fill the request. It does this by checking the eDirectory context of the requesting client for the specific information or license unit being requested.

4. If the requested resource is available, the LSP fills the request. If the LSP cannot fill the request, it searches for a resource. The LSP will start searching in its current container and then work its way upward in the tree.

5. Once the search is complete, the LSP returns a license status (i.e. available/not available) to the client library.

6. The library returns status to the application.

7. The application determines action based upon the status of license units.

Installing NLS

NLS v5.02 is installed automatically with NetWare 6. NetWare 4.x and NetWare 5.x servers will be upgraded to NLS v5.02 during the upgrade to NetWare 6. To verify that NLS was installed and is running properly, check the following:

▸ At the server console GUI, select Novell ⇨ Install, and then look for an NLS entry.

▸ Check that NLSLSP.NLM is running on the server. To do this, enter the `modules nls*` command at the server console or through RConsoleJ.

▸ With ConsoleOne, check that there is an LSP object in the container where the server is installed. It will have the name NLS_LSP_*servername*. You can also view this object through iManage.

Managing NLS Licenses

Novell typically distributes licenses in an *envelope*, which is a file with the extension .NLF (Novell License File). The envelope contains one or more license certificates. Envelopes allow you to install more than one license certificate at a time into License Container objects. For example, if you have purchased three products in a suite, you can use an envelope to simultaneously install license certificates for all three products. In some cases you will also see individual license certificates. They are files with an extension of .NLS.

Installing license certificates

When adding license certificates to the eDirectory tree, you should know where in the tree you want to install the license certificate. This location or context will determine who can use the license units associated with that license certificate.

For more information on installing and configuring iManage, see Chapter 3.

X-REF

To Install license certificates through iManage, complete the following steps:

1. Open iManage and select Roles and Tasks.

2. In the Task frame, select License Management and then Install a License.

3. Browse to and select the license file and select Next. NetWare 6 licenses are normally found on a diskette in the folder A:\LICENSE. Some NLS-enabled applications also link their license certificates to a separate activation key. This key is stored in a file with a .KEY extension or can be entered manually to unlock the license certificate.

4. Choose the license(s) you want to install and select Next. NetWare 6, for example, includes both a server license unit and a group of user license units in each .NLF file.

5. Specify the context where you want the license certificates installed and select Install. If no License Container object exists in the context that you specify, one will be created. If a server license is being installed you will also need to specify the server to which this license should be applied.

6. Select Done to exit the license installation routine.

You can also use this process to allow only designated servers to grant requests for license units. This is known as a *server assignment*. Some products require that a license certificate have a server assignment before the certificate can be used. The following guidelines apply to server assignments:

▶ Only one server assignment can be made for each license certificate.

▶ No other server can allow use of units from that license certificate.

▶ A server with a server assignment can have multiple license certificates assigned to it.

Delete an NLS license

To delete license certificates through iManage, complete the following steps:

X-REF

For more information on installing and configuring iManage, see Chapter 3.

1. Open iManage and select Roles and Tasks.

2. In the Task frame, select License Management and then Delete a License.

3. Browse to the appropriate license and select OK. Remember to browse into the license container to choose a specific license object. You may also select an entire license container, if desired.

TIP

You cannot move a license certificate from one location to another. To move a license certificate, delete it from its current location and then install it to the new location.

CHAPTER 2

NetWare Clients

Instant Access

Configuring Novell client

This client is the traditional NetWare client and is still required for some functionality, including many administrative tasks.

- ▶ Novell provides two versions of the NetWare client with NetWare 6: one for Windows 95/98 and one for Windows NT/2000. They are available on the NetWare 6 Client CD-ROM.

- ▶ Once installed, you can configure the Novell client by using the Novell client property pages. Right-click on the red "N" icon in the system tray and select Novell Client Properties.

- ▶ To configure the login for a Novell client user, create a login script. Login scripts can be associated with Container, Profile, and User objects. A login script can control what happens when a user logs into your Novell network.

- ▶ If you are upgrading many existing Novell or Microsoft clients for NetWare 6, you can use the Automatic Client Upgrade (ACU) feature to automate this process. Place ACU commands in a profile or container login script to detect if the client software needs to be installed, and then the ACU updates the workstation automatically, if necessary, when the user logs in.

Working with NICI client

NICI client (Novell International Cryptographic Infrastructure) provides cryptographic services to client-side applications and services.

- ▶ In NetWare 6 the client-side applications and services include: Deployment Manager, Advanced Audit, Native File Access, Novell Modular Authentication Service (NMAS) and Certificate server.

- ▶ NetWare 6 includes NICI client versions 1.5.7 and 2.0.2 on the NetWare 6 Client CD-ROM. They can actually be installed side-by-side to make sure that every application has what it needs.

Integrating NMAS client

Novell Modular Authentication Services (NMAS) allow you to supplement or replace the traditional Novell password authentication mechanism with alternative mechanisms such as Smart Cards, Tokens, and Biometrics.

▶ The NMAS client provides framework within which authentication methods can be configured and integrated with Novell eDirectory to provide a flexible and seamless authentication process.

▶ The NMAS client can be installed from the NetWare 6 Client CD-ROM.

Mapping drives to servers with NetDrive client

Novell NetDrive lets you map a drive to any server without using the traditional Novell client.

▶ With NetDrive, you can access your files on any server and modify them through standard Windows utilities such as Windows Explorer.

▶ The NetDrive client can be installed from the NetWare 6 Client CD-ROM.

Accessing files with Native File Access Pack (NFAP)

NetWare 6 offers a way to access the NetWare file system using a workstation's native file access protocols.

▶ NFAP supports Windows CIFS, Apple AFP, and UNIX/Linux NFS.

▶ NFAP can be installed during the NetWare 6 installation or after by using Deployment Manager or the graphical server console.

Updating to the latest client software

▶ Novell frequently updates its client software.

▶ Check on Novell's Support Web site's software download page at `http://download.novell.com/` for the latest versions of the NetWare clients.

Introduction to Novell Clients

On a NetWare network, workstations traditionally use special Novell client software to access NetWare servers. (Workstations are often called *clients* because they request services from the network.) This client software enables the workstation to communicate with the network. However, with the release of Netware 6, Novell is accelerating its move away from a large, monolithic client and toward small, service-specific clients and clientless services. Web-based management, iFolder, iPrint, and Native File Access are just a few ways that NetWare 6 lets you move your network in this direction.

Does that mean Novell client is no longer necessary? Absolutely not. Novell client is still required for advanced authentication and many administrative tasks associated with NetWare and Novell eDirectory. So, although you may not automatically install the Novell client on every workstation, you will still need it for several aspects of your network's operation.

This chapter explains how to install and configure the traditional Novell client software on the both Windows 95/98 and Windows NT/2000 workstations. This chapter describes how to use the Automatic Client Upgrade (ACU) feature to simplify the process of upgrading numerous workstations to the latest NetWare 6 client software. It also explains how to remove the client software, should that become necessary.

NOTE Novell no longer supports Client32 for DOS/Windows 3.1x. However, if you still need it, the final release of this client is available on Novell's software download page at `http://download.novell.com/`. Similarly, the NetWare client for Macintosh, available alternatively through Novell and third party partners, is no longer available. However, NetWare 6 supports Mac users through the Native File Access Pack, which is described later in this chapter.

In addition to the traditional Novell client software, Novell has collected other modular client pieces on the NetWare 6 Client CD-ROM. These include the NICI client, the NMAS client and the NetDrive client. This chapter will present overviews and installation procedures for these client pieces. Some service-specific clients, such as that for iPrint and iFolder, are not included on the NetWare 6 Client CD-ROM and will be discussed in their appropriate product sections.

Finally, this chapter presents Novell Native File Access Pack (NFAP), a new client option for NetWare 6 that may well eliminate the need for traditional NetWare clients for many network users.

The Traditional Novell Client

The Novell client installation program automatically copies all necessary NetWare files to the workstation, and edits any configuration files that require modification. In order to have full administrative capabilities on the NetWare network, you must use Novell's client software instead of that provided by Microsoft.

You can choose one of three methods for installing the Novell client on your workstation:

- ▶ Install the client software directly from the NetWare 6 Client CD-ROM.

- ▶ Upgrade existing workstations by copying the installation files from the CD-ROM to a network directory. This makes the update files readily accessible to any workstation attached to the network.

- ▶ You can download the latest Novell client from Novell's software download page at `http://download.novell.com/`. Periodically, Novell releases updated clients with new features, so the client files on the Internet may be newer than those on the NetWare 6 Client CD-ROM. It's a good idea to check this location occasionally for updates.

The installation procedure for Windows 95/98 and Windows NT/2000 workstations is identical, so you can use the installation, configuration, and removal instructions regardless of the version of Windows you are running. However, before you can install the client, your workstation must meet the following requirements:

PLATFORM	HARDWARE REQUIREMENTS	SOFTWARE REQUIREMENTS
Windows 95/98	486 processor or better Minimum 28MB free disk space Minimum 16MB RAM	Novell recommends using Windows 95 version A with the latest service packs from Microsoft installed. Have access to Windows 95/98 CAB files, either on CD-ROM or hard drive.
Windows NT/2000	Follow minimum recommended hardware requirements from Microsoft. Minimum 24MB RAM	Windows NT must have Service Pack 3 or later. Have access to Windows NT/2000 system files, either on CD-ROM or hard drive.

For either platform, if you are installing a new client, you will also need either a CD-ROM drive or an Internet connection to access the Novell client install files. If you're upgrading an existing workstation that already has a connection to the network, you can run the installation program from a network directory instead.

Once these hardware and software requirements have been met, you are ready to install the client software.

Installing the Client Software

To install the Novell client software on a Windows 95/98 or Windows NT/2000 workstation, complete the following steps:

NOTE

You can use the following procedure whether you're installing a new network workstation or upgrading an existing one. If you are upgrading an existing workstation, the installation program will detect existing settings (such as the protocol used, the network board, and optional features) and use those same settings as the default settings for the upgraded workstation.

1. Install a network board in the workstation according to the manufacturer's documentation and connect the workstation to the network. It's a good idea to record the board's configuration settings, such as its interrupt and port address.

TIP

You may want to use a worksheet such as the "Workstation Installation and Configuration" worksheet in Appendix B.

2. (Optional) If you are planning to upgrade a workstation and want to run the installation program from the network, create a directory called CLIENT under SYS:PUBLIC, and copy the contents of the NetWare 6 Client CD-ROM to the newly created network directory. Also, copy the WINSETUP.EXE file from the root of the CD-ROM to the new installation directory.

NOTE

You can create the CLIENT directory on any NetWare volume, but make sure users have Read and Filescan rights to the folder so they can locate the installation files. For more information on file system rights, see Chapter 6.

3. Run WINSETUP.EXE.

- If you're installing from the CD-ROM, insert the Client CD-ROM and WINSETUP.EXE will start automatically. If it does not, run WINSETUP.EXE from the root of the NetWare 6 Client CD-ROM.

- If you're upgrading an existing workstation and are running the installation program from the network, run WINSETUP.EXE from the directory you created in Step 2.

4. Select a Language for the client installation.

5. Select the client you would like to install (see Figure 2.1). The installation program will automatically detect your workstation OS and not allow you to install the wrong client.

FIGURE 2.1 *NetWare 6 Client Installation screen*

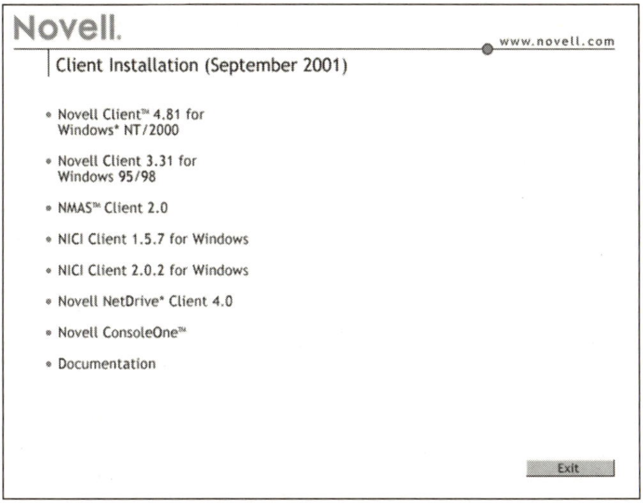

Novell.

www.novell.com

Client Installation (September 2001)

- Novell Client™ 4.81 for Windows* NT/2000
- Novell Client 3.31 for Windows 95/98
- NMAS™ Client 2.0
- NICI Client 1.5.7 for Windows
- NICI Client 2.0.2 for Windows
- Novell NetDrive* Client 4.0
- Novell ConsoleOne™
- Documentation

Exit

6. To accept the license agreement, select Yes.

7. At the Installation Option screen, choose either Typical or Custom installation and select Install. If you select Custom, continue with Step 8. If you choose Typical installation, skip to Step 13. The Typical installation configures the Novell client as follows:

- In addition to the Novell client, Typical install adds NDPS, Novell Workstation Manager, and ZENworks Application Launcher.

- Both IP and IPX protocols.

- Directory-based authentication (NDS).

8. Select the client components you want to install and select Next. If the installation program detects that any of these options are already installed on this workstation, those options will be checked.

9. Choose the network protocol(s) to support and select Next.

   - *IP only*: Installs only the IP protocol. The workstation will be able to communicate only with IP servers, and will not be able to communicate with IPX servers.

   - *IP with IPX Compatibility mode*: Installs the IP protocol, but allows the workstation to communicate with IPX networks if the servers have IPX Compatibility mode and a Migration Agent installed.

   - *IP + IPX*: Installs both protocols, allowing the workstation to communicate with either type of server.

   - *IPX only*: Installs only the IPX protocol, allowing the workstation to communicate with IPX servers, but not directly with IP servers.

10. Choose NDS login connection and select Next. A Bindery connection should only be chosen if NetWare 3 is the primary server environment.

11. (Conditional) If you selected Workstation Manager as a component to install, enter the eDirectory tree to be used by Workstation Manager, and select Next.

12. Select Finish to complete the installation. The installation program will automatically detect and load most LAN drivers for common network adapters. If it cannot detect your network board, it will prompt you to select one. You will need to specify a location for the LAN driver your network adapter requires.

13. At the Installation Complete screen, select Reboot to load the Novell client.

When the workstation reboots, it will automatically connect to the network and present you with a Login screen.

Removing the Client Software

To remove the Novell client software from a Windows 95/98 or Windows NT/2000 workstation, use the Network control panel. The Novell client uninstall will remove all client components from the workstation, but will leave behind a minimal "footprint" in the Windows registry. That way, if you reinstall the client at a later time the installation program can automatically load the same settings that were used previously.

To remove the Novell client from Windows 95/98 complete the following steps:

1. Open the Network Control Panel Applet by selecting Start ➪ Settings ➪ Control Panel and then selecting Network. Alternatively, you can access this utility via Network Neighborhood.

2. Select Novell NetWare client from the list of installed network services and select Remove.

3. Select Yes to confirm your decision.

4. Reboot the workstation to complete the client removal.

To remove the Novell client from Windows NT/2000 complete the following steps:

1. Open the Network control panel by selecting Start ➪ Settings ➪ Control Panel and then selecting Network and Dial-Up Connections. Alternatively, you can access this utility via My Network Places.

2. Select Local Area Connection and then select Properties.

3. Select Novell client for Windows 2000 from the list of installed network services and select Uninstall.

4. Select Yes to confirm your decision.

5. Reboot the workstation to complete the client removal.

The Client Login

At the Novell Login screen, select Advanced to see the various options available for managing user login.

NDS tab

The NDS tab, shown in Figure 2.2, allows you to specify the eDirectory tree, name context, and server to use during login. All users should specify their eDirectory tree and name context. A server only needs to be specified if connection to a NetWare 3 server is needed.

Script tab

The Script tab (see Figure 2.3) is used to manage the execution of login scripts. It allows you to specify whether or not to run scripts; whether or not to display the login results window (and close it automatically); and which Profile and User Login scripts to execute. The Variables button allows you to specify values for any script variables that might be included in the login scripts.

► • ◄

F I G U R E   2.2   *Novell Client Login screen*

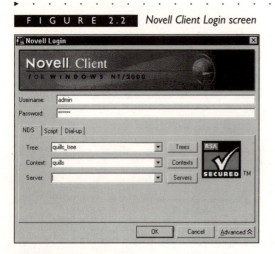

► • ◄

F I G U R E   2.3   *Script tab on the Novell Client Login screen*

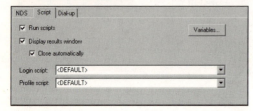

Dial-up tab

The Dial-up tab, shown in Figure 2.4, is only used if a user is connecting to the network via a modem connection. It allows you to configure a client to automatically dial in to the network whenever a user attempts to login. The Dial-Up tab taps into the Windows Dial-Up Networking information. You can select a dialing entry from the Windows phone book and a Windows dialing location profile. This option is used only rarely.

F I G U R E   2 . 4 *Dial-Up tab on the Novell Client Login screen*

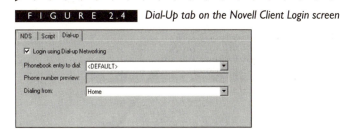

Configuring the Client

After you have installed the Novell client software, you can configure the client software by modifying its properties. The client properties enable you to specify information such as login preferences, protocol settings, default capture settings, and so on. To open the client property pages, right-click the red "N" icon in the system tray and click Novell Client Properties (see Figure 2.5).

F I G U R E   2 . 5   *Novell Client Configuration pages*

There are several different configuration pages available in Novell client properties.

▶ *Client*: The Client page lets you define basic login preferences, similar to the NDS tab in the Novell Login screen.

▶ *Location profiles*: Location profiles allow you to save a specific login configuration so that users don't have to enter login information manually. Location profiles are especially powerful for users who log in from multiple locations (i.e. office, home, laptop, etc.).

▶ *Advanced login*: Advanced login options let you hide certain aspects of the Novell Login screen to prevent users from making changes.

▶ *Contextless login*: Specify the use of an eDirectory catalog for login. This allows users to authenticate using their common name only, rather than having to remember their entire name context.

▶ *Service location*: The Service location page is used to configure the client for the use of Service Location Protocol (SLP). You can specify where and how the client will request network services. For more information on SLP, see the NetWare 6 documentation.

▶ *Advanced settings*: Advanced settings allow you to configure a host of network communications details.

▶ *Advanced menu settings*: Advanced menu settings gives you full control over the client network environment, including what network resources are available, and how they are offered to the network user.

▶ *Default capture*: This page lets you configure a user's NetWare print jobs.

▶ *Protocol preferences*: Protocol preferences let you define the usage order for network protocols and name resolution protocols. The listed protocols will be used in the order specified.

▶ *(Conditional) Single sign-on*: Novell client for Windows NT/2000 adds the Single sign-on tab, which allows you to store the workstation-specific password in eDirectory so that it can be automatically presented as part of a NMAS or single sign-on authentication, if available.

▶ *(Conditional) DHCP settings*: Novell client for Windows NT/2000 adds the DHCP settings to configure the client DHCP environment.

Upgrading Clients with ACU

If you are upgrading many existing workstations to the new Novell client for NetWare 6, you can use the Automatic Client Upgrade (ACU) feature to automate this process. With the ACU, you place ACU commands in a profile or system login script to detect if the client software needs to be installed, and then the ACU updates the workstation automatically, if necessary, when the user logs in.

You can also use the ACU process to upgrade workstations that are currently running Microsoft client for NetWare networks.

The ACU feature works best in situations when your workstations have similar configurations, because you define a common set of instructions for updating all the workstations in the same way.

To use the ACU process to upgrade a workstation to the Novell client, complete the following steps:

1. Create a directory called CLIENT under SYS:PUBLIC, and copy the contents of the NetWare 6 Client CD-ROM to the newly created network directory. Also, copy the WINSETUP.EXE file from the root of the CD-ROM to the new installation directory.

NOTE
You can create the CLIENT directory on any NetWare volume, but make sure users have Read and Filescan rights to the folder so they can locate the installation files. For more information on file system rights, see Chapter 6.

2. (Conditional) If you are upgrading Windows 95/98 workstations, copy the Windows CAB files from the Windows 95/98 installation CD-ROM to the new directory. CAB files are found in the WIN95 or WIN98 directory. If you are upgrading Windows NT/2000 workstations, copy the I386 directory from the Windows NT/2000 installation CD-ROM to the new directory.

3. Using ConsoleOne, create a group object called ACU.

4. Give the ACU group read and file scan rights to the new directory you created in Step 1.

> See Chapter 5 for more information about creating groups and rights assignments.

X-REF

5. Assign each user whose workstation you want to upgrade as a member of the group ACU.

6. Edit the WINSETUP.INI file to specify configuration options you want to use during the upgrade. This file is located together with WINSETUP.EXE in the CLIENT directory that you created in Step 1. This file determines whether the workstation's current client software is old and needs to be upgraded to the newer version.

   a. By default, the upgrade runs automatically when the user logs in. However, you can set it so that the user can choose whether or not to upgrade at that time. To display the screen that lets the user choose whether to upgrade the software, add the following command to the [AcuOptions] heading: `DisplayFirstScreen=Yes`. If the user chooses to skip the upgrade, the upgrade prompt will appear again the next time he or she logs in.

   b. By default, the upgrade will automatically reboot the workstation when it is finished. However, if you want to let the user decide whether or not to reboot the workstation, add the following command to the [AcuOptions] heading: `DisplayLastScreen=Yes`.

7. Add the following command to launch WINSETUP.EXE upon login, substituting the name of your server. For example, `:@\\server\SYS:PUBLIC\WIN98\WINSETUP.EXE`. This command can be placed in an individual script, a container script, or a profile script, depending on how many users you want to upgrade.

> If you want the old client configuration to be backed up on the workstation instead of just being replaced by the new client software, you can add the option /RB (for "rollback") to the end of this command. This option will copy the current software configuration to NOVELL\CLIENT32\NWBACKUP.

TIP

Now, the next time the users in the group log in, their workstations will be upgraded automatically to the new Novell client. For more information on ACU options, see the Novell online documentation.

Other Novell Clients

In addition to the traditional Novell client, there are three other clients included on the NetWare 6 Client CD-ROM. They are:

- ▸ NICI client
- ▸ NMAS client
- ▸ NetDrive client

In addition to these three feature-specific clients, there are a few others that are installed automatically with their respective product software. Each of these clients will be discussed as part of its product overview in other chapters throughout this book.

NICI Client

The Novell International Cryptographic Infrastructure (NICI) is the modular foundation for all crypto-services offered in Novell products and services. NICI client provides cryptographic services to client-side applications and services. NICI client has received FIPS 140-1 (Level 1) certification, which is as good as it gets for client-based cryptographic services.

X-REF

For more information on NICI and other NetWare 6 security services, see Chapter 6.

There are two versions of NICI client included on the NetWare 6 Client CD-ROM: version 1.5.7 and version 2.0.2. They can actually be installed side-by-side to make sure that every application that requires cryptographic services has access to those features that it needs. The following NetWare 6 services rely upon NICI client:

- ▸ *Deployment Manager*: NICI client 2.0.2
- ▸ *Novell Advanced Audit*: NICI client 1.5.7 and 2.0.2
- ▸ *Native File Access*: NICI client 1.5.7
- ▸ *Novell Modular Authentication Service (NMAS)*: NICI client 2.0.2
- ▸ *Novell Certificate server*: NICI client 2.0.2

To install NICI client, complete the following steps:

1. Insert the NetWare 6 Client CD-ROM. The CD-ROM will autoplay and present you with the Novell client installation menu. If the CD-ROM does not autoplay, run WINSETUP.EXE from the root of the Client CD-ROM.

2. Select NICI Client X.X.X for Windows. Select whichever version of NICI client is required for the services you need.

3. At the NICI client Welcome screen, select Next.

4. At the License Agreement screen, select Yes.

5. At the Setup Complete screen, select Finish to complete the installation.

NMAS Client

Novell Modular Authentication Services (NMAS) allow you to supplement or replace the traditional Novell password authentication mechanism with alternative mechanisms such as Smart Cards, Tokens, and Biometrics. NetWare 6 includes the NMAS Starter Pack, which offers two alternative authentication methods. NMAS Enterprise Edition, which is sold as an add-on product, adds support for many third-party authentication methods, multi-factor authentication, and graded authentication.

The NMAS client provides a framework within which authentication methods can be configured and integrated with Novell eDirectory to provide a flexible and seamless authentication process.

For more information on NMAS see Chapter 6.

X-REF

To install the NMAS client, complete the following steps:

1. Insert the NetWare 6 Client CD-ROM. The CD-ROM will autoplay and present you with the Novell client installation menu. If the CD-ROM does not autoplay, run WINSETUP.EXE from the root of the Client CD-ROM.

2. The latest version of the Novell client and NICI client 2.0.2 are required for installation of the NMAS client. Make sure they are installed prior to installing the NMAS client.

3. Select NMAS client 2.0.

4. At the NMAS Installation screen, make sure that the NMAS client checkbox is checked and select OK. The installation routine will review the versions of the Novell client and NICI client to make sure that all prerequisites have been met.

5. At the Novell License screen select Accept.

6. Select the login methods you want to use and select Next.

   - *Simple password*: This authentication method is used with Native File Access Pack to provide unencrypted password support required for Local Windows and NFS authentication.

   - *X509 certificate*: This authentication method provides digital certificate-based login to the Novell environment.

7. At the Optional NMAS Features screen, select Next. Select the Enable Disconnected Login checkbox if you want to require users to enter their eDirectory password even while they are disconnected from the network. This is only used in conjunction with Novell's Single Sign-On product, which can be purchased as an add-on to NetWare 6.

8. At the Install Complete, screen select OK. Select the Restart Later radio button if you don't want the client workstation to restart immediately.

When the workstation reboots you will see the new NMAS Login screen.

For more information on configuring and using NMAS login methods see Chapter 6.

X-REF

NetDrive Client

Novell NetDrive lets you to map a drive to any server without using the traditional Novell client. This means that with NetDrive, you can access your files on any server and modify them through standard Windows utilities such as Windows Explorer.

To install the NetDrive client, complete the following steps:

1. Insert the NetWare 6 Client CD-ROM. The CD-ROM will autoplay and present you with the Novell client installation menu. If the CD-ROM does not autoplay, run WINSETUP.EXE from the root of the Client CD-ROM.

2. Select Novell NetDrive client 4.0.

3. At the Welcome screen, select Next.

4. At the License Agreement screen, select Yes.

5. At the Destination Location screen, browse to the location where the NetDrive client should be installed and select Next.

For more information on using NetDrive see Chapter 10.

X-REF

Native File Access Pack

Novell Native File Access Pack (NFAP) lets Macintosh, Windows, and UNIX workstations access and store files on NetWare servers without installing the Novell client. NFAP is installed on the NetWare 6 server and provides "instant" network access. Just plug in the network cable, start the computer, and you've got access to servers on your network.

NFAP lets client workstations access the NetWare 6 file system using the same protocols that they use internally to perform local file operations such as copy, delete, move, save, and open. Windows workstations perform these tasks using the Common Internet File System (CIFS) protocol; Macintosh workstations use the AppleTalk Filing Protocol (AFP); and UNIX/Linux computers use the Network File System (NFS) protocol. This not only eliminates the overhead of a special network client, but also allows users to perform network tasks using the same familiar tools that they use to work on their local drives.

Native File Access Pack Requirements

NFAP requires NetWare 6 server and at least one Administrator Workstation running the Novell client.

NetWare server requirements

To check your server's configuration, select Novell, and then Install from the NetWare server GUI. The server must have the following configuration to run Novell Native File Access Software:

- ► NetWare 6 server.
- ► Novell Modular Authentication Service (NMAS) version 2 or later. NMAS will be automatically installed or upgraded during the NFAP installation. NMAS Starter Pack is automatically upgraded to NMAS Starter Pack 2.0. NMAS Enterprise Edition is upgraded to NMAS Enterprise Edition 2.0.

- ▸ (Conditional) Prior to the NFAP installation, load the Macintosh Name Space on each Traditional NetWare volume that will support Mac clients. To load Macintosh Name Space to a volume, enter the following at the server console: `ADD NAME SPACE MACINTOSH TO VOLUME volume_name`.

- ▸ (Conditional) If the server is currently supporting Mac clients through a traditional NetWare for Macintosh client, unload AFP.NLM and APPLETLK.NLM from the server.

- ▸ (Conditional) If you are going to use NFAP for NFS clients (UNIX/Linux), note that traditional NetWare volumes support only NFS v2. NSS volumes support both NFS versions 2 and 3.

- ▸ (Conditional) If Novell BorderManager Enterprise Edition version 3.5 or later is running in the same tree as the NetWare server, a Login Policy Object (LPO) must exist. For more information on LPOs see the Novell BorderManager documentation. To create a LPO in your tree, do the following:

    a. Log in to the server running BorderManager.

    b. Run NetWare Administrator from the SYS:public\win32 directory.

    c. From the Object menu, click Create ⇨ Login Policy ⇨ OK.

    d. (Conditional) If the server running BorderManager does not have a local NDS replica, complete the following: From NetWare Administrator, select the Security container and the LPO; click Trustees of This Object ⇨ Add Trustee; select the Server object of the server running BorderManager; deselect all Object rights; click Selected Properties ⇨ SAS: Policy Credentials; and then from Property Rights, click Read/Write ⇨ OK.

Admin workstation requirements

In order to manage Native File Access, there must be at least one administrative workstation with the following characteristics:

- ▸ Windows 95/98 running Novell client for Windows 95/98 version 3.21.0 or later OR Windows NT/2000 Novell client for Windows NT/2000 version 4.80 or later.

- ▸ NICI client version 1.5.7 or later. The NICI client is required to perform password administration using ConsoleOne.

A suitable Novell client and NICI client are available on the NetWare 6 Client CD-ROM. Alternatively, the latest versions of the clients can be downloaded from `http://support.novell.com/filefinder/`.

NFAP client requirements

To access NetWare servers running NFAP, computers must be connected to the network and running one of the following operating systems:

▶ Mac OS version 8.1 or later, Mac OS X.

▶ Windows 95/98/ME, Windows NT version 4, Windows 2000. Windows computers must be running Client for Microsoft Networks, which is a standard Windows networking component. It can be installed by selecting Control Panel ➪ Network ➪ Add ➪ Client ➪ Microsoft.

▶ Any version of UNIX or Linux that supports NFS v2 or NFS v3.

Installing Native File Access Pack

After you have met the prerequisites described above, you can install the NFAP remotely through Deployment Manager. Make sure you are logged in as a User with administrative rights to eDirectory and the NetWare server. To install Novell NFAP, complete the following steps:

1. At the administrative workstation, insert the NetWare 6 Operating System CD-ROM. Run Deployment Manager (NWDEPLOY.exe) from the root of the CD-ROM.

2. Select Install NetWare 6 Products in the left pane of Deployment Manager.

3. Select the Target server from the list of available servers and then select Next.

4. Provide authentication information to connect to the Target server and select OK. If you have any problem connecting, select Details and Connect by Address. Then supply the IP address of the server to which you want to attach.

5. At the Components screen, select Novell Native File Access Pack and select Next. Deselect any other products.

6. Select the native file protocols you wish the NetWare 6 server to support and select Next. The installation will check for NMAS and install it if needed.

7. (Conditional) If you are installing Windows CIFS support, complete the following steps (otherwise, skip to Step 13):

8. At the Native File Access for Windows screen, make your desired selections and select Next.

- *Server name*: Choose a server name (15 characters max) that CIFS clients will use to access the server. The default CIFS name is the server name with "_W" added to the end (e.g. SERVER1_W).

NOTE

NFAP server names *must* be distinct from the regular NetWare server name so that service advertisement protocols function properly on the network.

- *Server comment*: This can be any descriptive text that Windows users will see when they look at the details of the server object in Network Neighborhood.

- *Enable unicode*: This option enables international language support (double-byte characters). If this is needed, you must also create a text file (UNINOMAP.txt) in the SYS:ETC directory on the server. This file should list ASCII substitutions for any unmappable UNICODE characters that might be encountered. For more information on this file, see the NetWare 6 documentation.

9. At the Windows Authentication screen, make your desired selections and select Next. If users will authenticate using eDirectory, select Local. If users will authenticate through an NT domain, select Domain. Local authentication requires the creation of a simple password to authenticate to the NetWare server, but is not required for Domain authentication. Creating simple passwords is discussed later in this chapter.

NOTE

When NFAP is configured for Domain authentication, it is not possible to change the simple password or the eDirectory password using Windows' native Change Password feature. To change the password, you must use Windows' domain management utilities.

10. At the Windows IP Addresses screen, specify the addresses to which NFAP should be bound, and then select Next. If you have multiple IP addresses bound on your server, you can specify those addresses that should have CIFS support bound. If nothing is specified, CIFS support will be bound to all bound addresses.

11. At the Windows Share Point screen, make your desired selections and select Next. Here you can specify the entry point into the NetWare file system for CIFS clients.

- *Directory*: Specify the full path to the desired entry point, including volume name, and end with a back slash (for example: DATA1:Graphics\Bitmaps\). If nothing is specified, the CIFS client will see all NetWare volumes.

- *Sharename*: Specify a name for the entry point CIFS clients will see in Windows Explorer.

- *Connection limit*: If you wish to limit the number of simultaneous users, specify a maximum number of CIFS connections here.

- *Comment*: This can be any description that Windows clients will see for the share point in Windows Explorer.

12. At the Windows Context screen, make your desired selections and select Next. Specify all contexts that contain Windows users that need CIFS access to the NetWare server. These contexts will be search paths used to authenticate CIFS users. This list of eDirectory contexts is maintained in SYS:ETC\CIFSCTXS.CFG and can also be updated after installation.

WARNING

The NFAP authentication process does not currently support multiple users with the same common name, even if those users are in different contexts. NFAP authentication will search the specified contexts until it finds a matching name, and error out if the password is incorrect, rather than searching the rest of the specified contexts for any other matching common names.

13. At the Summary screen, review the proposed installation and select Finish to install NFAP.

14. At the Installation Complete screen, select Close. Restart the server to load all the necessary NFAP modules.

Configuring Native File Access Pack

After NFAP has been installed, you need to configure User objects and assign simple passwords before users will be able to access the network. The User object specifies attributes and information about the network resources a user can access. The User object will automatically have a NetWare password, but to use native protocols, you must also create a simple password for each User object. The following section covers the process for creating simple passwords.

Creating simple passwords

Simple passwords are necessary because of the lack of strong authentication methods for Local Windows authentication. They're also necessary for NFS, which supports only clear text authentication. Thus, to prevent the eDirectory password from becoming compromised, Novell has created a secondary password suitable for use in these less secure situations. To create a simple password, complete the following steps:

NOTE

If the simple password is different than the eDirectory password, the user would enter the simple password when accessing the network with native protocols and the eDirectory password when logging in with the Novell client software.

1. Make sure you are logged as a User with administrative rights to the eDirectory tree and launch ConsoleOne.

X-REF

For more information on ConsoleOne see Chapter 3.

2. Browse to a User object. If you need to create a new User object first, browse to the appropriate container, right-click on it, select New, and then User.

3. To assign a simple password, right-click the User object, select Properties. Select the Login Methods tab and choose Simple Password.

4. Select Set Password, then enter and confirm the simple password in the two fields provided.

5. Select OK to close the User object properties screen. Repeat these steps for each User object that needs a simple password.

If you want to create passwords for many network users, use NetWare Remote Manager. To set multiple simple passwords, complete the following steps:

X-REF

For information on installing and configuring NetWare Remote Manager, see Chapter 3.

1. Open the Web browser at your workstation and access the server you want to manage by entering the DNS name or IP address in the address (URL) field. If you are using a port other than port 80 for Web-based management, remember to add the port number to the end of the IP address. The default alternate port is 8008.

2. Accept the SSL certificate from the server. Your browser must have SSL 2.0 and SSL 3.0 (if supported) enabled in order to use NetWare Remote Manager.

3. When the login dialog appears in the browser, enter the required information.

4. In the left pane, select Manage eDirectory and then NFAP Security.

5. Make your desired selections and select Set to apply the simple password changes.

   - *NDS context*: A randomly generated simple password will be created for each User object found in the specified context.

   - *Traverse context tree for user objects*: The entire tree will be searched for User objects and random passwords will be created for each one.

   - *Send password to user*: Each User object that receives a simple password will be notified via e-mail of their new, randomly-generated simple password. To use this feature, NetWare Remote Manager must be setup to perform mail notification using the Access Mail Notification Control page.

   - *User supplied password*: Instead of generating a random password for each user, the text entered in this field will be the simple password for all users receiving new simple passwords.

   - *Generate script file*: To create a script file that will perform simple password creation based on the selections you make, select this option. Once created, the script filename can be entered into the Process Script File box in order to generate simple passwords.

   - *Process script file*: Enter a script filename here that defines how simple passwords are to be created.

NOTE You can also use NetWare Remote Manager to create a simple password for a single user by entering that user's name in the Username Context field and the desired password in the New Password field. Select Set to apply the changes.

You have now created simple passwords for user objects in NetWare. Users can now use their native access methods (Network Neighborhood, Chooser, etc.) to access network resources. When prompted, they will enter their NetWare username and the corresponding simple password.

Configuring CIFS access

With NFAP installed and passwords configured, nothing else is necessary to allow Windows users to access the NetWare file system. They can use Windows Explorer to browse and search for files through Network Neighborhood or My Network Places. They can map network drives to their defined share point and assign it a drive letter. Since access to NetWare files is handled by CIFS, Windows users can copy, delete, move, save, and open network files just like they do with any Windows-based drive resource.

Configuring AFP access

With NFAP installed and passwords configured, nothing else is necessary to allow Mac users to access the NetWare file system. They can use Chooser or the Go menu to access network files and even create aliases. Since access to NetWare files is handled by AFP, Mac users can copy, delete, move, save, and open network files just like they do with any Windows-based drive resource.

Configuring NFS access

Native NFS file access requires a few more steps before it can be used by a UNIX/Linux client. There are several terms that you should be familiar with if you have not worked with NFS previously and are implementing NFAP for NFS.

- *NFS server*: NFS server software is installed as part of the NFAP for NFS installation. It enables NFS clients to access a NetWare file system as if it were a local directory on the UNIX/Linux workstation. Any client that supports the NFS protocol can also access NetWare files using the NFS server.

- *File system export*: Before UNIX/Linux users can access the NetWare file system it must be made available to the NFS client. This process is called exporting the file system. During the export, you can define who should access the information and how it is accessed.

- *File system mount*: Once the NetWare file system is exported, an NFS client can import it into its local file system. Once imported, the specified portion of the NetWare file system will be available as though it were part of the local UNIX/Linux file system.

- *Network Information Service (NIS)*: NFAP for NFS also permits a NetWare server to function as a NIS server. This is not required for native file access, but is a useful additional service for UNIX/Linux clients. NIS is a widely used "Yellow Pages" for the UNIX/Linux environment. Similar to eDirectory, NIS servers act as central repositories for common information about users, groups, and hosts that reside on the network. With NIS server software loaded, eDirectory can function as a NIS repository and can respond to NIS requests from any NIS client.

After NFAP for NFS is installed you will have to start the NFS server. To do this, type **NFSSTART** on the server console. This is an NCF file that will load all the necessary modules. This command can also be placed in the AUTOEXEC.NCF so that the NFS server is loaded automatically when the server boots.

When NFAP for NFS is installed it extends the eDirectory schema to support new NFS objects (see Figure 2.6). There are three new objects that you will see after installing NFAP for NFS.

FIGURE 2.6 *NFS objects in the Novell eDirectory tree*

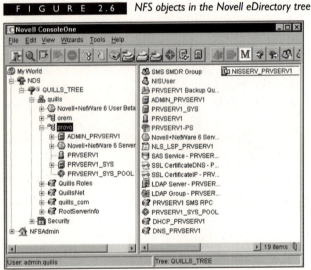

▶ *NFSAdmin*: The NFSAdmin object gives you access to the exported file structures that will be made available to NFS users.

▶ *NISUser*: The NISUser object is used to provide a link between NetWare and the root user on a UNIX/Linux client. This link is used internally for managing data flow between the two systems.

▶ *NISSERV_<servername>*: The NIS server object is created for those that might want to use Novell eDirectory as a NIS data repository. It is not used for NFS file access. For more information on NIS services, see the NetWare on-line documentation.

Exporting a NetWare directory

To export part of the NetWare 6 file system for use by NFS clients, complete the following steps:

1. Run ConsoleOne from the server where NFAP was installed. This will ensure that you have the appropriate snap-ins installed.

2. In the left pane, open the NFSAdmin object and then the NFS server object that appears beneath NFSAdmin.

3. Right-click the Exports object and then select Export New Path.

4. At the Export New Path screen (see Figure 2.7), make your desired selections and select OK.

FIGURE 2.7 *Creating an NFS export on a NetWare 6 server*

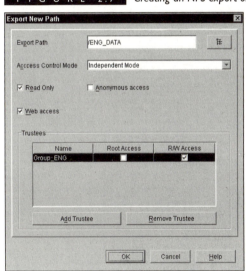

- *Export path*: Browse to the entry point in the NetWare file system for NFS clients.

- *Access control mode*: Independent mode is the only available choice; meaning that eDirectory and NFS file permissions will be managed separately.

- *Read only*: Check this box to permit only Read-Only access to the exported directory, regardless of individual user permissions. If this box is not checked, users will have Read/Write access.

- *Anonymous access*: Check this box to allow generic access to the exported directory through the UNIX user NOBODY and group NOGROUP.
- *Web access*: Check this box to allow WebNFS access to the exported directory.
- *Trustees*: In this field you can give users specific trustee permissions that will override the Read Only option listed above. You can specify either Root permissions or Read/Write permissions.

Once created, the new Exported directory will show up in the right pane with a name equivalent to the export path that was specified during its creation.

Mounting an exported directory

Once a NetWare 6 directory has been exported for NFS clients, it is imported into a remote file system for access. UNIX systems use the MOUNT command to accomplish this. To mount an exported directory on a UNIX/Linux system, complete the following steps:

1. Use the MKDIR command to create a directory that will hold the NetWare 6 NFS export. For example: `MKDIR NW6Files`.

2. Use the MOUNT command to link the new directory to the NetWare 6 export. For example: `MOUNT <server identifier>:/eng_data/ linux /NW6`.

IMPORTANT   The server identifier is the IP address or DNS name of the NetWare 6 server on which you created the NFS Export. Make sure to use both the colon and forward slash between the server identifier and the volume name. The target import directory must be an absolute path from NFS root and is separated from the source path by a <space>.

For more information on the UNIX/Linux MOUNT command, refer to your system's MAN pages.

CHAPTER 3

Novell Management Tools

Instant Access

Using ConsoleOne

ConsoleOne is a Java-based tool for managing your network and its resources.

- ▶ It can be launched by running CONSOLEONE.EXE from where it was installed (default: SYS:PUBLIC\MGMT\CONSOLEONE\1.2\BIN).
- ▶ By default, it lets you manage:
  - Novell eDirectory objects, schema, partitions, and replicas
  - NetWare server resources
- ▶ If you install other Novell products, additional capabilities are snapped in to ConsoleOne automatically.
- ▶ It is installed during the NetWare 6 installation, but can also be re-installed or installed locally from the NetWare 6 Client CD-ROM.
- ▶ ConsoleOne also supports remote server console access through a Java applet called RConsoleJ.
- ▶ To access the NetWare 6 server console remotely, launch ConsoleOne, browse to the desired server, select Tools, and then Remote Console.

Working with Web Manager

Web Manager is a Web-based utility for managing all NetWare 6 Web services. It also functions as a home page for all NetWare 6 Web-based management tools.

- ▶ To access Web Manager, open your Web browser and enter your Web server's domain name or IP address, followed by a colon and the Web manager port, which by default is 2200. For example:

  ```
  https://www.quills.com:2200
  ```

  or

  ```
  https://137.65.1923.1:2200
  ```

Accessing iManage

iManage is used to configure role-based management of your NetWare 6 network. It currently supports Licensing, iPrint, DNS/DHCP, and basic eDirectory management.

- ▶ You can start iManage from the Web Manager interface. Alternatively, you can load iManage directly by appending the iManage path (/eMFrame/iManage.html) to the Web Manager URL. For example:

```
https://www.quills.com:2200/eMFrame/iManage.html
```

or

```
https://137.65.192.1:2200/eMFrame/iManage.html
```

▶ To force iManage into Simple mode to support Federal accessibility guide-lines, use the Simple mode path (/eMFrame/Simple.html). For example:

```
https://www.quills.com:2200/eMFrame/Simple.html
```

or

```
https://137.65.192.1:2200/eMFrame/Simple.html
```

▶ You will be prompted to authenticate using a valid eDirectory username. Users will only have access to iManage features for which they have been assigned rights.

Using NetWare Remote Manager (NoRM)

NetWare Remote Manager (NoRM) is used for remote management of NetWare 6 servers.

▶ You can start NoRM from the Web Manager interface, or you can bypass the Web Manager home page and go directly to NoRM. To do this, open your Web browser and enter your Web server's domain name or IP address, followed by a colon and the port number, which by default is 8009. For example:

```
https://www.quills.com:8009
```

or

```
https://137.65.192.1:8009
```

▶ You will be prompted to authenticate using a full eDirectory username, including leading dot. For access to all NoRM features, the user should have supervisory rights to the NetWare server.

Working with iMonitor

iMonitor is used for Web-based management of Novell eDirectory in your NetWare 6 network.

▶ You can start iMonitor by launching NoRM, and then browsing to and selecting NDS iMonitor in the left-side frame. Alternatively, you go straight to iMonitor by appending the iMonitor path (/nds) to the NoRM URL. For example:

```
https://www.quills.com:8009/nds
```

or

```
https://137.65.192.1:8009/nds
```

▶ . . . . ◀

Introduction to Novell Management

Since the release of NetWare 4 in the mid-1990s, Novell has been working toward a consolidated management interface from which all administrative tasks can be performed. Since that time, the primary issue hampering this effort has been how to deliver that management interface.

From NWAdmin

The first version of a centralized management interface was NWAdmin. NWAdmin was a Windows-based utility that delivered a graphical interface that allowed administrator's to see the whole network from a directory-centric perspective rather than a server-centric perspective. It relied on the Novell client to provide network communications and access. NWAdmin also defined the standard look and feel for graphical management utilities that is still largely adhered to today.

NWAdmin supported an extendable "plug-in" architecture so new functionality could be added as necessary to manage new features and new products. This was accomplished through Windows-based programming techniques common at the time.

However, with the explosion of the Internet many began to question the assumption that Microsoft Windows would be the only desktop operating system in use at modern organizations. Rather than write a different version of NWAdmin for every possible workstation OS, Novell moved toward a more open and standards-based management architecture based on Java programming techniques. Java promised the ability to "write once, run anywhere", which was critical to Novell's management plans.

To ConsoleOne

So, with NetWare 5 in 1998, Novell introduced its second-generation administrative utility known as ConsoleOne. Similar to NWAdmin, ConsoleOne is an extendable management architecture that supports snap-ins to extend its capabilities. Its Java-based design allowed it to run on both workstations and the NetWare server itself, providing the first ever graphical server console. However, it still required some type of Novell client support for network communications and access. In the years since its release, ConsoleOne has achieved respectable performance, a major deficiency in its early versions, and is now the preferred tool for universal management of Novell and third-party products and services.

And NetWare Web Manager

With the release of NetWare 6, Novell is making the final management interface transition necessary to support its One Net initiative. ConsoleOne untied the management console from Windows, and now, NetWare Web Manager unties the management console from the Novell client. Similar to ConsoleOne, Web Manager is built of modular components that can be extended as needed to support new products and features. Perhaps most importantly, Novell no longer has to worry about creating and maintaining client software for any platform on which it wants to support management capabilities. NetWare Web Manager promises a true platform-independent management interface that can be used from any workstation at any location to perform network management and maintenance of any kind.

The first release of NetWare Web Manager and its component utilities does not provide every feature that is currently available in ConsoleOne, so it will be important for you to understand the current capabilities of these new interfaces. This chapter provides an introduction to the primary Novell management utilities, from NWAdmin to NetWare Web Manager. It will provide requirements and installation information for each utility, as well as an overview of its features and capabilities.

First, we will present ConsoleOne, which is still the most comprehensive management interface for NetWare 6. We will show how ConsoleOne can be used for both local and remote server administration as well as full eDirectory management.

Next we will present the new generation of Web-based management tools, starting with NetWare Web Manager and then moving to its primary components, including NetWare Remote Manager (NoRM), iManage, and iMonitor. These browser-based utilities will grow to include all ConsoleOne features over time and promise much more flexibility for network administrators looking to get their jobs done from any place at any time.

ConsoleOne

NetWare 6 includes ConsoleOne v1.3.2, which includes several improvements from previous 1.2x versions (see Table 3.1).

TABLE 3.1	ConsoleOne v1.3.2 Feature Improvements
FEATURE	**DESCRIPTION**
Accessibility	In support of new Federal regulations, ConsoleOne now supports improved accessibility for those with disabilities, such as screen reader support and keyboard equivalents for all mouse-based actions.
Partition checks	ConsoleOne can now walk a selected replica ring to check for inconsistencies and synchronization problems.
Platform support	ConsoleOne now supports Linux, Solaris, and Compaq Tru64 systems, in addition to Windows and NetWare.
DNS federation	If you use DNS federation in your network, ConsoleOne now supports making rights and membership assignments across trees.
Improved templates	Create trustee assignments and volume space restrictions through a template.
Auxiliary classes	Administrator's can now define custom eDirectory objects with Aux Class properties.
File system management	Manage the properties of multiple files, folders, or volumes simultaneously.

ConsoleOne is a Java-based tool for managing your network and its resources. By default, it lets you manage:

- ► Novell eDirectory objects, schema, partitions, and replicas
- ► NetWare server resources

If you install other Novell products, additional capabilities are snapped in to ConsoleOne automatically. For example, if you install Novell eDirectory, the capability to configure the LDAP interface to eDirectory is snapped in to ConsoleOne automatically.

Since ConsoleOne is a Java-based application, and it has a similar look and feel across all platforms, as shown in Figure 3.1.

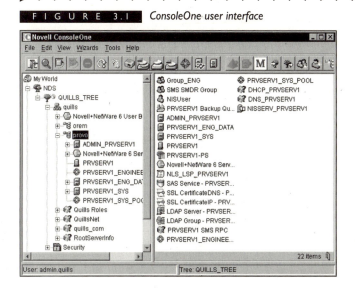

F I G U R E   3.1   *ConsoleOne user interface*

ConsoleOne Basics

Before looking at specific administrative tasks that are described through-out this book, it's a good idea to get a feel for the basics of ConsoleOne admin-istration. If you need a more detailed introduction to ConsoleOne see the NetWare 6 on-line documentation.

Organizing objects into containers

The whole purpose of using eDirectory to manage your network is that it allows you to organize network resources so they can be managed more easily. A principal way of doing this is to organize objects into logical groupings known as containers. Because of inheritance rules, objects in a container are security-equivalent to the container itself; so general object rights can be man-aged at the container level rather than the individual object level.

For more information on eDirectory tree design see Chapter 5. For information on eDirectory security see Chapter 6.

X-REF

Creating and manipulating objects

Once you have located the objects you want to manage, you can change their behavior by modifying their properties. You can also create, delete, move, and rename objects as needed. To do any of these, right-click the object(s) you want to manage and select the desired operation from the drop-down menu. For example, to create a new object do the following:

1. Right-click on the container in which you want the object stored, select New, and then the type of object you want to create. ConsoleOne will automatically limit the list of object types to those that are valid for the selected container.

2. Enter a name for the object.

3. Specify any other required or optional information, and then select OK.

IMPORTANT If you are attempting to modify a service-specific object for which you don't have a snap-in, ConsoleOne will only show you a generic list of properties. Make sure you have a snap-in installed for all the objects with which you will be working.

ConsoleOne 1.3.2 also allows you to modify the properties of multiple objects of the same type simultaneously. To do this, complete the following steps:

1. Select the objects using one of the following methods:
   - In the right pane, Shift+click or Ctrl+click multiple objects of the same type
   - Click a group or template object to modify its members
   - Click a container to modify the objects it contains

2. With the appropriate objects highlighted, select File from the menu bar, and then Properties of Multiple Objects.

3. If you selected a container in Step 1, in the dialog box double-click the object type that you want to modify; otherwise, skip this step.

4. On the Objects to Modify page, make sure only the objects that you want to modify are listed.

5. On the other property pages, make any changes you would like to apply to all selected objects, and then select OK.

Browsing and finding objects

In the left pane, see the eDirectory container, which holds the eDirectory trees you are currently logged in to. If you log into multiple trees, you will see them all listed here. To log into a new eDirectory tree, select the NDS Authenticate button on the ConsoleOne toolbar and specify the tree name, context, username, and password.

If you are using DNS tree federation with NetWare 6, you can access containers in other trees without logging in. To do this, complete the following steps:

1. In the ConsoleOne menu bar, select View, and then Set Context.

2. Enter the full DNS name for the eDirectory context you are trying to access, including an ending dns and period (.). For example:

```
testing.provo.quills.com.dns.
```

3. Click OK.

Once you are in an eDirectory tree or context and its objects are listed in the right pane, you typically browse to an object by opening container objects in the left pane until you arrive at the object.

Customizing views

ConsoleOne gives you the flexibility to customize views in both the left and right panes. However, except for window size, position, and view title, other custom viewing settings are lost when you exit ConsoleOne.

You can define the Topmost object in the left pane by doing one of the following:

▶ If the object is a container that's below the current top object, right-click the container object and select Set as Root.

▶ If the object is a container that's above the current top object, double-click in the left pane until the desired container appears.

▶ If you want to reset My World as the Top object, right-click in the left pane and select Show My World.

The right pane in ConsoleOne defaults to what is known as the Console view. This is the most-used view for managing directory and server resources. However, you can switch back and forth between the Console view and other views, such as the Partition and Replica view, by right-clicking an object in the right pane, selecting Views, and then the desired view.

X-REF

For more information on the Partition and Replica view see Chapter 5.

Regardless of which view the right pane contains, you can show or hide the view title at the top of the right pane by selecting View from the menu bar and then Show View Title. A check mark is added to or removed from the menu item, depending on whether the view title is being shown or hidden.

Installing ConsoleOne

ConsoleOne will be installed automatically during the NetWare 6 server installation to SYS:PUBLIC\MGMT\CONSOLEONE\1.2. Furthermore, any products installed on the server will automatically place their ConsoleOne snap-ins in the correct location (SYS:PUBLIC\MGMT\CONSOLEONE\1.2\SNAPINS) to function with this version. However, this means that different servers with different product sets may not have all the necessary snap-ins to manage services network-wide. So if you are doing service-specific management ,you should run ConsoleOne from a server where the service is actually installed.

If you want to install ConsoleOne on a workstation or an existing server, it is available on the NetWare 6 Client CD-ROM.

TIP

If you want to synchronize ConsoleOne snap-ins across servers, you can simply copy them from the \SNAPINS directory on one server or workstation to that on another.

To install and run ConsoleOne on one of its supported operating systems, complete the instructions in the following sections.

Windows

You can install and run ConsoleOne on a Windows workstation or server, or you can run it remotely from a NetWare or Windows server to which you have a mapped or shared drive.

IMPORTANT

If you install and run ConsoleOne from a Windows workstation or server, you will have to manually copy the snap-in files for newly-installed products from the NetWare server on which those products are installed.

The following system requirements apply to ConsoleOne in the Windows environment:

OS version	Windows 95/98 with Novell client 3.2 or later
	Windows NT/2000 with Novell client 4.7 or later
RAM	64MB minimum
	12MB recommended (required for generating ConsoleOne reports)
Processor	200 MHz or faster
Disk space	38MB (required for a local installation only)
Video resolution	800x600x256 colors (minimum)

Complete the following steps to install ConsoleOne on a Windows work-station or server:

1. Close any ConsoleOne sessions that are currently running.

2. Insert the NetWare 6 Client CD. If the CD does not autoplay, run WINSETUP.EXE from the root of the CD-ROM.

3. At the Novell Client Installation screen select Novell ConsoleOne and follow the on-screen prompts to complete the installation. If you do not need ConsoleOne reporting, you can choose not to install that snap-in.

TIP

If you are installing on a Windows server and you will run ConsoleOne remotely through drive sharing, don't forget to share the folder where you install ConsoleOne.

Once installed, executing CONSOLEONE.EXE from the location where you installed it starts ConsoleOne. If you installed ConsoleOne locally, you will have a shortcut on your desktop.

ConsoleOne accessibility

To enable the new ConsoleOne Accessibility features for a Windows environment you must first install the Java Access Bridge. The Java Access Bridge exposes the Java Accessibility API in a Windows DLL so that Windows Assistive Technologies can interact with Java applications that use the Java Accessibility API.

To set up the Java Access Bridge for use with ConsoleOne, complete the following steps:

1. Download the Java Access Bridge from the Java Access Bridge Web site at http://java.sun.com/products/accessbridge.

2. Unpack the Java Access Bridge into the C:\ACCESSBRIDGE-1_0 directory and run the following command:

```
C:\ACCESSBRIDGE-1_0\INSTALLER\INSTALL
```

TIP

For more information on installing and configuring the Java Access Bridge, see the Java Access Bridge readme (http://java.sun.com/products/accessbridge/README.txt).

3. Place a copy of the following files in your \CONSOLEONEEXT folder. By default, this folder is at C:\NOVELL\CONSOLEONE\1.2\.

```
JACCESS-1_3.JAR
```

```
ACCESS-BRIDGE.JAR
```

4. Place a copy of following file in your \JRE\LIB folder. By default, this folder is at C:\NOVELL\CONSOLEONE\1.2\.

`ACCESSIBILITY.PROPERTIES`

5. Copy the following files to your Windows DLL directory (for example, C:\WINNT\SYSTEM32 or C:\WINDOWS\SYSTEM):

`JAVAACCESSBRIDGE.DLL`

`WINDOWSACCESSBRIDGE.DLL`

NetWare

In addition to being installed during the NetWare 6 installation, you can install ConsoleOne v1.3. on existing NetWare servers. The following system requirements apply to ConsoleOne in the NetWare environment:

OS version	NetWare 5 Support Pack 3 or later
RAM	Use NetWare recommended minimums At least 128MB recommended
Processor	200 MHz or faster
Disk space	38MB available
Video resolution	800x600x256 colors (minimum)

IMPORTANT ConsoleOne v1.3 is compatible with existing ConsoleOne v1.2 snap-ins, but NOT with v1.1 snap-ins. If you have any older applications that use these snap-ins, then ConsoleOne v1.3 should not be installed on that server.

Complete the following steps to install ConsoleOne on an existing NetWare server:

1. At the Server console, type **JAVA –EXIT** to unload Java and any Java applications running on the server.

2. Make sure network users exit any ConsoleOne sessions currently in use.

3. From a Windows client, map a drive letter to the root of the server's SYS volume.

4. From the same workstation, insert the NetWare 6 Client CD-ROM. If the CD does not autoplay, run WINSETUP.EXE from the root of the CD-ROM.

5. At the Novell Client Installation screen, select Novell ConsoleOne and follow the on-screen prompts to complete the installation. If you do not need ConsoleOne reporting, you can choose not to install that snap-in.

Once ConsoleOne has been installed on the server, you can start the NetWare GUI and ConsoleOne simultaneously by typing the following command:

C1START

If the GUI is already started, select the Novell button in the lower-left corner, and select ConsoleOne from the menu. You will be required to authenticate to eDirectory before ConsoleOne will load.

You can also run ConsoleOne remotely from a Windows computer. First make sure you have a drive mapped to the SYS: volume of the NetWare server, and then you can create a shortcut to CONSOLEONE.EXE at the location where you installed it.

Linux

This is the first version of ConsoleOne that will run on a Linux system. You can run it locally or remotely from another system through an X terminal session, provided the remote computer has an X Windows subsystem.

NOTE This release of ConsoleOne for Linux has been tested only on the IBM 1.3 Java Runtime Environment (JRE). This JRE is included in the ConsoleOne installation package in case you don't have it. If you do have it, you can choose not to install it.

The following system requirements apply to ConsoleOne in the Linux environment:

OS version	Red Hat OpenLinux 6 or later, or Caldera eDesktop 2.4 or later, or Caldera eServer 2.3
RAM	128MB recommended
Processor	200 MHz or faster
Disk space	with JRE installation: 32MB without JRE installation: 5MB
Video resolution	800x600x256 colors (minimum)

IMPORTANT

This release of ConsoleOne is not compatible with eDirectory versions prior to v8.5. If the installation routine detects an unsupported version of eDirectory, it will abort the installation.

Complete the following steps to install ConsoleOne on an existing Linux server:

1. At the Linux system, mount the NetWare 6 Client CD-ROM and browse to the /consoleone folder.

2. Start the installation by typing the following at the system prompt: **c1-install**

3. Follow the on-screen prompts to complete the installation. Remember, if you already have the IBM JRE v1.3 installed, you can skip that portion of the installation.

NOTE

You can uninstall ConsoleOne by entering *c1-uninstall* at the system prompt. Both c1-install and c1-uninstall include some optional parameters for running in unattended mode or installing/uninstalling individual components. For details on the command syntax, type *c1-install -h* or *c1-uninstall -h* at the system prompt.

Both the install and uninstall routines maintain a log file in the /var directory that you can review at any time.

Use the following command to start ConsoleOne from either a local session or an X terminal (remote) session:

```
/usr/ConsoleOne/bin/ConsoleOne
```

Solaris

This is the first version of ConsoleOne that will run on a Solaris system. You can run it locally or remotely from another system through an X terminal session, provided the remote computer has an X Windows subsystem.

NOTE

This release of ConsoleOne for Solaris has been tested only on the Sun 1.2.2-5a Java Runtime Environment (JRE). This JRE is included in the ConsoleOne installation package in case you don't have it. If you do have it, you can choose not to install it.

The following system requirements apply to ConsoleOne in the Solaris environment:

OS version	Solaris 2.6 or 7 with the latest patch applied (download Solaris patches at `http://sunsolve.sun.com/`.) Solaris 8
Disk space	with JRE installation: 64MB without JRE installation: 10MB
Video resolution	800x600x256 colors (minimum)

IMPORTANT

This release of ConsoleOne is not compatible with eDirectory versions prior to v8.5. If the installation routine detects an unsupported version of eDirectory, it will abort the installation.

Complete the following steps to install ConsoleOne on an existing Solaris server:

1. At the Solaris system, mount the NetWare 6 Client CD-ROM and browse to the /consoleone folder.

2. Start the installation by typing the following at the system prompt: **c1-install**

3. Follow the on-screen prompts to complete the installation. Remember, if you already have the Sun 1.2.2-5a JRE installed, you can skip that portion of the installation.

NOTE

You can uninstall ConsoleOne by entering *c1-uninstall* at the system prompt. Both c1-install and c1-uninstall include some optional parameters for running in unattended mode or installing/uninstalling individual components. For details on the command syntax, type *c1-install -h* or *c1-uninstall -h* at the system prompt.

Both the install and uninstall routines maintain a log file in the /var directory that you can review at any time.

Use the following command to start ConsoleOne from either a local session or an X terminal (remote) session:

```
/usr/ConsoleOne/bin/ConsoleOne
```

Tru64 UNIX

This is the first version of ConsoleOne that will run on a Tru64 system. You can run it locally or remotely from another system through an X terminal session, provided the remote computer has an X Windows subsystem.

NOTE

This release of ConsoleOne for Tru64 has been tested only on the Compaq 1.2.2 Java Runtime Environment (JRE). This JRE is included in the ConsoleOne installation package in case you don't have it. If you do have it, you can choose not to install it.

The following system requirements apply to ConsoleOne in the Tru64 environment:

OS version	Compaq Tru64 UNIX 5.0a or later
RAM	64MB minimum 128MB recommended
Processor	200 MHz or faster
Disk space	with JRE installation: 20MB without JRE installation: 5MB
Video resolution	800x600x256 colors (minimum)

IMPORTANT

This release of ConsoleOne is not compatible with eDirectory versions prior to v8.5. If the installation routine detects an unsupported version of eDirectory, it will abort the installation.

Complete the following steps to install ConsoleOne on an existing Tru64 server:

1. At the Tru64 system, mount the NetWare 6 Client CD-ROM and browse to the /consoleone folder.

2. Start the installation by typing the following at the system prompt: **c1-install**.

3. Follow the on-screen prompts to complete the installation. Remember, if you already have the Compaq 1.2.2 JRE installed you can skip that portion of the installation.

NOTE

You can uninstall ConsoleOne by entering c1-uninstall at the system prompt. Both c1-install and c1-uninstall include some optional parameters for running in unattended mode or installing/uninstalling individual components. For details on the command syntax, type c1-install -h or c1-uninstall -h at the system prompt.

Both the install and uninstall routines maintain a log file in the /var directory that you can review at any time.

Use the following command to start ConsoleOne from either a local session or an X terminal (remote) session:

```
/usr/ConsoleOne/bin/ConsoleOne
```

ConsoleOne Limitations

Even though it has been around for quite a while, there are still some things ConsoleOne cannot do. Furthermore, with the new NetWare Web Manager tools on the horizon, some new network management tasks are bypassing ConsoleOne completely and going straight to the new stuff. Keep the following things in mind when you are using ConsoleOne.

- ▶ ConsoleOne is sluggish on older hardware, particularly if it doesn't have adequate RAM. No one ever said "write once, read anywhere" was cheap!

- ▶ Older products may not have ConsoleOne snap-ins. For these situations you will have to use NWAdmin, as described earlier in this chapter.

- ▶ A few new features, such as NetWare 6 licensing and iPrint management, are accessed through the new iManage interface and are not available from ConsoleOne.

- ▶ If you are performing operations on a large number of objects (more than 1000), then some ConsoleOne features — such as searches, selecting multiple objects, and displaying total object count — may produce inaccurate or partial results. NWAdmin is better at handling operations on large numbers of objects.

NetWare Web Manager

NetWare Web Manager is the management tool responsible for managing the NetWare Web services, which are new to NetWare 6. However, by adding links to other browser-based management utilities, such as NetWare Remote Manager, it also functions as a kind of "home page" for Novell's Web-based management tools.

For its internal operations, Web Manager leverages a NetWare port of the industry-leading Apache Web server that is new to NetWare 6. This leaves Enterprise Web server available for your eCommerce needs without further burdening it with network management overhead.

For more information on NetWare Web services, see Chapter 10. For more information on both the Apache and Enterprise Web servers see Chapter 9.

X-REF

While you can perform basic eDirectory object management with Web Manager, it leaves the bulk of this activity to ConsoleOne, discussed previously, and NetWare Remote Manager, discussed later in this chapter. In addition to providing a home page for Novell's Web-based management tools, Web Manager's main purpose is to provide the interface for configuring and managing the Web services in NetWare 6.

One of the primary advantages of using NetWare Web Manager is that you can easily access other browser-based management interfaces — including NetWare Remote Manager and iManage — and configure various services from any remote workstation that has Internet access. With Web Manager you can accomplish the following tasks either locally (from within your WAN or LAN) or remotely:

▶ *Manage the Enterprise Web server*: To manage the Web server, select your server name located under NetWare Enterprise Web server.

For more information on Enterprise Web server see Chapter 9.

X-REF

▶ *Manage user authentication to your Enterprise Web server*: Web manager supports authentication via either eDirectory or a local database. Novell recommends using eDirectory because it will manage both authentication and access rights. However, if your Web server contains mostly public information, then authentication will not be a major issue, and the local database mode will work fine.

▶ *Modify Web Manager settings*: To manage NetWare Web Manager settings, select the Admin Preferences icon in the top frame of the Web Manager home page.

▶ *Manage eDirectory trees or objects from a remote location*: From the Web Manager home page, select your server name located under Novell directory services. To manage users and groups specific to the Enterprise server, select the server name under NetWare Enterprise Web server, and then click the Users and Groups icon in the top frame of Web Manager.

Installing Web Manager

NetWare Web Manager is installed automatically during the installation of NetWare 6. After the installation, use a Web browser from a client computer in your network to access Web Manager. As you make configuration changes to the Web services available in NetWare 6, configuration files on the NetWare 6 server will be modified to support your changes.

In order to access Web Manager from an Internet connection outside your firewall, you will need to make sure that TCP port 2200 is opened through the firewall to the IP address of your Web server. Port 2200 is the default port through which you will access the Web Manager interface. If desired, this port can be changed as long as it doesn't conflict with any other service on the NetWare 6 server.

To use Web Manager, you must be using a 4.x or newer Web browser such as Internet Explorer or Netscape Communicator. The browser must have Java or JavaScript enabled on your Web browser to use Web Manager, because all of the configuration forms and other management tools require one or both of these forms of Java to function. To enable Java on your browser, complete the instructions in the following sections that correspond to the browser you are using.

Internet Explorer 4 or higher

To enable Java on Internet Explorer 4 or higher, use the following steps:

1. From the Internet Explorer browser window, click Tools ➪ Internet Options.

2. Select the Advanced tab.

3. Under Microsoft VM, check JIT Compiler for Virtual Machine Enabled box.

4. Click OK. You will have to restart your workstation to complete the installation.

Netscape Navigator

To enable Java on Netscape Navigator, use the following steps:

1. From the browser window, click Options ➪ Network Preferences.

2. Select the Language tab and make sure Java and JavaScript are checked.

3. Click OK.

Netscape Communicator

To enable Java on Netscape Communicator, use the following steps:

1. From the Communicator browser window, click Edit ⇨ Preferences.

2. Select the Advanced category in the left column.

3. Check the Enable Java and Enable JavaScript check boxes.

4. Click OK.

To access Web Manager, open your Web Browser and enter your Web server's domain name or IP address, followed by a colon and the port number, which by default is 2200. For example:

```
https://www.quills.com:2200
```

or

```
https://137.65.192.1:2200
```

Configuring Web Manager

There isn't a lot you need to do to get Web Manager set up once it is installed. Figure 3.2 shows the most basic Web Manager home page. As additional Web services are installed, such as Enterprise Web server, FTP, and Web Search server, new links will be added into Web Manager. There are also a few configuration tasks of which you should be aware.

FIGURE 3.2 *NetWare Web Manager interface*

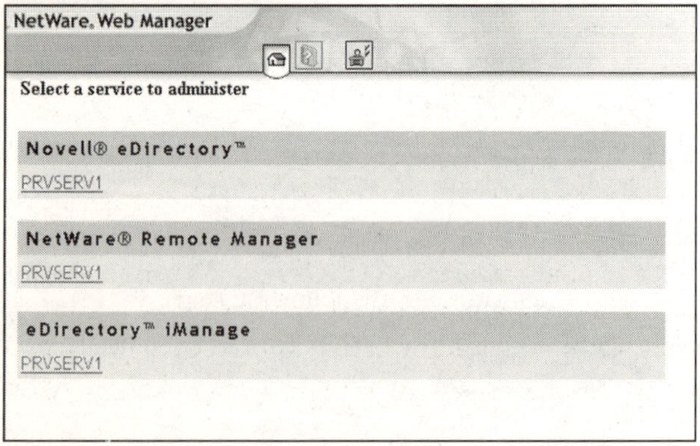

NetWare. Web Manager

Select a service to administer

Novell® eDirectory™
PRVSERV1

NetWare® Remote Manager
PRVSERV1

eDirectory™ iManage
PRVSERV1

NOTE

The first time you select a Web Manager link, you may be prompted to accept an unknown certificate. If so, select Yes to continue or View Certificate to install the server certificate in your browser. Installing the certificate will prevent this message from appearing in the future.

Changing Web Manager's port

By default, Web Manager secures its communications with SSL, using the server certificate that was created during the NetWare 6 installation. To give you a little added dose of security, though, you can change the Web Manager port number.

If you decide to do this, using a port number of 49152 or higher is the best bet. Ports below 49152 may be assigned for use by other services and should not be used. Pick an unassigned port between 49152 and 65000.

SMART LINKS

For a complete list of registered port numbers, visit the Internet Assigned Numbers Authority (IANA) Web site at `http://www.iana.org/assignments/port-numbers`.

To change NetWare Web Manager's port number, complete the following steps:

1. From the NetWare Web Manager home page, click the Admin Preferences icon.

2. In the Web Manager Port field, type the port number you want NetWare Web Manager to use.

3. Click OK.

4. Restart the server for the settings to take effect.

Enabling/disabling encryption

By default, Secure Sockets Layer (SSL) is used to secure Web Manager communications by encrypting all information going out or coming in to Web Manager. When enabled, you must use HTTPS to access Web Manager.

NICI and Novell Certificate server provide all the cryptographic underpinnings of Web Manager. They are installed by default as part of the NetWare 6 installation. Certificate server provides the cryptographic key pairs and server certificate used by Web Manager.

X-REF

For more information on NICI and Certificate server see Chapter 6.

To enable or disable encryption in Web Manager:

1. Open the Web Manager home page and select Admin Preferences.

2. Under Encryption, click On to enable, or Off to disable SSL.

3. From the Server Certificates drop-down list, select the Server Certificate object you want to use for SSL encryption.

4. Click OK.

Web Manager log files

The Apache Web server logs the activities of all services running on it, including Web Manager. These log files track who has visited, what has been accessed, and what errors, if any, have occurred.

NOTE   The Enterprise Web server maintains its own log files. To view Enterprise Web server log files, select your Web server link under NetWare Enterprise Web server on the Web Manager home page, and then select the Server Status icon.

The Apache log files are stored in the default Common Log Format (CLF) that provides a fixed amount of information about Apache Web server activity.

The Access log file records information about requests to the server and the responses from the server. The Error log file lists all the errors the server has encountered, including unsuccessful login attempts and any other informational messages.

To configure logging options for Web Manager, complete the following steps:

1. From the Web Manager home page select the Admin Preferences icon and then Log Settings.

2. In the Access Log field, specify the path where you want NetWare Web Manager to store the Access log file. By default this file is stored on the NetWare 6 server at SYS:NOVONYX/SUITESPOT/ACCESS-SERV/ LOGS/ACCESS.TXT. Leaving this field blank deactivates access logging.

3. In the Error Log field, specify the path where you want NetWare Web Manager to store the Error log file. By default this file is stored on the NetWare 6 server at SYS:NOVONYX/SUITESPOT/ACCESS-SERV/ LOGS/ERRORS.TXT. Leaving this field blank deactivates error logging.

4. Click OK to save the new settings.

To view an access log or an error log, complete the following steps:

1. From the NetWare Web Manager home page, select the Admin Preferences icon and either View Access Log or View Error Log.

2. In the Number of Entries field, type the number of lines you want the access log to display.

3. If you want to filter the log entries for a specific type of work, enter it in the Only Show Entries With field. This entry is case sensitive, so be specific!

4. Click OK to have your viewing options take effect. Use the Reset button to re-run the search and update the log file view.

iManage

NetWare 6 ships with version 1.0 of iManage, which is a browser-based tool, used for administering, managing, and configuring Novell eDirectory objects. iManage uses Role Based Services (RBS) to give you a way to focus the user on a specified set of tasks and objects as determined by their role(s). What users see when they access iManage is based on their role assignments in eDirectory.

In this first release of iManage you can define management roles to administer Novell Licensing Services (NLS), iPrint, DNS/DHCP services, and some basic eDirectory object management. Over time the list of iManage-supported services will grow significantly.

As with other NetWare 6 Web-based management tools, iManage leverages the Apache Web server that is new to NetWare 6.

For more information on Apache Web server for NetWare see Chapter 9.

X-REF

Installing iManage

iManage is installed automatically during the installation of NetWare 6. However, if it has been uninstalled for any reason, iManage can be manually re-installed through Deployment Manager or the graphical server console. To install iManage via Deployment Manager, complete the following steps:

1. Make sure you are logged in as a user with administrative rights to eDirectory and the NetWare server.

2. At the workstation, insert the NetWare 6 Operating System CD-ROM. Run Deployment Manager (NWDEPLOY.exe) from the root of the CD-ROM.

3. Select Install NetWare 6 Products in the left pane of Deployment Manager.

4. Select the target server from the list of available servers, and then select Next.

5. Provide authentication information to connect to the target server and select OK. If you have any problem connecting, select Details and Connect by Address. Then supply the IP address of the server to which you want to attach.

6. At the Components screen, select Novell iManage and select Next. Deselect any other products.

7. Specify the location and name for the iManage container that will hold the various administrative roles, and then select Next.

8. At the Summary screen, select Finish to install iManage on the target server.

To use iManage, you must have Internet Explorer v5 or higher, Netscape Communicator v4.6 or 4.7, or Netscape 6.1. Make sure that Java or JavaScript is enabled on your Web browser. For steps on doing this, see the sections on Web Manager in this chapter.

iManage is accessible only through the Web Manager port, but it is possible to bypass the Web Manager home page, if desired. You can open iManage in either of the following modes:

▶ *Regular Mode*: This is the default mode for Internet Explorer and Netscape 6.1 (see Figure 3.3). Its interface is very similar to that of NoRM. From Web Manager, open iManage by selecting the appropriate server name listed under the eDirectory iManage heading. At the Authentication dialog, enter the full username, with leading dot, the password of a user with administrative rights to this server, and then select OK. Alternatively, you can bypass the Web Manager home page and go directly to iManage. To do this, open your Web Browser and enter your Web server's domain name or IP address, followed by a colon and the port number, which by default is 2200. Then append the path /eMFrame/iManage.html. For example:

```
https://www.quills.com:2200/eMFrame/iManage.html
```

or

```
https://137.65.192.1:2200/eMFrame/iManage.html.
```

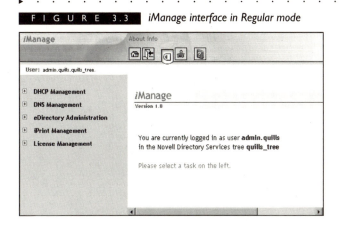

FIGURE 3.3 iManage interface in Regular mode

NOTE

You may be prompted to accept an unknown certificate if this is the first time you have tried to open NoRM. If so, select Yes to continue or View Certificate to install the server certificate in your browser. Installing the certificate will prevent this message from appearing in the future.

▶ *Simple Mode*: This is the default mode for Netscape 4.6 and 4.7 (see Figure 3.4). It provides the same functionality as Regular mode, but with an interface optimized for accessibility by those with disabilities (for example, expanded menus for blind users who rely upon spoken commands). To force iManage into Simple mode, you can bypass the Web Manager home page. Enter your Web server's domain name or IP address, followed by a colon and the port number, which by default is 2200. Then append the path /eMFrame/Simple.html. For example:

```
https://www.quills.com:2200/eMFrame/Simple.html
```

or

```
https://137.65.192.1:2200/eMFrame/Simple.html.
```

Using either interface, you will only have access to those features to which you have rights. For full access to all iManage features, authenticate as a user with Supervisory rights to the eDirectory tree.

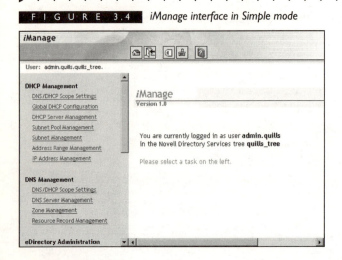

FIGURE 3.4 *iManage interface in Simple mode*

iManage Basics

As shown in Figures 3.3 and 3.4, iManage is organized into three main sections, or frames:

- *Header frame*: The Header frame is located at the top of the screen. It contains links to the Home, Roles and Tasks, Configuration, and Help pages, as well as an Exit link to close the browser window.

- *Navigation frame*: The Navigation frame is located on the left side of the screen. It lists different management tasks, organized into groups, which are available to the user that has just authenticated. For this release of iManage, that includes one or more of the following:

  - DHCP management

  - DNS management

  - eDirectory administration

  - iPrint management

  - License management

- *Main Content frame*: The Main Content frame occupies the middle-right of the screen. When you select a link in the Header or Navigation frames, the appropriate page will be displayed in the Main Content frame.

TIP

If you ever see the Looking Glass icon next to a field in iManage, you can use it to browse or search the tree for specific objects to use in creating, defining, and assigning roles.

Role-Based Management with iManage

The role-based services available through iManage are represented by objects in eDirectory. The new object types include:

- ▶ *RBS collection*: A container object that holds all RBS role and task objects for an eDirectory tree. You specify the location for this object during NetWare 6 installation.

- ▶ *RBS role*: Specifies the tasks that users (members) are authorized to perform. Defining a role includes creating an RBS Role object and linking it to the tasks that the role can perform. RBS roles can only be created in an RBS Collection container.

- ▶ *RBS module*: A container inside of the RBS collection that organizes available RBS Task objects into functional groups. RBS modules let you assign users responsibility for specific functionality within a product or service.

- ▶ *RBS task*: Represents a specific function, such as resetting login passwords. RBS Task objects are located only in RBS Module containers.

- ▶ *RBS scope*: Represents the context in the tree where a role will be performed, and is associated with RBS Role objects. This object is dynamically created when needed, then automatically deleted when no longer needed.

WARNING

Never change the configuration of an RBS Scope object. Doing so can have very serious consequences and could potentially break the system.

Configuring role-based services

During the iManage installation, the schema of your eDirectory tree was extended to support the RBS object types specified above. It also created an RBS Collection container for your role-based services and installed the iManage plug-ins to support all currently available product packages. However, you can complete these tasks manually from iManage, so everything is ready to go.

To install RBS schema extensions, complete the following steps in iManager:

1. Select the Configure button.

2. Select Role Based Services Setup and then Extend Schema.

3. Select OK to add the new Role Based Services schema extensions to the tree.

To create the RBS Collection container, complete the following steps:

1. Select the Configure button.

2. Select Role Based Services Setup ⇨ Create RBS Collection.

3. In the Create RBS Collection screen, enter the requested information and select OK.

- *Name*: Enter a name for the RBS Collection object.

- *Container*: Specify a context for the RBS Collection object.

To install product packages, complete the following steps in iManager:

1. Select the Configure button.

2. In the Install Plug-In screen, make your desired selections and select OK.

3. Highlight the desired plug-in and specify which RBS collection in which to put it.

Defining RBS roles

RBS roles specify the tasks that users are authorized to perform. The tasks that RBS roles can perform are exposed as RBS Task objects in eDirectory. RBS tasks are created automatically during the installation of product packages. They are organized into one or more RBS Module containers, each of which corresponds to a different type of functionality within the product.

Create and assign an RBS Role object by completing the following steps in iManage:

1. Select the Configure button.

2. Select Role Management and then Create Role.

3. In the Name screen, enter the requested information and select Next.

- *Role name*: Specify a name for the Role object.

- *Collection*: Specify an RBS Collection to hold the object.

- *(Optional) Description*: Enter a role description, if desired.

4. In the Tasks screen, make your desired selections and select Next.

- *All tasks*: Lists all available tasks for the role you are creating.

- *Assigned tasks*: Move the tasks you want assigned to this role from the All Tasks menu to the Assigned Tasks menu.

5. In the Associated Objects screen, specify an object to which to assign the role in the Object Name field and select Add. When all assignments have been made, select Next.

6. In the Set the Scope screen, specify a scope for each object to which this role is assigned and select Next. The scope defines where in your tree the assigned object can perform the role-based tasks. The Inheritable checkbox defines the scope including all sub-containers.

7. In the Summary screen, select Done to complete the creation of the RBS role.

Once created, you can modify RBS roles by completing the following steps in iManage:

1. Select the Configure button.

2. Select Role Management and then Modify Role.

3. In the Modify Roles screen, make the desired changes. Select the Task icon to add/remove tasks from a role. Select the Members icon to add/remove members from a role or redefine scopes of existing members of a role.

To delete any RBS object from your tree, complete the following steps in iManager:

1. Select the Configure button.

2. Select Role Management and then Delete RBS Object.

3. In the Delete RBS Objects screen, specify the full name and context of the RBS role you want to delete and select OK.

NetWare Remote Manager

If a good acronym is a sign of a successful product, then NetWare Remote Manager (NoRM) is well on its way to greatness! NoRM was formerly known as NetWare Management Portal, which is currently available for NetWare 5.1. NoRM provides most of the functionality of the console Monitor utility, together with functionality from several other console utilities, but also NoRM makes it available from a Web browser.

You can use NoRM to monitor your server's health, change the configuration of your server, or perform diagnostic and debugging tasks. The following list outlines some of the major tasks you can perform with NoRM:

- *Manage server health*: Monitoring the health status of one or more servers, building groups of servers to monitor together, and accessing eDirectory health and troubleshooting tools (iMonitor)

- *Configure server environment*: Managing disk partitions; viewing information about hardware adapters, hardware resources, and processor(s); loading or unloading NLM programs, LAN drivers, or disk drivers (also uploading new NLMs from NoRM); monitoring server disk space and memory resources; accessing files on volumes and DOS partitions; managing server connections; configuring SET parameters; scheduling console commands to run; and shutting down, restarting, or resetting a server

- *Troubleshoot server problems by*: Finding CPU hogs, finding high memory users, tracing ABEND sources, locating server process hogs, finding disk space hogs, seeing who is using a file

If you are familiar with NetWare Management Portal, which is available for NetWare 5.1, you will note some changes in NoRM for NetWare 6.

- *Look and feel*: NoRM layout has been changed to conform to other Novell web based utilities, such as iMonitor and iManage. The navigation frames have also been renamed and regrouped to better identify the tasks associated with the links.

- *Console Screens link*: From this link on the Console Screens page, a Java Applet allows you to view and run all the console screens just as though you were using the keyboard at the server console.

- *Console Commands link*: From this link you can access a list of all the console commands. Viewing and printing them is now much easier.

- *Logging in*: When you point your browser at NoRM, you will be prompted to authenticate before seeing any pages.

- *Admin and Non-Admin views*: If you log in to NetWare Remote Manager as a user with Supervisor rights to the server object, you can access and perform all management options. If you log in as a user without these rights, you can only see the volumes, directories, and files to which you have rights. You can view files where you have read access rights and upload files into directories where you have write access. No management functions are available.

- *Disk partition operations*: As an alternative to using ConsoleOne to create, change, or remove partitions, volumes, and pools, you can now use the Disk Partition Operation features in NoRM.

> ► *Profile CPU execution per NLM program*: On multiprocessor servers, you can view how each NLM program is distributing its activity across the available processors.

As you can see, NoRM is a very robust management utility that promises extremely flexible operation for today's NetWare administrators.

Installing NoRM

NetWare Web Manager is installed automatically during the installation of NetWare 6. The PORTAL and HTTPSTK NLM programs must be loaded on the server. Entries are placed in the AUTOEXEC.NCF to accomplish this.

After the installation, use a Web browser from a client computer in your network to access NoRM. In order to access NoRM from an Internet connection outside your firewall, you will need to make sure that TCP port 8009 is opened through the firewall to the IP address of your Web server. Port 8009 is the default port through which you will access the Web Manager interface. If desired, this port can be changed as long as it doesn't conflict with any other service on the NetWare 6 server.

To use NoRM, you must have a 4.x or newer Web browser such as Internet Explorer or Netscape Communicator. Make sure that Java or JavaScript is enabled on your Web browser. For steps on doing this, see the sections on Web Manager in this chapter.

NoRM is accessible in three ways, from Web Manager, directly, or from the server console.

To open NoRM from Web Manager:

1. Open Web Manager and select the appropriate server name listed under the NetWare Remote Manager heading.

NOTE

You may be prompted to accept an unknown certificate if this is the first time you have tried to open NoRM. If so, select Yes to continue or View Certificate to install the server certificate in your browser. Installing the certificate will prevent this message from appearing in the future.

2. At the Authentication dialog enter the full username, with leading dot, and password of a user with administrative rights to this server, and then select OK.

To open NoRM directly:

1. Open your Web browser and enter your Web server's domain name or IP address, followed by a colon and the port number, which by default

is 8009. For example: `https://www.quills.com:8009` or `https://137.65.192.1:8009`.

2. You may be prompted to accept the unknown certificate as noted above. At the Authentication dialog enter the full username, with leading dot, and password of a user with administrative rights to this server, and then select OK.

To open NoRM from the server console:

1. Select the Novell button from the console GUI.

2. Select Utilities and NetWare Remote Manager (see Figure 3.5).

NOTE

If you don't log in as a user with administrative rights to the server, you will not have access to all pages necessary to manage your server remotely. You will see only pages that display the volumes, directories, and files for which you have trustee rights. In this case, you can view files (where you have read access), and upload files into directories where you have write access. You will not have access to any other management functions.

► • ◄

F I G U R E   3.5   *NetWare Remote Manager interface*

NetWare Remote Manager	Novell NetWare 6 Server Version 5.60, September 13, 2001

Authentication (*admin*)

🔲 **PRVSERV1**   **Novell.**

Diagnose Server
  Health Monitor
  Profile / Debug
  Run Config
  Report
Manage Server
  Volumes
  Console Screens
  Connections
  Set Parameters
  Schedule Tasks
  Console
  Commands
  View Memory
  Config
  View Statistics
  Down / Restart

Volume Management

Volumes

Info	Name	Attributes	Mounted
ⓘ	SYS	N/A	YES
ⓘ	_ADMIN	N/A	YES
ⓘ	NETWARE6	N/A	YES
ⓘ	ENG_DATA	N/A	YES

Local Server Partitions

Drive
  C:\

Partition Management

  Disk Partitions

Novell Links:

After logging in, your session for NetWare Remote Manager remains open until you close all your browser windows at that workstation. To log out of NetWare Remote Manager, close all the browser windows at the workstation from which you logged in.

NoRM Basics

NoRM presents a little more complicated interface than that of Web Manager because of the number of tasks it can perform.

NoRM interface components

Similar to iManage, NoRM is organized into three main sections, or frames:

▸ *Header frame*: The Header frame is located at the top of the screen. It contains general information about the server and links to the Volumes, Health Monitor, and Configuration pages, as well as an Exit link to close the browser window. In addition to the Health Monitor button, selecting the semaphore icon next to your server name will also take you to the Server Health Monitor. By default, the Volumes page is always displayed when NoRM first starts.

▸ *Navigation frame*: The Navigation frame is located on the left side of the screen. It lists different management tasks, organized into groups, that you can perform with NoRM. Each link takes you to the specific page(s) for performing that task. The list of available tasks in the Navigation frame can change based on the services and NLMs that you have loaded on the server.

▸ *Main Content frame*: The Main Content frame occupies the middle-right of the screen. When you select a link in the Header or Navigation frames, the appropriate page will be displayed in the Main content frame. If an Information icon appears in the upper right corner of the page, you can view help for the page that is displayed in the main content frame.

Configuring NoRM

You can access the Configuration Options page either by selecting the Configure icon in the center of the Header frame or selecting the NetWare Remote Manager logo in the upper left corner of the Header frame. To access the Configuration Options page, you must be logged in as a user with supervisor rights to the server to which you are attaching. The NoRM Configuration settings are organized into three groups:

▸ **NetWare Remote Manager configuration options:** The following settings are used to configure NoRM views (see Figure 3.6):

FIGURE 3.6 *NoRM Configuration Options screen*

NetWare Remote Manager Configuration Options	
View Hidden Set Parameters	NO
View Hidden Console Commands	NO
View Hidden Files or Folders	NO
View System Files or Folders	NO
Enable Accessibility Options	NO
Restart NetWare Remote Manager (PORTAL.NLM)	RESTART
Enable Emergency account (SADMIN user) and set password.	
Disable Emergency account (SADMIN user) and clear password.	

- *View hidden SET parameters*: Toggles whether or not hidden SET parameters are visible in the list of available SET parameters in NoRM and on the server console.

- *View hidden console commands*: Toggles whether or not hidden console commands are visible in the list of available console commands. This can be helpful for discovering undocumented commands.

TIP

Even if hidden, any SET parameter or console command can still be activated from either NoRM or the server console as long as the proper syntax is known.

- *View hidden files or folders*: Toggles whether or not files and folders with the Hidden attribute set will appear in the page lists on NoRM or on the server console.

- *View system files or folders*: Toggles whether or not files and folders with the System attribute set will appear in the page lists on NoRM or on the server console.

- *Enable accessibility options*: Disables dynamic refresh of NoRM pages in order to conform with new Federal accessibility guidelines. With this option enabled, Health Monitor pages will not refresh until a manual page refresh is performed. For more information on accessibility options see the NetWare 6 on-line documentation.

- *Reset NetWare Remote Manager (PORTAL.NLM)*: If you make any changes to settings in this group, you must reset NoRM for the changes to take effect.

- *Enable emergency account (SAdmin) and set password*: SAdmin is a backup supervisor account that can be used when the Admin account or eDirectory is not working properly. It lets you perform maintenance tasks that do not require eDirectory. SAdmin is created when NoRM is installed. It copies the value of the Admin password for its own.

As the Admin password changes over time, the SAdmin password will not change. Make sure you keep track of your original Admin password or reset the SAdmin password when you change the Admin password to keep them in sync.

WARNING

- *Disable emergency account (SAdmin) and clear password*: Disables the emergency user account created by NoRM when it is installed.

► **HTTP logging controls:** The following settings control log files in the NoRM environment (see Figure 3.7):

FIGURE 3.7 *NoRM HTTP Logging Controls screen*

HTTP Logging Controls

Turn Debug Screen ON	
Turn Logger ON	
View Current HTTP Log File	View
Reset Current HTTP Log File	Reset
Log Only Errors to Log File	YES
HTTP Log File Rollover Size (in megabytes)	8

- *Turn Debug screen on*: When instructed by Novell Technical Services, turn this setting On to help debug a problem with the HTTPSTK module. You must also click the Turn Logger On button. The debug console screen journals debug information for the HTTP stack running on the server, so it can be reviewed for troubleshooting purposes.

This option will create significant server overhead and should not be used under normal operation.

WARNING

- *Turn logger on*: If logging has been turned off, clicking this button will turn it on.

- *View current HTTP log file*: The log file contains the following information: an entry number; the date and time stamp in Greenwich mean time (GMT); host name; the program making the call; the level of the call (whether it's done by the server or by users); and a description of the entry itself with information including the IP address of the source machine making the request, messages, status, etc.

- *Reset current HTTP log file*: This option clears the current log and begins a new one. Restarting the log is useful if you have made a configuration change to your server and want to begin a new logging session.

- *Log only errors to log file*: This option controls whether or not all requests are logged to the file. When logging only errors to the file, it will take much longer to fill the file to its maximum size, but casual access to the server is not tracked.

- *HTTP log file rollover size (in megabytes)*: This option sets a maximum size for the HTTP log file. If the available space on your volume SYS: is limited, you might want to limit the log file to a smaller size. If you want to gather more information over a longer period of time in the log file, you might want to increase the rollover size. When the file is full, the file is deleted and restarted. Automatic rollover guarantees that if logging is on, the log file always reflects the most recent activity on the server.

▶ **HTTP Interface Management:** The following settings control the basic configuration of NoRM (see Figure 3.8):

- *Change default port*: Allows you to select a different default TCP port for unencrypted access to NoRM. The default value is port 81.

- *Change alternate port*: Allows you to select a different default TCP port for unencrypted access to NoRM. The default alternate port is 8008.

- *Change SSL port*: Allows you to select a different default TCP port for encrypted (SSL) access to NoRM. The default alternate port is 8009.

FIGURE 3.8 *HTTP Interface Management settings*

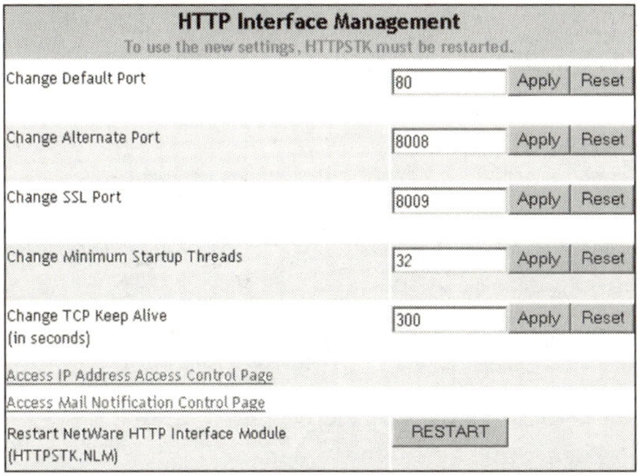

- *Change minimum startup threads*: This setting lets you define the number of worker threads that are created for NoRM at startup. At least one thread is required and other threads will be created as needed. These initial work threads will be built between the server and browser-based clients. Default is 32. However, if memory is low, you might want to set this to 4 and let more threads be created as needed.

- *Change TCP keep alive (in seconds)*: This option lets you change the timeout for TCP sessions in NoRM. Default is 300 seconds (5 minutes).

- *Access IP Address Access Control page*: From this page you can limit access to NoRM. You can specify IP addresses for workstations or specify a subnet and subnet mask for ranges of workstations from which to give access. Restricting access in this way can help secure remote access to your server.

- *Access Mail Notification Control page*: From this page you can specify a primary mail server, an alternate mail server, up to eight users in the notification list, and a Mail From identification. You can control which items to be notified about on the Health Monitor page.

- *Reset NetWare HTTP Interface module (HTTPSTK.NLM)*: Changes to settings in this group require that HTTPSTK.NLM be reloaded. Select this button to perform the reload remotely.

By clicking the word Novell in the upper-right portion of the header frame, you can access the Novell Support Connection at `http://support.novell.com/`. From this site, you can get current updates, locate troubleshooting information, or open an on-line support incident.

Customizing NoRM

You can add text, graphics, and custom links to the home (Volumes) page of NoRM by creating an HTML file named PRTLANNC.HTM, which contains the HTML code you want to add, and placing it in the server's SYS:\LOGIN directory. Any information in this file will appear at the bottom of the home page. See the NetWare 6 on-line documentation for more information.

Because this file will be used as part of the HTML code that generates the front page, do *not* include the <body> and </body> tags.

NOTE

▶ • ◀

iMonitor

NetWare 6 ships with iMonitor v1.5. It is accessible as a component of NoRM. It provides eDirectory management and repair capabilities similar to the server management capabilities offered by NoRM. The goal of iMonitor is to provide a Web-based alternative, and eventual replacement, for many of the traditional eDirectory management and troubleshooting tools such as DSBrowse, DSTrace, DSDiag and much of DSRepair.

While iMonitor runs on NetWare 6 (and NetWare 5.1), it is capable of gathering information from most any version of eDirectory, including NDS version 4.11 or higher, and NDS or eDirectory running on any supported platform (NetWare, Windows NT/2000, Solaris, Linux, and Tru64).

While iMonitor does provide tree-wide management, it is designed to get "down in the weeds" just like the console-based tools that you may have used in the past. It keeps track of the activities of the DSAgent running on each eDirectory server, so you can get an accurate picture of what is happening at any given time.

The following list identifies some of the major features offered by iMonitor in NetWare 6:

▶ *General eDirectory tasks*: This category of features includes search for eDirectory object(s), status of DirXML in your environment (if applicable), both pre-configured and customizable eDirectory reports, and detailed eDirectory error code and troubleshooting references.

► *Monitor eDirectory agent health*: This includes synchronization status, detailed synchronization information, known eDirectory servers, and partition and replica status for this server.

► *Browse eDirectory agent*: This lets you view eDirectory objects and attributes from the perspective of the server as well as viewing eDirectory schema on the server.

► *Configuring eDirectory agent*: Configure partition lists, replication filters, background processes, agent triggers, login settings, schema and partition synchronization, and database cache settings.

► *Server-centric tasks*: This includes web-based versions of DSTrace, simplified DSRepair, and a background process scheduler. These services are only available for the server from which iMonitor is running.

Installing iMonitor

iMonitor is installed automatically during the installation of NetWare 6. Since it shares resources with NoRM, the PORTAL and HTTPSTK NLM programs must be loaded on the server. Entries are placed in the AUTOEXEC.NCF to accomplish this.

After the installation, use a Web browser from a client computer in your network to access iMonitor. To access iMonitor from an Internet connection outside your firewall, you will need to make sure that TCP port 8009 is opened through the firewall to the IP address of your Web server. Port 8009 is the default port through which you will access the Web Manager interface. If desired, this port can be changed as long as it doesn't conflict with any other service on the NetWare 6 server.

To use iMonitor, use Netscape v4.06 or higher or Internet Explorer v4 or higher. Make sure that Java or JavaScript is enabled on your Web browser. For steps on doing this see the Web Manager sections of this chapter.

To access iMonitor, open NoRM and browse down to the Manage eDirectory heading in the left column, then select NDS iMonitor.

Alternatively, you can open iMonitor directly by opening your Web browser and entering your Web server's domain name or IP address, the NoRM port number (8009), and the iMonitor path (/nds). For example:

```
https://www.quills.com:8009/nds
```

or

```
https://137.65.192.1:8009/nds
```

You may be prompted to accept a certificate. At the Authentication dialog, enter the full username, with leading dot, and password of a user with administrative rights to this server, and then select OK to display the screen shown in Figure 3.9.

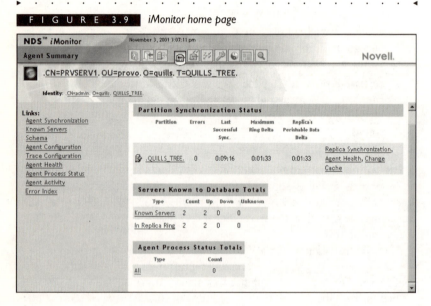

FIGURE 3.9   *iMonitor home page*

As with NoRM, your iMonitor session remains open until all browser windows at your workstation are closed.

iMonitor Basics

Because it is a component of NoRM, iMonitor adheres largely to the same page layout as NoRM and iManage.

iMonitor interface layout

There are four possible frames to an iMonitor page:

▸ *Header frame*: The Header frame is located at the top of the screen. It contains general links such as Help, Search, NoRM Home, and Logout. In addition to these, the header contains links to specific iMonitor features, including Agent Summary (iMonitor Home), Agent Configuration, Trace Configuration, Repair, DirXML Summary, and Reports.

▶ *Navigation frame*: The Navigation frame is located on the left side of the screen. It lists different management tasks, organized into groups, which you can perform with NoRM. Each link takes you to the specific page(s) for performing that task.

▶ *Main Content frame*: The Main Content frame occupies the middle-right of the screen. When you select a link in the Header or Navigation frames, the appropriate page will be displayed in the Main Content frame.

▶ *(Conditional) Replica frame*: When needed, the Replica frame will appear in the lower left corner of the iMonitor frame. This will happen when another replica of the requested data exists, or when another replica may have a different view of the information being presented in the Main Content frame. From the Replica frame you can change the replica that you are using to view the requested data.

The amount and type of information that you see in iMonitor is dependent on your current eDirectory identity and the version of the DSAgent with which you are currently working. As new versions of eDirectory are released, they will be updated to provide more information to iMonitor. Therefore, older versions of eDirectory, or NDS, while still accessible via iMonitor, may not provide the same level of detail offered by a NetWare 6 server running eDirectory 8.6.

Modes of operation

iMonitor can function in one of two possible modes. You don't need to do anything to select between the two modes; iMonitor handles it automatically. However, it is important to understand them in order to properly interpret iMonitor data and navigate the eDirectory tree.

▶ *Direct mode*: Direct mode is used when iMonitor is gathering information or executing an operation on the same server from which iMonitor is running. The server-centric iMonitor features mentioned above, which include DSTrace, DSRepair, and Background Scheduler are only available from direct mode. Direct mode gives you full access to all iMonitor features and is faster than Proxy mode, which is described next.

▶ *Proxy mode*: Proxy mode is used when iMonitor is gathering information or executing an operation on a server other than that on from which iMonitor is running. Proxy mode makes it possible to gather information and statistics from older versions of eDirectory or NDS. Proxy mode is the default method of operation for iMonitor; meaning that once iMonitor is opened it will continue to run from the specified server until explicitly told to switch to an instance of iMonitor on a different server.

iMonitor chooses the mode based on the URL request submitted from your browser. If the URL contains a server query, then iMonitor will use Proxy mode. If no server query is present, iMonitor will run the query against the local DSAgent using Direct mode.

Configuring iMonitor

The default configuration of iMonitor is suitable for most environments. However, iMonitor offers a configuration file, SYS:SYSTEM\NDSIMON.INI, that allows you to customize iMonitor if desired (see Figure 3.10). It lets you change both the general execution of iMonitor, as well as customize specific iMonitor features. For more information on iMonitor see the NetWare 6 on-line documentation.

F I G U R E   3 . 1 0 *Excerpt from iMonitor Configuration file*

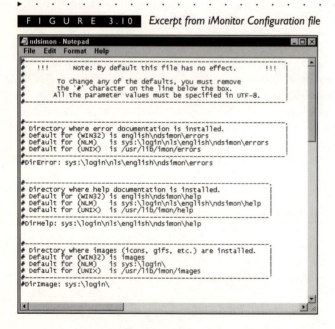

Remote Management with ConsoleOne

Much of the server management that previously required access to the NetWare 6 server console could now be done with NoRM, as discussed previously. NoRM lets you perform most management tasks that normally require access to the server console from a remote workstation or even from across the Internet. However, to manage any version of NetWare 5 or NetWare 6 remotely, you can use RConsoleJ, which is part of ConsoleOne. While RConsoleJ does not offer the flexibility of NoRM, it can save significant time by letting you manage servers to which you have a LAN/WAN connection.

NOTE

If you have Netware 4.x or earlier servers on your network, you will have to use the DOS-based RConsole utility that shipped with these versions of NetWare. Consult your server documentation for more information.

RConsoleJ is a Java applet that provides a server "window" on your workstation from which you can use console utilities, load/unload NLMs, and change server configuration just as if you were using the server's actual keyboard and monitor. Using RConsoleJ enables you to access the server from any workstation on the network, which gives you greater freedom when administering your network.

RConsoleJ requires the IP protocol to connect to NetWare servers remotely. However, if you want to use it to connect to a server that is running IPX only, you can do so by routing RConsoleJ communications through a secondary proxy server, which has both IP and IPX protocol stacks loaded. The proxy server acts as a gateway between RConsoleJ and the IPX server.

Because RConsoleJ is part of ConsoleOne, you can run it from any platform that supports ConsoleOne, including Windows, NetWare, Linux, Solaris, and Tru64.

To set up your network for RConsoleJ, you will have to do the following:

- ▶ Setup the target server, which is the server you want to access remotely.

- ▶ (Conditional) Install proxy software on an IP server if the target server is only running IPX.

- ▶ Install RConsoleJ software on the workstation or server from which you want to run the remote console session.

Setup the Target Server

The target server is the server whose console you want to access during the remote console session. The target server can be running either IP or IPX.

To prepare a target server, complete the following steps:

1. At the server console prompt load the following NLM:

RCONAG6

2. Enter the password you want administrators to use when accessing the target server from RConsoleJ. You do not need an eDirectory password, because RConsoleJ does not use eDirectory.

3. Enter the TCP port number for the unencrypted session. The default value is 2034. If the server communicates using IPX only, enter −1 to disable TCP listening. To enable listening over a dynamically assigned port, enter 0.

4. Enter the TCP port number for the secure session. The default port number is 2036. Ensure the Key Material object named SSL CertificateDNS has been created.

The Secure connection is available only on IP and not on IPX.

NOTE

5. Enter the SPX port number on which RCONAG6 will listen for a proxy server. The default port number is 16800. If the server communicates using IP only, enter −1 to disable SPX listening. To enable listening over a dynamically assigned port, enter 0.

(Conditional) Configure an RConsoleJ Proxy Server

This server will act as a middleman between the RConsoleJ client, which only communicates via IP and a NetWare server running on IPX. To do this, the RConsoleJ proxy server, must have both IP and IPX protocol stacks loaded.

1. At the server console prompt, enter the following command:

RCONPRXY

2. Enter the TCP port number on which RCONPRXY will listen for RConsoleJ. The default value is 2035. To enable listening over a dynamically assigned port, enter 0.

Once the NetWare server is running the RConsoleJ Proxy agent, the RConsoleJ client can communicate through it with the IPX target server.

(Conditional) Automating RConsoleJ Agents

If you want to have the NetWare server automatically load the necessary RConsoleJ modules at startup, put a command to run LDRCONAG.NCF in the server's AUTOEXEC.NCF file. LDRCONAG.NCF contains all the necessary RConsoleJ commands necessary to support RConsoleJ.

Since loading these modules requires you to specify a remote password, you can encrypt it for storage in LDRCONAG.NCF. To create an encrypted remote password complete the following steps:

1. Type the following command:

   ```
   RCONAG6 ENCRYPT
   ```

2. Enter the password you want to use for remote console sessions.

3. Enter the other required port information as outlined in the previous section. The system will display the encrypted password value and a message prompting if the RCONAG6 command should be written to the SYS:SYSTEM\LDRCONAG.NCF file. To include the RCONAG6 command with your encrypted password in the LDRCONAG.NCF file, enter **Y**.

4. The system places a LOAD RCONAG command into the LDRCONAG.NCF file with the encrypted password as a parameter. To autoload RCONAG6.NLM with an encrypted password on startup, use either NWCONFIG or EDIT to open the AUTOEXEC.NCF file. At the end of the file, enter the following:

   ```
   LDRCONAG
   ```

5. Save and exit the AUTOEXEC.NCF file.

The server will now automatically load the necessary remote modules and your encrypted password whenever it is started.

Running the RConsoleJ Client

To run RConsoleJ from a supported workstation or NetWare 6 server, do the following:

NOTE

If you are running RConsoleJ from a NetWare server, you can start it directly from the server GUI by selecting the Novell button and then selecting Programs and RConsoleJ. You can then continue with Step 3 below.

1. Open ConsoleOne and browse to the server object you want to control.

2. Right-click the server object and select Remote Console.

3. In the RConsoleJ screen, shown in Figure 3.11, specify the required information and select Connect.

RConsoleJ access screen

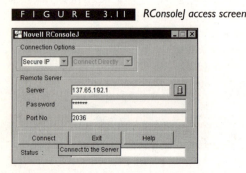

- *Connection options*: Specify whether you are connecting via Secure or Unsecure IP. If you are using Unsecure IP you can choose whether to connect directly or through a proxy.

- *Remote server*: Specify the target server's name for a direct connection or the Proxy server's name for a proxy connection. Enter the remote password. The Port number will be automatically inserted unless you have changed it from the default.

PART II

Delivering One Net

In This Part

Novell's vision of One Net is a world in which all types of networks work together to simplify the complexities of modern business and provide the power and flexibility needed to succeed in the economy of the twenty-first century.

The one thing you don't have the luxury of doing in today's net world is dictate the software, hardware, and architecture across the entire reach of your network. By definition, One Net integrates myriad technologies, platforms, and architectures in such a way that the underlying complexity is masked from the user. Users see what they need (and nothing more), when they need it, from any net connection anywhere in the world!

The three chapters in Part I of this book introduced NetWare 6, the various Novell clients, and the suite of management tools that let you keep everything running smoothly. From an administrator's perspective, it is easy to see how NetWare 6 is achieving its goal of One Net. There are several installation and upgrade options; clients no longer demand prerequisites or make assumptions about platform; and management tools are fully net-enabled, so you can administer from home in your pajamas if you want.

But all the One Net love in the world isn't going to change the fact that for you, as a network administrator, the complexity of the net isn't hidden. You will see it every day, and you will need to know how to perform those tasks that keep the Net functioning smoothly.

Chapter 3 introduced the NetWare 6 administrative tools. Part II of this book introduces the administrative techniques and tools used to keep the foundation of One Net strong and steady. Chapters 4 and 5 will demonstrate how to use those tools for day-to-day administration of NetWare 6 servers and Novell eDirectory. Chapter 6 provides an overview of the absolutely critical area of network security, and how eDirectory solves many of the traditional problems associated with managing authentication and access control. Chapter 7 introduces the other aspect of network computing that touches just about everybody: printing. NetWare 6 has made it easier than ever to configure a robust printing architecture that gives users the freedom to print from anywhere to anywhere with the click of a button.

CHAPTER 4

NetWare 6 Server Management

Instant Access

Optimizing performance

▶ To monitor performance, use NetWare Remote Manager (NoRM). You can also use MONITOR.NLM from the server console.

▶ To optimize performance, use NoRM or MONITOR.NLM to change server parameters. You can also set parameters individually using SET commands from the server console.

▶ You can manage a virtual memory swap file using NoRM. You can also use the SWAP console utility.

▶ To see a history of errors that have occurred with the server, the volume, or TTS, use a text editor or EDIT.NLM to read the error log files: SYS$LOG.ERR, VOL$LOG.ERR, TTS$LOG.ERR, BOOT$LOG.ERR, and ABEND.LOG.

▶ Logger captures server messages to the server console so you can read them for diagnostic purposes. You can also dump the contents of Logger to a file for offline diagnosis.

Running Java applications

▶ To run Java applications or applets on a server, specify a Just In Time (JIT) compiler and load JAVA.NLM on the server.

Protecting the server

▶ To use an Uninterruptible Power Supply (UPS) to protect the server from power outages, use UPS_AIO.NLM or third-party UPS-management software.

▶ To protect the server and network from virus infections, use virus scanning software, assign executable files the Execute Only or Read-Only attributes, and warn users against loading files from external sources.

▶ To keep faulty NLMs from corrupting server memory, you can load them in a protected address space using either NoRM or the PROTECTED load command from the server console.

Maintaining the server

▶ If you are unsure of a server's name, you can display it with the NAME console utility.

▶ To display the server's hardware information, use the links in the Manage Hardware section of NoRM. You can also use CONFIG, CPUCHECK, and LIST DEVICES from the server console.

▶ To see the version of NetWare that is running on a server, look in the header of NoRM, or look in the General ⇨ Server Information tab of the Server object in ConsoleOne. You can also use the VERSION console command.

▶ To view a list of the server's volumes and the name spaces they support, open the Volumes page in NoRM or use the VOLUMES console command.

▶ To bring down the server, use the DOWN console command.

▶ To reboot the server, use the RESTART SERVER console command.

▶ Keep abreast of current patches and updated modules by checking http://support.novell.com regularly.

▶ To control the server from a workstation, use Console Screens in NoRM or the RConsoleJ utility in ConsoleOne.

▶ To control server startup activities, use the server startup files: AUTOEXEC.NCF and STARTUP.NCF. (Edit these files by using EDIT.NLM or NWCONFIG.)

▶ To manage workstation connections, open the Connections page in NoRM. You can also use MONITOR.NLM. Manage login from ConsoleOne User object properties.

▶ To monitor or modify a server's time, open and use the TIME, SET TIME, and SET TIME ZONE console commands.

▶ TIMESYNC.NLM manages time synchronization between servers in an eDirectory tree.

▶ To unload or display currently loaded NLMs, open the Modules page in NoRM. You can also use the UNLOAD and MODULES console commands.

Managing storage devices

▶ To add a new hard disk or replace an existing one, use NWCONFIG.NLM.

▶ To protect network data by mirroring hard disks, use ConsoleOne to manage partitions, NSS pools, and Volumes. You can also use the MIRROR STATUS, REMIRROR PARTITION, and ABORT REMIRROR console commands. NWCONFIG.NLM is no longer used for disk management.

▸ To protect network data from bad blocks on the hard disk, use the Hot Fix feature. Set up Hot Fix during installation or when creating a new partition. Monitor the number of bad blocks found from the Volumes page in NoRM.

▸ To mount CD-ROMs as network volumes, load CDROM.NLM.

▸ To add or remove a PCI Hot Plug adapter, use NCMCON.NLM.

Managing routing between servers

▸ To list networks, use the DISPLAY NETWORKS console command.

▸ To list servers, open the Known Servers page in iMonitor or use the DISPLAY SERVERS console command.

▸ To execute protocol configuration commands made using INETCFG.NLM, use the INITIALIZE SYSTEM and REINITIALIZE SYSTEM console utilities.

▸ To configure protocols, use INETCFG.NLM.

▸ To configure IPX, AppleTalk, and TCP/IP protocols, use INETCFG.NLM.

▸ To configure RIP/SAP packet filtering, use FILTCFG.NLM.

▸ To display routing information, use the TRACK ON and TRACK OFF console utilities.

NetWare Server Basics

There are many different tasks associated with managing a NetWare 6 server, from monitoring performance to adding or changing server hardware, to accounting for customer usage. NetWare 6 brings a new management paradigm to many of these standard operations. This chapter will present you with the available options for performing server maintenance and management. Some of them are brand new, some are tried and true, but the move is definitely toward remote, clientless management tools that give you all the power of NetWare's traditional console-based utilities. Specific administrative tasks that will be covered in this chapter include:

- ▶ Protecting the server
- ▶ Monitoring and optimizing server performance
- ▶ Performing regular server maintenance
- ▶ Installing or replacing server hardware, such as hard disks and network boards
- ▶ Working with CD-ROMs as network volumes
- ▶ Managing startup files
- ▶ Synchronizing time between all the network servers

The behavior of a NetWare 6 server is configured and managed in two ways: Console utilities and NetWare Loadable Modules (NLMs). New with NetWare 6, NetWare Remote Manager exposes these tools for use from a remote workstation. Similarly, the remote console capabilities of ConsoleOne also make server management more flexible by making the server console accessible from any workstation on your LAN/WAN.

Console Utilities

Console utilities are used to change or view some aspect of the NetWare 6 server. They ship as part of the core operating system. Console commands are accessible either directly from the console or remotely through RConsoleJ or NoRM.

To see a list of all supported console commands, select the Console Commands option in NoRM or type **HELP** at the server console. Figure 4.1 shows the NoRM Console Commands page. To see a brief description and example of any console command, select the Information link next to the command in NoRM or type **HELP** at the server console.

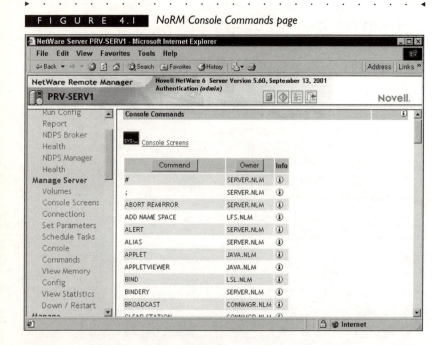

FIGURE 4.1 NoRM Console Commands page

NetWare Loadable Modules

NetWare Loadable Modules (NLMs) are software modules dynamically linked to the NetWare operating system to extend the capabilities or provide additional features. Many NLMs are automatically installed with the NetWare operating system. Others are optional; you can load them if your particular situation requires them. There are four common types of NetWare Loadable Modules you can use to add different types of functionality to your server: NLMs, Name Space modules, LAN drivers, and Storage drivers (also called disk drivers). Additional types of NLMs, such as PSMs (Platform Support Modules), also exist. Table 4.1 lists the four most common types of NLMs.

TABLE 4.1 *Different Types of NLMs*

NLM TYPE	EXTENSION	DESCRIPTION
NLM	.NLM	Changes or adds to the server's functionality. Such an NLM might allow you to back up network files, add support for another protocol, or add support for devices such as a CD-ROM drive or a UPS (Uninterruptible Power Supply).
Name Space module	.NAM	Allows the operating system to store Macintosh, OS/2, Windows NT, Windows 95/98, or NFS files, along with their unique file formats, long filenames, and other characteristics.
LAN driver	.LAN	Enables the operating system to communicate with a network board installed in the server.
Storage driver	.CDM and .HAM	Enables the operating system to communicate with a storage device (such as a hard disk) and its controller board (also called adapter) installed in the server. The .CDM driver (Custom Device Module) drives the storage device. Its accompanying .HAM driver (Host Adapter Module) drives the storage device's adapter. You need both drivers for a single storage device. The .CDM and .HAM drivers replace the older .DSK drivers used in previous versions of NetWare.

Many NLMs have their own status screen that is available on the server console. To view the various status screens that are active on your server at any given time, select Console Screens from NoRM. Figure 4.2 shows the NoRM Console Screens page. From the server console itself, you can use Alt+Esc to cycle through the available status screens, or use Ctrl+Esc to bring up a list of available screens from which you can select.

FIGURE 4.2 *Console screens in NoRM*

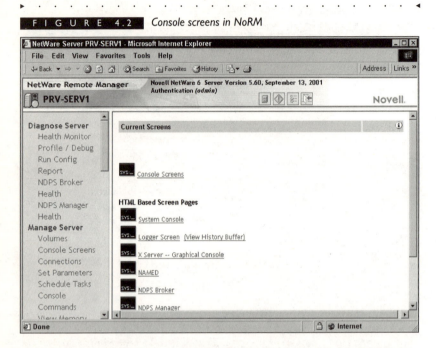

To load or unload NLMs, it is more effective to use the List Modules link in NoRM. Enter the full name, including path, to the NLM you want to load and select the Load Module button. You can check the box to view the System console during module load to make sure it loads properly.

Similarly, you can unload an NLM by selecting it from the list of loaded modules and then selecting Unload. This is equivalent to typing **UNLOAD** *<module>* from the server console.

TIP

One powerful feature of NoRM is the ability to define groups of servers and create a custom home page from which those servers can be managed. Select the Build Group option in NoRM, select the servers you want in the group, and then select Build Server Group. Once created, you can easily move from server to server as necessary to perform your administrative tasks.

Stopping and Starting the Server

If you need to shut down or restart your NetWare 6 server, first notify users so they have time to save their work and close any files they are using on that server. Once this is done, select DOWN or RESTART in NoRM. Three options will be available, as shown in Figure 4.3.

TIP

You can send a broadcast message to all users attached to a server by selecting the Connections link in NoRM. Simply type your message into the Broadcast Message field and select Send.

FIGURE 4.3 *DOWN, RESTART, and RESET server options in NoRM*

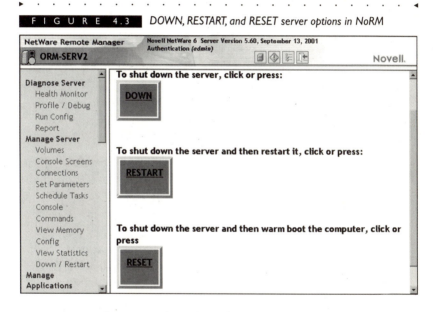

- ▸ *DOWN*: This option shuts down the server and returns the server console to a DOS prompt. From the DOS prompt, you can turn off the computer, reboot it, or restart the server. This is equivalent to typing **DOWN** from the server console.

- ▸ *RESTART*: This option unloads and then automatically reloads the NetWare operating system without returning to DOS first. This command is equivalent to typing **RESTART SERVER** from the server console.

- ▸ *RESET*: This option not only shuts down the server and returns it to DOS, but also performs a reset of the computer hardware (warm reboot). If your server is configured to load automatically on boot up, NetWare 6 will automatically reload after the hardware has rebooted. This is equivalent to typing **DOWN** from the server console and then doing a "three finger salute" (Ctrl+Alt+Del) to reset the hardware.

To start NetWare 6 from DOS, change to the \NWSERVER directory and load SERVER.EXE. This loads the NetWare operating system on the computer, turning it back into a server. During the NetWare 6 installation, commands to automatically load SERVER.EXE will be added to your computer's AUTOEXEC.BAT file unless you specifically choose not to have them added.

Running Java Applications on the Server

NetWare 6 includes an updated Java Virtual Machine (JVM), which allows Java-based applications and applets to run better than ever. Complete the following steps to load the JVM on the server and to install and run an application or applet on the server:

1. Copy the application or applet files to the default Java directory on the server. The default directory is SYS:JAVA\CLASSES. This directory is included in the CLASSPATH environment variable, so the server will be able to find the application or applet without users having to specify the path.

2. Specify a Just In Time (JIT) compiler for the server to use. This will improve the performance of Java-based applications. NetWare 6 ships with the Symantec JIT compiler v1.3, or you can install another manufacturer's JIT compiler.

3. Java is loaded by default when NetWare 6 loads. If it has been unloaded for whatever reason, you can restart Java by loading JAVA.NLM on the server. Once JAVA.NLM is loaded you can view Java information from NoRM by selecting the Java Application Information link, which is shown in Figure 4.4.

4. You can start a new Java Applet by selecting Start New Application and typing the **APPLET *<html_file>*** command, substituting the applet's filename for *<html_file>*.

5. To execute a Java-based application, the command you type depends on how you want the application to run. Use one of the following commands, substituting the application's name for *<class>*:

   • If the application doesn't require user input, or if it runs in a graphical user interface, use the JAVA *<class>* command.

- If the application is text-based and requires user input, use the JAVA -NS <class> command to bring up a separate console screen for the application.

- If you want to designate a specific amount of virtual memory for the application to use, use the JAVA –VM<size> <class> command, substituting the amount of memory (in megabytes) for <size>. The default size is 32MB.

Java information in NoRM

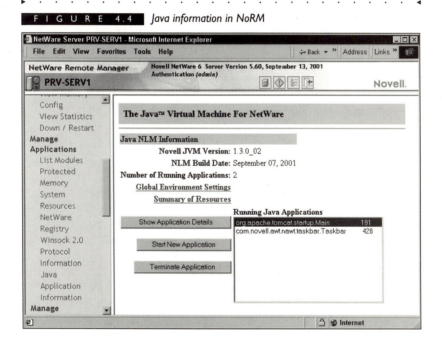

You can view detailed statistics on any Java application running on NetWare 6 by selecting Show Application Details in NoRM.

TIP

If you need to terminate a Java process for any reason, do the following from the NoRM Java Application Information screen:

I. Select the application from the list of running Java applications. This can be done from the server console by typing **JAVA –SHOW** and noting the ID of the process you want to shut down.

2. Select Terminate Application, then select OK to confirm that this application should be unloaded. This is equivalent to typing **JAVA –KILL** *<id>* at the server console, substituting the ID of the Java process you want to terminate for *<id>*.

Managing a NetWare Server

In the preceding sections you can see how NoRM permits us to manage most any aspect of a NetWare 6 server from any workstation with Browser access to the network, even over the Internet! The following sections review several of the other types of day-to-day server management you need to perform on a NetWare 6 network.

Protecting the Server

Protecting the server is a very important safeguard that cannot be overlooked. Damage to the server can affect the entire network. The activities covered in the following sections can help you protect your server.

Physical damage

If the server is in an exposed public area where anyone can have access to it, accidents can, and will, happen. For example, someone may unplug the power cord or turn off the server, thinking it had been left on accidentally.

Be sure to store the server in a locked room. In fact, you may also want to remove its keyboard and monitor, and access it only with the Remote Console feature when necessary.

Secure the server to a desk or counter if you are in an earthquake-prone area. Even a small shake can knock a computer to the floor.

Electrical power problems

Because electrical power is not always consistent, you need to ensure your server will not be damaged and files won't be corrupted if a brownout, surge, spike, or outage occurs.

Use a UPS for the server. This provides the server with a backup battery in case of a power outage, which allows enough time for the UPS to shut down the server cleanly, leaving no open files exposed to corruption.

While attaching every workstation to a UPS may not be feasible, you should at least use surge suppressors on workstations and peripherals (such as printers) to prevent electrical surges from damaging equipment.

Typically, UPS manufacturers provide software to manage their UPS products. You should use the manufacturer's software to manage your UPS whenever possible. However, if you don't have software from the UPS manufacturer, you can use NetWare's UPS_AIO.NLM to support the UPS attached to a serial port on the server.

Use the following steps to install a UPS on a server using Novell's UPS_AIO.NLM. Use this module if your UPS is connected through a serial port.

1. Attach the UPS to the server using the manufacturer's instructions.

2. Load the UPS hardware driver on the server.

3. Load an AIO device driver on the server. AIOCOMX.NLM is the default driver that comes with NetWare.

4. Load UPS_AIO.NLM on the server, specifying the correct options in the UPS_AIO options format (see Table 4.2).

TIP

If you want the UPS to be configured the same way every time the server is rebooted, put this same command in the server's AUTOEXEC.NCF file.

T A B L E 4 . 2	*UPS_AIO Options*
OPTION	**DESCRIPTION**
Downtime = *value*	The time, in seconds, that the server will run on battery power before shutting down. Default: 300. Values: Minimum 30 seconds (no maximum).
MSGDelay = *value*	The time, in seconds, before the system sends a message to users about the approaching shutdown. Default: 5. Values: Minimum 0 (no maximum).
MSGInterval = *value*	The time, in seconds, between broadcasts. Default: 30. Values: Minimum 20 (no maximum).
DriverType = *value*	The AIO device driver type. See the manufacturer's documentation for the type. Default: 1 (AIOCOMX). Values: 1, 2, or 3.
Board = *value*	The AIO board number. If you use AIOCOMX, the board number is displayed when you load AIOCOMX. If you use another driver, see the manufacturer's documentation for the number. Default: 0.

(continued)

T A B L E 4 . 2	UPS_AIO Options (continued)
OPTION	**DESCRIPTION**
Port = *value*	AIO port number. If you use AIOCOMX, the port number is displayed when you load AIOCOMX. If you use another driver, see the manufacturer's documentation for the number. Default: 0.
Signal_High	Sets normal RS232 signaling state to High. Use the High setting only if your system uses high values instead of low values to determine if the power is low. See the manufacturer's documentation for more information. Default: none.

Viruses

Unfortunately, software viruses are a fact of life. Use a third-party product to check for viruses and to disinfect your network if one is found. Several companies are manufacturing virus detectors for NetWare networks.

Because new viruses are being created continually, keep your virus detection software up to date (get all available updates of the software, follow manufacturer's procedures for updating, and so on).

If necessary, establish policies against users loading their own software on the network or downloading software from outside online sources or email messages, or provide diskless workstations to the users.

To prevent viruses from infecting executable files, you can assign those files the Execute Only file attribute. You can also remove the Modify right from the directory that contains the executable files and assign the Read-Only attribute to the executables. If a user still has the Modify right to a file, the virus can change the Read-Only attribute to Read-Write, infect the file, and then change the attribute back. Therefore, it's important to remove the Modify right from the user, if you are going to use the Read-Only attribute for virus protection.

Hardware Failures

To protect your server from hard disk problems, the NetWare feature called Hot Fix monitors any bad blocks that develop on the hard disk. (Hot Fix is explained in the section "Using Hot Fix," later in this chapter.) For more protection, you can use disk mirroring and disk duplexing to store identical copies of all network files on two disks, so if one disk goes bad, the data is still available from the other. This protection feature is explained in the section on disk mirroring and duplexing, later in this chapter.

NOTE

Another critical feature for protecting against hardware-related features in NetWare 6 is NetWare Cluster Services (NCS) and the ability to use shared storage in a Storage Area Network (SAN). For more information on high availability server clusters, see Chapter 12.

Faulty NLMs

Occasionally, an NLM may exhibit problems using the server's memory. It may corrupt the server's memory or overwrite memory being used by another process, causing the server to *ABEND*, a term which stand for an "abnormal end" — a serious error that causes the process to hang, and can hang the server as well.

Usually, this sort of problem is limited to third-party NLMs that have not been fully tested, or perhaps an NLM being developed and tested. If you have an NLM that you suspect is being troublesome, or if you are developing an NLM and want to test it in a safe environment, you can use the Protected Address Space feature of NetWare 6.

NOTE

All NLMs from Novell have been thoroughly tested and should not require that you load them in protected address spaces. However, some default applications, such as the JVM, load in protected memory automatically, to protect the server from external applications.

With this feature, you can load the suspect NLM in a protected area of memory, where the core operating system processes are insulated from the actions of this module. Not all NLMs can be loaded in a protected memory space, because of the memory management that is employed, so you should test any NLM you want to run in protected memory before committing to this solution. Modules running in a protected address space use what is known as virtual memory, in which data the module is using can be swapped out of system memory and moved to disk, so other processes can use the same physical memory space.

You can load an NLM into a protected address space from NoRM by doing the following:

I. Select the Protected Memory link. This screen also gives you a view of applications operating in protected memory and settings for memory protection SET parameters.

2. Select one of the following options:

   - *Load NCF file protected*: Many third-party applications will create an NCF script to load the necessary modules. Use this option to make sure all modules loaded from the specified NCF file are loaded into protected memory.

   - *Load module protected*: Use this option to load a single NLM into protected memory.

3. Enter the full name, including path, of the module or NCF file that you want to load in the appropriate field, and then select the corresponding button.

Monitoring and Optimizing Server Performance

When you monitor the server's performance, you look for key indicators that the server is functioning at an optimal level. Some of the things you should monitor include the utilization percentage of the server's processor, the number of cache buffers and packet receive buffers being regularly used, and the server's memory allocation.

Every network has different needs and usage patterns. By default, server parameters are set so that the server will perform well on most networks. In addition, the server is self-tuning, meaning that it will gradually adjust itself over time to accommodate changing usage patterns. However, you should be aware of what constitutes "normal" for your server(s). That way you be able to effectively plan for future network and server needs as well as noticing any unusual changes that might indicate a potential problem.

The best way to do this is to regularly view the Server Health Monitoring page in NoRM, as shown in Figure 4.5. The Health Monitor is broken down into major groupings of server health. Selecting one of the links on the Server Health Monitoring page takes you to more specific information about the current state of the server with regards to that category.

Health Monitor also allows you to set thresholds for server performance that can generate automated alerts to the administrative staff when they are passed.

Server parameters, also called SET parameters, control the NetWare 6 server environment. They set Maximum, Minimum, and Thresholds levels for many aspects of the server's internal operations.

FIGURE 4.5   *Server Health Monitoring page in NoRM*

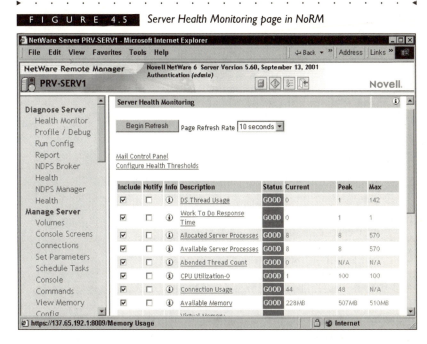

You can use NoRM to adjust SET parameters by selecting the Set Parameters link as shown in Figure 4.6. This can also be done from the server console with MONITOR.NLM. SET parameters come in two types: persistent and non-persistent. Persistent SET parameters are those that will maintain their state even if the server is shut down. Non-persistent SET parameters will reset to their default value when the server restarts. To avoid this problem, you place non-persistent SET parameters in your AUTOEXEC.NCF and/or STARTUP.NCF, so they are set automatically to the desired value whenever the server starts.

After NetWare 6 is first installed, it will optimize itself over a period of time by leveling adjustments for low-usage times with peak-usage bursts. Over a week or two the server will settle on an optimal setting for each SET parameter. However, if you already know where the server should be set, or if you are not satisfied with the server's self-tuned settings, you can configure any SET parameter manually.

The following sections describe some of the ways to monitor and optimize your server's performance.

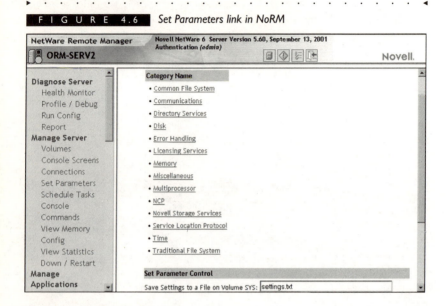

FIGURE 4.6   *Set Parameters link in NoRM*

Cache memory

Running out of cache memory is one of the biggest causes of poor server performance in a NetWare environment. Prior to NetWare 6 there were a number of cache parameters related to directory, open files applications, and the like. One of the major changes between NetWare 5 and NetWare 6 is the use of the NSS file system as the default file system for NetWare 6 an the SYS volume. With NSS you get a completely redesigned caching system that eliminates most of the cache monitoring with which you may be familiar.

NSS introduces a much simplified caching system with only two cache pools to worry about: the NSS pool, and the OS pool. The OS pool, as its name implies, is used to supply the memory needs of all OS-related processes, including packet receive buffers. The NSS pool is used for everything else, including directory, files, server applications, and so on.

When NetWare 6 is installed, the total available cache memory is balanced between the OS and NSS cache pools. The default balance is 60% NSS pool and 40% OS pool. You can change this setting from NoRM by selecting Set Parameters ⇨ Novell Storage Services ⇨ NSS Cache Balance Percent. The NSS system will automatically re-allocate memory between the two pools to keep them functioning at an optimal level.

You can review the current server statistics related to cache memory through the following links in the Health Monitor of NoRM. If you are familiar with it, you can also set these values using MONITOR.NLM from the server console.

▶ *Cache performance*: Provides both a textual and graphic overview of memory allocation on the server to which you are attached through NoRM. Also provides links to specific memory allocations within the general pools. The Available Memory link brings you to this same page.

▶ *Available ECBs*: Event Control Blocks (ECBs) are another name for packet receive buffers. You can get an overview of ECB allocation from this page. It also lists all modules currently assigned ECBs. The Packet Receive Buffers link brings you to this same page.

If the server seems to be slowing down or losing workstation connections, see how many ECBs are allocated and how many are being used. You may need to increase the minimum and/or maximum numbers of packet receive buffers. To do this from NoRM, select Set Parameters ➪ Communications and scroll down to the Minimum and Maximum Packet Receive Buffers settings. You can also decrease the New Packet Receive Buffer wait time.

After a couple of days of average network usage, check to see how many packet receive buffers are being allocated, and compare that with the maximum number. If the two numbers are the same, increase the maximum value by 50 buffers. Continue to monitor the buffers periodically and increase the maximum value until the allocated number no longer reaches the maximum.

Virtual memory

NetWare 6 includes support for virtual memory to help utilize memory more efficiently. Any modules that are loaded in protected memory will utilize virtual memory. With virtual memory, data that hasn't been accessed recently can be moved back to disk, where it is temporarily stored in a swap file. When the data is requested again, it is restored back into memory. Data in the swap file can still be accessed more quickly than from its permanent location on the disk, while at the same time allowing existing RAM to be used more efficiently. This helps reduce the possibility of encountering low memory conditions on the server.

A swap file is created automatically for the SYS volume. You can create additional swap files for each volume if you wish. The swap files don't necessarily need to reside on the volume for which they're designated, but it's a good idea to have one swap file per volume.

View, create, and delete swap files from NoRM by selecting Health Monitor ➪ Available Memory ➪ Swap File Size. This will open the Swap File

Configuration utility as shown in Figure 4.7. You can also use the SWAP command to set swap file parameters from the server console.

Swap File Configuration utility in NoRM

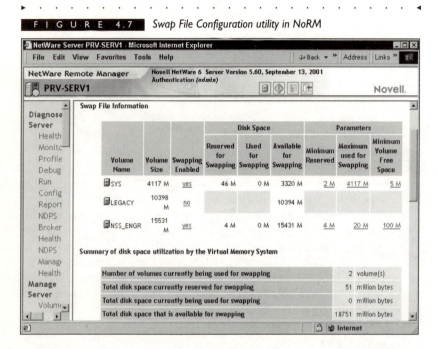

To create a new swap file, select the No link in the Swapping Enabled column next to the volume for which you want to create a swap file. If you don't specify any parameters, this will create a swap file with a minimum size of 2MB, a maximum size of the entire volume size, and will leave a minimum of 5MB of free space on the volume. However, you can set any of these parameters as you see fit by typing the desired value into the appropriate field.

To delete a swap file from a volume, select the Yes link in the Swapping Enabled column next to the volume for which you want to delete the swap file and select Disable.

Error logs

You can monitor several different error log files to see if your network has generated any error messages. You should make a practice of reviewing these files on a regular basis to ensure that nothing out of the ordinary is happening to your network.

You can view log files from any workstation using a standard text editor. However, you can also view these files from NoRM — particularly useful when you only have an Internet connection to the server without the Novell client — by completing the following steps:

NOTE You can view log files from the system console using EDIT.NLM. However, LOGGER.TXT, which is stored on the Boot partition, is not available in this manner. Remember, you can also run NoRM from the server GUI by selecting the Novell button, and then selecting Utilities ⇨ NetWare Remote Manager.

1. Select the Volumes link in NoRM. NoRM will open to this link as its home page.

2. Select the volume or partition where the log file is stored, usually either SYS or C:\.

3. Browse to and select the log file you wish to view.

The error log files you should monitor include the following:

▸ SYS$LOG.ERR — Logs error messages for the server. It is stored in the server's SYS:SYSTEM directory. All of the messages or errors that appear on the server's console are stored in this file.

▸ BOOT$LOG.ERR — Logs all the errors that occur during server startup. This file is stored in the SYS:SYSTEM directory.

▸ LOGGER.TXT — Is a file that captures all console messages. This is particularly useful during system initialization. LOGGER.TXT is stored on the boot partition of the server.

▸ ABEND.LOG — Tracks any ABENDs that may have happened on the server. (An ABEND, which is short for "abnormal end," is a serious error that stops the server from operating.) Because of the robust ABEND recovery features in NetWare 6, you may not be aware that the server has ABENDed unless you view this file. This file is created on the server's boot partition but gets copied to SYS:SYSTEM when the server restarts.

▸ VOL$LOG.ERR — Logs error messages for a volume. This log file is only used with traditional NetWare volumes. Each volume has its own log file, which is stored at the root of the volume. Any errors or messages that pertain to the volume are stored in this file.

▸ TTS$LOG.ERR — Logs all data that is backed out by the NetWare Transaction Tracking System (TTS). This log file is only used with traditional NetWare volumes. This file is stored in the SYS volume. To allow this file to be created, use MONITOR.NLM to turn the TTS Abort Dump Flag parameter to On.

To limit the size of SYS$LOG.ERR and BOOT$LOG.ERR, select Set Parameters ⇨ Error Handling from NoRM and change the appropriate log file parameters. You can also set these parameters from the server console with MONITOR.NLM.

▸ *Server log file state*: This parameter defines what should happen if the server log reaches its size limit. Valid options are 0-2. Default is 2.

- 0: Takes no action (logging will effectively stop)
- 1: Clears the log file (all previously saved data is lost)
- 2: Renames the log file and starts a new one

▸ *Server log file overflow size*: Sets the maximum size for SYS$LOG.ERR in Bytes.

▸ *Boot error log file state*: This parameter defines what should happen if the boot error log reaches its size limit. Valid options are 0-3. Default is 3.

- 0: Takes no action (logging will effectively stop)
- 1: Clears the log file (all previously saved data is lost)
- 2: Renames the log file and starts a new one
- 3: Causes a new log file to be created every time the server is rebooted

▸ *Boot error log file overflow size*: Sets the maximum size for BOOT$LOG.ERR in bytes.

To limit the size of VOL$LOG.ERR and TTS$LOG.ERR on traditional NetWare volumes, select Set Parameters ⇨ Traditional File System from NoRM and change the appropriate log file parameters. You can also set these parameters from the server console with MONITOR.NLM.

▸ *Volume log file state*: This parameter defines what should happen if the server log reaches its size limit. Valid options are 0-2. Default is 2.

- 0: Takes no action (logging will effectively stop)
- 1: Clears the log file (all previously saved data is lost)
- 2: Renames the log file and starts a new one

▶ *Volume TTS log file state*: This parameter defines what should happen if the TTS log reaches its size limit. Valid options are 0-2. Default is 2.

- 0: Takes no action (logging will effectively stop)
- 1: Clears the log file (all previously saved data is lost)
- 2: Renames the log file and starts a new one

▶ *Volume log file overflow size*: Sets the maximum size for VOL$LOG.ERR in bytes.

▶ *Volume TTS log file overflow size*: Sets the maximum size for TTS$LOG. ERR in bytes.

Performing Regular Server Maintenance

From time to time, you may find you need to perform some type of maintenance on your server. For example, you may need to add a new hard disk, load the latest patches (bug fixes or enhancements) on the server, or clear a workstation connection. The following sections explain how to do some of these common maintenance tasks.

Displaying information about the server

Just about all the server information you will ever need is available in NoRM. Utilities with identical functionality are also available from the server console. Table 4.3 lists the types of information about the server you can see and the console utilities you can use to display that information.

T A B L E 4.3	*How to Display Server Information*	
TYPE OF INFORMATION	NORM PAGE	CONSOLE UTILITIES
Server name	Header Frame	NAME, CONFIG
Tree name	Run Config Report	CONFIG
Bindery context	Run Config Report	CONFIG
Network board info	Run Config Report	CONFIG
Storage devices	Disk/LAN Adapters	LIST STORAGE ADAPTERS
Loaded NLMs	List Modules	MODULES
Processor speed	Processors	SPEED, CPU CHECK

(continued)

TABLE 4.3 *How to Display Server Information (continued)*

TYPE OF INFORMATION	NORM PAGE	CONSOLE UTILITIES
Processor status	Processors	DISPLAY PROCESSORS
Version number	Run Config Report	VERSION
Current SET parameters	Set Parameters	DISPLAY ENVIRONMENT
SET parameters not at default	Set Parameters	DISPLAY MODIFIED ENVIRONMENT
Mounted volumes	Volumes	VOLUMES

Installing patches and updates

No software product is going to be perfect, no matter how thoroughly it has been tested. And because of today's tight development schedules and competitive marketplace, the reality is that there is already a list of known defects before the product even ships. NetWare 6 is the most thoroughly tested and most stable product ever to be released by Novell, but that doesn't mean that unforeseen flaws or unexpected behaviors won't crop up.

To fix these problems, Novell releases software patches and updated modules that can be installed on your NetWare server. Once tested, NetWare 6 patches will be rolled into a Support Pack. Not all individual patches or updates are needed for every customer, but Support Packs usually contain enough fixes that they are a good idea for the majority of NetWare 6 users.

All NetWare patches come with installation instructions and an automated installation routine to make sure all the files get to the right places.

Novell releases Support Packs, patches, and updates in a variety of ways. The best way to keep track of the recommended updates is through Novell's Minimum Patch List. Individual patches are available from Novell's Support Web site, and all patches and updates are also included on the Support Connection Library—a collection of CDs regularly produced by Novell Technical Services division and sent to subscribers.

Novell's Minimum Patch List is located at `http://support.novell.com/misc/patlst.htm`. Individual patches are available from Novell's Support Web site at `http://support.novell.com`. For more information about all of the Support Pack and update sources, see Appendix C.

Monitoring workstation connections

Some types of server maintenance require that you break a workstation's connection to the server or that you prevent users from logging in while you're completing the maintenance task. Use the utilities listed in Table 4.4 to perform these tasks.

TABLE 4.4	Ways to Monitor Workstation Connections	
TASK	**NORM PAGE**	**CONSOLE UTILITY**
See connected workstations	Connections	MONITOR
See open files	Connections (select a connection)	MONITOR (select a connection)
Clear connections	Connections	MONITOR (press Del)
Prevent user login	None (use ConsoleOne)	DISABLE LOGIN
Re-enable login	None (use ConsoleOne)	ENABLE LOGIN

TIP

While there isn't a specific option in NoRM for disabling/enabling user login, you can still use the console command from NoRM by selecting Console Screens ⇨ System Console.

Adding Network Boards

Whenever you add a new network board to the server, use NWCONFIG. NLM to configure and load the appropriate LAN driver (also called a network driver) for the board. NWCONFIG will automatically detect and load most network drivers, but you can also manually load the driver you want.

To add a network board to a server, first install the board according to the manufacturer's instructions. Then, load NWCONFIG.NLM by typing the following command at the server's console:

```
NWCONFIG
```

From the main menu of NWCONFIG, select Driver Options, and then choose Configure Network Drivers. From there, you can tell NWCONFIG whether you want it to discover and load the appropriate driver, or whether you want to load it manually. You can also use these options to configure the driver to the options you prefer.

Working with Hard Disks

One of the most annoying problems that can happen to a server is a hard disk failure. There are several NetWare features, explained in the following sections, which can help you monitor and work with your server's hard disks.

For information on managing NSS, partitions, and volumes on hard disks, see Chapter 8.

X-REF

Using Hot Fix

NetWare provides a feature called Hot Fix, which monitors the blocks that are being written to a traditional NetWare volume on a disk. When NetWare writes data to the server's hard disk, NetWare writes the data, and then verifies that the data was written correctly by reading it again (called read-after-write verification). When a bad block is encountered, the data that was being written to that block is redirected to a separate area on the disk, called the "disk redirection area," and the bad block is listed in a bad block table.

Some manufacturers' hard disks maintain their own version of data redirection and do not need to use NetWare's Hot Fix feature. If your disk does use Hot Fix, the size of the redirection area is set up by default when you first create a volume on the disk. However, Hot Fix is required for mirroring drives, which is described in a later section in this chapter.

You should monitor the NetWare Hot Fix statistics periodically to see if a disk is showing a high number of bad blocks and is filling up the allocated redirection area. To see the number of redirection blocks being used, use the Volumes page in NoRM, which happens to be the home page. You can also use MONITOR.NLM (Choose Storage Devices from the main menu, and then select a "hot fixed" partition from the list of partitions displayed. Press Tab to see the entire information screen for this partition.

Track the number of bad blocks being found (Used Hot Fix Blocks) over time, so you can see if the disk suddenly starts to generate bad blocks at an undesirable frequency. If more than half of the total Hot Fix blocks have been used for redirected data, or if the number of redirected blocks has increased significantly since the last time you checked it, the disk may be going bad. You should use the manufacturer's documentation to try to diagnose the disk problem or replace the disk drive.

A useful worksheet for tracking Hot Fix bad blocks can be found in Appendix B.

TIP

Disk mirroring and duplexing

Another way to protect your network data from possible disk corruption is to implement disk mirroring, which ensures that data is safe and accessible even if one disk goes down. When you mirror disks, both disks are updated simultaneously with network data so that both disks contain identical copies of all network files. If one disk fails, the other takes over so that the network operates normally. Users don't typically see any difference in services.

If the mirrored disks are using the same disk controller board, it's simply called *disk mirroring*. If the mirrored disks are using separate disk controller boards, it's called *disk duplexing*. Disk duplexing provides more security than disk mirroring, because it duplicates not only the disk but also the controller channel. Disk duplexing also increases the performance of data reads, because the server sends the reads to both controllers. Whichever controller is least busy services the requests.

With mirrored or duplexed disks, if a disk problem causes the server to stop, you should turn off the server, remove the bad disk, restart the server, and then replace the bad disk as soon as possible. When you install the new disk, the server will remirror the new drive with the existing one, which also means the server will copy all the data onto the new disk automatically.

WARNING

Using disk mirroring or duplexing does not eliminate the need for making regular backups of your network. Always have a current backup of your network data before you change disks or change the server's hardware configuration.

You can use the utilities shown in Table 4.5 to work with mirrored disks.

T A B L E 4 . 5	Utilities Used to Manage Mirrored Disks	
TASK	**NORM PAGE**	**CONSOLE UTILITY**
Configure mirroring or duplexing	None (use ConsoleOne)	NWCONFIG.NLM
Status of mirrored disk partitions	Disk/LAN Adapters	MIRROR STATUS
Stop re-mirroring of a disk	None (use ConsoleOne)	ABORT REMIRROR
Restart re-mirroring process	None (use ConsoleOne)	REMIRROR PARTITION

Recovering data from an out of sync disk

Once a hard disk is unmirrored, its status is listed as either Not Mirrored or Out of Sync on the Disk Partition Mirroring Status list.

When a hard disk is listed as Out of Sync, the operating system does not recognize any volume information on it. Use this procedure to recover data from an Out of Sync partition.

1. From ConsoleOne, open the tree you want.

2. Right-click on the Server object and select Properties.

3. Select Media ⇨ Partitions.

4. Select a Partition that contains the data you want to recover, click Mirror ⇨ Resync.

This initiates the resynchronization process for the mirror group that contains the partition you selected.

Adding a hard disk

To install a new hard disk in a server, complete the following steps:

IMPORTANT

If your server or disk subsystem supports hot swapping or adding of disks, follow the manufacturer's instructions for adding a new disk drive.

1. Down the server and turn off its power (or the power to the disk's subsystem).

2. If necessary, install a new disk controller board.

3. Install the hard disk and cable it to the server according to the manufacturer's instructions.

4. If necessary, configure the computer to recognize the new disk.

5. Reboot the server.

6. To load the disk driver, load NWCONFIG.NLM. Choose Driver Options, and then choose Configure Disk and Storage Device Drivers. Then select either Discover and Load an Additional Driver, or Load an Additional Driver, and follow the prompts to load the driver.

X-REF

Once a driver is loaded, you will continue configuring storage devices with ConsoleOne to create partitions and volumes. For more information about working with NetWare 6 storage services, see Chapter 8.

Replacing a hard disk

To replace an existing hard disk in a server, complete the following steps:

IMPORTANT

If your server or disk subsystem supports hot swapping or adding of disks, follow the manufacturer's instructions for adding a new disk drive.

1. Back up the files on the existing hard disk.

2. If the disk is mirrored, use ConsoleOne to dismount all of the disk's volumes and to unmirror the disk.

3. Bring down the server and turn off its power (or the power to the disk's subsystem).

4. Remove the original disk.

5. Install the new disk and cable it to the server as necessary, according the manufacturer's instructions.

6. If necessary, configure the computer to recognize the new disk.

7. Reboot the server.

8. To load the disk driver, load NWCONFIG.NLM. Choose Driver Options, and then choose Configure Disk and Storage Device Drivers. Then select either Discover and Load an Additional Driver, or Load an Additional Driver, and follow the prompts to load the driver.

X-REF

Once a driver is loaded, you will continue configuring storage devices with ConsoleOne to create partitions and volumes. For more information about working with NetWare 6 storage services, see Chapter 8.

9. Restore data to the new hard drive.

Using PCI HotPlug Hardware

If your server uses PCI HotPlug technology, you can add and remove PCI disk and network adapters without having to turn off the server. When you install NetWare 6 on the server, the installation program detects whether your server supports HotPlug and has the appropriate driver. If it does, it automatically installs the necessary modules. It also adds commands to the AUTOEXEC.NCF file to load the PCI bus driver and load NCMCON.NLM.

NCMCON is the management utility that enables you to monitor, install, and remove PCI adapters. When it is loaded on the server, it constantly monitors the status of PCI slots and the adapters in them, and displays any change of status.

To remove a PCI HotPlug disk or LAN adapter, complete the following steps:

1. Load NCMCON.NLM by typing the following command at the server prompt:

NCMCON

2. Choose the slot into which PCI adapter is installed and select Remove Adapter.

3. When the slot status changes to Powered Off and the slot's green LED goes out, you can safely remove the adapter.

To install a PCI HotPlug disk or LAN adapter, complete the following steps:

1. Load NCMCON.NLM by typing the following command at the server prompt:

NCMCON

2. Install the PCI adapter into the HotPlug slot.

3. When prompted to decide if you want to supply power, answer Yes. The green LED will light up, and NCMCON will try to automatically detect and load the adapter's drivers.

4. If you choose No, select the slot and adapter from the main menu. Then choose Add Adapter or Power On Slot (whichever option appears). NCMCON will then try to automatically detect and load the driver.

Working with CD-ROMs

With NetWare, a CD-ROM mounted in a drive that is attached to the server can appear as a NetWare NSS volume. Users on the network can access the CD-ROM just like any other volume, except that it is read-only.

> **For more information on NSS volumes, see Chapter 8.**

X-REF

Because a CD-ROM is read-only, do not enable file compression or block sub-allocation on such a CD-ROM volume.

To mount a CD-ROM as a NetWare volume, use CDROM.NLM, which supports High Sierra, ISO 9660, and HFS (Apple) extensions. (This means you can access Mac files on the CD-ROM from a Mac workstation.)

Complete the following steps to install a CD-ROM drive and mount it as a NetWare volume:

1. Bring down the server and turn off its power.

2. If necessary, install a new disk controller board for the CD-ROM drive.

3. Install the CD-ROM drive and cable it to the server as necessary, according to the manufacturer's instructions.

4. If necessary, configure the computer to recognize the new drive.

5. Reboot the server.

6. To load the disk driver for the CD-ROM, load NWCONFIG.NLM. Choose Driver Options ⇨ Configure Disk and Storage Device Drivers, and then select either Discover and Load an Additional Driver, or Load an Additional Driver, and follow the prompts to load the driver.

7. In the CD-ROM drive, insert the CD-ROM you want to be mounted as a volume.

8. Load CDROM.NLM on the server by typing the following command at the server's prompt:

    CDROM

9. If you want the CD-ROM to be mounted as a volume every time the server is rebooted, put the following command in the AUTOEXEC.NCF file:

    LOAD CDROM

Loading CDROM.NLM on the server automatically loads two separate modules: CD9660.NSS (which supports ISO 9660-standard CD-ROMs), and CDHFS (which supports HFS CD-ROMs, used in Macintosh systems).

Loading CDROM.NLM also automatically mounts the CD-ROM that is in the drive. Once loaded, you can use the Volumes page in NoRM to see the CD-ROM volume listed as an active volume on the server. You can dismount and mount the CD-ROM just like any other volume on the server.

Modifying Server Startup Activities

When you start up or reboot the NetWare server, its boot files execute in the following order:

1. The DOS system files load, including CONFIG.SYS and AUTOEXEC.BAT, which sets up a basic environment and can be set to automatically execute SERVER.EXE.

2. SERVER.EXE runs the NetWare operating system on the computer, which turns the computer into the NetWare server. NWSERVER.EXE is located in the \NWSERVER directory.

3. STARTUP.NCF, which is stored in the Boot partition with SERVER.EXE, automates the initialization of the NetWare operating system. It loads disk drivers, name space modules to support different

file formats, and may execute some SET parameters that modify default initialization values.

4. AUTOEXEC.NCF, which is stored in SYS:SYSTEM, loads the server's LAN drivers, sets time parameters, specifies the server name and ID (formerly the IPX internal net number), mounts volumes, and then performs optional activities — such as loading application or utility NLMs you specified to load automatically, and executing additional SET parameters.

5. Additional .NCF files, if they've been created, can be called from the AUTOEXEC.NCF file or executed from the server's console. They are normally stored in SYS:SYSTEM.

The STARTUP.NCF and AUTOEXEC.NCF files are created automatically during the installation process. They contain commands that reflect the selections you made during installation. Several other .NCF files are created during the NetWare 6 installation or when other services are installed.

You can edit these .NCF files after installation to add new commands or modify existing ones. Table 4.6 describes the utilities you can use to edit the STARTUP.NCF and AUTOEXEC.NCF files.

IMPORTANT

When using a text editor, make sure you save the NCF file as a plain text document to prevent any formatting characters from being inserted, and be sure the .NCF extension is preserved.

There are several ways to modify .NCF files, both from the server console and from a client workstation. Furthermore, any server-based method can be accessed remotely through RConsoleJ in ConsoleOne.

T A B L E 4.6	Tools for Editing .NCF files
TOOL	**DESCRIPTION**
Text editor	Any text editor can be used to modify an NCF file from a Windows workstation. Simply browse to the desired file and open it with your editor. You may have to use the Open With option to specify the editor for the .NCF file extension.
EDIT.NLM	A text editor on the server that lets you manually edit the files. Type **EDIT** at the server console, and then enter the full name, including path, of the desired file.

TOOL	DESCRIPTION
NWCONFIG.NLM	Lets you modify the same options you set during installation. Automatically updates the appropriate file with the new information you've specified. Also lets you manually edit the files by choosing NCF files options.
MONITOR.NLM	Lets you add, delete, or modify SET parameters by selecting them from menus. Automatically updates the appropriate file with the new information you've specified.

TIP

You can also open EDIT.NLM from Console Screens in NoRM and edit an NCF file from there.

NetWare Time Synchronization

While time synchronization is vital to the proper function of Novell eDirectory, it does not implement time synchronization. Rather, eDirectory requires the underlying Network Operating System (NOS) platform to provide a fully time-synchronized environment in which eDirectory can operate.

Novell implemented a proprietary time sync model for NetWare with the release of NetWare 4. However, since eDirectory is now used across multiple NOS platforms it must be able to synchronize time with non-NetWare servers and/or networks. To do this, Novell has extended the NetWare time sync modules to support an industry standard time synchronization protocol known as Network Time Protocol (NTP).

There are four types of timeservers supported in a NetWare 6 environment. :

▶ *Single reference*: Uses its own internal clock, or an external time source, to determine network time. This eDirectory time is then communicated to secondary time servers and network clients. The Single Reference timeserver is the master source for network time.

▶ *Reference*: Uses its own hardware clock, or external time source, to determine network time. Reference servers replace the Single Reference timeserver in more complex network environments. The Reference server participates with other timeservers in a voting process to determine a consensus time. When a reference server is used, NetWare uses a hybrid time sync strategy. However, as will be seen, other participants in the time synchronization process will converge toward the Reference server time.

▶ *Primary*: Name notwithstanding, a Primary timeserver does not generate network time. Primary timeservers participate in a polling process with other Primary servers and the Reference server. During the polling process, each Primary timeserver "votes" on the correct network time. From this process, a consensus network time emerges. Each Primary timeserver synchronizes its internal clock to the consensus network time and helps distribute that time to all interested parties.

▶ *Secondary*: Secondary timeservers receive network time from Single Reference, Reference, Primary, or other Secondary timeservers. Secondary timeservers are slaves that do not participate in the time polling process, but simply receive and pass-on the consensus network time.

The choice of a time synchronization strategy is largely dependent on the size and complexity of your network. You have your choice of a default strategy, appropriate for smaller networks, or a more complex "Time Provider Group" strategy, which is more efficient in a large network environment. Configuring either of these environments is done with the TIMESYNC.CFG file, as shown in Figure 4.8. TIMESYNC.CFG is stored in SYS:SYSTEM.

F I G U R E   4.8   *Sample TIMESYNC.CFG file*

```
                  Current File "SYS:SYSTEM\TIMESYNC.CFG"

# TimeSync.Cfg is now updated automatically,
# when changes are made on the System Console

# TIMESYNC Configuration Parameters

Configured Sources =    ON
Directory Tree Mode =   ON
Hardware Clock =    ON
Polling Count =    3
Polling Interval =    600
Service Advertising =    OFF
Synchronization Radius =    2000
Type =    SINGLE

# TIMESYNC Configured time source list
```

Default time synchronization

The default time synchronization strategy is suitable for smaller networks with less than 30 servers in the network and no WAN connections. The default time synchronization strategy utilizes SAP in an IPX environment and SLP in an IP environment to locate and query the Single Reference server. Figure 4.9 shows a default time sync configuration.

FIGURE 4.9 *Sample default time sync configuration*

Single Reference
(Time Provider)

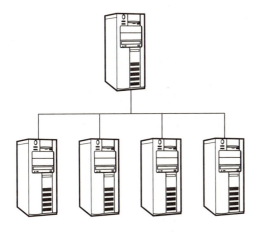

Secondary Time Servers
(Time Consumers)

Under the default strategy, the first server installed into an eDirectory tree is designated as a Single Reference timeserver. All subsequent servers installed into the tree are designated as Secondary timeservers. In this scenario, the Single Reference server defines the network time and responds to all queries regarding network time. Obviously, as the network grows and/or WAN links are added, this single source for network time will become a bottleneck. If this Single Reference server has to be contacted across a WAN link, this time synchronization method will also add unnecessary traffic to expensive WAN links.

Time Provider Group

More complex environments should implement a Time Provider Group (TPG), or groups. A TPG consists of a centrally located Reference server, and between two and seven Primary servers that will distribute the network time to all servers in the network, as shown in Figure 4.10. This strategy spreads the task of distributing network time out across multiple servers. It also makes it possible to limit the amount of time synchronization traffic that needs to traverse costly WAN links.

F I G U R E 4.10   *Sample TPG configuration*

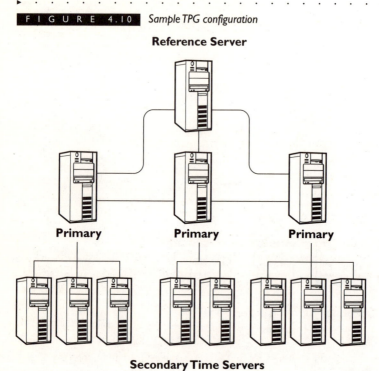

Reference Server

Primary   **Primary**   **Primary**

Secondary Time Servers

In a well-designed network environment, it is easy to determine the optimal locations for the various timeservers. The Reference server should exist at the "hub" of the network, perhaps at a corporate headquarters to which all satellite or branch offices are connected. The Reference server will normally receive its time from a highly accurate external time source such as an atomic clock, radio clock, or Internet time source. These time sources may be contacted through dial-up connections or across the Internet.

Primary servers should be strategically placed at the largest branches and distribute time information to Secondary servers at their own site as well as any small satellite sites in their area.

Time sync advertisement

In addition to these synchronization strategies, you will have to decide on either automatic or manual advertisement of time synchronization.

▸ *Automatic advertisement*: By default, NetWare 6 advertises its configuration automatically using SLP in TCP/IP networks or SAP in IPX networks. The advantage of automatic advertisement is ease of implementation. Timeservers will communicate without any intervention from the administrator. However, this background communication consumes network bandwidth, which can be a big issue on WAN links and other slow network connections.

▸ *Manual advertisement*: Also known as Configured Lists, the administrator manually defines the source of network time for each server in its TIMESYNC.CFG file. Reference and Single timeservers may get their time from either their internal clocks or from an authoritative time source such as an atomic clock, radio clock, or Internet time source.

Configuring your time sync environment

TIMESYNC.NLM is responsible for all time sync operations that take place in the NetWare environment. It loads automatically when the server starts. At that time, TIMESYNC.NLM reads the TIMESYNC.CFG file to determine how it should act. As with NCF files, TIMESYNC.CFG can be viewed or modified with text editors, EDIT.NLM, or MONITOR.NLM (select Server Parameters ⇨ Time). Eight of the parameters are set when the server is installed and will seldom have to be modified.

▸ TIMESYNC configuration file

▸ Start of daylight savings time

▸ End of daylight savings time

▸ Daylight savings time offset

▸ Daylight savings time status

▸ New time with daylight savings time status

▸ Time zone

▸ Default time server type

The remaining parameters are used to configure and reset the time sync environment. They are outlined in Table 4.7.

TABLE 4.7	TIMESYNC.CFG Parameters	
PARAMETER	**DEFAULT**	**VALUES DESCRIPTION**
Configured sources	Default: OFF	Set ON if a list of time sources is used.
Directory tree mode	Default: ON	Only time packets from the same directory tree will be recognized when setting time. OFF lets timeservers from other directory trees adjust time for this server. This parameter applies to Secondary timeservers only.
Polling count	Default: 3	Defines how many time packets to exchange during time polling cycle. Increasing this number will add network traffic needlessly.
Polling interval	Default: 600 sec	Defines the time to wait between time polling cycles. This value should be the same for every server in the tree.
RESET	N/A	Resets internal time sync variables and clears the configured server list.
Restart flag	N/A	Restarts the time sync service. Similar to unloading and reloading TIMESYNC.NLM.
Service advertising	Default ON	Determines whether or not SAP/SLP advertisement will be used. Turn this off when using Configured lists.
Synchronization radius	Default: 2000 msec	Defines how close a server's time has to be to network time in order to be considered in sync.
Time adjustment	[+ | -]hh:mm:ss [AT date and time]	Schedules a time adjustment on a Single, Reference or Primary timeserver

PARAMETER	DEFAULT	VALUES DESCRIPTION
Time sources	Timeserver to query	Configured list of timeservers that this server will query for network time. Multiple time sources can be configured, so that if one does not respond, the server will query the next on the list.
Type	Single, Reference, Primary, Secondary	Defines the type of timeserver

Using NTP with NetWare 6

The first decision you need to make when integrating TIMESYNC and NTP environments is the direction of the time flow. Do you want NTP to receive time from TIMESYNC or vice versa? Both options are equally valid, but some environments lend themselves more to one method over another. The random mixing of NetWare and NTP servers is not recommended.

Novell time sync experts recommend using NTP over WAN links and then letting the NetWare TIMESYNC environments at each site receive their time by NTP. To configure TIMESYNC to receive time from NTP, edit the TIMESYNC.CFG file on the Reference or Single server and change the Time Source to point to an NTP server.

CHAPTER 5

Novell eDirectory Management

Instant Access

Managing eDirectory objects

▶ To create and manage eDirectory objects, use the Java-based ConsoleOne utility. Certain services, and their associated objects, are managed from iManage.

Managing replicas and partitions

▶ To manage replicas and partitions, use ConsoleOne.

▶ To manage the eDirectory schema, use ConsoleOne.

Managing bindery services

▶ To set a bindery context, use the SET BINDERY CONTEXT parameter, which you can execute from the server console or through the Server Parameters option in MONITOR.NLM.

▶ To display bindery context(s), open the Agent Configuration in iMonitor or use the CONFIG console command.

Managing WAN traffic

▶ To prevent WAN links from being kept open excessively, use the WAN Traffic Manager feature in ConsoleOne to restrict routine WAN traffic to specific times or days (or to other limits you specify).

Using indexes

▶ eDirectory manages most popular indexes automatically, with no intervention on your part.

▶ You can view the list of default indexes with ConsoleOne by selecting the Indexes tab in Server object ⇨ Properties. You can also create custom indexes from this same page.

Merging eDirectory trees

▶ To merge eDirectory trees, use DSMERGE.NLM.

Using additional services with eDirectory

▶ Use LDAP services for eDirectory to allow LDAP clients to access eDirectory information. Configure LDAP through the LDAP Server and LDAP Group objects in eDirectory.

▶ Use Novell DNS/DHCP services to integrate DNS and DHCP address management into eDirectory. Configure DNS and DHCP using iManage.

Troubleshooting

▶ To monitor eDirectory messages, use Trace from iMonitor or one of the DSTrace utilities from the server console.

▶ To repair the eDirectory tree, use DSREPAIR.NLM. You can also perform a limited number of DSRepair activities from iMonitor.

What Is eDirectory?

In order to understand Novell eDirectory, you must first invert the standard view of network architecture. Many people assume that since the directory requires a Network Operating System (NOS) on which to run that it is part of the NOS. In reality, it is just the opposite. The directory defines the "world" of your network. As such, network servers are part of the directory, not vice versa. This is a critical shift in thinking if you are going to work effectively with directories in today's complex computing environments.

In simplest terms, eDirectory is a distributed and replicated database of network information that provides your network with four key services:

▶ *Discovery*: eDirectory makes it possible to browse, search and retrieve information about the network. You can search for objects such as users, printers, and applications, or for specific properties of objects such as names, phone numbers, and configurations.

▶ *Security*: eDirectory provides a central point for authentication and access control across your entire network. You can grant specific rights to users or groups of users, control the flow of data across the network, and protect sensitive or personal information through the use of cryptographic technologies. Most importantly, eDirectory provides the foundation for managing security across networks, so you can safely and efficiently communicate with partners, suppliers, and customers without having to create a separate infrastructure to do so.

▶ *Storage*: eDirectory is at its heart a database. As such, it includes the capabilities to safely and securely store network data and protect it from corruption. It also provides a way to classify different data types, so you can manage the type of data in eDirectory and how it may be used. Finally, eDirectory allows you to split the database into discrete pieces and distribute those pieces across multiple servers to provide fault tolerance and improved performance for network users.

▶ *Relationship*: eDirectory allows you to model relationships between objects on the network. This allows you to move configuration information away from specific devices and make it global. Practically, this means that users can receive the same profiles, privileges, and services regardless of location, type of connection, or device. Furthermore, users no longer have to connect to each server with a separate user account. eDirectory moves authentication to the network level from the individual server level.

Novell released its first version of eDirectory, then known as NetWare Directory Services, in 1993 with NetWare 4. It has been in constant improvement since that time, making it the most advanced and used directory in the world. The name was changed to Novell Directory Services with the release of NetWare 5 in 1998. Since then, Novell's directory has been modularized so it can be installed on platforms other than NetWare — including Windows NT/2000, Sun Solaris, Linux, Compaq Tru64, and soon IBM AIX. It has also been configured with a powerful new database that makes it possible to support vast numbers of objects in a single tree. In light of these many changes, Novell Directory Services (NDS) has been rechristened Novell eDirectory. The following sections provide you with an overview of eDirectory architecture, design considerations, common administrative tasks, and the tools for doing them.

eDirectory Architecture

There are three main aspects to the eDirectory architecture:

- ▶ Physical eDirectory database
- ▶ Rules governing eDirectory data
- ▶ Organization of data in eDirectory

Physical eDirectory Database

At its lowest physical level, eDirectory is a database. A typical database comprises a dataset together with methods of searching and retrieving specific data from the dataset. eDirectory is an object-oriented, hierarchical database. A hierarchical database maintains data (objects) in a logical tree structure. Specific objects are located by traversing (walking) the tree. Each object in the eDirectory database is uniquely identifiable by a combination of the object name, or Common Name (CN) together with information describing the location of that object within the tree, or Context. Figure 5.1 shows a possible tree structure and the relationship between object name and logical position within the directory. The combination of Common Name and Context is known as the Distinguished Name.

The underlying eDirectory database is organized as a *b-tree*, which those of you with a programming background will recognize as a well-known type of data structure. B-trees are ordered, or sorted, trees in which the root node always stores values at the midpoint of the sorted value set. As new elements are added, the tree automatically re-orders itself. The eDirectory b-tree nodes contain multiple elements, each of which is a directory object.

F I G U R E 5 . 1 Possible eDirectory tree structure (location determines name)

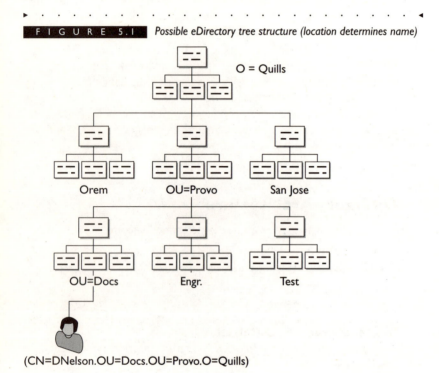

(CN=DNelson.OU=Docs.OU=Provo.O=Quills)

The result of these two characteristics is a data structure in which a huge number of elements can be stored, and stored elements can be located very quickly.

The eDirectory database also makes extensive use of indexing. Data is sorted in a variety of ways in order to decrease the time required to locate a given piece of data even more. Each index is a smaller b-tree structure that is automatically updated whenever any relevant piece of the database is added, changed, or deleted. When a query is received by eDirectory, internal logic determines what index, if any, should be used to most efficiently respond to the query. Figure 5.2 shows you the default indices created by eDirectory. You can also add custom indices (note the entry highlighted in Figure 5.2) by completing the following steps:

F I G U R E 5 . 2 *Default eDirectory indices*

Name	State	Type	Rule	Attribute
Aliased Object Name	Online	Operational	Value	Aliased Object ...
CN	Online	Auto Added	Value	CN
CN_SS	Online	Auto Added	Substring	CN
dc	Online	Auto Added	Value	dc
DNIP:CfgPreferences	Online	System	Value	DNIP:CfgPrefere...
Equivalent To Me	Online	System	Value	Equivalent To Me
Given Name	Online	Auto Added	Value	Given Name
GUID	Online	Operational	Value	GUID
mail stop	Online	User	Value	mailstop
Member	Online	System	Value	Member
NLS:Common Certificate	Online	System	Value	NLS:Common Cert...
Obituary	Online	Operational	Presence	Obituary
Reference	Online	System	Value	Reference
Revision	Online	System	Value	Revision
Surname	Online	Auto Added	Value	Surname
uniqueID	Online	Auto Added	Value	uniqueID
uniqueID_SS	Online	Auto Added	Substring	uniqueID

1. Launch ConsoleOne and browse to a NetWare 6 server.

2. Right-click on the Server object and select Properties.

3. Select the Indexes tab. This will show you all currently created indices and their state.

4. Click Add. Enter a name for the new index, the attribute on which it should be sorted.

5. In the Rule field, select Value to create an index based on values of the specified attribute. Select Presence to create an index based on whether or not the specified attribute has a value.

6. Click OK to save your Index configuration. Click OK again to save the changes.

Rules Governing eDirectory Data

Rules defining valid object types, where they can be stored, and what can be done with each of the object types are maintained within the eDirectory schema. The schema provides the structure to the eDirectory tree. The schema is comprised of a set of object classes. Object classes describe the types of objects that can be created in eDirectory. Each object class contains a set of attributes that specifies the type(s) of data that can be stored within each object. In this way, the schema creates the logical view of the eDirectory data that network administrators and users make use of every day.

Novell provides a base set of object classes in eDirectory but has recognized that they cannot account for every possible use of the directory. To address this, the eDirectory schema is extensible, meaning that third parties are free to define new object classes and attributes in order to extend eDirectory capabilities.

Organization of Data in eDirectory

eDirectory organization has two aspects, the physical organization and the logical organization. Physical organization of data in eDirectory revolves around its distributed nature and the need to provide fault tolerance for the eDirectory database. Each "piece" of the total eDirectory database is known as a partition. In order to make the data contained in a given partition more secure and accessible, multiple copies of that partition can be stored across the network. This process of creating and maintaining multiple partition copies is known as replication, as shown in Figure 5.3. Replication is an extremely powerful capability, and Novell has designed eDirectory with a complex set of checks and balances in order to maintain the integrity of directory data across the distributed environment.

▶ . . . . ◀

eDirectory partitions and replicas

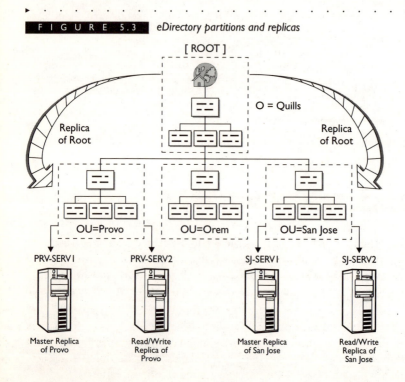

The logical organization of data in eDirectory determines how data will be presented to users and administrators. The logical organization is what you "see" when you look at eDirectory. The schema controls this logical eDirectory organization. The schema essentially defines the types of data that can be stored in eDirectory and the acceptable set of operations that can be performed on that data.

First, the eDirectory schema defines a class of objects that can store other objects. These are known as Container objects, or simply Containers. Containers are the building blocks used to create the structure of the eDirectory tree. Objects that cannot hold other objects are known as Leaf objects. Leaf objects define the actual network resources available in the eDirectory tree.

Each class of Leaf object contains a unique set of attributes that describes the data and functionality associated with that object. Leaf objects might include users, printers, network routers, applications, or even other databases. Because the eDirectory schema is fully extensible, new object classes can be defined and created within eDirectory by anyone who might need them

eDirectory Tree Design

A key purpose of implementing a network directory is to make the operation of the network more efficient and easy to use. Unfortunately, this means that the directory cannot be rolled out without any consideration for the environment into which it is being inserted. There are a few basic rules that should be followed when designing an eDirectory tree:

- ▸ The top of the tree reflects physical layout.
- ▸ The bottom of the tree reflects organizational structure.
- ▸ Organize objects to facilitate access and administration.
- ▸ Partition and Replicate for scalability and fault tolerance.

Top of the Tree Should Reflect Physical Layout

The top one or two levels of an eDirectory tree form the foundation for everything that will come later. If these levels are not configured properly the whole tree will suffer. Similar to the construction of a house, the eDirectory tree foundation needs to be stable and not prone to changes in structure.

The stable part of an organization tends to be its capital assets (i.e. buildings and equipment). Organizational structure might change and merge, but it still generally uses the same physical facilities. Make use of this stability by designing the foundation of the eDirectory tree around physical locations.

There are four main points to address when designing the top levels of the eDirectory tree:

- ▶ Name the tree [Root]
- ▶ Determine use of Country and Locality objects
- ▶ Define the Organization object
- ▶ Define location-based Organizational Unit objects

When you name your eDirectory tree, you are naming the [Root] object. Make the name descriptive and unique. It should also be different from other container objects. Many use the following tree name convention: Organization Name_TREE.

Next you have to decide how to create the first level in your eDirectory tree. This involves determining whether or not you are going to incorporate the use of a Country (C) or Locality (L) objects into your eDirectory tree design, as shown in Figure 5.4.

▶ • ◀

F I G U R E   5 . 4   *eDirectory Country and Locality objects*

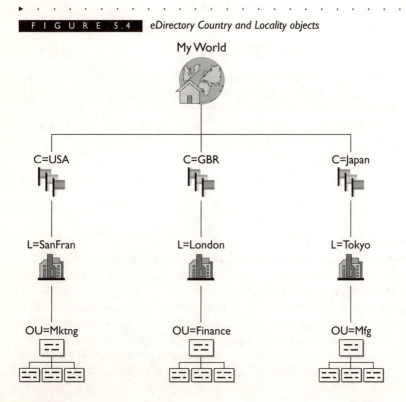

In most cases, the use of Country and Locality objects does not make sense. However, if it is important to comply with X.500 naming syntax in order to interact with external X.500 directories, then these objects can be used. Other than that, it is probably easier to start with the Organization (O) object and define geographical regions under the organization as Organizational Unit (OU) objects, as shown in Figure 5.5.

F I G U R E   5 . 5   *Sample eDirectory tree*

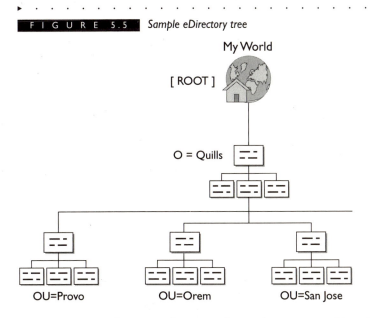

Next you must determine the name of your Organization object. Normally, this is the first level of the tree and simply using the organization name is a good way to go.

Finally, define subsequent levels of the tree around the physical network infrastructure currently employed (or planned) by the organization. Regional sites are usually defined as level two organizational units. A third level may also be appropriate for larger organizations to designate branch offices. Usually, three levels dedicated to the geographical structure of the organization will accommodate even the largest organizations.

The opposite is true for smaller companies. In some cases where the company is located at a single site the physical levels can be eliminated altogether, if desired. However, this strategy is not recommended if there is any chance the company will grow into multiple sites in the future. The lack of containers based upon physical sites will make it much more difficult to expand the eDirectory structure as the organization grows.

The Bottom of the Tree Reflects Organizational Structure

The bottom portion of the tree is where all the action will be. Unlike the top of the tree, we fully expect adaptation and evolution to occur over time at the lower levels of the tree. This means we need to design flexibility into the system.

For this reason, the lower levels of the eDirectory tree will grow based not on physical locations, but on organizational structure, as shown in Figure 5.6. The best way to visualize the eDirectory tree at this point is to look at a current copy of your company's "Org Chart". You will need to understand the divisions and/or departments that operate at each physical site in order to create the lower levels of the eDirectory tree.

► · ◄

FIGURE 5.6 *Lower levels of eDirectory tree designed around organizational structure*

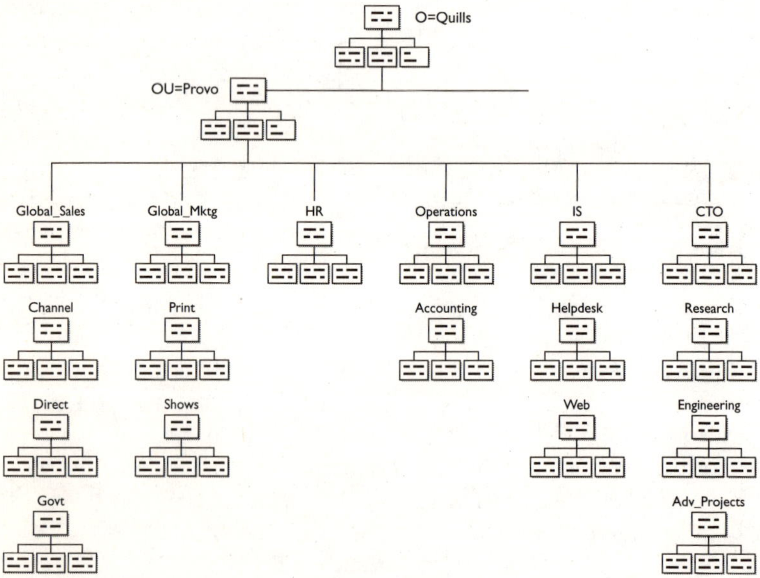

The reason that organizational containers are so useful at this level is that they allow us to group resources together. We can put the users in the marketing department together with their printers, servers, and applications. Then those users and resources can be managed together. As we will see in the next section, this grouping also allows us to minimize the overhead associated with maintaining replica integrity and currency.

Locate Objects to Facilitate Access and Administration

Now that you have the general tree design and containers created, how should you organize all the Leaf objects that will populate the eDirectory tree? The two primary considerations are:

▶ Make it as easy as possible for users to access the resources they need

▶ Make it as easy as possible to centrally control and administer network resources

In most cases you will be able to place resources such as servers, printers, and departmental applications in the same container with the users who will need access to those resources. However, if users in multiple containers will share resources, place those resources one level above the user containers. This makes the resource much easier to locate.

Furthermore, if we group users based upon common needs, we can manage things like access controls, login scripts, and policies from the container level, rather than managing each user individually. Only the exceptions to the general container rules need to be specifically managed. Management by exception is tremendously powerful as a tool for reducing complexity and increasing efficiency.

One last consideration when designing the bottom levels of your eDirectory tree is the use of Bindery services. Bindery services provides compatibility between eDirectory and applications written for older versions of Novell NetWare (i.e. v2.x and v3.x). These older versions of NetWare maintained a server-specific database of user and resource information known as the Bindery. Our first recommendation is to eliminate the need for Bindery compatibility, upgrading these legacy applications if at all possible. Bindery compatibility inherently reduces the efficiency of eDirectory and increases the complexity of the network.

If it is not yet possible to eliminate these older applications, they can still be installed on newer versions of NetWare by creating Bindery contexts on your NetWare servers on which they will run. A Bindery context allows access to the objects stored in a specific eDirectory container as if they were Bindery objects. Basically, eDirectory data is "mapped" to the old Bindery model so that legacy applications can access it.

Bindery context is defined in the AUTOEXEC.NCF of each eDirectory server. Up to 16 different Bindery contexts can be specified in a list, separated by semi-colons. Create or modify that list by editing the AUTOEXEC.NCF directly, or through MONITOR.NLM (select Directory Services). You can also set Bindery contexts through NWCONFIG.NLM.

The problem with Bindery contexts arises from the fact that the server on which the Bindery context is set must hold a replica of the Bindery Context container. If several Bindery contexts are defined for legacy applications used throughout the organization, this will increase the number or replicas (and the overhead required to maintain them) dramatically. So, if Bindery contexts must be used, it is best to consolidate all Bindery applications on a few servers. Users who will make use of those applications should also be grouped together. This can be done either by putting them in the same container(s) or by creating special group objects and placing the group in the Bindery Context containers.

X-REF

Group objects will be discussed further in Chapter 6.

Partition and Replicate for Scalability and Fault Tolerance

As a distributed database, eDirectory requires a mechanism for dividing the entire database into discrete chunks that can be installed on different servers across the organization. This is done through a process of partitioning and replicating the database.

Partitions

eDirectory allows the creation of partitions in order to distribute the directory database across the network. A copy of a given eDirectory partition is known as a *replica*. By creating multiple replicas of a given partition, you build fault tolerance into the directory architecture. If a server holding a Partition replica fails, the partition is still available from other replica servers.

Locating those portions of the eDirectory database close to those users that make use of them dramatically increases eDirectory performance. It also greatly reduces network traffic associated with directory queries. This is particularly important when multiple sites are connected by costly WAN links. The last thing we want to do is use WAN link bandwidth for background operations like searching for a server or printer.

When the first eDirectory server is installed, a [Root] partition is automatically created and a replica of that partition is stored on the eDirectory server. Once [Root] exists, the rest of the directory can be built by adding the necessary Container and Leaf objects.

As other eDirectory servers are installed, replicas of [Root] should be created to provide fault tolerance. If you maintain a small network at a single site the [Root] partition may be all you need. Replicate it to two or three servers for fault tolerance and you are done. However, if your network environment is more complex, more work should be done to create an efficient eDirectory environment.

Planning your eDirectory partition strategy is similar to planning the top levels of the eDirectory tree. Partition creation should follow the physical network infrastructure. WAN links should always be considered boundaries between partitions. This eliminates the need for eDirectory to pass background traffic across these links. Refer to Figure 5.5 for a view of partitioning along geographical lines.

Each Child partition should then be replicated to multiple servers at the site that partition is serving.

Once partitions have been created based upon the physical boundaries, it is not usually necessary to partition the bottom layers of a tree. However, there are two possible exceptions to this:

- A Child partition might also be further partitioned in order to limit the number of partition replicas that exist across the network. A large numbers of replicas for any given partition will increase the background traffic required for synchronization. It also complicates partition repair operations that may be necessary. A good rule of thumb is to try to limit the total number of replicas of a given partition to ten or fewer.

- If you are using Filtered replicas to create specific views of eDirectory information, it is entirely acceptable to further divide a Child partition.

The goal of your partitioning strategy should be a small [Root] partition and a Child partition for every physical site in the network. The [Root] partition should end up containing only [Root] and the Organization object. The reason for this will be explained in the next section.

Replicas

A *replica* is a physical copy of an eDirectory partition. By default, the first replica created is designated as the Master replica. Each partition will have one, and only one, Master replica. Other replicas will be designated as Read/Write, Read-Only, and Subordinate reference. There are five types of eDirectory replicas:

- *Master replica*: The Master replica contains all object information for the partition. Objects and attributes maintained in the partition can be modified from the Master replica. These changes are then propagated to other servers holding replicas of this partition. Furthermore, all changes to the partition itself, such as creating other replicas or creating a Child partition, must be performed from the perspective of the server that holds the Master replica.

▶ *Read/Write replica*: A Read/Write replica contains the same information as the Master replica. Objects and attributes maintained in the partition can be modified from the Read/Write replica. These changes are then propagated to other servers holding replicas of this partition. Any number of Read/Write replicas can be created. However, for the sake of overall directory performance it is recommended that the total number of partition replicas not exceed ten. This type of replica cannot initiate partition operations.

▶ *Read-Only replica*: The Read-Only replica contains all the same information as the Master and Read/Write replicas. Users can read, but not modify, the information contained in these replicas. The replica is updated with changes made to the Master and Read/Write replicas. In practice, Read-Only replicas are seldom used since they are unable to support login operations. The login process requires updating some directory information. Since a Read-Only replica does not support directory updates, it cannot provide login services. One potential use is maintaining a backup copy of a partition. The Read-Only replica will receive all partition updates but will not participate in the update process in any way.

▶ *Filtered replica*: The Filtered replica can be either a Read or a Write replica. They are designed to provide specific services or applications, including other directories, with only the eDirectory information they need. Creating replicas that only contain certain types of objects and/or specific subsets of object attributes accomplishes this goal. For example, a Filtered replica might hold only User objects with their associated name, phone number, and email address for a corporate directory application.

NOTE

These replica types exist primarily to eliminate the single point of failure in an eDirectory environment. A recommended design goal is three replicas, one Master and a combination of Read/Write and/or Read-Only replicas. As stated above, the Read-Only replica is seldom used, so most eDirectory implementations will focus on Master and Read/Write replicas in their production environments.

▶ *Subordinate references*: Subordinate references are special replica types that provide connectivity between the various partitions that exist in an eDirectory environment. Subordinate references are internal replicas and are not visible to end-users or configurable by administrators. A Subordinate reference contains a list of all servers that hold replicas of a Child partition. eDirectory uses this list to locate the nearest replica of a Child partition so it can "walk" down the tree when searching for an object. Figure 5.7 shows how Subordinate references are distributed across servers.

A partition's Subordinate reference is stored on all servers that hold a replica of that partition's parent. Subordinate references effectively point to Child partition(s) that are not stored on that particular server. The distributed nature of eDirectory allows servers to hold replicas of the Parent partition but not all of the corresponding Child partitions.

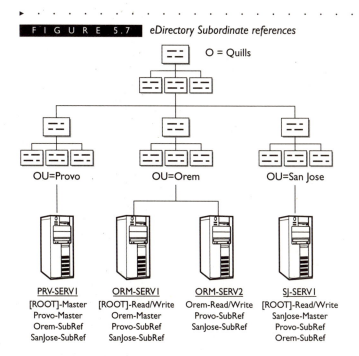

FIGURE 5.7 eDirectory Subordinate references

O = Quills

OU=Provo   OU=Orem   OU=San Jose

PRV-SERV1	ORM-SERV1	ORM-SERV2	SJ-SERV1
[ROOT]-Master	[ROOT]-Read/Write	Orem-Read/Write	[ROOT]-Read/Write
Provo-Master	Orem-Master	Provo-SubRef	SanJose-Master
Orem-SubRef	Provo-SubRef	SanJose-SubRef	Provo-SubRef
SanJose-SubRef	SanJose-SubRef		Orem-SubRef

The eDirectory replication strategy is a balancing act between the need to provide consistency across the directory and the limitations of network hardware and bandwidth. You should follow three rules when creating your replication strategy:

▶ *Don't replicate across WAN links*: WAN links represent one of the most costly network resources. To clutter up these links with unnecessary eDirectory traffic would be a terrible mistake. To avoid this, all copies of a given partition should be maintained locally. The one situation where this rule might not apply (there's always at least one exception, isn't there?) is the case of a small satellite office with only one server. In that case it is more important to protect the eDirectory database by placing a replica across a WAN link than it is to preserve the WAN link bandwidth itself. Fortunately, a partition that contains only one server will not usually generate a lot of eDirectory traffic.

▶ *Replicate to limit subordinate references*: Even though Subordinate references don't participate in the normal eDirectory replica update process, its still a good idea to limit the number of Subordinate references to reduce complexity. There are two ways to do this:

- Limit the number of Child partitions that are created. This is only partially controllable since we always want to define WAN links as partition boundaries. However, this does argue for limiting the number of additional partitions that are created within a single site.

- Store both Parent and Child partition replicas on the same server wherever possible. If multiple partitions are going to exist at a single site, try to distribute replicas such that Parent and Child partition replicas are stored together.

▶ *Replicate to improve eDirectory performance*: The final reason to replicate is to provide the best possible performance for network users. If the partition and replication guidelines in this chapter are followed, a user will find most of his or her resources within the local partition. Occasionally it may be necessary to access a resource "on the other side of the world". These situations require eDirectory to traverse, or "walk" the tree to locate the requested resource. As we previously noted, these searches start at [Root] and proceed down the tree until the requested object is located. Placing replicas of [Root] at strategic locations, such as communications hubs, can facilitate these searches. In order to do this without significantly increasing the overall replication burden, the [Root] partition must be small (only the [Root] object and the Organization object) and the number of [Root] replicas should not exceed three or four.

Managing eDirectory

Once you have an understanding of the basics of eDirectory architecture and design, it is important to understand the activities and tools necessary to maintain eDirectory on a day-to-day basis.

As with the rest of the administrative capabilities of NetWare 6, eDirectory management tools are being focused in flexible new Web-based utilities. Unfortunately, eDirectory administration has only made it part way for the release of NetWare 6. Novell has released a fabulous new tool for monitoring eDirectory in iMonitor. iMonitor consolidates the monitoring and data gathering aspects of several console-based tools, such as DSTrace, DSRepair, and DSBrowse. It also includes the reporting functionality of DSDiag.

Because of its passive nature, however, there are not a lot of actual maintenance tasks that can be performed from iMonitor yet. Looking forward, expect to see many of the partition and schema management capabilities migrate to iManage where they will be managed as eDirectory roles. The iMonitor interface is shown in Figure 5.8.

X-REF

For information on installing and configuring both iMonitor and iManage see Chapter 3.

FIGURE 5.8 *The iMonitor user interface*

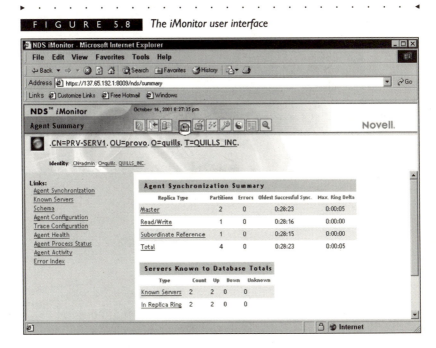

Fortunately, all the active maintenance functionality is available from ConsoleOne. ConsoleOne now provides a Partition and Replicas view for performing all standard partition and replica operations, as shown in Figure 5.9. This functionality was formerly accessed through NDS Manager. Furthermore, for those operations that are not yet available directly, ConsoleOne offers RConsoleJ for remote access to the server console, from which you can run DSRepair, DSTrace, or any other console command or utility.

F I G U R E   5 . 9   *ConsoleOne Partition and Replicas view*

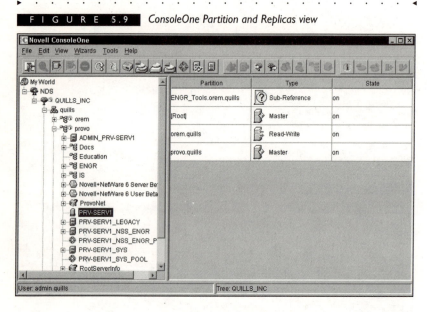

This section will give you an overview of common eDirectory tasks and the tools used to perform them. eDirectory management tasks can be organized into five main categories:

- ► Partition operations
- ► Replica operations
- ► eDirectory repair
- ► Monitoring eDirectory
- ► Managing synchronization

X-REF

Managing of specific eDirectory objects is covered in the appropriate chapter on that topic. For example, User and Group object management is covered in Chapter 6, while Printer object management is covered in Chapter 7.

Partition Operations

There are four primary partition operations that you will be required to make. The toolbar buttons for performing these operations are on the far right in ConsoleOne. Figure 5.10 identifies the buttons on the toolbar that you can use for partition operations.

NOTE

If you aren't running ConsoleOne in at least 1024x768 resolution, you may not see all the toolbar buttons.

- ▶ Create a Partition
- ▶ Merge a Partition
- ▶ Prune and Graft a Partition
- ▶ Check Partition Continuity

> ▶ . . . . ◀

FIGURE 5.10   *Partition operations in ConsoleOne*

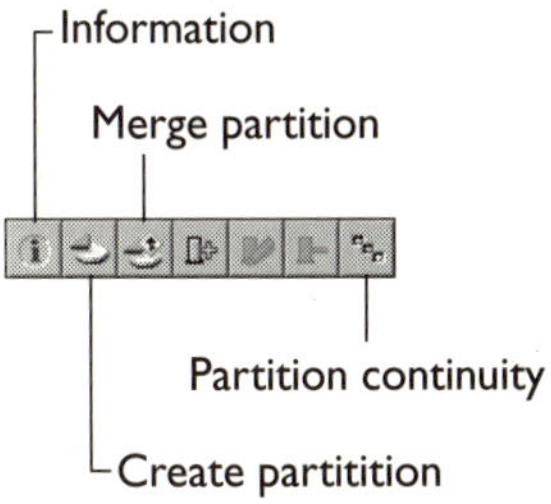

┌ Information

  Merge partition

      Partition continuity

└ Create partition

IMPORTANT

eDirectory does a great deal of work when performing partition operations. In larger eDirectory environments, each of the operations described in the following sections can take a significant amount of time to process completely. Furthermore, each operation will have to complete before the next can begin. Make sure you take this into account when planning these tasks.

Create partition

The first operation we want to look at is creating a partition. As mentioned earlier, partitioning the tree serves to break up the eDirectory database up into chunks that can be distributed across multiple servers for fault tolerance and increased performance. Use the Partition and Replicas view in ConsoleOne (refer to Figure 5.9) to create partitions.

If you want to create a new partition, complete the following steps:

1. From the ConsoleOne Partition and Replica view, browse to and select the container that will be the root of the Child partition.

2. Select the Create Partition button from the toolbar (refer to Figure 5.10). You could also select the Edit drop-down menu and select Create Partition.

3. Confirm that the proper container name is displayed in the Create Partition window and select OK.

4. Select Close at the message that eDirectory is processing your request.

NOTE

By default, the Master replica of the new partition is created on the server that maintains the Master replica of the Parent partition. Read/Write replicas are stored on servers that maintain Read/Write replicas of the Parent partition. You can move or change replica placement after the partition has been created, if desired.

Merge partition

Sometimes you want to consolidate partitions. This may be particularly true if you are moving from an older NDS environment to a much more scalable eDirectory tree. To merge a partition with its parent complete the following steps:

1. From the ConsoleOne Partition and Replicas view, browse to and select the root container of the partition you want to merge.

2. Select the Merge Partition button from the toolbar (refer to Figure 5.10). You could also select the Edit drop-down menu and select Merge Partition.

3. Confirm that the proper container name is displayed in the Merge Partition window and select OK. All replicas for the Child partition will be removed and all data from the Child partition will be distributed to the replicas maintained for the Parent partition.

4. Select Close at the message that eDirectory is processing your request.

Move a partition

The partition move operation is commonly known as a prune and graft. It involves moving a partition and all its associated containers and objects from one location in the tree to another. Hence, pruning a branch from one part of the tree and grafting it in somewhere else. This is the most complex of the partition operations, so note the following qualifications before attempting a partition move:

▶ You cannot move a container unless it is a partition root. If you want to move a container that is not a partition you first need to define it as a partition. Then you can move the container to its new location and merge it with its new Parent partition.

▶ This operation is only available to partitions that do not have any subordinate (Child) partitions. If you want to move a partition with subordinates, you will have to merge the subordinates into the Parent partition first.

▶ When you move a partition, you must follow eDirectory containment rules that define what type of objects can be placed in each type of eDirectory container object. For example, you cannot move an organizational unit directly under the root of the tree, because the containment rules for [Root] only allow Locality, Country, Organization, or Security objects, and not Organizational Unit objects.

If you want to prune and graft a partition, complete the following steps:

1. From the ConsoleOne partition and replica view, browse to the container you want to move.

2. Right-click the container and select Move. You could also select the File drop-down menu and select Move.

3. Specify the new location for the container in the Move window and select OK. Choose Create an Alias for all objects being moved if you want users to be able to continue accessing those objects from their original directory context. This is usually a good idea at least until all users have been notified of the change in location.

Check partition continuity

Partition continuity helps you identify whether any of a partition's replicas are experiencing synchronization errors. To do this, it walks the replica ring, examining all servers that hold replicas of the selected partition to make sure that each server has the same information.

If each server holding a replica of the chosen partition does not have an identical replica list, or if a replica cannot synchronize with the eDirectory tree for any reason, the Partition Continuity table displays one or more errors. Errors appear as exclamation points inside the replica icons.

The Partition Continuity table, shown in Figure 5.11, displays the replicas for the selected partition. To read the table, follow the column and row for a given server to where they meet. That cell will indicate the type of replica stored on that server.

You might also see icons representing unreadable replicas. This may not indicate that the servers can't talk, only the client running ConsoleOne was unable to contact the server for information.

▶ · ◀

F I G U R E 5.11   *Partition Continuity table in ConsoleOne*

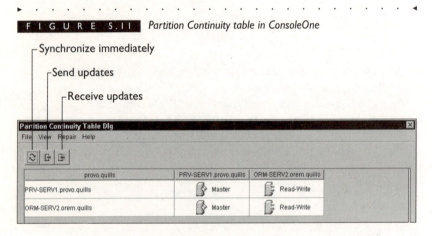

To check the continuity of any partition, complete the following steps:

1. In ConsoleOne partition and replica view, browse to and select the container for which you want to check continuity.

2. Select the Partition Continuity button from the toolbar (refer to Figure 5.10).

The Partition Continuity screen also lets you perform some basic repair operations. These operations were formerly available in NDS Manager and can still be performed from the DSRepair console utility. The buttons for performing these operations are identified in Figure 5.11.

X-REF

DSRepair is discussed in detail in Appendix A.

▶ *Synchronize immediately*: Forces an immediate synchronization of partition information across all replica servers.

▶ *Send updates*: Instructs the specified server to immediately send a copy of its partition information to all other replica servers for this partition. Receiving servers will add any new data to their partition information, but will not over write existing partition data.

▶ *Receive updates*: Forces the specified server to immediately receive a copy of the partition information from the Master replica. All existing data will be over written by the data from the Master replica.

Replica Operations

Now that you have eDirectory partitions created and situated within the tree, you may notice that the default placement for the replicas is less than perfect. After all, you probably don't want all Master replicas on one server, and you want to avoid replicating across expensive WAN links, as discussed previously. Similar to partition operations, replica operations are accomplished from the ConsoleOne Partition and Replicas view. There are three primary replica operations, as shown in Figure 5.12:

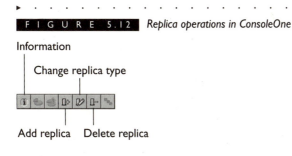

FIGURE 5.12 *Replica operations in ConsoleOne*

Information

Change replica type

Add replica   Delete replica

NOTE

You will see Subordinate reference replicas listed in the ConsoleOne Partition and Replicas view. However, Subordinate references are not manageable by ConsoleOne, so their placement is purely informational.

Add replica

If you want to place a partition replica on a server that does not currently have a copy of that partition, complete the following steps:

1. From the ConsoleOne Partition and Replicas view, browse to and select the container for which you want to create a new replica.

2. In the right pane, highlight one of the existing replicas and select the Add Replica button from the toolbar (refer to Figure 5.12). You could also select the Edit drop-down menu and select Add Replica.

3. In the Add Replica screen, provide all the required information and select OK.

   • *Partition*: Confirm that the proper container name is displayed.

   • *Replica*: Specify or browse to the server object where the new replica should be stored. Specify the type of replica that you want to create: Read/Write, Read-Only, Filtered Read/Write or Filtered Read-Only.

Change replica type

Sometimes it is useful to be able change the type of an existing replica. For example, if a Master replica is stored on a server and it is going down for a hardware upgrade you can change an existing Read/Write replica to be the Master so that eDirectory partition operations can continue normally.

NOTE

You cannot change the type of a Master replica since a Master replica must exist for every partition. If you want to change a Master replica, change an existing Read/Write replica to be the new Master, and the existing Master will automatically be converted to a Read/Write.

If you want to change the type of a replica, complete the following steps:

1. From the ConsoleOne partition and replica view, browse to and select the container whose replica you want to change.

2. In the right pane, highlight the replica you want to change and select the Change Replica Type button from the toolbar (refer to Figure 5.12). You could also select the Edit drop-down menu and select Change Replica Type.

3. In the Change Replica Type screen, provide all the required information and select OK.

   • *Partition*: Confirm that the proper container name is displayed.

   • *Replica*: Specify the type of replica that you want to create: Master, Read/Write, Read-Only, Filtered Read/Write or Filtered Read-Only.

NOTE

You cannot create a Master replica from a Filtered replica.

Delete replica

Sometimes, when partitions have been merged or moved, a given replica is no longer necessary. To delete an existing replica from a server, complete the following steps:

1. From the ConsoleOne Partition and Replicas view, browse to and select the container for which you want to delete a replica. You can also browse to and select the server object that holds the replica you want to delete.

2. In the right pane, highlight the replica you want to delete and select the Delete Replica button from the toolbar (refer to Figure 5.12). You could also select the Edit drop-down menu and select Delete Replica.

3. In the Delete Replica screen, confirm that the correct partition and server name are listed and select Yes.

Monitoring and Maintaining eDirectory

This section identifies some common administrative tasks that will help you effectively monitor the operation of eDirectory in your network and make little repairs as they are found. After all, the one thing more impressive than resolving a serious network problem is preventing it from occurring in the first place. While this is not always possible, a program of active monitoring and proactive maintenance will go a long way toward getting you home on time at night.

Some of these tasks can be performed in multiple ways by using different utilities. Of course, you can use the method with which you are most comfortable, but take the time to explore and learn the new Web-based tools, because they are the future of Novell administration and management.

For more information on Novell management tools, see Chapter 3.

X-REF

The following tasks are a starting point for maintaining your eDirectory environment. By monitoring eDirectory process execution you can see every type of communication activity and whether any errors are being reported. Traditionally, monitoring eDirectory is handled through the server-based DSTrace tool. However, you can also use iMonitor to keep track of the activities of eDirectory processes through its trace interface, as shown in Figure 5.13.

The server-based DSTrace tool is described in detail in Appendix A.

X-REF

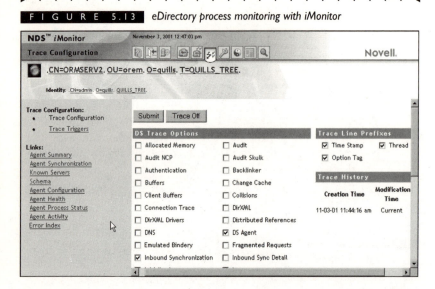

F I G U R E   5.13   *eDirectory process monitoring with iMonitor*

To access the iMonitor Trace page, select DSTrace from the NoRM navigation frame, or click Trace Configuration from the iMonitor header frame.

DSTrace in iMonitor gives you access to all the process monitoring capabilities of DSTrace. To start tracing eDirectory activity, complete the following steps:

1. From the Trace Configuration page, check the eDirectory process(es) that you want to monitor and click Submit.

> For more information on the individual options listed here, see Appendix A.

X-REF

2. To see a live view of the trace, click the View button next to the Current trace session under the Trace History heading.

3. To stop a trace, click Trace Off. Because of the added overhead and the size to which log files can grow, you usually want to run DSTrace for enough time to gather the information for which you are looking.

Verify the version of eDirectory

Even if you don't apply updates immediately, it's a good idea to be aware of what updates exist and, more importantly, those issues they are intended to resolve. Keep track of the versions that you have installed on your servers, so as you review Novell support documents, you can keep an eye out for any problems that might relate to your environment.

NOTE

With the release of NetWare 6, Novell is implementing a new versioning scheme that will eliminate the inconsistencies that have previously existed. You will note that the version of eDirectory is very different. Instead of seeing 8.6.x or 86.xx, you will see 10110.xx. This versioning will be permanent from this point forward. NetWare 6 shipped with version 10110.20 of Novell eDirectory.

You can check the version of eDirectory that you are currently running on any server in the following ways:

▶ *iMonitor*: Select Known Servers. The DS revision for all known eDirectory servers is listed.

▶ *DSRepair*: Look in the header for the DS version.

▶ *Server console*: Type **MODULES ds*** and look for the entry for DS.NLM.

Review Novell's support web site, `http://support.novell.com`, on at least a quarterly basis for updates to eDirectory files and utilities.

Verify that time is synchronized

Check the time sync status for each partition in the tree every couple of weeks. Keep an eye out for synthetic time messages that might keep background processes from completing properly.

You can check the status of time synchronization in the following ways:

▶ *NoRM*: Select Health Monitor. Browse to and select TimeSync Status. This will show you the time sync status for the server to which you are currently connected. To check another server, switch to it by selecting Managed Server List, under the Access Other Servers heading and select the server to which you want to connect.

▶ *DSRepair*: Select Time Synchronization from the main menu. This method will show you the synchronization status of all servers known by the server from which you run DSRepair.

▶ *Server console*: Type **TIME SYNC** and review the server's time sync information. This only lets you know if this single server is synchronized.

If time is not synchronizing properly you may run into problems with the timestamps that are maintained on eDirectory objects. Timestamps indicate when the object was last synchronized.

Probably the best-known eDirectory timestamp issue is synthetic time. Synthetic time is when an eDirectory object has a modification timestamp ahead of current network time. If the period between current time and synthetic time is small, this problem will correct itself. However, if the period is large, then it is possible to resolve the problem manually by reviewing the eDirectory communications processes to be sure that all replicas are communicating properly. Using DSRepair, perform a check on the Master replica, such as a full unattended repair, to be sure that it does not contain any errors, and that it is receiving current updates properly.

Timestamps can be repaired in two ways:

▶ Use DSRepair to repair timestamps and declare a new epoch. To use this option, load DSRepair with the -a parameter. Select Advanced Options ⇨ Replica and Partition Operations. Select the partition with which you want to work, and choose Repair timestamps and declare a new epoch.

▶ Identify the replica(s) with the synthetic timestamps and rebuild those replicas using the Receive All Objects operation:

• *ConsoleOne*: Browse to and select the container on which you are going to work and select the Partition Continuity button from the toolbar. In the Partition Continuity table, highlight the replica you need to repair and select Receive Updates.

• *DSRepair*: Select Advanced Options ⇨ Replica and Partition Operations. Select the partition to work with and select View replica ring. Select the replica to be repaired and choose Receive all objects for this replica.

WARNING

This operation generates a large amount of eDirectory-related traffic as timestamps for all replicas are reset.

Verify replica synchronization

You can view synchronization status from several different perspectives. However, making sure that all replicas of a given partition are synchronizing properly is probably one of the best ways to keep track of things. Check this every couple of weeks.

You can check the sync status of a replica ring in the following ways:

▶ *iMonitor*: Select Agent Synchronization, as shown in Figure 5.14. Repeat for each eDirectory server in the network.

▶ *DSRepair*: Select Advanced Options ⇨ Replica and Partition Operations. Select the partition you want to check, and choose Report Synchronization Status of All Servers.

F I G U R E   5 . 1 4   *Agent Synchronization Summary page in iMonitor*

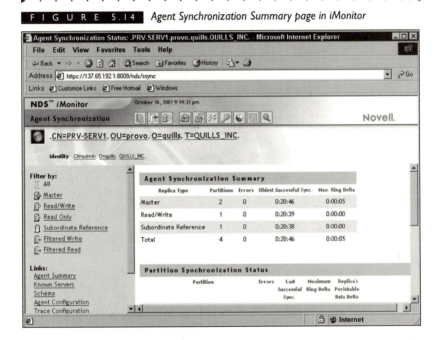

If you begin to notice inconsistencies in replica rings, you can use the following general steps to diagnose and resolve the problems:

1. Identify all servers that host replicas of this partition and the type of replica on each server.

• *iMonitor*: Select Agent Synchronization, and then select the Replica Synchronization link beside the partition with which you need to work.

• *DSRepair*: Select Advanced Options ⇨ Replica and Partition Operations. Select the partition to work with and select View replica ring.

2. Examine the server hosting the Master replica since it functions as the authoritative source for partition information. If the Master replica is the source of the problem, designate one of the Read/Write replicas as a new Master:

   - *ConsoleOne*: Follow instructions outlined in the previous section on replica operations.

   - *DSRepair*: From the server that you want to host the new Master replica, load DSRepair with the -a parameter. Select Advanced Options ➪ Replica and Partition Operations. Select the partition with which to work, and choose Designate this server and the new Master replica.

3. Once a healthy Master replica exists, you can receive updates on the server that is having synchronization problems to eliminate any inconsistent objects:

   - *ConsoleOne*: Browse to and select the container on which you are going to work and select the Partition Continuity button from the toolbar. In the Partition Continuity table, highlight the replica you need to repair and select Receive Updates.

   - *DSRepair*: Select Advanced Options ➪ Replica and Partition Operations. Select the partition to work with and select View replica ring. Select the replica to be repaired, and then Receive all objects for this replica.

4. Monitor the replica ring after making repairs to make sure that it is successfully sending updates between all replica-hosting servers. You can perform a send updates operation from the Master replica by doing the following:

   - *ConsoleOne*: Browse to and select the container on which you are working and select the Partition Continuity button from the toolbar. In the Partition Continuity table, highlight the server with the Master replica select Send Updates.

   - *DSRepair*: Select Advanced Options ➪ Replica and Partition Operations. Select the partition to work with, and then select View replica ring. Select the Master replica, and then Send all objects to every replica in the ring.

Check external references

External references are pointers to eDirectory objects not stored in replicas on the current server. The check examines each External reference and makes sure that it links to a valid eDirectory object. Performing this check on a weekly basis makes sure that queries are able to traverse the tree properly.

You can do one of the following to check External references:

▶ *iMonitor*: Select Agent Process Status and review the data under the External Reference Status heading.

▶ *DSRepair*: Select Advanced Options ⇨ Check External References.

One nice thing about the External reference check is that it will list any "obituaries" in your tree. *Obituaries* are references to deleted objects that are maintained until word of the deletion has been propagated to all servers hosting replicas of the affected partition. It is possible for obituaries and other types of External references to become corrupt or get "stuck" in the tree.

One thing that can cause this is problems with network addresses. To resolve network referral problems do the following:

▶ Identify the actual assigned IP or IPX addresses for each server involved.

  • *iMonitor*: Select Known Servers. Select the link for the server you want to look at, and then select Network Addresses in the Navigator frame.

  • *Server Console*: Run CONFIG.NLM on each server you want to check.

▶ Check network addresses to make sure that the addresses stored by eDirectory match those being reported by the servers in their SLP or SAP broadcasts. In DSRepair, select Advanced Options ⇨ Servers known to this database. Select the server with which you want to work, and then Repair all network addresses. Repeat this for each server hosting eDirectory replicas in the network.

▶ More severe problems may require a rebuild of replicas that have received invalid network address information, as described in the previous section on verifying schema synchronization.

Check the eDirectory schema

Anytime you make changes to the eDirectory schema, confirm that all servers hosting eDirectory replicas are properly receiving schema updates. You can check the schema synchronization status in iMonitor by selecting Agent Process Status, and then reviewing the data under the Schema Sync Status heading. You can also force a schema sync by selecting Agent Configuration ⇨ Agent Triggers. Check the Schema Synchronization box and select Submit.

You can also view the schema sync as it occurs with DSTrace. For information on using DSTrace see Appendix A.

TIP

It is possible that an eDirectory server, due to communications problems or corruption of synchronization time stamps, will fail to receive schema updates as they are applied to the eDirectory environment. The resulting schema inconsistencies can be resolved by doing the following:

▶ Identify the server that is reporting schema errors. This will be the server that has not received the schema updates properly. In iMonitor, force schema synchronization by selecting Agent Configuration, and Agent Triggers. Check the Schema Synchronization box and select Submit. Before doing this, make sure that DSTrace is configured to report Schema Sync messages and that it is currently logging in iMonitor.

See Chapter 3 for information on configuring DSTrace in iMonitor.

X-REF

▶ Once the server has been identified, one potential solution is to declare a new epoch on the server. Load DSRepair with the -a parameter. Select Advanced Options ⇨ Replica and Partition Operations. Select the partition with which you want to work, and then choose Repair time stamps and declare a new epoch.

Review tree for unknown objects

On a monthly basis, search eDirectory for unknown objects. To do this complete the following steps:

1. From ConsoleOne select the Edit drop-down menu and select Find.

2. Select the tree level from which to start your search.

3. Select Unknown as the object type.

Unknown objects can indicate resources that have not been properly installed or removed from the tree. However, it may also indicate ConsoleOne does not have a snap-in capable of recognizing that object type, so don't immediately assume that unknown objects need to be deleted.

It is also possible to get eDirectory object and attribute inconsistencies when replicas of the same partition, for whatever reason, have different information stored about the same eDirectory object or object attribute. In order to isolate the server(s) that have the faulty information, it is necessary to unload eDirectory on other servers. This type of troubleshooting can only be done in off hours.

In order to troubleshoot this type of problem, do the following:

1. Identify all servers that host replicas of this partition and the type of replica on each server.

   - *iMonitor*: Select Agent Synchronization, and select the Replica Synchronization link beside the partition with which you need to work.

   - *DSRepair*: Select Advanced Options ➪ Replica and Partition Operations. Select the partition to work with and select View replica ring.

2. Unload eDirectory by entering **UNLOAD DS.NLM** at the server console:

3. Use ConsoleOne to query the tree for the faulty objects and/or attributes. If they are correct, you know this server's replica is not faulty.

4. Repeat Step 3 until the faulty server(s) is (are) found.

5. To attempt to repair the problem, first attempt to receive updates at the faulty server:

   - *ConsoleOne*: Browse to and select the container on which you are going to work and select the Partition Continuity button from the toolbar. In the Partition Continuity table, highlight the replica you need to repair and select Receive Updates.

   - *DSRepair*: Select Advanced Options ➪ Replica and Partition Operations. Select the partition to work with and select View replica ring. Select the replica to be repaired and Receive all objects for this replica.

6. If that fails, attempt to send all objects from one of the known good servers. If possible, use the master for this operation.

   - *ConsoleOne*: Browse to and select the container on which you are working and select the Partition Continuity button from the toolbar. In the Partition Continuity table, highlight the server with the Master replica and select Send Updates.

   - *DSRepair*: Select Advanced Options ➪ Replica and Partition Operations. Select the partition to work with and select View replica ring. Select the Master replica, and then Send all objects to every replica in the ring.

7. If that fails, the replica will have to be destroyed. At this point you may want to involve Novell Technical Support unless you are very comfortable with the use of advanced DSRepair switches. Load DSRepair with the -a parameter. Select Advanced Options ⇨ Replica and Partition Operations. Select the partition with which you want to work, and Destroy the selected replica on this server.

Managing eDirectory Traffic

Replication is an event driven process, meaning that it is initiated by the occurrence of some external trigger. A few of these trigger events include: adding, deleting, and moving directory objects, as well as modification of object attributes. Each trigger event is flagged as being "high convergence" or not. *High convergence* means that eDirectory considers this event to be more significant, and these events should be replicated as quickly as possible.

High convergence events are scheduled for fast synchronization (Fast Sync). Fast Sync occurs every 10 seconds by default. Other events are replicated using slow synchronization (Slow Sync). Slow Sync occurs every 30 minutes by default. Both of these sync processes serve to send the changed information out to each server that maintains a replica of the affected partition. Since only the actual database changes are replicated, as opposed to sending the entire partition, replication operations are generally small.

Since each directory operation is timestamped, the synchronization process relies heavily on the time synchronization processes described earlier in this chapter. During the eDirectory synchronization process each operation will be ordered based upon its timestamp and be applied to the eDirectory database in that order.

Using WAN Traffic Manager

If your network spans geographical areas, you may want to use the WAN Traffic Manager to control how often eDirectory information is synchronized across the network. WAN Traffic Manager enables you to control when routine eDirectory synchronization takes place, so that the traffic is minimized and/or confined to less active times of day.

WAN Traffic Manager is an optional feature of NetWare 6. You can select it for installation during the NetWare 6 installation process or you can install it after the fact using Deployment Manager.

You need to install WAN Traffic Manager on each server whose traffic you want to control. If servers that share replicas of the same partition are on opposite sides of a WAN link, all those servers should have WAN Traffic Manager installed if you want to control their traffic.

Creating a WAN traffic policy

To control the eDirectory traffic, you need to create a WAN traffic policy, which defines the rules that control how the traffic goes out on the network. This policy is stored as a property of each server object. If you have several servers that all require the same policy, you can create a LAN Area object, which contains a list of all the affected servers. Then you can assign the policy to that single LAN Area object, instead of to multiple individual servers.

NetWare 6 includes several predefined policies that may suit your situation. For example, one commonly used policy specifies that all routine updates should be performed between 1:00 and 3:00 a.m. You can also edit those policies to create customized policies for your network. For more detailed information about these predefined policies, see the Novell online documentation.

The following predefined policies are available in NetWare 6:

▶ *1-3AM Group*: These policies limit eDirectory traffic to be sent between the hours of 1:00 a.m. and 3:00 a.m.

▶ *7AM-6PM Group*: These policies limit eDirectory traffic to be sent between the hours of 7:00 a.m. and 6:00 p.m.

▶ *COSTLT20 Group*: These policies only allow traffic to be sent if the cost factor is less than 20. You can assign cost factors to destinations in units, such as dollars per hour or cents per minute.

▶ *IPX Group*: These policies allow only IPX traffic.

▶ *NDSTTYPS Group*: These policies are sample policies for limiting traffic to specific types of eDirectory traffic and events.

▶ *ONOSPOOF Group*: These policies allow eDirectory traffic to be generated only across existing WAN links that are already open.

▶ *OPNSPOOF Group*: These policies allow eDirectory traffic to be generated only across existing WAN connections that are already opened, unless the connection hasn't been used for at least 15 minutes. (It assumes the connection is being used for another purpose and is not available.)

▶ *SAMEAREA Group*: These policies allow traffic only between servers in the same network section (servers sharing a common network address).

▶ *TCPIP Group*: These policies allow only TCP/IP traffic.

▶ *TIMECOST Group*: These are additional policies that cover different types of time and cost restrictions.

The following sections explain how to set up a LAN Area object and how to assign a WAN policy to a server or LAN Area object.

Creating a LAN Area object

If you want to assign a single WAN policy to multiple servers, you can save time by creating a LAN Area object that contains a list of all the servers, and then assigning the policy to the LAN Area object. Complete the following steps to create a LAN Area object.

1. Launch ConsoleOne and browse to the container that you want to hold the LAN Area object.

2. Right-click the Container object and select New ⇨ Object.

3. Select WANMAN:LAN Area and click OK.

4. Enter a name for the new LAN Area object.

5. Check Define additional properties and click OK to create the object.

6. Provide the appropriate information for your LAN Area object and click OK to save your changes.

   - *(Optional) General*: Enter any specific information about this LAN Area object, for description and identification purposes.

   - *Members*: From this page, click Add to select the servers that will be members of this LAN Area object.

   - *(Optional) Costs*: This page lets you define costs with specific network destinations that WAN Manager can use in its policy calculations. Click Add TCPIP or Add IPX to define an address or address range to which you want to assign a delivery cost.

   - *Policies*: From this page you can define the policy that will govern your eDirectory background process communication. Click Load to select a pre-defined policy. Click Add to define a custom policy. Once you have selected the policy, you can use the Edit button to make changes to the policy itself.

When you are finished, the new LAN Area object, and its associated eDirectory traffic policies, will be active.

Using LDAP with eDirectory

Lightweight Directory Access Protocol (LDAP) services for eDirectory lets LDAP clients access information stored in eDirectory. LDAP is currently the preferred directory access protocol on the Internet. Because eDirectory lets you give different clients different levels of directory access, you can manage external, internal, and confidential information from the same directory. eDirectory also supports secure LDAP connections so that privileged users can access internal or private information securely without any special client software. All they need is a browser with LDAP support and connectivity to the LDAP server.

Installing LDAP Services

Novell LDAP Services for eDirectory are installed automatically during the NetWare 6 installation routine.

See Chapter 1 for more information on NetWare 6 installation options.

X-REF

Two types of objects are defined in the eDirectory schema to support LDAP Services:

► *LDAP Server object*: Use this object to configure the LDAP environment for a single LDAP server.

► *LDAP Group object*: Use this object to configure LDAP client access to eDirectory.

LDAP Services for eDirectory can be loaded and unloaded manually by loading or unloading the LDAP services NLM, which is NLDAP.NLM.

LDAP Server object

The LDAP Server object stores configuration information in eDirectory about an LDAP server. Figure 5.15 shows the LDAP Server object configuration page. The LDAP Server object is created in the same container as your server object. Each LDAP Server object configures one LDAP server.

To configure your LDAP server complete the following steps:

1. In ConsoleOne, right-click the LDAP Server object and select Properties.

2. Enter the configurable parameters in the property pages.

3. Select OK to save your settings when finished.

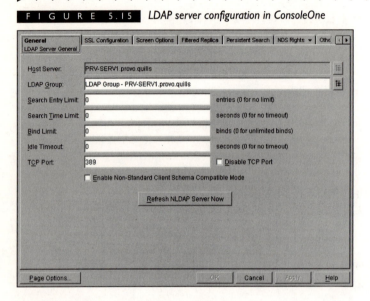

FIGURE 5.15 *LDAP server configuration in ConsoleOne*

There are five pages of configuration parameters for the LDAP Server object:

▶ *General*: Set the general configuration of your LDAP server on this page. The following entries are available:

- *LDAP group*: Specify the name of the LDAP group to which this server should belong.

- *Search entry limit*: Sets the maximum number of objects returned for any given search. Default is 500. This limit is independent of LDAP client settings.

- *Search time limit*: Sets the maximum time in seconds spent on any given search request. Default is 3600 seconds (1 hour).

- *Bind limit*: Sets the maximum number of simultaneous LDAP connections. This should be set based on the amount of available memory in the LDAP server. Each LDAP request takes ~160K of memory.

- *Idle timeout*: Defines the maximum time in seconds that an open LDAP connection can remain inactive before being closed. Default is 900.

- *TCP port*: Sets the TCP port used for LDAP on this server. Default is port 389. This should not be changed unless another service is already using port 389 on this server. Check Disable TCP port to force LDAP clients to use SSL connections on this server.

▶ *SSL configuration*: Sets the SSL configuration for this LDAP server with the following options:

  - *SSL port*: Sets the TCP port used for SSL connections on this server. Default is port 636. This should not be changed unless another service is already using port 636 on this server. Check Disable SSL port to prevent LDAP clients from using secure connections on this server.

  - *SSL certificate*: Specifies the digital certificate that is used for SSL encryption on this server. Certificate server creates this certificate during the server installation routine. You should not have to change this value.

▶ *Screen options*: This page is used to set LDAP trace parameters. Unless you have a specific problem you are tracking, keep trace options to a minimum because LDAP traces will consume processor cycles on the LDAP server.

▶ *Filtered replicas*: If you have configured a Filtered replica with specific search data, such as a corporate directory, you can specify that LDAP use this replica to perform its searches. If your Filtered replicas are configured for this purpose, they can improve search time significantly.

▶ *Persistent search*: Persistent search is an extension to the LDAP search operation that allows an LDAP client to receive active updates to a given query from the LDAP server. As data on the LDAP server changes, the client will be automatically notified of changes that affect their search.

LDAP Group object

The LDAP Group object allows you to configure user access to the LDAP server. By default, an LDAP Group object will be created for each LDAP Server object, but if you want to use the same user configuration for multiple LDAP servers you can combine them into a single LDAP group. The LDAP Group configuration page is shown in Figure 5.16.

F I G U R E   5 . 1 6   *LDAP Group configuration page in ConsoleOne*

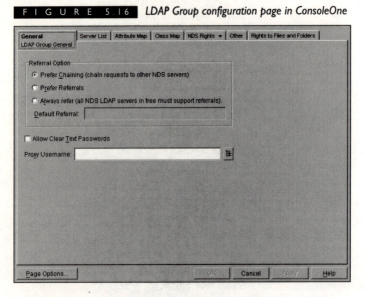

To configure the LDAP Group object, complete the following steps:

1. In ConsoleOne, right-click the LDAP Group object and then click Properties.

2. Enter the configurable parameters in the property pages. Each of the configurable parameters is described in the LDAP online help.

3. Select OK to save your settings when finished.

There are four pages of configuration parameters (General, Server list, Attribute map, and Class map) for the LDAP Group object:

▶ *General*: This page lets you set the referral options that define how the LDAP server will react if it is unable to process the LDAP request directly.

- *Prefer chaining*: Chaining causes the LDAP server to contact other LDAP servers to locate the requested data for the client, and then return the data to the client. Query work is server-intensive.

- *Prefer referrals*: A *referral* is a message returned to the client that tells it where it can go to get the requested information. Both LDAP clients and servers must support referrals, but this eliminates the first LDAP server as a "middle man" for the LDAP request.

- *Always refer*: This option prevents LDAP servers in the group from performing chained searches.

- *Allow clear text passwords*: If you want to perform eDirectory connections over non-SSL connections, you must set the clear text passwords within the LDAP Group object. This is not recommended since eDirectory passwords and usernames entered by LDAP clients can be captured by network monitoring equipment.

- *Proxy username*: Specifies the eDirectory user object to use as a proxy for anonymous LDAP bind requests. See the later section in this chapter on connecting via LDAP for more information.

▶ *Server list*: Shows the list of LDAP servers serviced by this LDAP group. You can add and delete servers from the group using this page.

▶ *Attribute map and Class map*: These pages let an administrator associate LDAP schema classes and attributes to corresponding eDirectory schema classes and attributes. A default set of mappings is defined when the LDAP group is created, but this leaves many LDAP classes and attributes unmapped. If you have specific needs you can map LDAP classes and attributes as needed.

NOTE

Since there are certain LDAP attributes (such as CN and Common Name) that map to the same NDS value, LDAP services support multivalue associations. However, the LDAP server will return the value of the first matching attribute it locates in the list. If you map multiple LDAP attributes to a single NDS attribute, make sure you order the list with the most important attributes at the top since they will take precedence.

Connecting Via LDAP

All LDAP clients bind or connect to eDirectory as one of the following types of users:

▶ [Public] user (anonymous bind)

▶ Proxy user (proxy user anonymous bind)

▶ Directory user (eDirectory user bind)

The type of bind the user authenticates with affects the content the LDAP client can access. LDAP clients access a directory by building a request and sending it to the directory. When an LDAP client sends a request through LDAP services for eDirectory, eDirectory completes the request for only those attributes to which the LDAP client has the appropriate access rights.

For example, if the LDAP client requests an attribute value (which requires the Read right) and the user is granted only the Compare right to that attribute, the request is rejected.

Standard login restrictions and password restrictions still apply; however, any restrictions are relative to where LDAP is running. Time and address restrictions are honored, but address restrictions are relative to where the eDirectory login occurred—in this case, the LDAP server. Also, since LDAP does not support grace logins, users can login to the server yet not be able to bind to LDAP.

Connecting as [Public]

An anonymous bind is an LDAP connection that does not contain a user-name or password. If an anonymous client requests an LDAP connection and the service is not configured to use a Proxy user, eDirectory authenticates them as a [Public] user.

[Public] is an unauthenticated eDirectory user. By default, [Public] is assigned only the Browse right to the objects in the eDirectory tree. [Public] can see objects only, it cannot browse object attributes. This is typically too limited for most LDAP clients. Although you can change the [Public] rights, this will give those rights to all users. To avoid this, use Proxy user (anonymous bind).

Connecting as a proxy

Proxy user (anonymous bind) allows LDAP to connect as a pre-defined eDirectory user. This gives you the flexibility to offer an anonymous connection that may actually be useful for something—like accessing public information—without potentially causing security problems by changing [Public].

The key concepts of Proxy user (anonymous bind) are as follows:

- ▶ All anonymous LDAP access is managed through the Proxy User object. Assign the Proxy user appropriate rights to all objects and attributes in eDirectory.

- ▶ The Proxy user cannot have a password or any password restrictions, such as password change intervals, because LDAP clients do not supply passwords during anonymous binds. Do not allow the Proxy user to change passwords.

- ▶ If desired, you can limit the locations from which a Proxy user can login by setting address restrictions on the Proxy User object.

For more information on creating and configuring eDirectory User objects see Chapter 6.

X-REF

The Proxy User object is enabled from the General page of the LDAP Group object that configures LDAP services for eDirectory. There is only one Proxy User object for all servers in an LDAP group.

To enable the Proxy User object in LDAP Services for eDirectory, complete the following steps:

1. In ConsoleOne, browse to and right-click the LDAP Group object.

2. Select Properties, and the General tab.

3. Enter the name of an eDirectory User object in the Proxy Username field.

Connecting as an eDirectory user

LDAP clients can also connect using regular eDirectory User objects. Once authenticated, the LDAP client is allowed access to any information to which the eDirectory user has rights.

The key concepts of eDirectory user binds are as follows:

▶ eDirectory user connections are authenticated to eDirectory with a username and password entered at the LDAP client.

▶ If a secure connection is not used, the eDirectory password will be transmitted in clear text on the path between the LDAP client and LDAP server.

▶ If clear text passwords are disabled, all eDirectory bind requests must be requested over a secure (SSL) connection or they will be rejected.

▶ If an eDirectory user password has expired, eDirectory bind requests for that user are rejected.

DNS and DHCP Services

Novell DNS/DHCP services in NetWare 6 integrate the Domain Name Service (DNS) and Dynamic Host Configuration Protocol (DHCP) into the eDirectory database. Integrating these services into eDirectory provides centralized administration and enterprise-wide management of network (IP) addresses, configuration, and hostnames.

DNS and DHCP manage the assignment and discovery of IP addresses on a network. By integrating this information into eDirectory, network administrators can now manage both DNS and DHCP information together with regular eDirectory information from a single, centralized location. The DNS/DHCP information is stored in the eDirectory database, so it is distributed and replicated just like other eDirectory data, making it easier to access and manage. The DNS/DHCP Management utility is available through iManage.

Installing DNS/DHCP Services

DNS/DHCP services can be installed as an optional service during the NetWare 6 installation routine. It can also be installed as a post-installation task through Deployment Manager. When you install DNS/DHCP services as an optional product during the server installation, the eDirectory schema is extended to support a variety of DNS- and DHCP-related objects. These objects help keep track of IP addresses, DNS and DHCP servers, configurations, host addresses, zones, and the like.

To install DNS/DHCP services from Deployment Manager, complete the following steps:

1. From the Deployment Manager opening screen, select Post-installation tasks and Install NetWare 6 products.

2. At the Target Server screen, select the server to which you want to install DNS/DHCP services and select Next. Authenticate the server you selected.

3. At the Components screen, select only Novell DNS/DHCP services and select Next.

4. At the Summary screen, select Finish to install DNS/DHCP services. At the Installation Complete screen, select Close.

With DNS/DHCP services installed on the network, an IP client can establish a connection with the network by leasing an IP address from a pool of available addresses, rather than requiring that the workstation be assigned a fixed address individually. This makes IP address management much easier.

Once connected to the network, the IP client can automatically detect available DNS name servers, through which it can translate domain names, for example www.novell.com, into its corresponding IP address, for example 137.65.168.1. This enables the client to communicate with the server properly. Domain names are a benefit to the human users of computers, not the computers themselves.

All DNS/DHCP configuration and management is handled through iManage. iManage is accessible through Web Manager.

For more information on the basics of iManage see Chapter 3.

X-REF

. . . .

There are several aspects to the configuration of DNS/DHCP services for your NetWare 6 network, but the three primary tasks are:

- ▸ Planning for DNS/DHCP
- ▸ Setting DNS/DHCP scope
- ▸ Configuring DHCP
- ▸ Configuring DNS

Planning for DNS/DHCP

There are three objects to which all DNS/DHCP servers need to have access:

- ▸ DNS/DHCP Group
- ▸ DNS/DHCP Locator
- ▸ RootServerInfo Zone

For this reason, it is best to place these objects together, in a separate container and partition that can be replicated to all points of the network where DNS/DHCP servers are located. Replicating these objects across the network will improve DNS/DHCP server performance.

Locate the DNS/DHCP container near the top of your eDirectory tree. You should also consider creating an Administrator Group object in this same container. Give the Administrator Group object read/write rights to all DNS/DHCP Locator Object attributes except the Global Data and Options fields. Once created, you can assign any User objects you want to be able to use iManage to configure DNS/DHCP, as members of this group.

X-REF

For more information on creating Group objects and assigning trustee rights see Chapter 6.

Consider the following eDirectory issues to maintain optimal performance when providing DNS/DHCP services on your NetWare network:

- ▸ *Where to locate DNS and DHCP servers*: Plan to locate your DNS and DHCP servers where they are physically close to the hosts that require their services. Plan to have one DHCP server in each partition of your network to minimize impact on WAN communications.

- ▸ *What replication strategy to employ*: Replicate the partition containing the DNS/DHCP Group and Locator objects to all parts of the network that use DNS/DHCP services to ensure access in the event of system unavailability or hardware problems.

> ▸ *How to provide fault tolerance*: When planning your DNS replication strategy, consider that replication is employed for load balancing when you provide multiple name servers within the DNS zone. Well-planned replication is the best way to provide fault tolerance for DNS/DHCP services.

Setting DNS/DHCP Scope

Setting the scope of the DNS/DHCP services specifies the context of the Locator object and the administrative scope for the session. Defining these two values first will improve performance in larger eDirectory environments because it eliminates the need to search for the Locator object and it restricts the retrieval of DNS/DHCP objects to the scope you specify to avoid searching the entire tree.

DNS/DHCP Scope settings will normally last only for the duration of the DNS/DHCP session. However, if you configure DNS/DHCP Scope settings for either DNS or DHCP Management, the settings apply across the session to both roles.

To configure DNS/DHCP Scope settings, complete the following steps:

1. In iManage, click DNS Management or DHCP Management ⇨ DNS/DHCP Scope Settings to open the DNS/DHCP Scope Settings window.

2. Enter the eDirectory context of the DNS/DHCP Locator object.

3. Enter the eDirectory context of the container object that will provide the administrative scope of the current session.

4. Click OK.

Configuring DHCP Services

Configuring the DHCP environment involves the following steps:

- ▸ Planning DHCP
- ▸ Creating DHCP objects
- ▸ Starting DHCP services

Planning DHCP

Before using DHCP for the first time, you need to gather a lot of network information:

> ▸ Make a list of all IP hosts to be served by the DHCP server. Include all devices that use network addresses on every segment of your network.

▶ Compile a list of current IP address assignments. Organize your lists of hosts and IP addresses by geographic location. For example, if your network is spread over a WAN, make a list for each location to help you organize the distribution of DHCP resources.

▶ You must have a list of all permanently assigned network addresses. You might also want to make a list of devices that are to be denied IP addresses and those hosts that are to receive strict address limitations.

Another major issue is deciding how long to set your client leases. You must strike a balance between the amount of network traffic and the amount of flexibility in the system. The longest lease provided by a DHCP server determines the length of time you might have to wait before configuration changes can be propagated within a network. Consider the following when setting lease times:

▶ Keep leases short if you have more users than IP addresses. Shorter leases support more clients, but increase the load on the network and DHCP server. A lease of two hours is long enough to serve most users, and the network load will probably not be significant. Leases shorter than this start to increase network and server load dramatically.

▶ Leases should be set twice as long as typical interruptions, such as server and communications outages. Decide how long your users should be able to go without contacting the DHCP server, and double it to get a recommended lease duration.

▶ Hosts that are advertising services on the network, such as Web servers, should not have an IP address that is constantly changing. Consider permanent assignments for these hosts. The deciding factor should be how long you want the host to be able to keep an assigned address.

The default of three days is usually a pretty good balance between the need for a shorter lease and a longer lease.

Creating DHCP objects

After you gather the necessary information, create the necessary objects to represent this information in eDirectory. Create a DHCP Server object from which to configure the DHCP environment. Create Subnet objects to represent each LAN segment. Create one or more Subnet Address Range objects to represent all your contiguous strings of IP addresses for each LAN subnet.

When a DHCP server makes or modifies address assignments, it updates the database. The partition where this database is stored should have at least two writeable replicas. Having only one replica might be unsafe due to a lack of fault tolerance, but three can be too costly in terms of replication overhead.

To create the necessary DHCP objects complete the steps in the following sections.

Creating a DHCP Server object   Use iManage to install a DHCP Server object in any of the following container objects, based upon the needs of your network: Organization, Organizational Unit, Country, or Locality.

1. From iManage, open the DHCP Management link and select DHCP Server Management.

2. Select Create Server from the drop-down menu and select OK.

3. At the Create DHCP Server screen, browse to and select the name of the server that will act as a DHCP server, and select Create.

4. At the Request Succeeded message screen, select OK.

Creating a Subnet object   Use iManage to create and set up a DHCP Subnet object for each of the subnets to which you will assign addresses, by completing the following steps:

1. From iManage, open the DHCP Management link and select Subnet Management.

2. Select Create Subnet from the drop-down menu, and select OK.

3. At the Create Subnet screen, enter the required information and select Create.

   • *Subnet name*: Specify a unique name for this Subnet object.

   • *eDirectory context*: Specify the eDirectory context where the subnet record will be stored.

   • *Subnet address*: Specify the IP subnet address.

   • *Subnet mask*: Specify the IP subnet mask.

   • *Default DHCP server*: Specify the DHCP server that will manage this subnet. By default, this server is assigned all address ranges created under the subnet.

4. At the Request Succeeded message screen, select OK. IP Address objects are simultaneously created to exclude routing and broadcast addresses.

Creating Subnet Address Range objects   Use iManage to create and set up Subnet Address Range objects for each pool of addresses you want to be dynamically assigned by DHCP. To create and set up a Subnet Address Range object, complete the following steps:

I. From iManage, open the DHCP Management link and select Address Range Management.

2. Select Create Address Range from the drop-down menu, and select OK.

3. At the Create Subnet Address Range screen. window, enter the required information and select Create.

- *Select the subnet*: Specify the subnet for which the address range is required from the drop-down menu.

- *Address range name*: Specify a unique name for the subnet address range.

- *Start address*: Specify the beginning of the address range.

- *End address*: Specify the end of the address range.

4. At the Request Succeeded message screen, select OK.

Optionally, you can also use iManage to create specific IP Address objects if you have certain addresses that need to be assigned to specific devices, or excluded from dynamic assignment. This requires you to specify the client's Media Access Control (MAC) address or client ID.

Starting DHCP Services

Once you have created the necessary DHCP objects in eDirectory, you can start DHCP services on your server by entering the following command at the server console prompt:

```
LOAD DHCPSRVR
```

You typically won't need to anything beyond this, but DHCPSRVR.NLM does support some command line parameters for specific functions, as noted in Table 5.1.

TABLE 5.1	DHCPSRVR.NLM Command Line Parameters
PARAMETER	**DESCRIPTION**
-d1	Turns on a screen log of DHCP packets on the NetWare server.
-d2	Turns on a screen log of debug statements and DHCP packets on the NetWare server.
-d3	In addition to -d2, this parameter sends the DHCP log to a file: SYS:ETC\DHCPSRVR.LOG.

(continued)

TABLE 5.1	DHCPSRVR.NLM Command Line Parameters (continued)
PARAMETER	**DESCRIPTION**
-h	Displays the command line syntax.
-py	Sets the global polling interval to every y minutes.
-s	Forces the DHCP server to read and write from the Master replica.

To enable DHCP services on a client workstation, simply configure the TCP/IP properties to obtain an IP address automatically. The next time the client starts up, it will send a request to the DHCP server for an IP address.

WARNING

Client configuration settings will override the configuration received from a DHCP server. The only exception is the hostname parameter set on the DNS Configuration tab of the TCP/IP Properties window.

For detailed information on DHCP configuration parameters see the NetWare 6 on-line documentation.

Configuring DNS Services

Similar to DHCP, configuring the DNS environment involves the following steps:

- ▶ Planning DNS
- ▶ Creating DNS objects
- ▶ Starting DNS services

Planning DNS

Consider the following issues and recommendations as you plan your DNS environment:

- ▶ You will configure a primary DNS name server, which is considered the authoritative source for DNS information. For load balancing and fault tolerance, plan to install a primary and at least one secondary name server.

- ▶ Secondary name servers receive their zone data from the primary name server. When it starts up, and at periodic intervals, the secondary checks with the primary to see if any information has changed. If the information on the secondary is older than that on the primary, a zone transfer occurs to update the secondary name server's information.

▸ If you are running a primary name server and providing DNS service for a zone, the size or geography of your network might require creating subzones within the zone.

▸ Novell recommends installing your NetWare 6 DNS name server as a primary to most efficiently take advantage of Dynamic DNS (DDNS). By doing this, if you make changes to the DHCP environment with iManage, those changes can be dynamically recognized by the primary DNS server. Secondary name servers, even non-NetWare secondary name servers, can transfer that revised data in from the primary.

▸ If your NetWare servers will operate as secondary DNS servers to a non-Novell master name server, one Novell secondary name server must be specified as the Dynamic DNS, or *Zone In* server (a server that receives zone transfer information from the master name server and updates eDirectory accordingly). Other NetWare secondary name servers can then transfer the information from eDirectory.

▸ If a name server cannot answer a query, it must query a remote server. This is particularly relevant for Internet domain queries. Novell's DNS/DHCP services allow you to configure primary and/or secondary name servers to act as forwarders. Forwarders that handle the off-site queries develop a robust cache of information. When using forwarders, configure the other name servers in your zone to direct their queries to the forwarder. The forwarder can typically respond to any given query with information from its cache, eliminating the need to pass an outside query to a remote server.

Creating DNS objects

There are three main types of DNS objects that you will create for your DNS environment. The following sections provide the steps for creating each type.

DNS Server object   The DNS Server object allows you to configure the operation of your DNS servers through eDirectory. To create a DNS Server object, complete the following steps:

1. From iManage, open the DNS Management link and select DNS Server Management.

2. Select Create Server from the drop-down menu and select OK.

3. At the Create DNS Server screen, enter the required information and select Create.

- *NCP server name*: Browse to and select the NetWare server that will act as a DNS server.
- *Host name*: Specify a unique host name for the DNS Server object.
- *Domain name*: Specify a domain name for the DNS server object.

4. At the Request Succeeded message screen, select OK.

DNS Zone object   Zones define the group of domains and/or sub-domains for which you have authority. All host information for a zone is maintained in a single, authoritative database. To create a DNS Zone object complete, the following steps:

1. From iManage, open the DNS Management link and select Zone Management.

2. Select Create Zone from the drop-down menu, and select OK.

3. At the Create DNS Zone screen, enter the required information and select Create.

- *Zone type*: Select Create New Zone. The IN-ADDR ARPA zone is used for reverse look-ups, translating an IP address into a domain name. For more information on IN-ADDR ARPA zones see the NetWare 6 on-line documentation.
- *eDirectory context*: Specify a location for the Zone object.
- *Zone domain name*: Specify a domain name for the Zone object.
- *Zone type*: Select Primary if this zone will be associated with the primary name server and will function as the authoritative source for domain information. Otherwise, select Secondary.
- *(Conditional) Name server IP address*: If this is a secondary zone, enter the IP address of the primary DNS name server from which this zone will receive its updates.
- *(Conditional) Assigned authoritative zone server*: If the primary DNS server is a NetWare server, select it from the drop-down list.
- *(Conditional) Name server information*: If the primary DNS server is not a NetWare server, specify its complete domain name and, optionally, its domain.

4. At the Request Succeeded message screen, select OK.

(Optional) Resource records   A resource record is a piece of information about a domain name. Each resource record contains information about a particular piece of data within the domain. To create a new resource record, complete the following steps:

1. From iManage, open the DNS Management link and select Resource Record Management.

2. Select Create Resource Record from the drop-down menu, and select OK.

3. At the Create Resource Record screen, enter the required information and select Create.

   - *Domain name*: Select the domain in which the resource record is to be created.

   - *(Optional) Host name*: Select the name of the host server. This binds a domain name with a hostname for a specific name server.

4. Specify the Resource Record (RR) type and select Create. Depending on the type of RR you are creating, you will be required to specify different types of record data. For more information on RR types, see the NetWare 6 on-line documentation.

5. At the Request Succeeded screen, select OK.

Starting DNS services

After you have created and set up a DNS Server object and a DNS Zone object, enter the following command at the DNS server console. After NAMED.NLM is loaded, the DNS server can respond to queries for the zone.

```
LOAD NAMED
```

You typically won't need to do anything beyond this, but NAMED.NLM does support some command line parameters for specific functions, as noted in Table 5.2. You can issue the LOAD NAMED command repeatedly to invoke different command line options. NAMED.NLM is only loaded the first time.

T A B L E 5.2	NAMED.NLM Command Line Parameters
PARAMETER	**DESCRIPTION**
-a	Turns on auto-detect of new zones (default setting)
-b	Turns off auto-detect of new zones

(continued)

T A B L E 5.2	*NAMED.NLM Command Line Parameters (continued)*
PARAMETER	**DESCRIPTION**
-f <scrpt.txt> [context]	Creates multiple zones using a text file in BIND bootfile format; specifying context enables zones to be created anywhere in the eDirectory tree
-h	Displays help information
-l	Enables a DNS server to login as an administrator to acquire rights to create and delete zones from the command line
-m <file.dat> [context]	Imports file.dat and creates a new primary zone; specifying context enables zones to be created anywhere in the eDirectory tree
-q	Disables verbose mode for debug messages (default setting)
-r <zone name>	Deletes and removes an existing zone from the zone database
-rp <characters>	Replaces listed characters with a dash (-) in host names for which resource records are dynamically created
-s [zone name]	Prints status information; zone name is optional
-u <file.dat>	Imports file.dat and updates the contents of a previously created zone
-v	Enables verbose mode for debug messages
-zi <zone name>	Forces named zone for zone-in transfer

To enable DNS services on a client workstation, simply configure the TCP/IP properties to obtain DNS server addresses automatically. The next time the client starts; it will perform a Dynamic DNS query and locate the primary DNS server.

CHAPTER 6

Users and Network Security

Instant Access

Creating users and groups

- To create User and Group objects, use ConsoleOne.
- To set up a template so all users you create receive a set of common characteristics; use ConsoleOne to create a Template object.

Ensuring login security

- To create account restrictions, access the user or group properties with ConsoleOne.
- To set or change passwords, access User object properties with ConsoleOne.

Working with eDirectory security

- To view or change eDirectory object or property rights, use ConsoleOne.

Dealing with directory and file security

- To view or change file system rights, use ConsoleOne.
- To view or change directory and file attributes, use ConsoleOne.

Securing the network from intruders

- To use NCP packet signatures, use the Packet Signing SET parameter to set the server to the appropriate signing level. Use the Advanced Settings page of the Novell client property pages to set the appropriate packet signing level on your Windows workstations.
- To set intruder detection, use ConsoleOne.
- To lock the server console, use SCRSAVER.NLM.
- To remove DOS and prevent NLMs from being loaded from insecure areas, use the SECURE CONSOLE console command.

An Overview of Network Security

Like no other time in the history of computing, regular users and small network administrators are being confronted with the issues of securing their networks. The Internet has uncovered the deficiencies in standards, protocols, and operating systems by allowing hackers and other n'er-do-wells the opportunity to test our networks from distant locations. Malicious viruses, worms, and Trojan Horses seek to infiltrate your network to harm and destroy.

And yet the most likely source of network attack is from your own users, whether out of malice or ignorance. Viruses can be introduced, security procedures circumvented, and sensitive systems and data left unprotected. Clearly, any effective security program is going to have to protect from both internal and external threats.

NetWare 6 offers a broad set of security features. Many of these features are implemented and managed through Novell eDirectory, which helps you develop a robust network security infrastructure without creating a management nightmare. NetWare 6 security concepts and features can be organized into five main categories:

- ▶ User-related objects
- ▶ Authentication
- ▶ Authorization
- ▶ Data security
- ▶ Other security features

Novell has always been adept at providing effective network security, primarily because NetWare is not an operating system that lends itself to simple security attacks. However, today's network security involves a lot more than assigning passwords to network users. Today's complex computing environments require advanced techniques for assuring that only those persons required to access network resources are able to do so. It is important to understand these basic topics in order to lay the groundwork for discussions of specific security products and features.

User-Related Objects

This might seem like an odd place to talk about User objects and related features, but critical security problems may arise from a misunderstanding of the ways in which eDirectory users can be assigned trustee rights. There are three main objects that are used to organize your network users. You can use ConsoleOne to create and manage each of these types of objects. (Users can also be assigned specific task-based privileges through the role-based administration features in iManage.)

See Chapter 3 for more information on ConsoleOne and for more information on configuring and using iManage.

X-REF

- ▶ User object
- ▶ Group object
- ▶ Organizational role

These objects form the foundation from which network services and privileges are ultimately delivered. After all, User-related objects define the human elements of your network. Immediately after a new NetWare 6 and eDirectory installation, the only User object that exists is Admin. While it may be comforting to think of a network of one, you are going to have to create user accounts for each and every one of your users. Once users have been created, they can begin working on the network. In most cases, users on a network will notice very little difference from working on a standalone computer. They still use the applications they were using before. They still open, save, and delete files the same way. They can still play the same games—but only if you let them!

And that's the goal of network security, to prevent users from taking some action, either unintentionally or intentionally, that might compromise the integrity of the network or expose network resources in such a way that can cause harm to the network or the organization. There are several levels of network security in today's networks, and NetWare 6 gives you a great deal of control over each.

The User Object

To create an eDirectory User object, complete the following steps:

I. (Optional) Create a directory for all users' home directories. For example, you may want to create a network directory called Users on volume VOL1.

For more information on NetWare 6 volumes, see Chapter 8.

X-REF

2. Launch ConsoleOne and browse to the container that will hold the new user or users.

3. Right-click the container object and select New ⮞ User from the drop-down menu.

4. In the New User dialog box, as seen in Figure 6.1, specify the desired information and click OK. The required fields have been so noted below:

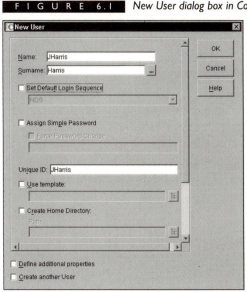

FIGURE 6.1 *New User dialog box in ConsoleOne*

- *Name*: (Required) Enter the desired login name for this user. This is the name the user will enter when he or she authenticates to eDirectory.

- *Surname*: (Required) Specify the last name of this user. This field is required so you can perform name-based searches on eDirectory.

- *Default login sequence*: (Conditional) If you have installed NMAS, you will see this field, which lets you define the sequence for multi-factor authentication. More information on NMAS is available later in this chapter.

- *Assign simple password*: The simple password is used with the Native File Access Pack (NFAP) with those protocols that do not support encrypted authentication.

X-REF

For more information on NFAP and simple passwords see Chapter 3.

- *Unique ID*: (Required) This field is populated with the contents of the Name field by default. The Unique ID field must contain a globally unique object name that can be used during LDAP searches. You can change this value manually, if desired.

- *Use template*: Specify the template object from which User object properties should be copied. Templates are discussed in more detail later in this chapter.

- *Create home directory*: This option will create a personal directory for the user, at the path you specify and using the directory name you specify.

- *Assign eDirectory password*: Select this option and you can either specify the user password or force eDirectory to prompt the user for a password upon their first login.

WARNING

It is possible to create an eDirectory User object without a password, but it is highly discouraged due to the network security breach that results.

- *Define additional properties*: If desired, you can define more specific user information once the User object is created. For more information on additional User object properties see the Novell on-line documentation.

- *Create another user*: Check this option if you want ConsoleOne to automatically return to the New User window after this User object has been created. This option and the Define additional properties option are mutually exclusive.

If you plan to assign many of your users some identical properties, you can use a User Template object. The Template object will automatically apply default properties to any new user you create using the template. However, it does not apply those properties to any users that existed before you created the user template. Network administrators often use a template to automatically grant default eDirectory and file system rights to users.

To create a User Template object, complete these steps:

1. (Optional) Create a directory for all users' home directories. For example, you may want to create a directory called Users on VOL1.

2. Launch ConsoleOne and browse to the container that will hold the new User Template object.

3. Right-click the container object and select New ⇨ Object from the drop-down menu. Browse to the Template object type and click OK.

4. At the New Template window, specify the desired information and click OK.

   - *Name*: Specify a name for this Template object.

   - *Use template or user*: If you want to base this template on an existing template or User object, check this box and specify the path to the model object.

   - *Define additional properties*: Similar to the User object, check this box to enter or change specific template details. The Template Properties page mirrors that of a User object.

   - *Create another template*: Check this option if you want ConsoleOne to automatically return to the New Template window after this Template object has been created. This option and the Define additional properties option are mutually exclusive.

In addition to Template objects, it is easy to simultaneously edit the same information for several users. Suppose a whole department moves to a different floor in the building. If you've entered the location or address information in those users' Details pages, you can update the information quickly.

From ConsoleOne, browse to the container that holds the User objects you want to update. In the right pane, highlight all the desired User objects using Shift+click or Ctrl+click. Right-click the collection of objects and select Properties of Multiple Objects. Any changes you make from this window will be applied to all the User objects you selected.

The Group Object

Group objects are used to apply a common set of trustee rights to different User objects. User objects assigned to a group are made security equivalent to that group; meaning that anything to which the Group object has rights, its member users will also have rights. Creating a group is very similar to creating a user. Complete the following steps to create a group and assign group membership to a user.

1. Launch ConsoleOne and browse to the container that will hold the new user Group object.

2. Right-click the container object and select New ⇨ Group from the drop-down menu.

3. At the New Group window, specify the desired information and click OK.

- *Name*: Specify a name for this Group object.

- *Define additional properties*: Check this box to define specific group properties, such as group members and group trustee rights.

- *Create another group*: Check this option if you want ConsoleOne to automatically return to the New Group window after this Group object has been created. This option and the Define additional properties option are mutually exclusive.

Group members can be added both during the creation of the Group object and afterward. To add group members, open the Members tab. Click the Add button and browse to the user, or users, that you want to add. You can select multiple users in the same container by using Shift+click or Ctrl+click.

The Organizational Role

Organizational roles function like groups of one. (They can have multiple occupants for process redundance.) They use explicit security equivalence to provide specific rights to a user who needs to be able to perform a specific task. Organizational roles are generally used to grant some degree of administrative ability for a tree or branch of the tree.

Complete the following steps to create an organizational role and assign occupancy to a user.

1. Launch ConsoleOne and browse to the container that will hold the new Organizational Role object.

2. Right-click the container object and select New ⇨ Object from the drop-down menu. Browse to the Organizational Role object type and click OK.

3. At the New Organizational Role window, specify the desired information and click OK.

- *Name*: Specify a name for the Organizational Role object.

- *Define additional properties*: Similar to the Group object, check this box to define specific details for the organizational role and to assign an occupant of the role.

- *Create another organizational role*: Check this option if you want ConsoleOne to automatically return to the New Organizational Role window after this object has been created. This option and the Define additional properties option are mutually exclusive.

Once the Organizational Role object is created, you can add additional occupants by right-clicking the object and selecting Properties.

Authentication

Authentication provides the doorway for access to network resources. Without a strong authentication mechanism, sensitive network resources are essentially laid bare for anyone to access. The primary authentication method currently used with eDirectory is the username/password combination. However, Novell Modular Authentication Service (NMAS) is now available, which makes it possible to integrate more advanced authentication methods into the NetWare environment.

Novell Modular Authentication Service

NMAS is designed to help you protect information on your network. NMAS brings together additional ways of authenticating to eDirectory in your NetWare 6 environment.

NMAS is bundled with NetWare 6 and provides limited NMAS functionality. It provides an authentication method for simple passwords, as required by Native File Access Pack. Simple passwords provide a secondary authentication mechanism for those protocols, such as NFS and CIFS, which do not support encrypted authentication.

NMAS Enterprise Edition is available as an add-on product for NetWare and adds the following:

- Several additional login methods
- Support for multiple login methods per login sequence (multi-factor authentication)
- Support for graded authentication
- Expanded ConsoleOne management
- RADIUS support

To provide this functionality, NMAS introduces three new concepts to NetWare authentication:

- ▶ Login factors
- ▶ Login methods and sequences
- ▶ Graded authentication

Login factors

NMAS uses three different approaches to logging in to the network, known as *login factors*. These login factors describe different items or qualities a user can use to authenticate to the network:

- ▶ *Password authentication*: Also referred to as "something you know," password authentication is the traditional network authentication method. It is still responsible for the lion's share of network authentication that goes on, including LDAP authentication, browser-based authentication, and most other directories.

- ▶ *Device authentication*: Also referred to as "something you have," device authentication uses third-party tokens or smart cards to deliver the secret with which you authenticate to the network.

- ▶ *Biometric authentication*: Also referred to as "something you are," biometric authentication uses some sort of scanning device that converts some physical characteristic into a digital pattern that can be stored in eDirectory. When a users attempts to authenticate, his or her biometric pattern is compared against that which is stored to see if they match.

NOTE

NMAS provides support for password authentication only. Device and biometric login factors are supported with NMAS Enterprise Edition.

Login methods and sequences

A *login method* is a specific implementation of a login factor. Novell has partnered with several third parties to create a variety of options for each of the login factors described earlier in this chapter. A *post-login method* is a security process that is executed after a user has authenticated to eDirectory. One such post-login method is the workstation access method, which requires the user to provide credentials in order to unlock the workstation after a period of inactivity.

Once you have decided upon and installed a method, you need to assign it to a login sequence in order for it to be used. A *login sequence* is an ordered set of one or more methods. Users log in to the network using these defined login sequences. If the sequence contains more than one method, the methods are presented to the user in the order specified. Login methods are presented first, followed by post-login methods.

Graded authentication

An important feature that is available only through NMAS Enterprise Edition is *graded authentication*, which allows you to "grade," or control, access to the network based on the login methods used to authenticate to the network. Graded authentication operates in conjunction with standard eDirectory and file system rights to provide very robust control over data access in a NetWare 6 environment.

There are three main elements to graded authentication:

► *Categories*: NMAS categories represent different levels of sensitivity and trust. You use categories to define security labels. There are three secrecy categories and three integrity categories by default: biometric, token, and password.

► *Security labels*: Security labels are combinations of categories that assign access requirements to NetWare volumes and eDirectory objects and properties. NMAS Enterprise Edition comes with eight security labels defined:

  • Biometric & password & token

  • Biometric & password

  • Biometric & token

  • Password & token

  • Biometric

  • Password

  • Token

  • Logged in

► *Clearances*: Clearances are assigned to users to represent the amount of trust you have in them. In the clearance, a read label specifies what a user can read and a write label specifies locations to which a user can write. Clearances are compared to security labels to determine whether or not a user has access. If a user's read clearance is equal to or greater than the security label assigned to the requested data, the user will be able to view it. If a user's write label data is labeled at the read label and below, a user can write data that is labeled between the read label and the write label.

Installing NMAS

There are two pieces to NMAS, the server installation and the NMAS client software.

Installation of the client is described in Chapter 2.

X-REF

NMAS is one of the default services installed with NetWare 6. It is also installed automatically with any service that requires its services, such as NFAP. However, if it has been removed for any reason, you can install it manually from either Deployment Manager or the graphical server console.

To install NMAS from Deployment Manager, complete the following steps:

1. Insert the NetWare 6 Operating System CD-ROM at the workstation. Run NWDEPLOY.EXE from the root of the CD-ROM.

2. Open Post-Installation tasks and select Install NetWare 6 products.

3. At the Target Server screen, select the server to which you want to install NMAS and click Next. Authenticate as an admin user at the root of the tree.

4. At the Components screen, click Clear All. Check the box next to Novell Modular Authentication Service and click Next.

5. At the Summary screen, click Finish to install NMAS.

6. Click Close. Close Deployment Manager by clicking Cancel ⇨ Yes.

You can configure the evaluation version of NMAS Enterprise Edition by completing the following steps:

1. Launch ConsoleOne and browse to the Security container.

2. With the Security container highlighted, you will see a Login Policy object in the right panel of ConsoleOne.

3. Right-click the Login Policy object and select Properties.

4. Select the Evaluation tab. Check Enable Enterprise Edition Evaluation (A fine example of alliteration, by the way) and click OK to save your changes.

With the evaluation copy enabled, you will be able to explore all the NMAS features introduced above, such as multi-factor authentication, graded authentication, and third-party login methods (should you have any you want to try out). You will get annoyance messages when using the advanced features, just to remind you that you haven't purchased a license yet, but all features are fully enabled.

For more detailed information on NMAS Enterprise Edition see the Novell on-line documentation.

eDirectory Login Controls

In addition to the actual login process, eDirectory provides a variety of login controls designed to help secure the network. Those controls are found in the properties of each User object. To see them, double-click on a User object in ConsoleOne and select the Restrictions tab. These restrictions are not configurable through Group or Container objects, so it is important to create users through templates to automate the configuration of these controls. Templates are discussed in detail elsewhere in this chapter. The various types of restrictions offered by eDirectory include:

- ▶ Password restrictions
- ▶ Login restrictions
- ▶ Time restrictions
- ▶ Address restrictions
- ▶ Intruder lockout

NOTE

You will see one other tab in ConsoleOne for Account Balance. This is a "leftover" from a server accounting feature that is no longer supported.

Login controls can be set on individual User objects, or they can be defined at the container level, where they will be automatically applied to all users in that container. To get to the login restrictions pages available through eDirectory, complete the following steps:

I. Launch ConsoleOne and browse to the object where you want to set login controls.

2. Right-click the object and select Properties.

3. Select the Restrictions tab and you will see a subpage for each of the controls listed previously. Select the appropriate page.

4. Make your desired changes and select OK to save your changes. Each of the login control pages is described in more detail in the following sections.

Password restrictions

The Password Restrictions page allows you to set password characteristics for eDirectory users, as shown in Figure 6.2. By default, the only selected option is Allow user to change password. However, this will not provide any significant degree of security, so you will want to enable some of the other options.

Time Variables with ConsoleOne

Time values in ConsoleOne are interpreted as UTC time, or Greenwich Mean Time (GMT). This affects how you set any type of expiration parameter. For example, if you want a user's password to expire at a specific time, you need to take into account the time zone offset between your location and GMT. Mountain Standard Time (MST) is 7 hours earlier than GMT, so if you want the password to expire at 1:00am in Utah you would have to set the expiration time to 8:00am GMT (8:00 − 7:00 = 1:00).

It is possible to force ConsoleOne to use the local time rather than UTC by setting an environment variable on the workstation from which ConsoleOne is running. Consult the documentation for your particular workstation operating system to determine how this is done.

Since ConsoleOne is Java-based, and not a native Windows application, it does not recognize the Windows-based time zone information. In order to set system-level time zone information for Windows 95/98 or Windows NT/2000, add the TZ= environment variable to a login script or the AUTOEXEC.BAT file. For example, SET TZ=MST7MDT will instruct the system to use Mountain Standard Time instead of GMT when displaying time information. This information will be available to non-Windows applications such as ConsoleOne.

F I G U R E   6 . 2 *Password Restrictions page in ConsoleOne*

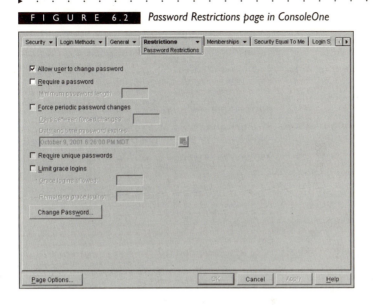

▶ *Require a password*: Checking this box forces users to set an account password. It also enables all other password options. Associated with this option is a Minimum password length field that can be used to require passwords of at least a given number of characters. Default is 5, but the value can be set from 1 to 128 characters.

▶ *Force periodic password changes*: This field allows you to require users to change their password regularly. Associated with this option is a Days between forced changes field that defines how often the password must be changed in days. Default is 40, but the value can be set between 1 and 365 days.

▶ *Date and time password expires*: With this option you can define a specific password expiration. It also shows when the password will next expire. When the user resets his or her password, the system will automatically reset this date forward by the number of days specified in the Days between forced changes field.

▶ *Require unique passwords*: Checking the Require unique passwords option allows eDirectory to track the last 8 passwords used with this account and prevents the user from re-using these old passwords.

NOTE

eDirectory does not implement any pattern recognition algorithms that force users to change the password to a significantly different value. Users can change the value by a single character and eDirectory will not complain. Similarly, eDirectory does not have an option for requiring numeric or special characters as part of the password.

▸ *Limit grace logins*: This option limits the number of times a user is allowed to login after their password has expired. Associated with it are two fields. The Grace logins allowed field allows the administrator to set how many grace logins will be permitted. The default is 6, but the value can be set between 1 and 200. The Remaining grace logins field tracks how many grace logins remain before the account is locked out. The administrator can also reset this value in order to give an expired account more time to reset their password, if necessary.

▸ *Change password (button)*: This button allows an authorized user to reset the password on a user account immediately.

Login restrictions

The Login Restrictions page allows you to control the ability of a user to login to the network, as shown in Figure 6.3.

FIGURE 6.3 *Login Restrictions page in ConsoleOne*

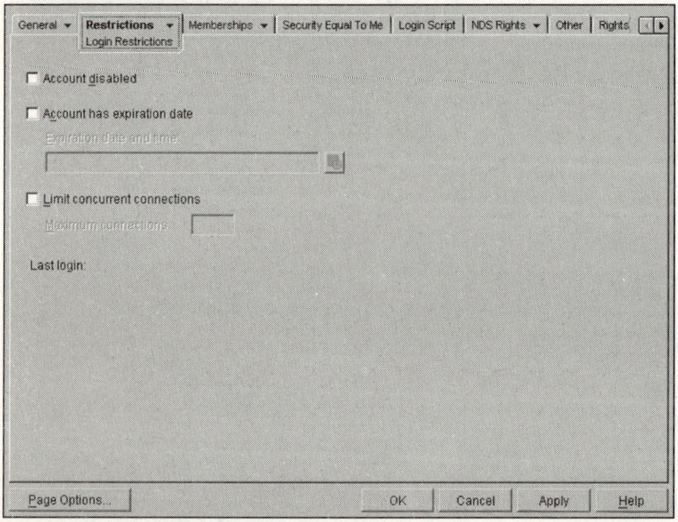

- ► *Account disabled*: Checking this box disables the user account and prevents future login attempts. However, this will not affect a user that is currently logged in.

- ► *Account has expiration date*: Checking this box allows you to set a date when the user account will be automatically disabled. This option might be used for contract employees or consultants who will be working for a predefined period of time.

- ► *Limit concurrent connections*: Check this box to define how many times the same account can be used to login from different workstations simultaneously. If enabled, the default is 1, but any value between 1 and 32,000 can be selected.

Time restrictions

The Time Restrictions page enables you to limit the time(s) of day when a user can access the network, as shown in Figure 6.4. By default there are no restrictions.

Simply click and drag the cursor over the time(s) that you want the user account locked out. Each grid square is 30 minutes. If a user is logged in when his or her lockout period is reached, they will be issued a 5-minute warning, after which they will be automatically logged out.

FIGURE 6.4 *Time Restrictions page in ConsoleOne*

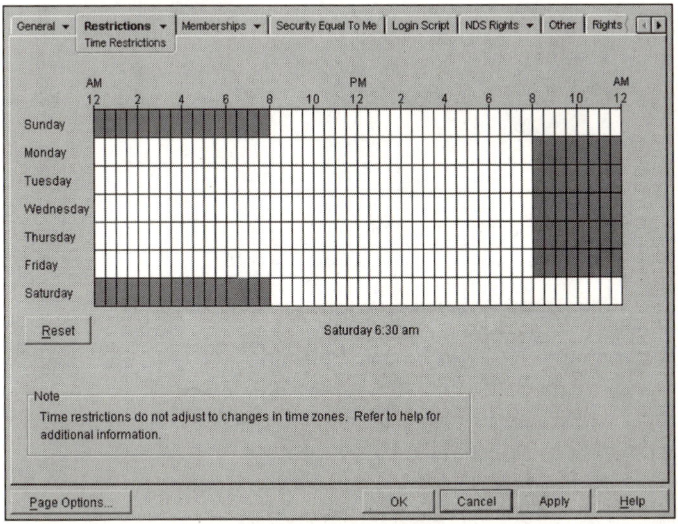

NOTE

One important caveat to time restrictions is that they are governed by the user's home time and not their current time. For example, if a user in New York takes a trip to Los Angeles and is going to dial in to their home network, the time in New York rather than the time in Los Angeles will determine the time restriction. A 6:00pm EST time restriction would shut the user down at 3:00pm PST. While that may give your employee time to get in a round of golf, it may not be what you intended when configuring the time restriction in the first place.

Address restrictions

The Address Restrictions page can be used to tie a user account to a specific workstation, as shown in Figure 6.5, thereby forcing them to login from that hardware location only.

FIGURE 6.5 *Address Restrictions page in ConsoleOne*

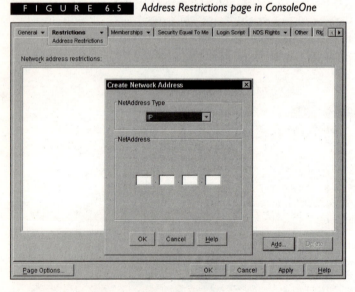

In today's world of dynamic addressing and roaming users, this option is not as useful as it once might have been, but in very security-conscious environments, it can still be necessary. However, TCP/IP functionality is severely limited by the fact that the utility assumes a Class B subnet mask (255.255.0.0) for all IP addressing—not very practical in today's overloaded IP world.

Intruder lockout

The Intruder Lockout page is useful only after a user account has been locked out. Intruder lockout refers to the disabling of a user account after a certain number of unsuccessful login attempts have been made. To re-enable a locked out account, the administrator unchecks the Account locked box on this page, as shown in Figure 6.6. The other three entries simply provide information about the status of the locked account.

FIGURE 6.6   *Resetting the Intruder Lockout page in ConsoleOne*

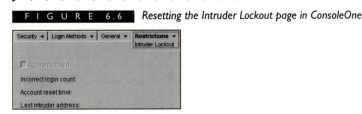

The actual intruder detection system is configured at the container level rather than the user level. In order to configure your intruder detection environment, complete the following steps:

1. Launch ConsoleOne and browse to the container object that holds the users for whom you want to enable intruder lockout.

2. Right-click the container and select Properties.

3. Click on the General tab and select the Intruder Detection page, which is shown in Figure 6.7.

4. Make your desired selections and click OK to save your changes.

   - *Detect intruders*: Check this box to enable the intruder detection system for this container. Associated with this checkbox are fields that allow you to set the number of incorrect login attempts before intruder lockout is activated — default is 7 — and the interval within which the unsuccessful attempts must occur — default is 30 minutes.

   - *Lock account after detection*: Check this box to enable the account lockout feature. Associated with this checkbox are fields that allow you to specify the time period for which the account will remain locked — default is 15 minutes. At the end of this period, the account will be reactivated automatically.

▶ . . . . ◀

FIGURE 6.7 *Enabling Intruder Detection features in ConsoleOne*

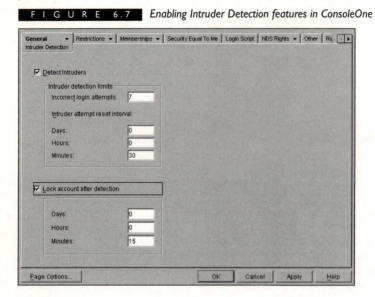

▶ . . . . ◀

Authorization

Now that users have authenticated to the network, you must provide them with access to all the resources they need. This also entails preventing them from accessing resources that they do not need. It wouldn't do to have sensitive documents describing future products open to and accessible to just anyone. The reality of the corporate world is that some resources must be maintained as "need to know."

While determining exactly who needs access to what is a decision beyond most network administrators, Novell eDirectory provides powerful tools for implementing those decisions. This section discusses eDirectory access control concepts and how they work together to provide proper access to objects in the eDirectory tree.

Access Control Lists

Access Control Lists are stored in each eDirectory object to identify those other objects that have been granted some sort of control over it. Each object in an eDirectory tree maintains two types of access rights. The first set of rights is entry rights. Entry rights define how an object can be manipulated by other directory entities, as described in Table 6.1:

TABLE 6.1	*Valid Entry Rights in eDirectory*
ENTRY RIGHT	**DESCRIPTION**
Browse	Allows a trustee to discover and view the object in the eDirectory tree.
Create	This right applies only to container objects. It allows the trustee to create new objects within the container.
Delete	Allows a trustee to delete the object.
Rename	Allows a trustee to rename the object.
Supervisor	Allows a trustee full access to the object and its attributes.

The second set of rights is property rights. Property rights define how the attributes associated with an object can be manipulated. eDirectory property rights are described in Table 6.2:

TABLE 6.2	*Valid Property Rights in eDirectory*
PROPERTY RIGHT	**DESCRIPTION**
Compare	Allows a trustee to compare, or see if an attribute contains a given value.
Read	Allows a trustee to read an attribute value. This right confers the compare right.
Write	Allows a trustee to add, delete, or modify an attribute value. This right confers the add or delete self right to the attribute.
Add self (delete self)	Allows a trustee to add or delete its name as an attribute value (if applicable).
Supervisor	Assigns a trustee all attribute rights.

When entry and/or property rights are conferred to an eDirectory entity, that entity becomes a trustee of the conferring object. The list of trustees, and the specific object and property rights they have been granted, is maintained in an Access Control List (ACL) associated with each eDirectory object. Figure 6.8 shows a representative ACL as seen from ConsoleOne.

eDirectory Access Control List in ConsoleOne

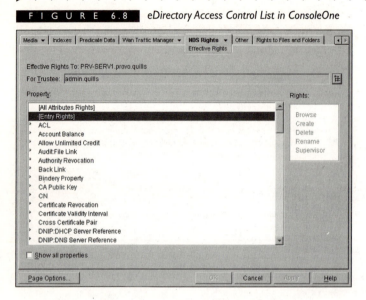

The ACL contains three pieces of information about a trustee assignment: trustee ID, protected attribute ID, and privilege set.

▶ *Trustee ID*: This field identifies the object that is being granted rights. It can also contain one of the special entry references outlined in Table 6.3:

▶ *Protected attribute ID*: This field specifies the type of right that is being granted. It also specifies how that right is to be applied. Rights can be assigned to a specific property, to all properties, or to the object itself.

▶ *Privilege set*: This field lists the right(s) that have been granted. In the eDirectory schema, most object classes specify a default access template that is used to create an ACL attribute for a new object. This default template provides basic access control for the new entry, allowing it to function in the Directory. Different object classes have different default ACL templates to reflect their different needs. For example, the default ACL template for the User object grants the write right to its own login script attribute. This allows users to change their personal login scripts as necessary.

TABLE 6.3	Special Trustee References in eDirectory
REFERENCE	**DESCRIPTION**
Inherited rights filter	eDirectory uses this reference to mask or filter privileges rather than granting rights.
[Public]	eDirectory uses this reference to grant rights to all objects in the eDirectory tree, including both authenticated and non-authenticated objects.
[Root]	eDirectory uses this reference to grant rights to all authenticated entries.
Creator	eDirectory uses this reference to grant all rights to the client that created the object.
Self	eDirectory uses this reference to allow objects to add or delete themselves as values of attributes and to grant the object rights to its own attributes.

Inheritance

Inheritance is one of the most powerful — and sometimes frustrating — concepts in eDirectory security planning. It is similar to the security equivalence concepts (discussed previously) in that it deals with the determination of effective rights at any given point in the eDirectory tree. On the one hand, inheritance promises to save untold amounts of work by automating the assignment of rights in the eDirectory tree. On the other hand, because of the way that inheritance works, things sometimes don't happen exactly as you might have planned.

Novell has been using inheritance for a long time to apply rights to the NetWare file system. If a user was granted rights at a specific directory, those rights implicitly applied to everything from that point down in the directory structure — until explicitly removed. The same principle applies to eDirectory: If a user is granted rights at a given container object, those rights are implicitly applied to each object in the tree from that point downward — until explicitly removed.

eDirectory implements inheritance through a dynamic model. This means that rights are calculated in real-time whenever an eDirectory object attempts to perform any directory operation. To do this, eDirectory starts at [Root] and walks the tree down to the object, building a set of effective rights for that object along the way. If the effective rights for that object permit the requested operation, then it is allowed to continue. If not, the operation is denied.

At first, it might seem very inefficient to traverse the eDirectory tree from [Root] each time effective rights need to be calculated — and it would be — except that eDirectory resolves this inefficiency through the use of external references.

External references exist to protect database integrity by storing information about partitions that do have local replicas. In other words, the Master replica of a child partition will maintain an external reference to [Root]. In order to determine the effective rights for a user, eDirectory need only consult the locally stored external references instead of potentially crossing the entire network to find the information it needs. This reduces network traffic and increases the speed of eDirectory tremendously.

For more information on external references, see Chapter 5.

X-REF

Inherited Rights Filters

Inherited Rights Filters (IRF) are used to restrict inheritance in a directory tree. IRF use looks pretty straightforward on the surface, but it can cause all kinds of interesting situations to arise. More calls have been logged to Novell's Technical Support groups because administrators got carried away with controlling every single aspect of eDirectory security instead of just trusting the environment to handle things properly.

Don't implement IRFs unless you are absolutely sure you understand the consequences of doing so.

WARNING

That said, it is sometimes desirable to limit the flow of rights through the eDirectory tree — either to segment administration or to isolate sensitive sections of the tree. If this becomes necessary, IRFs are the way to go. Just remember that less is usually more in this case. If you find yourself creating a large number of IRFs it may be a sign of some fundamental eDirectory design issues.

See Chapter 5 for more information on eDirectory tree design.

X-REF

The first thing to recognize about IRFs is that they can filter supervisory rights in eDirectory, unlike supervisory rights in the NetWare file system. This makes it possible to limit the control of admin users higher up in the tree, but it also threatens to destroy your ability to administer the directory tree properly.

To configure an IRF, complete the following steps:

1. Launch ConsoleOne and browse to the container to which you want to add an IRF.

2. Right-click the container and select Trustees of this Object.

3. Click on the NDS Rights tab and select the Inherited Rights Filters subpage. Click Add Filter to create an IRF.

4. At the Add Property page, select the property for which you want to define an IRF and click OK. You can create an IRF for Entry Rights, for All Properties, or for specific properties.

5. Uncheck those rights that you want to be blocked by the IRF and select OK to save your changes. The IRF properties page is shown in Figure 6.9.

FIGURE 6.9 *IRF properties in ConsoleOne*

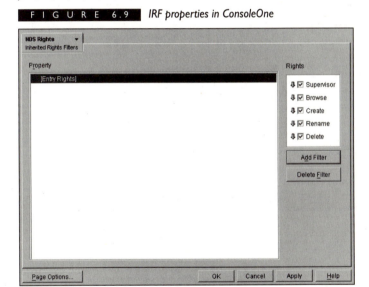

It is very important that you remember the dynamic nature of rights calculation in eDirectory. For example, if you are going to create a container administrator and filter administrative rights to that container from above, you had better create the new Admin object first. If you set the IRF first, you will find yourself "locked out" — unable to define a user with administrative control for the container. IRFs are a two-edged sword.

IMPORTANT

Explicit Rights

Explicit rights are those rights specifically assigned to an object at some point in the eDirectory tree. When one object is given specific rights to another it is called a trustee. To assign explicit rights, complete the following steps:

1. Launch ConsoleOne and browse to the object to which you want to add a trustee.

2. Right-click the object and select Trustees of this Object.

3. Click Add Trustee. Browse to the eDirectory object to which you want to assign trustee rights and click OK.

4. At the Rights Assigned to Selected Objects page, define the appropriate rights for this trustee and select OK. This page is shown in Figure 6.10.

   • *Property*: Select the type of rights you want to configure for this trustee. If you want to assign specific property rights only, click Add Property to select specific properties from a list.

   • *Rights*: Check the rights for this property type that you want granted to this trustee. You can assign entry rights, all property (attribute) rights, specific property rights, or any combination of the three.

   • *Inheritable*: If you are assigning a trustee to a container object, you can check the Inheritable box if you want those rights to flow down to other objects within the container.

FIGURE 6.10   *Assigning explicit trustee rights in ConsoleOne*

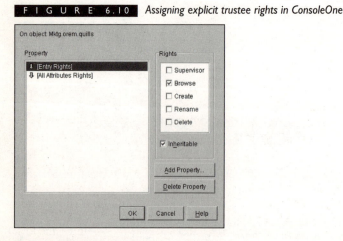

Assigning explicit rights is a very straightforward process, but as with IRFs there are some caveats. For example, unlike security equivalence, explicit assignments are not additive. An explicit assignment preempts the implicit rights that a user might have had through inheritance. Making explicit rights assignments can easily eliminate rights that existed previously. Make sure you understand what is being provided through inheritance and security equivalence, and how your explicit assignment will affect those existing rights, before making manual changes to trustee rights.

Security Equivalence

Security equivalence in eDirectory is used to assign one object identical eDirectory rights to those already assigned to another object. eDirectory offers explicit and implicit security equivalence. Under the rules of inheritance described previously, security equivalence will continue to flow down from the point it is granted. In other words, if JHarris in Provo.Quills is granted equivalence to the Admin object, those rights will be granted at [Root] just like they are for admin. Equivalence provides a method to grant users in one area of the eDirectory tree rights to objects in another.

TIP

Using security equivalence is not an efficient way to manage access. If you find yourself using lots of security equivalences it is a strong indication of a poor eDirectory tree design. See Chapter 5 for more information on eDirectory design.

Implicit security equivalence occurs automatically when an object is inserted into the eDirectory tree. Every eDirectory object has security equivalence with the following objects:

▶ The [Root] object

▶ The [Public] trustee

▶ Each container between it and [Root]

Security equivalence to these objects and trustees provides basic access to eDirectory so that the new object can perform basic network tasks, such as navigating the directory, locating servers, and initiating an authentication request. Beyond that, they are pretty helpless until you grant them more specific trustee rights.

Explicit security equivalence is identical to implicit security equivalence — except the network administrator has to assign the equivalence manually. Use explicit security equivalence whenever one user needs identical explicit rights as another but cannot get those rights through normal inheritance or implicit security equivalence. To assign explicit security equivalence, complete the following steps:

1. Launch ConsoleOne and browse to the object to which you want to make another object security equivalent.

2. Right-click the container object and select Properties.

3. Select the Security Equal To Me tab.

4. Click Add. Browse to the object that you want to be security equivalent and click OK

5. Click OK to save the security equivalence.

The Danger of Explicit Security Equivalence

Not all uses of explicit security equivalence are appropriate. For example, some administrators have used security equivalence to make their User object equivalent to the Admin object. This gives them all rights associated with the Admin object. The danger in this is that when you derive your rights from another object, those rights are never specifically recorded in your object. For example, if JHarris.Provo.Quills is security equal to Admin.Quills, whenever JHarris attempts to perform some directory operation, eDirectory will look at the effective rights of admin. If admin has sufficient rights to perform the operation, then JHarris, as a security equal, is granted permission as well.

Can you see the danger? Sometime down the road JHarris is happily administering eDirectory. Why keep the Admin object around when it is never used? Except that the instant the object is deleted, JHarris loses all his administrative rights because they are derived from the Admin object and not explicitly assigned.

Even worse, unless some other object has been explicitly granted supervisory rights to the eDirectory tree, deleting the Admin object may delete the ability to administer eDirectory at all.

Explicit security equivalence can be a powerful tool, but you can end up laying a trap for yourself — or others who might come after you. In most cases, the explicit security equivalence should be restricted to use with Group objects. For assigning specific rights to a single object, it is often best to assign those rights directly, rather than to rely on another object to supply them.

Explicit security equivalence is most often used with Group objects, which were discussed earlier in this chapter. Each member of an eDirectory group is assigned as security equal to the Group object. In this way each user receives the rights associated with that group. Because security equivalence is cumulative, an object's implicit and explicit security equivalence will be added together in order to determine its effective rights.

Effective Rights

The whole point of all the preceding rights controls is to ensure that a given user, or other eDirectory object, has the appropriate rights on the network to do what's needed. Effective rights are the cumulative result of all the different rights tools working together. In the end, there are eight different ways that one object can get rights to another:

- ▶ 1) Object 1 is a trustee of Object 2. Therefore, Object 1 has explicit rights to Object 2.

- ▶ 2) A parent container of Object 1 is a trustee of Object 2. Therefore, Object 1 has rights to Object 2 due to implicit security equivalence.

- ▶ 3) Object 1 has explicit security equivalence to Object 3, which is a trustee of Object 2. Therefore, Object 1 has trustee rights to Object 2, which are equivalent to Object 3.

- ▶ 4) [Public] is a trustee of Object 2. Therefore, Object 1 has rights to Object 2 through implicit security equivalence to [Public].

- ▶ 5) [Public] is a trustee of a parent container of Object 2, and those rights flow down the tree due to inheritance. Therefore, Object 1 has rights to Object 2 through the combination of implicit security equivalence and inheritance.

- ▶ 6) Object 1 is a trustee of one of Object 2's parent containers, and those rights flow down the tree to include Object 2 due to inheritance.

- ▶ 7) A parent container of Object 1 is a trustee of a parent container of Object 2. Therefore, Object 1 has rights to Object 2 through a combination of explicit rights, implicit security equivalence, and inheritance.

- ▶ 8) Object 1 is security equivalent to Object 3, which is a trustee of a parent container of Object 2. Therefore, Object 1 has rights to Object 2 through the combination of explicit security equivalence and inheritance.

NOTE

Inherited rights filters cannot affect the effective rights in cases 1–4, because no inheritance is being used. However, IRFs can modify or eliminate the effective rights provided in cases 5–8, because they depend on inheritance.

With eight different ways to derive effective rights between two objects, it's easy to see how rights issues can get complicated very quickly. In most cases, the best solution is to let inheritance do the work of assigning rights wherever possible. The default combination of implicit security equivalence and dynamic inheritance is suitable for 90 percent of the directory installations out there.

Assign rights through containers and let them flow downward. As your directory tree evolves over time, situations may arise that cannot be satisfied by inheritance alone. If this happens, use groups, explicit assignments, and IRFs sparingly to address these exceptions.

When using IRFs, be careful that a single object doesn't become a point of failure. Consider what might happen if a User object is corrupted, or if that user becomes malicious. Always have a second or third option for accessing a branch of the tree that is restricted. Just as the military establishes a chain of command so that the mission can continue if one man is lost, eDirectory administrators have to make sure that proper access can continue — or at least be repaired — if the default method of access is lost.

TIP

One way of doing this is to create a secondary user object with full administrative rights, and then add a Browse IRF to that object. This effectively hides the secondary admin from view, but provides emergency administrative access should it be necessary.

Role-Based Administration

A new, and highly anticipated, instance of authorization is the ability to assign specific administrative roles to users in the eDirectory tree. While this was possible in a limited fashion with the use of organizational roles, iManage offers you a previously impossible level of control and ease-of-use. Over the next year you will see a greatly expanded set of roles that can be configured and managed from iManage.

X-REF

For more information on configuring role-based administration with iManage, see Chapter 3.

Data Security

The whole point of eDirectory-based security concepts such as authentication and authorization is to provide a secure environment within which data can be used and protected. The mantra of the twenty-first century is "Information is Power," and you want to be sure you aren't sharing your competitive advantage with your competitors.

NetWare 6 leverages eDirectory to extend the idea of authorization to the server file system. The NetWare file system is manageable through the Server, Volume, Folder, and File objects in eDirectory. In this way, you can manage file access through the same tools used to manage the rest of your network.

You can implement two different types of security tools in the file system, either together or separately, to protect your files:

- ▶ *Trustee rights*: These are equivalent to entry rights for eDirectory objects. Trustee rights define the possible actions that can be taken with Volume, Folder, and File objects, and who or what can perform those actions.

- ▶ *Attributes*: Unlike trustee rights, which define acceptable behavior for different users and groups, attributes define the characteristics of individual Volume, Folder, or File objects. Because attributes trump trustee rights, they control the activities of all users, regardless of which trustee rights are assigned.

File System Trustee Rights

File system trustee rights allow users and groups to work with files and directories in specific ways. Each right determines whether a user can do things such as see, read, change, rename, or delete the file or directory. File system rights obey inheritance rules just like directory rights. When rights are assigned to a file, they define a user's allowable actions for that file only. When rights are assigned to a directory, they affect a user's allowable actions on not only the directory itself but also everything stored within that directory.

Although file system rights are similar in nature to the eDirectory rights for objects and properties (described earlier in this chapter), they are not the same thing. File system rights are separate from eDirectory rights. They affect only how users work with files and directories. eDirectory rights affect how users work with other eDirectory objects.

There are eight different file system trustee rights. You can assign any combination of those file system rights to a user or group, depending on how you want that user or group to work.

Table 6.4 describes the available file system rights and how they affect directory and file access.

T A B L E 6 . 4 *File System Rights*		
FILE SYSTEM RIGHT	**ABBREVIATION**	**DESCRIPTION**
Read	R	Directory: Allows the trustee to open and read files in the directory.
		File: Allows the trustee to open and read the file.
Write	W	Directory: Allows the trustee to open and write to (change) files in the directory.
		File: Allows the trustee to open and write to the file.
Create	C	Directory: Allows the trustee to create subdirectories and files in the directory.
		File: Allows the trustee to salvage the file if it was deleted.
Erase	E	Directory: Allows the trustee to delete the directory and its files and subdirectories.
		File: Allows the trustee to delete the file.
Modify	M	Directory: Allows the trustee to change the name, directory attributes, and file attributes of the directory and its files and subdirectories.
		File: Allows the trustee to change the file's name or file attributes.

FILE SYSTEM RIGHT	ABBREVIATION	DESCRIPTION
File scan	F	Directory: Allows the trustee to see the names of the files and subdirectories within the directory. File: Allows the trustee to see the name of the file.
Access control	A	Directory: Allows the trustee to change the directory's IRF and trustee assignments. File: Allows the trustee to change the file's IRF and trustee assignments.
Supervisor	S	Directory: Grants the trustee all rights to the directory, its files, and its subdirectories. It cannot be blocked by an IRF. File: Grants the trustee all rights to the file. It cannot be blocked by an IRF. Note that the Supervisor right can be added or removed only at the entry point to the file system (where you go from directory object to file system object).

Inheriting file system rights

Just like eDirectory rights, file system rights can be inherited. This means that if you have file system rights to a parent directory, you can also inherit those rights and exercise them in any file and subdirectory within that directory. Inheritance keeps you from having to grant users file system rights at every level of the file system.

You can block inheritance by removing the right from the IRF of a file or subdirectory. As with directory objects, every directory and file has an inherited rights filter, specifying which file system rights can be inherited from a parent directory. By default, file and directory IRFs allow all rights to be inherited.

Inheritance can also be blocked by granting a new set of trustee rights to a subdirectory or file within the parent directory. As with the eDirectory rights, inherited and explicit file system rights are not additive. Explicit assignments replace the inherited rights from a parent directory.

File system security equivalence

Security equivalence for file system rights works the same way as security equivalence for eDirectory rights (explained earlier in this chapter). You can assign one user to have the same eDirectory rights and file system rights as another user by using the Security Equal To Me tab in an object's properties page.

NOTE

Remember: You are still subject to the shortcomings of security equivalence as described previously.

File system effective rights

Just as with eDirectory rights, determining which file system rights a user can actually exercise in a file or directory can be confusing at first. A user's *effective file system rights* are the file system rights that the user can ultimately execute in a given directory or file. The user's effective rights to a directory or file are determined in one of two ways:

► The user's inherited rights from a parent directory, minus any rights blocked by the subdirectory's (or file's) IRF

► The sum of all rights granted to the user for that directory or file, through direct trustee assignment and security equivalences to other users

Working with file system trustee rights

To see or change a user's trustee assignments, complete the following steps:

1. Launch ConsoleOne and browse to the point in the file system, volume, folder, or file with which you want to work.

2. Right-click the container and select Properties. Select the Trustees tab.

3. Click Effective Rights. Browse to the User object for which you want to view file system rights and click OK.

4. The user's effective rights will be listed in black type, as shown in Figure 6.11.

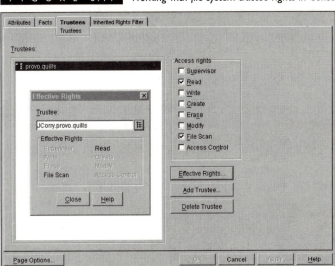

You can make a user a trustee of a File System object by doing the following:

1. From the Trustees page, click Add Trustee. Browse to the desired User object and click OK.

2. Check those explicit file system rights that you want to grant the user and click OK.

If the user is already a trustee, simply highlight the appropriate User object in the Trustees window and perform Step 2 above.

Changes to explicit security equivalence are done using the same process described previously in the "Authorization" section of this chapter.

File and Directory Attributes

Another important NetWare security tool for securing files and directories is attributes. *Attributes* are properties of files and directories that control what can happen to those files or directories. Attributes, which are also called *flags*, are different from trustee rights in several ways:

▶ Attributes are assigned directly to files and directories, whereas rights are assigned to users.

- ▶ Attributes override rights. In other words, if that directory has the Delete Inhibit attribute, you can't delete the directory even if you've been granted the erase right.

- ▶ Likewise, attributes don't grant rights. Just because a file has the Read-Write attribute doesn't mean you can write to it if you don't have the write right.

- ▶ Attributes affect all users, including the admin user.

- ▶ Attributes affect some aspects of the file that rights do not, such as determining whether or not the files in a directory can be purged immediately upon deletion.

File and directory attribute types

There are eight attributes that apply to either files or directories. There are an additional six that apply only to files. These attributes are listed in Table 6.5.

TABLE 6.5	File and Directory Attributes		
ATTRIBUTE	FILE	DIRECTORY	DESCRIPTION
Delete inhibit	X	X	Prevents users from deleting the file or directory.
Hidden	X	X	Hides the file or directory so it isn't listed by the DOS DIR command or in the Windows File Manager and can't be copied or deleted.
Purge immediate	X	X	Purges the file or directory immediately upon deletion. Purged files can't be salvaged.
Rename inhibit	X	X	Prevents users from renaming the file or directory.
System	X	X	Indicates a system directory that may contain system files (such as DOS files). Prevents users from seeing, copying, or deleting the directory. (However, does not assign the System attribute to the files in the directory.)

ATTRIBUTE	FILE	DIRECTORY	DESCRIPTION
Don't migrate	X	X	Prevents a file or directory from being migrated to another storage device.
Immediate compress	X	X	Compresses the file or directory immediately.
Don't compress	X	X	Prevents the file or directory from being compressed.
Archive needed	X		Indicates that the file has been changed since the last time it was backed up.
Execute only	X		Prevents an executable file from being copied, modified, or deleted. Use with caution! Once assigned, it cannot be removed, so assign it only if you have a backup copy of the file. You may prefer to assign the Read-Only attribute instead of the Execute Only attribute.
Read-only	X		Allows the file to be opened and read, but not modified. All NetWare files in SYS:SYSTEM, SYS:PUBLIC, and SYS:LOGIN are read-only. Assigning the Read-Only attribute automatically assigns delete inhibit and rename inhibit.
Shareable	X		Allows the file to be used by more than one user simultaneously. Useful for utilities, commands, applications, and some database files. All NetWare files in SYS:SYSTEM, SYS:PUBLIC, and SYS:LOGIN are shareable. Most data and work files should not be shareable, so that users' changes do not conflict.

(continued)

TABLE 6.5	File and Directory Attributes (continued)		
ATTRIBUTE	FILE	DIRECTORY	DESCRIPTION
Transactional	X		When used on database files, allows NetWare's Transaction Tracking System (TTS) to protect the files from being corrupted if the transaction is interrupted.
Don't suballocate	X		Prevents a file from being suballocated. Use on files, such as some database files, that may need to be enlarged or appended to frequently. (See Chapter 8 for information on block suballocation.)

Assigning file and directory attributes

To assign attributes to a file or directory, complete the following steps:

1. Launch ConsoleOne and browse to the folder or file with which you want to work.

2. Right-click the object and select Properties.

3. Select the Attributes tab, which is shown in Figure 6.12. Check the desired attributes and select OK to accept your changes.

There are three other File Status boxes on the Attributes page. These are informational and indicate the following:

▶ *File compressed*: Indicates whether or not the selected file or folder is stored in a compressed format on the NetWare volume.

▶ *Can't compress*: Indicates that selected file compression would not achieve any significant space savings on this file.

▶ *File migrated*: Indicates that the selected file has been moved to a secondary storage system, such as tape.

FIGURE 6.12 *Working with file and folder attributes in ConsoleOne*

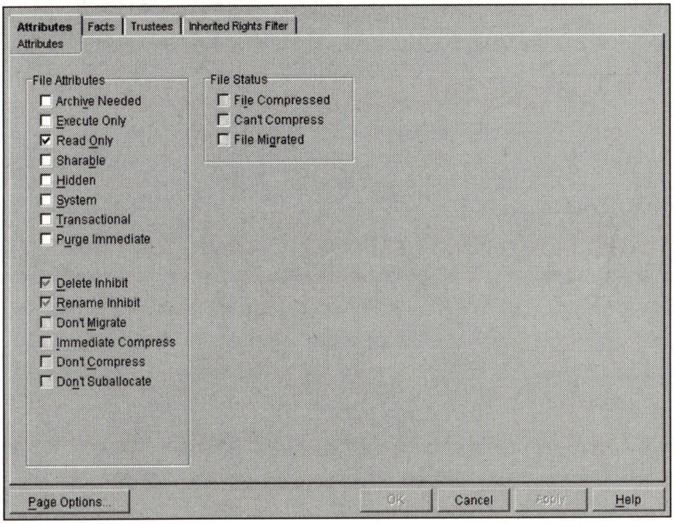

Login Scripts

One other point of interaction between directory and file system is the login script. The eDirectory login script is a batch file that outlines basic operations that should be performed every time the user logs into the network. Login script operations can include environment variables, drive mappings, program execution, and message display.

NCP Packet Signature

NCP Packet Signature is a feature designed to prevent a would-be hacker from spoofing a network connection. Spoofing involves hijacking a connection by forging network packets that appear to be from a legitimate user connection. This feature requires workstations and servers to automatically "sign" each NCP packet with a signature and to change the signature for every packet.

Packet Signature is an optional security feature and can slow down network performance on busy networks. Since spoofing requires access to a physical network connection, you may prefer not to use packet signatures if your network is in a relatively trusted environment, or if the threat of intruders stealing sensitive information is low.

There are four levels of NCP Packet Signature, which must be set on both workstations and servers. If the levels on the workstation and server don't form an allowable combination, the two computers will not be able to communicate with each other.

To set the signature level on a server, use MONITOR.NLM and select Server Parameters, and then choose the NCP category. If you prefer, you can type the following SET command at the server's console prompt:

```
SET NCP PACKET SIGNATURE OPTION=number
```

Replace *number* with the signature level (0 through 3) you want the server to use. After the server has been booted, you can execute the SET command to increase the signature level. If you want to decrease the level, however, you have to reboot the server. Table 6.6 shows the NCP Packet Signature levels.

TABLE 6.6   *Server Levels for NCP Packet Signature*

LEVEL	DESCRIPTION
0	Does not sign packets.
1	Only signs packets if so requested by other entity.
2	Prefers to sign packets, but will still communicate with an entity that cannot sign.
3	Both entities must sign packets.

To set the signature level on a Windows workstation, complete the following steps:

1. Right-click the red "N" in the system tray and select Novell Client Properties.

2. Select the Advanced Settings tab and browse to Signature Level.

3. Select the appropriate level, 0-3, and click OK to save your changes.

Figure 6.13 shows how the signature levels on servers and workstations combine to either allow unsigned packets, force signed packets, or deny login.

FIGURE 6.13 *Packet signature operation between server and client*

Workstation Level

		0	1	2	3
	0	Unsigned	Unsigned	Unsigned	Login Denied
Server Level	1	Unsigned	Unsigned	Signed	Signed
	2	Unsigned	Signed	Signed	Signed
	3	Login Denied	Signed	Signed	Signed

Other Security Features

There are several other security features that you should consider as you install and configure NetWare 6.

Physical Server Protection

An important aspect of network security is to make sure the server itself is secure from tampering. This is a simple task but is often overlooked, leaving the network vulnerable to either deliberate or accidental damage.

If the server is sitting in an area that is easily accessible and isn't protected with a keyboard lock or password, a malicious user can easily access the server and wreak havoc. Less dramatic, but potentially just as damaging, is the accidental tampering that could occur. A janitorial employee could unplug the server to plug in the vacuum cleaner; a helpful employee could try to load a virus-infected file directly on the server; another employee could try to "fix" a printing problem while you're not around and end up in worse shape than before.

The following are some of the simple ways you can secure your server:

▶ Lock the server in a separate room. Just putting the server in a locked room can prevent much of the potential tampering that could occur.

- Lock the server's console with SCRSAVER.NLM, which loads a screen saver on the server. To do this, type **SCRSAVER** at the server's console. By default, this module will lock the server's console when the screen saver activates. To unlock the console while the screen saver is displayed, press any key, and then enter a username and password. The username must have valid access rights to the server, such as admin. The default time for the screen saver to activate is 10 minutes of inactivity. You can change this time delay, and you can specify whether or not the screen saver locks the console. Type **SCRSAVER HELP** for specific command line options.

- Prevent the loading of NLMs from anywhere but the specified search paths (by default, SYS:SYSTEM only) by using the SECURE CONSOLE command at the server console. SECURE CONSOLE also prevents anyone from accessing the operating system's debugger and from changing the server's date and time. To remove SECURE CONSOLE, you must reboot the server.

- Make sure that only authorized users have rights to SYS:SYSTEM.

- Use a secure password for remote console access. Load RCONAG6.NLM, from the AUTOEXEC.NCF with an encrypted password. Keep the remote console password secure, and change it periodically.

> For more information on using secure passwords for remote control access, see Chapter 4.

X-REF

- Maintain updated virus protection software, and regularly scan for viruses.

Novell Cryptographic Services

Starting with NetWare 5, Novell has provided a comprehensive security infrastructure. It provides the foundation for delivering advanced security solutions with NetWare and eDirectory. The Novell International Cryptographic Infrastructure (NICI) provides all cryptography-related services to eDirectory and its related services. Novell Certificate server provides a public key infrastructure that integrates with today's standards-based security systems.

NICI and Certificate server work largely behind the scenes to provide critical services to your network. Hopefully, you won't have to do much with them directly, but it is good to know a little about them in order to better understand how your network operates.

NICI

NICI is a modular security framework that is responsible for all crypto-graphic services in the NetWare and eDirectory environments. The advantage of using NICI as a security foundation is that it eliminates the need to build cryptographic functionality into each application. Because of varied export laws across countries, applications would have to be written in several different versions if they were to be used worldwide.

NICI consolidates all cryptographic functionality into eDirectory. Applications leverage the existing cryptographic infrastructure and do not have to worry about multiple versions. It also means that all security management can take place from eDirectory management tools. The modular nature of NICI allows for the support of varied cryptographic export laws through the policy manager in NICI. NICI prevents the insertion and use of cryptographic modules that would violate export laws. Because of this, NICI has received export approval from the United States. All applications that leverage NICI for their cryptographic functions will only need to pass a cursory export review, rather than having to endure the whole process.

Certificate server

Certificate server is a set of services that implements a Public Key Infrastructure (PKI) to create key public key pairs, generate certificates, import externally generated certificates, and revoke expired or invalid certificates.

PKI is also referred to as *asymmetric encryption*. Asymmetric encryption algorithms were developed in the 1970s as a way to avoid having to transmit cryptographic keys to those who needed to be able to decrypt secure messages. Asymmetric encryption utilizes a mathematically related key pair instead of a single key in order to provide the encryption and decryption capabilities. When a message is encrypted using an asymmetric key it can only be decrypted using the other half of the key pair.

In a PKI, each person is assigned a key pair and one of those keys is published as the public key (see Figure 6.14). The other is carefully guarded as the private key. If someone wants to send you a secure message, they encrypt it using your public key and send it out. They know the only person who can decrypt that message is the person with the other half of the key pair — you!

Switching to the receiving end of that secure message (see Figure 6.15), you decrypt the message using your private key and find out that it is a note from the sender (except that you can't be sure they were actually the person that authored it. What if someone is attempting to impersonate the sender by sending you a "forged" message? Well, PKI also solves this problem by providing the ability to electronically "sign" a message.

F I G U R E   6.14   *Asymmetric encryption in action*

F I G U R E   6.15   *Electronic certificates in action*

The next hurdle for PKI is creating repositories for all of the public keys that are in use. Public keys are stored, together with vital statistics about the owner, in a standard certificate format known as X.509. These certificates can then be stored in large databases known as Certificate Authorities (CA). Certificate server provides organizations the ability to use eDirectory as a CA. Cryptographic keys and certificates can be created and/or managed by eDirectory. Certificate server can also interact with external entities such as Verisign or Entrust through the use of standard communication protocols and certificate formats. Certificate server supports the dominant standards in the security space. You can make eDirectory the hub for all their security needs from secure authentication and resource access, to secure communications with external parties and non-repudiation of business critical communications.

Creating server certificates

When NetWare 6 is installed, all the necessary security objects are created automatically, including an Organizational Certificate Authority (CA) and the necessary key pairs to support cryptographic activities. During the installation, two different server certificates are created, one for DNS and one for IP. These certificates are used to create secure SSL connections with client workstations. You can also create other server certificates, as needed, to support additional secure services on your NetWare 6 server. To create a server certificate, complete the following steps:

1. Make sure you are logged in to the eDirectory tree as an administrator with supervisory rights to the container in which the server resides.

2. Launch ConsoleOne and browse to the server's container.

3. Right-click the container object and select New ➪ Object.

4. Select NDSPKI:Key Material from the list of possible objects and click OK.

5. After the Server Certificate Wizard opens, specify the requested information and click Next.

   - *Certificate name*: Specify the name of your server certificate. This name will be combined with the server name to create a unique name for the Server Certificate object.

   - *Creation method*: Select the method for creating the certificate. Standard uses typical certificate parameters, while Custom lets you define each option manually. Import lets you specify a PKCS#12 file from which to get the necessary data.

Follow the prompts from there to complete the installation. If you select Custom, be prepared to supply the following information:

- ▶ CA that will sign the certificate (default: your Organizational CA)
- ▶ Key size (default: 2048 bits)
- ▶ Key type (default: SSL)
- ▶ The server to which the certificate will be assigned
- ▶ Algorithm for creating the certificate (default: SHA-1)
- ▶ How long the certificate will remain valid (default: 2 years)
- ▶ Certificate root (default: your Organizational certificate)

Creating user certificates

In order to make use of a PKI, users must have key pairs and certificates of their own. Complete the following steps to create a user certificate:

1. Make sure you are logged in to the eDirectory tree as a user with supervisory rights to the User objects as well as rights to read objects in the security container.

2. Launch ConsoleOne and browse to the User object that will host this certificate.

3. Right-click the User object and select Properties. Double-click the Security tab and select the Certificates subpage.

4. Click Create to open the User Certificate Wizard. Specify the requested information and click Next.

- *Server:* Specify the server that will generate the cryptographic key pair.

- *Certificate nickname*: Specify the name of the user certificate. This name will be combined with the User object name to create a unique Certificate object name.

- *Creation method*: Select the method for creating the certificate. Standard uses typical certificate parameters, while Custom lets you define each option manually.

Follow the prompts from there to create the user certificate. If you select Custom, be prepared to provide the same type of information as previously specified for the server certificate.

Novell Advanced Audit

Audit is an important feature for monitoring the status of your network security. An audit service can tell you how the network is being used and by whom. It can track important or sensitive actions and help identify potential security breaches.

Prior to NetWare 6, Novell offered a server-based audit utility known as AuditCon. AuditCon was a framework for creating a NetWare-based audit service. Now, with the release of NetWare 6, Novell is beginning to move away from a server-based audit solution to a network-based audit solution integrated with eDirectory.

Novell Advanced Audit Service (NAAS) is the first release of this directory-enabled audit tool. It enables you to audit services running on the network. NAAS uses Novell eDirectory for storing policies and configuration information, and for managing access to the audited data. The main components of NAAS are:

▶ *Audit utility*: Provides a user interface for communicating with the audit framework. Using this utility, you can configure and view the audit policies, and view the audit data stored in the audit database.

▶ *Audit agent*: Resides on each machine that is hosting the services you want to audit. The agent performs the following tasks:

  • Collects audit events from the audited services based on the policy.

  • Stores the audit records locally and periodically forwards them to the Audit server.

▶ *Audit server*: Collects the audit records from the audit agents and stores them in the database. The Audit server also services queries from the Audit utility for reading these audit records and performs the necessary access control.

▶ *Audit database*: Stores the audit records.

For more information on NAAS, see the Novell on-line documentation.

CHAPTER 7

NetWare Printing Services

Instant Access

Installing and configuring NDPS

▶ Install NDPS as part of the server installation. It can be installed after the fact through Deployment Manager or the graphical server console.

▶ Configure NDPS broker, Print Services manager, and Printer objects through iManage ⇨ iPrint Management.

▶ After NDPS broker and Print Services manager are created, load BROKER.NLM and NDPSM.NLM on your NetWare 6 server to enable NetWare print services.

▶ Use the Manage Printers page in iManage to configure printer objects.

▶ Use the RPM Configuration page in iManage to configure automatic printer support for workstations.

Working with iPrint

▶ iPrint support is installed simultaneously with NDPS. To configure an NDPS printer for iPrint support, use the Manage Printers page in iManage to enable IPP support on that printer. IPPSRVR.NLM will be loaded automatically on the NetWare server that hosts the Print Services manager for that printer.

▶ The iPrint client is required to access and manage iPrint printers. Install the client by going to the iPrint home page on your NetWare 6 server at `http://<server_IP_address or DNS_name>:631/ipp`.

Defining print options

▶ To tell the printer how to print a job (paper form to use, format, and so on), open iManage ⇨ Manage Printer. Specify the printer and select the Configurations page to change printer configuration.

Printing jobs

▶ To print files from within an application, simply follow the application's normal printing procedures (making sure the application is configured to print to a network printer).

▶ To cancel or move a print job, open iManage ⇨ Manage Printer. Specify the printer and select the Printer Control ⇨ Jobs page.

How NetWare Printing Works

NetWare print services allow your network users to share printers that are connected to the network. With NetWare print services loaded, you can increase productivity and save on hardware expenses by allowing users to share a smaller number of printers than you would have to buy if each user had a standalone printer. (You may also be able to buy a single, more sophisticated printer instead of multiple lesser-quality printers.)

Another benefit is that users can send their print jobs to different printers for different purposes without having to copy the file to some other system before printing it. NetWare print services also enable you to prioritize print jobs, so important print jobs are sent to the printer ahead of less-important print jobs.

In standalone printing:

- ▶ A printer is connected directly to the serial or parallel port (usually LPT1) on the workstation.

- ▶ When the user prints a file, the print job goes from the application to the print driver, which formats the job for the specific printer. (The print driver is software that converts the print job into a format that the printer can understand.)

- ▶ Next the print job goes to the LPT port, and then directly to the printer.

- ▶ Often, the application has to wait until the print job is finished before it can resume working.

With NetWare print services:

- ▶ NetWare 6 provides two different ways to set up your printing services: NDPS (Novell Distributed Print Services) and iPrint, for standards-based printing that does not require the Novell client. If you are using queue-based printing from previous versions of NetWare, NDPS and iPrint can coexist with your legacy queue-based environment while you plan for a conversion to the new system.

- ▶ After setup, the print job goes to the network instead of directly to the printer, though this process is transparent to users.

- ▶ Then the network takes care of sending the print job to the correct printer.

NDPS is a new printing system designed by Novell, Hewlett-Packard, and Xerox that provides advanced printing features. Queue-based printing is the older system used in all previous versions of NetWare.

NDPS provides nominal support for queue-based printing. You can install NDPS and have it support existing print queues. However, because of the additional management overhead associated with queue-based printing, your best bet is to use this support as a transition mechanism to migrate toward NDPS and iPrint as your standard print environments, rather than continuing to use print queues through NDPS.

The first half of this chapter explains NDPS. The second half of this chapter presents the powerful new features of iPrint.

NDPS Printing

Novell Distributed Print Services (NDPS) is the powerful printing system first released with NetWare 5. Developed in conjunction with Hewlett-Packard and Xerox, NDPS provides normal network printing capabilities along with several features that weren't available in queue-based printing:

- Bidirectional communication so you can communicate with the printer, and the printer can communicate with you

- Event notification, so the printer can notify appropriate personnel when something occurs (such as the printer running out of toner)

- Automatic downloading of printer drivers and other printing resources to workstations that need them (such as fonts, banners, or printer definition files)

In addition, the printer manufacturer can embed NDPS software directly into a printer in order to provide smarter, more customizable features for network print users. These printers are called "NDPS-aware" to distinguish them from existing printers that do not have NDPS software embedded. There are currently a large number of NDPS-aware printers, and the list is still growing.

NetWare 6 no longer supports queue-based printing, but NDPS and queue-based printing systems can coexist on the same network. So if you want to take time to transition from your legacy queue-based system to NDPS, you can do so in a phased, orderly manner.

Understanding NDPS Printing

Before installing NDPS printing, it's important to have a good understanding of the components that make up NDPS. The following sections explain the NDPS components and how to use those components with the types of printers you have.

NDPS components

In a NetWare network, you can have multiple printers all working at the same time, and users from all over the network may be sending print jobs to those printers simultaneously. To take care of all that traffic and potential conflicts, NDPS uses the following software components:

► *NDPS printer agents*: A printer agent is a software entity that manages a printer. Every printer must have a suitable printer agent. NDPS-aware printers have their printer agents embedded. All other printers must have a printer agent created on the server. The printer agent for a printer performs the following tasks:

- It manages the printer's print jobs.

- It answers client queries about print jobs or printer attributes (such as whether the printer supports color printing).

- It receives notification from the printer when something goes wrong, or when a requested event occurs.

- It services existing queues from queue-based printing setups, so the NDPS printer can print jobs from those queues.

► *Gateways*: If a printer is not NDPS-aware and requires that a printer agent be installed on the server, a gateway must also be installed. The gateway translates NDPS commands into a language the printer can interpret. NetWare 6 includes vendor-specific gateways from Epson, Hewlett Packard, Kyocera, and Xerox, in addition to the generic Novell gateway. Manufacturer-specific gateways will offer more features customized for their specific printers. Novell's generic gateway will work for all printers, but provides fewer bells and whistles. For more information about vendor-specific gateways, consult the Novell on-line documentation or check the documentation from the specific vendor.

NOTE

As mentioned previously, gateways aren't necessary for NDPS-aware printers (those that have their own printer agents embedded).

▶ *NDPS manager*: The NDPS manager controls all the printer agents on a server. (If you're familiar with queue-based printing, the NDPS manager is similar to the print server.) If all of your printers are NDPS-aware and have embedded printer agents, you will not need NDPS manager. It's required only for printer agents that reside on the server.

▶ *NDPS broker*: The NDPS broker provides centralized management of printing services for all the printers on the network. By default, NDPS brokers are created automatically during the NetWare 6 server installation. However, because every server doesn't need to be a broker, the installation program analyzes the network to determine whether or not a broker needs to be installed. If an existing broker is within three hops of the server you're currently installing, the installation program will not install a broker automatically. If the nearest existing broker is four or more hops away, the installation program will install a broker on this server. In addition to the "three-hop" guideline, there may be other situations where you want to have the installation program create a broker. For example, you may want to have two brokers on a network for reliability—if one server goes down, the broker still exists on the other server. The NDPS broker provides three services:

- *Resource management service*: This service stores printing resources (mainly printer drivers, fonts, banners, and printer definition files) in a central location on the network. When a workstation needs a new printer driver, for example, the broker automatically downloads that driver from this central location.

- *Event notification service*: This service receives the event notifications that come from the printer agents and sends the notification out to users via predetermined methods. Users (or the administrator, or anyone else that has been specified) can be notified of printer events by NetWare pop-up messages on a workstation screen, in log files, via GroupWise email, or by other delivery methods that can be defined or developed.

- *Service registry service*: All NDPS printers advertise their availability and attributes, such as make, model, and address, through this service.

TIP

If your network is spread across a multiple geographical locations, connected by WAN links, you should plan to have a broker at each site. This reduces WAN traffic and lets the broker function more efficiently.

Which NDPS components do you need?

To summarize, if all the printers on your network are NDPS-aware, meaning they have NDPS printer agents embedded in them, the only NDPS software component you need on your network is an NDPS broker. The broker handles event notification, advertisement of printer availability, and automatic downloading of printer drivers and other resources. (You may need more than one broker, depending on the size of your network.)

If at least some of your printers are non-NDPS printers, you need to create:

▸ A printer agent for each non-NDPS printer

▸ A gateway so the non-NDPS printer can communicate with NDPS

▸ An NDPS manager to manage the printer agents on the server

▸ An NDPS broker

Planning NDPS Printing

As you plan your NDPS printing setup, keep in mind the following information about NDPS:

▸ NDPS supports both IP and IPX. If both protocols are available, NDPS defaults to using IP.

▸ NDPS can support legacy queue-based printing so you can plan an orderly transition to an NDPS printing environment. If you already have queues created from an existing system, you can assign a printer agent to accept jobs from one or more of those queues.

▸ To use NDPS printing natively, workstations must have the Novell client installed. However, NetWare 6 now offers iPrint, which is a standards-based thin-client printing solution that does not require the Novell client. iPrint is discussed later in this chapter.

▸ NDPS is managed from iManage in NetWare 6. While there is still some management capability from the console-based NDPS utilities that were first introduced in NetWare 5, iManage should become your best friend for managing your printing services.

If you consider each of the following suggestions before beginning the installation process, your NDPS installation may go more smoothly:

▸ If you're upgrading a network from a previous version of NetWare, you may find it easiest to install NDPS and then to make sure that all of the existing queues are assigned to new NDPS printer agents. That way, all of your users can continue to print normally using their existing client software on their workstations. You can then plan and execute the upgrade of user workstations to the new NDPS-aware client software much more efficiently.

▶ Although NDPS doesn't use print queues natively, you may still want to configure each printer agent so it has space on a volume to store files that are waiting to be printed. (This is called *job spooling*.)

▶ Decide which printers you want to be available to users' workstations automatically (which basically consists of automatically downloading the appropriate printer driver to the workstations). Make sure those printers' drivers are added to the broker's Resource Management database.

NOTE

If a user needs a printer driver that isn't in the database, he or she can install the driver from a diskette or other site.

▶ Plan which servers need to have an NDPS broker installed. Plan for at least one broker per geographic site (two brokers per site is better, in case one server goes down). Also, any server should be no more than three hops away from a broker.

▶ Create an NDPS Manager object on each server that will control NDPS printers. (One NDPS manager can support an unlimited number of printer agents.) You may want to assign printer agents on one server to multiple NDPS Manager objects (on other servers) to make sure that if one server goes down, network users can still print. Assigning printer agents to multiple NDPS managers also helps balance the load of printing traffic. (However, you should keep printer agents assigned to NDPS managers within the same geographical site, so that printing traffic isn't going across phone lines unnecessarily.)

▶ Once you have fully transitioned your printing environment to NDPS, you no longer need to provide the client-side support for print queues on your network. This means that you can remove all CAPTURE commands from batch files, login scripts, AUTOEXEC.BAT files, or other locations.

The following sections explain how to install and manage NDPS printing on your network.

Installing NDPS

NDPS is normally installed during the NetWare 6 installation, since printing is a core network service. However, NDPS can be installed after the fact from either Deployment Manager or the graphical server console. To install NDPS from Deployment Manager, complete the following steps:

1. Insert the NetWare 6 Operating System CD-ROM at the workstation. Run NWDEPLOY.EXE from the root of the CD-ROM.

2. Open Post-Installation tasks and select Install NetWare 6 products.

3. At the Target Server screen, select the server to which you want to install NDPS and click Next. Authenticate as an admin user at the root of the tree.

4. At the Components screen, click Clear All. Check the box next to iPrint/NDPS and click Next.

5. (Conditional) Choose how you want to resolve any IP resource conflicts and click Next. If you have other IP-based services already installed on your server, such as the Apache Web server, the Port Resolver software in NetWare 6 will ask you to configure the IP environment to avoid address conflicts, as shown in Figure 7.1.

    • *Single IP address*: Choose this option if you want to run multiple services through a single IP address on the server and choose different TCP ports for each service. For Web-based services this requires that you specify the port number as part of the URL (for example: 137.65.192.1:631). For example, since Apache Web server will grab the default SSL port of 443, you will want to specify an alternative address for use by NDPS if you choose to use the Single IP address method.

    • *Multiple IP addresses*: Choose this option if you want to bind multiple IP addresses to your NetWare 6 server and assign a different address to each service. This lets each service use its default TCP port(s). If you are using DNS to access NetWare 6 services, this option requires you to assign an appropriate DNS name to each IP address that you create. This method seems to avoid potential problems better than the Single IP address method, since it eliminates the issue of port conflicts all together.

For more information on managing DNS with NetWare 6 see Chapter 5.

X-REF

F I G U R E   7.1   *NetWare 6 Port Resolver at work*

6. At the Summary screen, click Finish. If you installed NDPS during the NetWare 6 installation, an NDPS Broker object was installed in your eDirectory tree by default. All three of the broker's services (resource management service, event notification service, and service registry service) are enabled.

TIP

If you want to turn off one or more of the broker's services, or if you want to prevent the broker from being installed on this server, click the Customize button on the Summary screen. From there, you can choose NDPS and make any modifications before the installation proceeds.

7. When the installation of NDPS is complete, click Close. Close Deployment Manager by clicking Cancel ⇨ Yes.

Configuring NDPS

There are several steps involved in configuring your NDPS printing environment. You configure and manage your NDPS environment through iManage. The following sections explain how to:

► Set up the NDPS broker on a server and add printer drivers to it if necessary.

► Create the NDPS manager.

► Decide whether or not you need to support legacy queue-based printing. (NDPS printers can be configured to service print queues, if necessary.) This is recommended only as a transitional strategy and not as an on-going print solution.

► Install printer support on workstations.

Configuring the NDPS broker

If you installed NDPS during the NetWare 6 server installation, you will be able to toggle through the available screens on the server console and find an NDPS Broker screen. This screen shows you that the broker NLM is loaded and active and that the services you selected, all three by default, are enabled.

If you have installed NDPS after the fact, you will need to manually create a Broker object in your eDirectory tree and load BROKER.NLM on your NetWare 6 server. To do this complete the following steps:

1. Launch Web Manager and select your server name under eDirectory iManage. Log in as admin and select iPrint Management in the navigation bar to open the NDPS management options.

2. Select Create Broker. At the Create Broker page, provide the necessary information and click OK.

   - *Broker name*: Specify a name for the Broker object.

   - *Container name*: Specify a location for the Broker object in the eDirectory tree.

   - *Enable services*: Select the services that you want to load on this broker. Broker services have been described previously. If you enable the Resource Management Service (RMS), you will need to specify the volume on which RMS information will be stored.

3. At the Operation Succeeded screen, click OK to complete the process.

4. Load BROKER.NLM on the appropriate server using the following syntax. Table 7.1 lists the switches you can use when loading BROKER.NLM.

```
load broker <broker name>/[startup parameter]
```

T A B L E 7.1	*BROKER.NLM Load Switches*
STARTUP PARAMETER	**DESCRIPTION**
noui	Loads the broker without displaying the user interface.
noipx	The NDPS manager will not support the IPX protocol.
noip	The NDPS manager will not support the IP protocol.
allowdup	The NLM will not check for two brokers using the same Broker object.

TIP

You should modify the AUTOEXEC.NCF to load BROKER.NLM automatically whenever the server restarts.

Once the broker is loaded, you need to load the iPrint client in order to perform certain management tasks from iManage. To do this, complete the following steps:

1. Launch your browser and point it to the URL for your NDPS service. For example: `http://137.65.192.81:631`.

NOTE

If you have installed NDPS to its own IP address you will not have to specify the TCP port number. You could also use the DNS name that has been assigned to the NDPS IP address, if one has been assigned.

2. At the iPrint client message screen, select OK.

3. At the File Download screen, select Run this program from its current location and click OK. At the security warning, click Yes.

4. At the Setup Language screen, select the language for the installation and click OK.

5. At the iPrint Client Setup screen, click Next. Accept the license agreement by clicking Yes.

6. At the Program Folder screen, click Next to install the iPrint client to its default location.

7. When the installation completes, click Finish to reboot your workstation.

Adding printer drivers or other resources to the broker   NetWare 6 ships with many printer drivers for common printers. However, as new printers and updated drivers are released by printer manufacturers, you may need to add a driver that is not included with the default set that shipped with NetWare 6.

You can also add new banner pages to the broker using the same procedure. To see the list of existing printer drivers and banners, and to add a new driver or banner to the broker, complete the following steps:

1. Launch Web Manager and select your server name under eDirectory iManage. Log in as admin. Select iPrint Management.

2. Click Manage Broker. Specify or browse to your NDPS Broker object and click OK.

3. Select the Resource Management Service tab to add a resource to your broker, as shown in Figure 7.2.

Resource Management Service tab in iManage

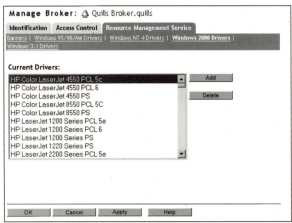

4. Select the subpage for the type of resource you want to add. A list appears, showing all resources of that type that are currently loaded.

5. Click Add and browse to the driver you want to add. Click OK and follow the prompts to add the driver or banner to your broker.

The new driver or banner will appear in the list of available resources in the Resource Management database.

Disabling a broker service   By default, all three of the broker's services are enabled when the broker is installed. If you want to disable (or re-enable) a service, do so from the NDPS Broker screen in the server console. To disable a broker service, complete the following steps:

1. From the server console prompt, press Ctrl+Esc to open the list of current screens and select NDPS Broker.

2. Highlight the service you want to disable, or enable, and press Enter.

3. Confirm your choice by selecting Yes.

Disable a broker service only if you're sure you do not need that service on your network or if that service is available on another server that is no more than three hops away.

Creating an NDPS manager on a server

To create an NDPS manager on your server, you have to create an NDPS Manager object in the eDirectory tree and then load NDPSM.NLM on the server. To do this, complete the following steps:

1. Launch Web Manager and select your server name under eDirectory iManage. Log in as admin and select iPrint Management in the navigation bar to open the NDPS management options.

2. Select Create Print Service Manager. At the Create Manager page, provide the necessary information and click OK.

- *Manager name*: Specify a name for the Broker object.
- *Container name*: Specify a location for the Broker object in the eDirectory tree.
- *Database volume*: Specify the NetWare volume where you want the print services manager database to reside.

3. At the Request Succeeded screen, click OK to return to the iManage home page.

4. From console of the appropriate server, load NDPSM.NLM using the following syntax (see Table 7.2 for the switches to use when loading NDPSM.NLM):

```
load ndpsm <Manager name> /[startup parameter]
```

T A B L E 7.2	*NDPSM.NLM Load Switches*
PARAMETER	**DESCRIPTION**
nodatabase	Load the NDPS manager without opening the database. The Database Options menu is displayed, which lets you examine, backup, restore, resynchronize, and uninstall the NDPS manager database. See earlier sections in this chapter for more information about the NDPS manager database.
noipx	The NDPS manager will not support the IPX protocol.
noip	The NDPS manager will not support the IP protocol.

PARAMETER	DESCRIPTION
dbvolume=full_DNS_volume name	Download the database from eDirectory and reconnect pointers to the local server where the command is executed. This is useful for moving the NDPS manager to a new volume.
dbvolume=nocheck	The NDPS manager will not validate that the database volume is local. This is used with clustering.
setens=broker_name	Set the event notification service to the specified broker for all printers associated this NDPS manager.
setrms=broker_name	Set the resource management service to the specified broker for all printers associated this NDPS manager.
qloadbalance	The NDPS manager evenly distributes the waiting print jobs among printers that are ready. This is used when pooling printers.
iprinton	The IPP attribute is turned on for all printers associated with the associated NDPS manager.
dnsname=NDPSM_DNS_name	This sets a DNS name to an NDPS Manager object. You will need to include the DNS information in your DNS lookup tables. If you included the DNS name before deploying printing with this manager, then you can easily move the NDPS manager to another server without disrupting printing.

You should modify the AUTOEXEC.NCF to load NDPSM.NLM automatically whenever the server restarts.

TIP

Creating network printers

To create an NDPS printer you must first create an NDPS Printer object in the eDirectory tree. (You must have already created an NDPS Manager object.)

You can configure the NDPS Printer object so that it services existing print queues, if desired.

To use iManage to create an NDPS printer, complete the following steps:

1. Launch Web Manager and select your server name under eDirectory iManage. Log in as admin.

2. Select iPrint Management and click Create Printer.

3. At the Create Printer page, shown in Figure 7.3, specify the required information and click Next.

   • *Printer name*: Specify a name for the Printer object.

   • *Container name*: Specify a context where the Printer object will be located.

   • *Manager name*: Specify the name of the NDPS manager that will manage this printer.

   • *Gateway type*: Specify the gateway that you want to use to communicate with your printer here. Select a third-party gateway if you know that is what you are using. In most cases, the Novell IPP gateway will be the right one. The Novell LPR gateway is for UNIX/Linux print support.

F I G U R E   7.3   *Creating an NDPS printer in iManage*

4. Specify the IP address or DNS name of your printer and click Next.

5. Select the appropriate printer driver(s) from the driver lists and click Next. You can select a driver for each type of Windows workstation platform: Windows NT/2000, Windows 95/98/Me, and Windows 3.1. These are the drivers that will be automatically downloaded to the client workstations when they install the printer.

6. At the Create Printer request succeeded message, click OK.

Once the printer is created, make sure spooling is configured properly by completing the following steps:

1. From iManage, select iPrint Configuration and click Manage Printer.

2. Specify the printer you just created and click OK.

3. At the Manage Printer page, select the Configuration tab and choose the Spooling page (see Figure 7.4).

4. From the Spooling page you can set the location of the spooling area (it defaults to the same location as the NDPS manager), restrict the amount of space available for spooling, and determine the print scheduling algorithm (default is First In, First Out).

F I G U R E   7.4   *Manage Printer pages in iManage*

If you need to service legacy print queues, select the Client Support tab from the Manage Printer page and click the QMS Support subpage. From there you can specify the print queues that you want this printer to service. NDPS offers PSERVER emulation so you don't need to load PSERVER.NLM on the server.

Once NDPS printers have been installed, managing them is relatively easy. Everything you need is located in iManage. The Printer Management pages shown in Figure 7.4 are a one-stop shop for managing user access, printer configuration, and print service support.

Installing printer support on workstations

When you create NDPS printers, NDPS allows you to designate specific printer drivers to be automatically downloaded and installed on workstations, so the users don't have to worry about installing their own printer support. The printers you specify will appear automatically on the user's installed printers list. This feature is known as Remote Printer Management (RPM). You can also use Remote Printer Management to designate a default printer and remove printers from workstations.

NOTE

You aren't required to designate printers to download and install automatically. Users can also install printer support manually. However, you will probably find that it saves time to designate automatic downloads instead.

With Remote Printer Management, you configure printer drivers and other information you want to be installed. When a user logs in, the workstation software checks the user's container object for any new printer information. If new printer information (such as a new driver to be downloaded) exists, the workstation is automatically updated.

Automatically installing printer support You can access Remote Printer Management from iManage by completing the following steps:

1. From iManage, select iPrint Management and click RPM Configuration.

2. Specify the object for which you want to configure Remote Printer Management and click OK. Valid object selections include Organization, Organizational Unit, Group, or User. Your choice will determine how broadly the RPM rules are applied.

3. At the RPM Configuration page, as shown in Figure 7.5, specify your desired configuration and click OK. You can specify enable/disable RPM, specify printers to install automatically, select a default printer, and even specify printers that should be removed if currently installed.

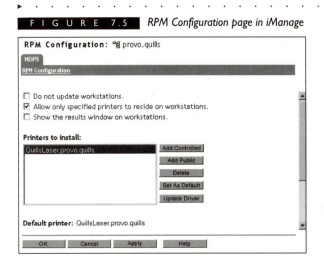

F I G U R E 7.5 *RPM Configuration page in iManage*

Manually installing printer support   If a required printer driver isn't automatically downloaded, users can still install the printer support on their workstations manually. This involves using the standard Windows printer installation tools to locate, specify, and install the appropriate print drivers.

This method requires knowledge about the printer they are trying to install and access to appropriate print drivers, which are often available from Windows printer libraries.

iPrint

As you can see from the previous sections, NDPS makes it much easier for network users to use network printing services. New with NetWare 6, iPrint takes ease of use one step further and aligns it with Novell's One Net initiative.

iPrint puts a Web interface on Novell's printing services and removes the dependence on the Novell client to access NetWare-based printing services. With iPrint, mobile employees, business partners, and even customers can be given access to your printers through existing Internet connections. iPrint uses the Internet Printing Protocol (IPP), an industry standard, to make it possible to seamlessly print over the Internet, thus making location-based printing a reality.

The benefits of IPP include the following:

► Enjoys broad vendor support

► Works over local networks as well as the Internet

► Provides encrypted print services via SSL or TLS

► Provides accessibility to print services from any platform (Windows, Macintosh, Linux, UNIX, and so on)

However, because iPrint is implemented on the foundation of NDPS, you get all the advantages of robust network printing services coupled with the interoperability and ease-of-use of an Internet standard. In addition to the benefits of IPP, iPrint offers the following capabilities:

► Global access to printers managed through eDirectory

► Web-based printer location tool and driver installation

► Ability to print from anywhere to anywhere

► Web-based user controls and printer status

► The benefit that printers don't have to be IPP-aware to function with iPrint

Installing iPrint

iPrint is installed together with NDPS. Since iPrint runs on NDPS, once you have NDPS configured, your iPrint environment is also largely configured. That's why I have put the NDPS information first in this chapter. You will do all NDPS configuration prior to configuring the iPrint specifics. The iPrint implementation of the IPP includes three main components:

► A print provider and a set of browser plug-ins that are installed on a user's workstation. The Novell client is not required.

► The IPPSRVR.NLM runs on your NetWare 6 server. If you configure an NDPS printer to support IPP printer, the NDPS Print Services manager automatically loads this NLM.

► HTML pages from which to install the iPrint client software and printers, as well as viewing and managing print jobs.

Setting up DNS for the Print Services manager

Each server that is running the Print Services manager loads IPPSRVR.NLM when iPrint is enabled for a printer associated with that manager. To provide additional stability to the printing environment, you should assign a DNS name for each Print Services manager that will host IPP printers. That way, if the Print Services manager is moved to a different server, the iPrint URLs for associated IPP printers will still work.

To enable DNS for each Print Services manager, first load NDPSM.NLM with the /dnsname command line switch using the following syntax:

```
NDPSM <NDPS_Manager> /dnsname=<DNS_Name_for_NDPS_Manager>
```

Once the Print Services manager is loaded with a DNS name, add a new resource record (A Record) to your DNS name server that links the new DNS name to the IP address of the NetWare 6 server hosting the Print Services manager.

For more information on configuring DNS see Chapter 5.

X-REF

Configuring iPrint printers

iPrint printers are just NDPS printers with a couple of additional features enabled. If you already have an NDPS printer installed, complete the following steps to configure it to support IPP. If you are installing the printer object itself, you can make these selections simultaneously with the NDPS printer installation, which was described in a previous section in this chapter.

1. From iManage, select iPrint Management and click Manage Printer.

2. At the NDPS Printer page, specify the Printer object for which you want to enable IPP printing and click OK.

3. At the Manage Printer page, select the Client Support tab and click the IPP Support page, as shown in Figure 7.6.

FIGURE 7.6 *IPP Support page for enabling iPrint printers in iManage*

4. Select Enable IPP access.

5. (Optional) If you want users to have to authenticate through eDirectory prior to using the printer, select Requires security. This is a good idea if the printer is going to be available over a public network such as the Internet.

6. Click Apply. The name that appears in the Accepted IPP URL(s) box is used when the printer is installed on a workstation.

7. Click OK to update the printer settings. IPPSRVR.NLM is automatically loaded on the server where the printer's Print Services manager is running.

TIP

To disable IPP print support on a printer, simply repeat the previous steps and uncheck Enable IPP access. Click Apply or OK to save your changes.

Enabling iPrint on all printers

Instead of enabling IPP support one printer at a time, you can enable all printers assigned with a particular Print Services manager. To do this, complete the following steps:

1. From iManage, select iPrint Management and click Enable iPrint Access.

2. Specify the Print Service manager for which you want to enable IPP printing.

3. At the Enable iPrint Access page, check the box next to Enabled and click OK. This will enable IPP on all printers assigned to this Print Service manager. You can also select printers individually by checking the box from the Enabled column next to each printer you want iPrint enabled.

4. (Optional) Use the same checkbox procedure in the Secure column to enable secure printing as needed for printers associated with this Print Services manager.

X-REF

More information on securing your printing services is provided later in this chapter.

Accessing iPrint Printers

In order for users to use iPrint, they need two components:

▶ The Novell iPrint client

▶ A printer to which they can print

When a user selects a printer to be installed by iPrint, iPrint checks to see if the Novell iPrint client is installed. If it is not installed, iPrint will walk the user through the client installation. Following this, the printer driver is downloaded and the printer installed in the user's Printer folder.

iPrint client files and printers can be quickly and easily installed from a Web page.

TIP

The iPrint client and appropriate printer drivers can also be distributed using ZENworks for Desktops. If you have this additional Novell product, consult the Novell on-line documentation for more information on automating client delivery and installation with ZENworks for Desktops.

The iPrint client has the following requirements for installation:

▶ Windows 95/98/Me or Windows NT/2000

▶ Web browser with JavaScript enabled, such as:

• Microsoft Internet Explorer 5.0 or later

• Netscape 4.76 (iPrint is not supported on Netscape 6)

From such a workstation, users browse to the iPrint URL, which, by default, is the following: `http://<server_IP_address or DNS_name>:631/ipp`

Figure 7.7 shows a sample iPrint Printers home page. If users will print through a secure port using SSL, specify port 443 rather than 631. This requires users to authenticate using their eDirectory usernames and passwords.

The iPrint Printers home page displays a listing of available printers and a link to install the iPrint client. Users simply select Install iPrint Client and follow the prompts to complete the client installation. If they try to install a printer before installing the iPrint client, they will be prompted to install the client first.

NOTE

The iPrint client requires the workstation to reboot to complete the installation. The iPrint client can be removed through the standard Remove Programs option in the Windows Control Panel. There is also an Uninstall option under the Novell iPrint program group in the Start menu.

▶ • • • • • • • • • • • • • ◀

F I G U R E   7 . 7   *Sample iPrint Printers home page*

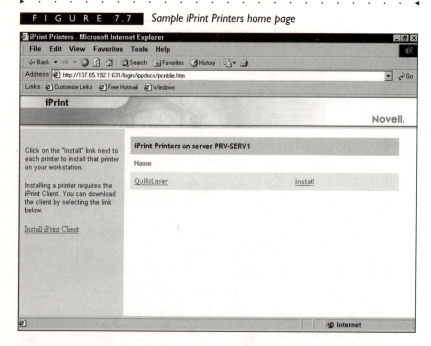

After the client is installed, users return to the same iPrint URL to install the necessary printer support. If you have associated a printer driver with each of your iPrint printers, it is automatically installed on the user's workstation. If a printer driver already exists on the workstation, it will be overwritten.

When the printer driver installs, a Printer icon is added to the user's Printers folder. From that point on, users access the printer through all the normal avenues. Because iPrint printers are also NDPS printers, you can make use of the Remote Printer Management (RPM) settings to specify default printers, remove existing printers, and so forth. For more information on RPM, see the sections on NDPS earlier in this chapter.

Default printer driver options

You can control how printer driver options are set when the printer driver is installed on a workstation. Printer driver defaults are kept in the INST.HTM file, which is stored in SYS:LOGIN\IPPDOCS on your iPrint server. Complete the following steps to change the printer driver default settings:

I. Open SYS:\LOGIN\IPPDOCS\INST.HTM using any text editor.

2. Search for the section heading PARAM NAME=driver-options, as shown in Figure 7.8. The setting occurs twice: once for Internet Explorer and once for Netscape browsers.

Printer driver options portion of INST.HTM

3. Replace the value after the colon (:) with the desired parameter for each option you want to change. Supported parameter values are listed in Table 7.3.

4. Save and close INST.HTM.

T A B L E   7 . 3   *Supported Printer Parameters for iPrint Printers*

PARAMETER	SUPPORTED VALUES
Orientation	landscape, portrait
Paper size	letter, lettersmall, tabloid, ledger, legal, statement, executive, A3, A4, A4small, A5, B4, B5, folio, quatro, 10x14, 11x17, note, env_10, env_12, env_14, csheet, dsheet, esheet, env_dl, env_c5, env_c4, env_c3, env_c65, env_b5, env_b6, env_italy, env_monarch, env_personal, fanfold_us, fanfold_std_german, fanfold_lgl_german, iso_b4, japanese_postcard, 9x11, 10x11, 15x11, env_invite, letter_extra, legal_extra, tabloid_extra, A4_extra, letter_extra_transverse, a_plus, b_plus, letter_plus, A4_plus, A5_transverse, B5_transverse, A3_extra, A5_extra, B5_extra, A2, A3_transverse, A3_extra_transverse

(continued)

TABLE 7.3	Supported Printer Parameters for iPrint Printers (continued)
PARAMETER	**SUPPORTED VALUES**
Copies	Enter the number of copies you want printed
Color	yes=color, no or false=monochrome
Duplex	simplex, horizontal, vertical
Collate	yes or true=collate, no=do not collate

iPrint client updates

Periodically, users will need to update their iPrint client. Each time a user starts his or her workstation; the iPrint client checks with the default printer to see if a newer version of the iPrint client exists. If necessary, a newer version of the client can be installed. You can control how this update takes place with the IPRINT.INI file.

IPRINT.INI is stored in SYS:\LOGIN\IPPDOCS on each server where iPrint is installed. It lets you specify whether or not the user should be prompted before a new client is installed, or if the update should be a "hands free" process.

Descriptive text for each entry in the IPRINT.INI is included in the file. You can view and edit the file using a text editor.

IMPORTANT

The IPRINT.INI file should be synchronized across all servers where iPrint is running.

Location-Based Printing

Location-based printing is one of the key values of iPrint. It lets users easily locate and install printers using one of two methods:

▶ *Printer list views*: With list views, you configure printer lists so they make the most sense for your users, such as by building, by office location, or by eDirectory context.

▶ *Printer maps*: Using the iPrint Map Designer, you can create maps of printer locations by using drag-and-drop technology. Once created, the maps are posted on a Web server for users to access. By looking at the maps, they locate a printer close to their location and simply click the Printer icon. The printer driver and iPrint client, if necessary, are then installed on the users workstation.

Creating printer lists

iPrint provides a default list of printers organized by Print Services manager. In order to create a custom list, you modify the iPrint HTML page, creating links to individual printers' IPP URLs. As previously mentioned, when you enable IPP support, a URL is listed in the accepted IPP URL list. This is the URL you will specify when creating a customized printer list.

Using the iPrint Map Designer tool, you can quickly create a map showing printer locations. The tool lets you import floor plans that can be used to drag and drop printers to actual locations. These maps are then published on a Web server so users can install printers that are closest to their location.

Creating printer maps

Creating printer maps requires that you use Microsoft Internet Explorer 5.5 or later and have the iPrint client installed on the workstation from which you will be creating the maps.

The iPrint Map Designer lets you create maps showing the physical locations of printers in a building by using background images of the building's floor plan. Once the map is created, use the iPrint Map Designer to modify or update your maps as necessary.

To create a printer map for your iPrint users, complete the following steps:

1. Get graphic images of your building floor plan(s). iPrint supports images in JPEG, GIF, and BMP formats. Copy all of the floor plan images to your iPrint servers and store them in SYS:LOGIN\IPPDOCS\IMAGES\MAPS.

2. To access the iPrint Map tool, do one of the following:

   • Map a drive to SYS:LOGIN\IPPDOCS\ and open MAPTOOL.HTM with Microsoft Internet Explorer.

   • With Microsoft Internet Explorer, open the `http://<server_address>:631/login/ippdocs/maptool.htm` iPrint URL, with *<server_address>* as the IP address or DNS name of the server where Print Services manager is running.

3. Select Background from the navigation frame on the left. Select a floor plan image from those you have copied to SYS:LOGIN\IPPDOCS\IMAGES\MAPS. Alternatively, you can retrieve and modify an existing map file by selecting Open and specifying (browsing to) the directory where the map is located.

4. To add a printer to the map, provide the following information:

- *Printer icon*: Select the type of printer icon you want to use
- *Printer icon size*: Select the icon size. This will be largely dependent on dimensions of your map background and the printer size.
- *Printer list*: Click the Browse icon and enter the DNS name of the appropriate Print Services manager. Click OK. You can also enter the IP address or DNS name of the NetWare 6 server where the Print Services manager is running. From the printer list, select the printer agent you want associated with this printer icon. If the printer is not listed, make sure you have IPP enabled for that printer.

NOTE

To add printers from different Print Services managers to the same map, first add the printers from the first Print Services manager, and then click the Browse icon and select a different manager.

- *Printer URL*: This field will be populated automatically by the URL created for the printer when IPP is enabled for the printer. You should not need to change the URL.
- *Mouse over text*: This field is populated automatically by the printer agent's name. You can override this information and enter any descriptive text you want to display when a user moves the mouse over the Printer icon.
- *(Optional) Printer Caption field*: Enter the information to display, using Enter to parse the information onto multiple lines.

5. Click Save, and save the map to SYS:LOGIN\IPPDOCS.

WARNING

If you click Refresh or exit Internet Explorer without saving the map, all changes since the last time the map was saved will be lost.

Repeat Step 4 for each printer you want to place on your map. You can edit a printer's information at any time by clicking the appropriate printer icon and changing the printer information fields as required. If you need to add or modify printers from a previously used Print Services manager, click a printer icon from that manager and the printer list will be populated with printers from that manager.

Hosting the maps on a Web server

After creating your maps, you need to post them on a Web server. Copy the contents of the \IPPDOCS directory and its subdirectories to the Web server in order for your maps and iPrint to work properly. You can link to your maps from your company's internal Web page or send the URL out to your users.

Printer Availability on Workstations

You might want printers to remove themselves automatically from a workstation. For example, you have a printer in your lobby for customers to use. When the customer leaves, you want the printer to be removed from the customer's laptop. Setting the persistence of the printer allows you to automatically remove the printer when the customer reboots his laptop.

Complete the following to set the persistence of a printer:

1. Using a text editor, open SYS:\LOGIN\IPPDOCS\INST.HTM.

2. Edit the file by searching for "persistence=". The setting occurs twice: once for Internet Explorer and once for Netscape browsers.

3. Replace the printer setting value — located after the comma (,) — with **reboot**.

4. Save the file.

Setting Up a Secure Printing Environment

NDPS is designed to take full advantage of eDirectory security and ease of management. And because iPrint runs on a foundation of NDPS, it is able to leverage those same directory-enabled advantages. Setting up a secure printing environment can be done on three different levels.

- *Print access control*: Create a secure printing management infrastructure by assigning users to User, Operator, or Manager roles. This restricts the list of those who can control printers, print services managers, and brokers.

- *Printer security levels*: Printer security levels control how access to printers is managed. By default, the client application will control print security, but this responsibility can be moved to the Print Services manager to provide greater security.

► *Securing iPrint with SSL:* This option not only encrypts print communications over the wire, but also requires users to authenticate before installing and printing to a printer.

Print Access Control

Printer security is ensured through the assignment of the Manager, Operator, and User Access Control roles, and by the strategic placement of printers and printer configurations.

> **X-REF**
>
> For more information on eDirectory access control in general, see Chapter 6.

The access controls for NDPS allow you to specify the access each User, Group, or Container object will have to your printing resources. It is important to remember that all NDPS print roles function independently. For example, assigning someone as a printer Manager does not automatically grant him or her the rights of a printer User.

In most cases, the default NDPS assignments will prevent any problems that this role independence might cause. For example, a printer Manager is automatically assigned as a printer Operator and User for that printer. Similarly, a printer Operator is automatically assigned as a User of that printer as well. You cannot remove the User role from an Operator, and you cannot remove the Operator and User roles from a Manager.

The creator of an NDPS object is automatically assigned to all supported roles for the type of object being created.

You can assign multiple Printer objects to a given Printer Agent, but simultaneously make different access control assignments to each Printer object. This means that users in different containers can be assigned different trustee rights to the same printer.

Printer roles

As previously alluded to, there are three roles associated with NDPS printing services: Manager, Operator, and User. Table 7.4 describes the rights granted to each role.

T A B L E 7 . 4	NDPS Print Roles and Their Associated Rights
ROLE	**ASSOCIATED RIGHTS**
Manager	NDPS tasks performed exclusively by the printer Manager are those that require the creation, modification, or deletion of NDPS Printer objects, as well as other eDirectory administrative functions. Printer Managers are automatically designated as printer Operators and Users as well, so they can perform all tasks assigned to the Operator role. Typical Manager functions include the following: — Modifying and deleting Printer objects — Adding or deleting Operators and Users for a printer — Adding other Managers — Configuring interested-party notification — Creating, modifying, or deleting printer configurations
Operator	Print Operators cannot create, modify, or delete eDirectory objects or perform other eDirectory administrative functions. Their management tasks include the following: — Performing all of the functions available through the Printer Control page — Pausing, restarting, or reinitializing printers — Reordering, moving, copying, and deleting jobs — Setting printer defaults, including locked properties — Configuring print job spooling
User	Print Users only have rights to submit and manage print jobs that they own. Users cannot copy, move, reorder, or remove jobs they do not own. To simplify administration, the container within which a printer resides is automatically assigned as a User for that printer. That way, all users in that container inherit printer User rights. You can delete the Container object as a printer User in order block access to the printer for users in that container.

To define the role assignment for a printer, complete the following steps:

1. From iManage, select iPrint Management and click Manage Printer.

2. In the NDPS Printer field, specify the printer for which you want to configure access controls and click OK.

3. At the Manage Printer page, select the Access Control tab, as shown in Figure 7.9.

4. Make your desired changes by adding or deleting members from the User, Operator, and Manager roles for this printer. eDirectory objects that can be assigned in these roles include: User, Group, or Container objects. Click OK to save your changes.

F I G U R E   7.9 *Access Control tab for defining printer management roles in ConsoleOne*

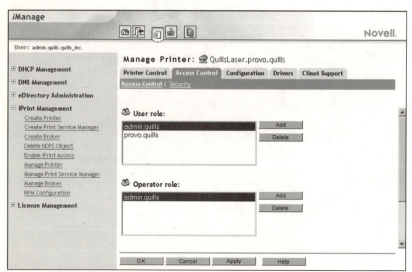

Print Services manager access controls

Print Services manager security is provided exclusively through the printer Manager role. Common administrative tasks related to the Print Services manager include the following:

- Creating Printer Agents and NDPS Manager objects
- Adding or deleting Operators and Users for a printer

- Adding other Managers
- Configuring interested-party notification
- Creating, modifying, or deleting printer configurations

NDPS broker access controls

There are two roles associated with the NDPS Broker object:

- *Manager*: NDPS tasks performed exclusively by the broker Manager are those that require the creation, modification, or deletion of Broker objects, as well as those that involve other eDirectory administrative functions. Typical Manager functions include the following:
  - Creating, modifying, and deleting Broker objects
  - Adding other Managers
  - Enabling or disabling brokered services
  - Adding resources to the Resource Management Service
  - Assigning or changing a broker password
- *Public access user*: A Public Access User is a role assigned to all individuals on the network who are users of printers receiving services and resources provided by the broker. This role is assigned by default and does not require specific administrative action by the broker manager.

You can also assign a password to the broker interface for increased security. After the broker loads on your NetWare server, navigate to the Broker screen and press F4.

Printer Security Levels

Printer security levels affect how rights to a printer are determined and enforced. There are three security levels:

- *Low*: Security is enforced by the client applications only
- *Medium (default)*: Security is enforced by NDPS manager, if print data integrity is involved. Otherwise, security is enforced by the client applications.
- *High*: Security is enforced by the NDPS manager for all operations.

As noted, the default security level is Medium. For sensitive print data, you can set the security level to High, but there is a trade-off between print performance and print security. To set a printer's security level, complete the following steps:

1. From iManage, select iPrint Management and click Manage Printer.

2. Specify the printer for which you want to change security levels and click OK.

3. At the Manage Printers page, select the Access Control tab and click the Security subpage.

4. In the Security Level field, set the level of security for this printer and click OK to save your changes.

IMPORTANT

As you can see, making security level changes will affect all print jobs going to this printer, so make sure you consider the consequences carefully.

Securing iPrint with SSL

Secure printing takes advantage of SSL, which requires users to authenticate using their eDirectory usernames and passwords. Users must authenticate once per eDirectory tree per session. The print data is encrypted, and all print communications use port 443. Without secure printing, the printer is available to anyone on the local network and print communications are not encrypted. Secure printing works in conjunction with the security level set for the printer.

Table 7.5 shows how access is determined, depending on the level of printer security and if secure printing is enabled or disabled.

T A B L E 7 . 5	*Effects of Printer Security and Secure Printing Options*	
PRINTER SECURITY LEVEL	**SECURE PRINTING DISABLED (NO SSL)**	**SECURE PRINTING ENABLED (WITH SSL)**
Low	Full access	eDirectory authentication
Medium	Check of user's effective rights	eDirectory authentication and check of user's effective rights
High	Users must use SSL and authenticate to eDirectory	Users will receive an error if they do not use SSL. eDirectory authentication, check user's effective rights, and connection verification are all required.

Saving Passwords for Secure Printers

When users print to a secure printer, they are prompted for the eDirectory username and password. Users can select to have their workstation remember their password for printing. For Windows NT/2000 users, passwords are saved on a per-user basis.

By default the Remember Password feature is enabled. To disable it, open SYS:\LOGIN\IPPDOCS\IPRINT.INI and set AllowSavePassword=0.

IMPORTANT

The IPRINT.INI file should be synchronized across all servers where iPrint is running.

Providing Transparent
Storage and Access

In This Part

Up to this point, the book has focused on the specific components and tasks necessary to get NetWare 6 ready to support the business needs of the twenty-first century. Part III looks at the specific features and offerings in NetWare 6 that make it the pre-eminent network operating system for conducting eBusiness.

Think for a minute about what you need to do business in today's world. You have far-flung employees, mobile users moving from site to site, partners and suppliers that need to provide and receive critical information, and the open access Internet — across which you need to send mission-critical and often confidential information. To manage all this you need to develop a new paradigm — a new way of looking at things — and NetWare 6 does just that.

Chapter 8 introduces you to the powerful features of Novell Storage Service (NSS), which provides unparalleled flexibility and security for your critical business data. After all, the data is what the network is all about, right?

Chapter 9 introduces the NetWare 6 Web servers. That's right, that's plural, as in two different Web servers. NetWare Enterprise Web server is the eBusiness and eCommerce foundation for NetWare 6. New to the game is Apache Web server for NetWare. Apache provides the "internal" Web services upon which you will rely to manage your One Net infrastructure. The tools that leverage the Apache Web server platform have been discussed at length in preceding chapters.

Chapter 10 introduces the new user tools for One Net. These tools finally make it possible to seamlessly and securely provide users with access to the information they need, regardless of location, time or anything else. After all, your job as a network administrator revolves around making sure that users get to what they need when they need it — and nothing more than that.

NetWare 6 just made your job a whole lot easier.

CHAPTER 8

File Storage and Management

Instant Access

Managing disk space

▶ To manage file compression, use NoRM or MONITOR.NLM to set file compression SET parameters.

▶ To limit users' disk space, use ConsoleOne.

Managing files

▶ To purge or salvage files that have been deleted, use ConsoleOne.

▶ To display information about files and directories, use ConsoleOne.

Backing up and restoring files

▶ To back up and restore network files, use NWBACK32, which can run from either a server (SBCON.NLM) or a workstation (NWBACK32.EXE). You can also use a third-party backup product.

Managing volumes

▶ To create, delete, or enlarge a traditional NetWare volume, use ConsoleOne.

▶ To create, delete, or enlarge an NSS volume, use ConsoleOne.

▶ To mount either a traditional or an NSS volume, use ConsoleOne.

▶ To dismount either a traditional or an NSS volume, use ConsoleOne.

▶ To mount a server's DOS partition as an NSS volume, load NSS support with the DOSFAT module.

▶ To repair a corrupted traditional NetWare volume, use VREPAIR.NLM.

▶ To repair a corrupted NSS volume, use REBUILD (which can be run from the NSS administration console utility).

▶ To add name space support to a volume, load the name space module on the server, and then use the ADD NAME SPACE *module* TO *volume* command at the server console.

Protecting database transactions

▶ To manage the NetWare Transaction Tracking System (TTS), use NoRM or MONITOR.NLM to change the appropriate SET parameters.

▶ To flag a file with the Transactional file attribute, use ConsoleOne.

▶ To re-enable TTS after it has been disabled, use the ENABLE TTS console utility.

Understanding the NetWare File System

NetWare enables you to manage files in many different ways. How you manage your files can contribute significantly to how well users can find files, how well your disk space is conserved, and how easy it is to restore the network files when something goes wrong.

When you first set up your server, you need to take into account how your file system will be structured. Several factors can affect how you organize your network files and applications. Careful planning can make it easier to back up and restore needed files and can also make it easier to assign trustee rights to large numbers of users.

The first step toward planning and managing an effective file system is to understand how NetWare uses volumes. A volume is the highest level in the file system hierarchy, and it contains directories and files. Each NetWare server has at least one volume, SYS, which contains all of the NetWare files and utilities. You can have additional volumes on a server if you want. Volumes help you organize files on the server.

With NetWare 6, you can choose to create two different types of volumes: Novell Storage Services (NSS) volumes or traditional NetWare volumes. The following sections explain the differences between traditional NetWare volumes and NSS volumes.

Traditional NetWare Volumes

If you have used previous versions of NetWare, you're familiar with traditional NetWare volumes. In NetWare 6, traditional volumes function exactly as they do in previous versions. Traditional volumes can support space-saving features such as block sub-allocation and file compression, as well as data preservation features, such as TTS (Novell's Transaction Tracking System) and disk mirroring.

A NetWare server can support up to 64 traditional volumes. When a traditional volume is created on a disk, a "segment" is also created on the disk to hold the volume. If you create two volumes on the disk, the disk will have two segments (also called volume segments). If you later decide to merge the two volumes into one, you will discover that the new single volume contains two segments. If you create a volume that spans multiple hard disks, the portion of the volume on each disk will be contained in a different segment.

Each volume can have up to 32 volume segments, which can all be stored on the same hard disk or scattered across separate disks. Letting volume segments reside on different disks enables you to increase the size of a volume by adding a new hard disk. In addition, by putting segments of the same volume on more than one hard disk, different parts of the volume can be accessed simultaneously, which increases disk input and output. However, the more segments a volume has, the slower the performance may be, so use this option carefully.

If you spread volume segments across disks, it is important to mirror the disks so a single disk's failure won't shut down the entire volume.

X-REF

For more information on disk mirroring see Chapter 4.

One hard disk can hold up to eight volume segments that belong to one or more volumes. However, a single segment cannot span multiple disks.

When you create a traditional volume, an eDirectory Volume object is automatically created at the same time. The Volume object is placed in the same context as the server. By default, the Volume object is named with the server's name as a prefix. For example, if the server's name is Sales, the Volume object for volume SYS is named Sales_SYS.

Even though NSS is now the default file system of NetWare, there are still a few times when traditional volumes should be used:

▶ Legacy applications, particularly older databases, may require traditional volume structures to function properly.

▶ NSS does not support the following features currently supported by traditional NetWare volumes:

- Block sub-allocation
- Auditing
- File name locks
- Data migration

NSS Volumes

Novell Storage Services (NSS) is a storage and file system that provides an efficient way to use all of the space on your storage devices. NSS is best used with systems that require the ability to store and maintain large volumes and numerous files or large databases.

NSS is the default storage and file system for NetWare 6. You use it to create, store, and maintain both traditional and NSS volumes. The NSS volumes are called logical volumes. When you install NSS, it creates a storage pool (SYS:) and an equal sized volume SYS.

NOTE

NetWare 5 ran NSS in parallel with the traditional NetWare file system. In NetWare 6, NSS replaces traditional volumes as the primary storage and management system, but NetWare 6 continues to support traditional volumes for legacy application support when necessary.

If you are new to NSS, you should be aware of the following data and storage management features available through NSS in NetWare 6:

► *NSS management*: ConsoleOne is the primary utility for configuring and managing both traditional and NSS logical volumes. Do not attempt to use NWCONFIG or NSS Menu with NetWare 6, because they are not compatible with some of the new NSS features.

► *Combine logical volumes in a single storage pool*: NSS uses storage pools, as shown in Figure 8.1. A storage pool is a specified amount of space you obtain from all your storage devices. Then you place all NSS logical volumes into the storage pool. This way you do not have to limit the number of volumes you have in a partition. You can only have one storage pool on a partition, but you can place an unlimited number of logical volumes in the pool.

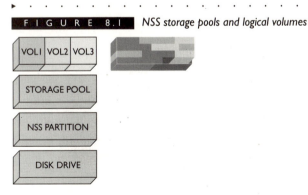

FIGURE 8.1 *NSS storage pools and logical volumes*

► *Create logical volumes*: The volumes you create from NSS storage pools are called logical volumes. A logical volume is a volume that is either set to a specific size, or one that can grow dynamically according to the amount of physical space assigned to the pool. This lets you add and store any size or any number of files you need without having to create other partitions. You can add any number of volumes to a storage pool as long as you have available physical space in the pool.

▶ *Overbook your storage pool*: Individual logical volumes cannot exceed the size of a storage pool. However, since you can create multiple logical volumes in a single storage pool, NetWare 6 permits the total space allocated to logical volumes to exceed the actual pool size. This feature, called overbooking, can be an efficient way to manage your file system since it lets your volumes grow organically over time instead of being locked into a rigid structure that may leave space unused.

▶ *Deactivate/activate logical volumes and storage pools*: You might need to temporarily prevent user access to storage pools or volumes to do maintenance. Instead of bringing down the server, you can deactivate individual storage pools. When you deactivate a storage pool, users will not have access to any of the volumes in that pool.

▶ *Fast error correction and data recovery*: Because NSS is a journaled file system, it can quickly recover data after a file system crash. Instead of scanning the file system for corruption, NSS replays the latest set of changes to make sure they were written correctly. The file system either recovers the changed information or returns it to its original condition prior to the transaction.

▶ *Immediately save data to disk*: The Flush Files Immediately feature saves your file data to disk immediately after you close the file instead of caching it in memory and waiting for the next disk write cycle. This prevents your data from being at risk between disk write cycles, at the cost of slower file system performance overall.

▶ *Retain previously saved files (snapshot)*: The File Snapshot feature keeps an original copy of all open files so they can be archived by your backup utility. By capturing the most recent closed copy of the file, Snapshot guarantees that you still have a solid copy of the file with which to work.

▶ *Transaction Tracking System (TTS)*: Transaction Tracking System protects database applications by backing out transactions that are incomplete due to a system failure. TTS can be enabled for the NSS file system or for the traditional file system, but not for both simultaneously. If you have both traditional and logical volumes on your server, TTS will support the traditional volumes by default. To enable TTS for your logical NSS volumes, you must add the DISABLE TTS command to your AUTOEXEC.NCF. Then enable TTS for those logical volumes that need it by typing the following command at the server console. You can also place the NSS transaction command in your AUTOEXEC.NCF so that TTS starts automatically on your NSS logical volumes.

```
nss/transaction=<volume name>
```

▸ *Review the modified file list*: NSS maintains a list of files that have been modified since the previous backup. To save time, your backup utility has to review only this list rather than scanning the entire file system for modified files.

▸ *Enable file compression*: NSS now supports file compression. This lets you decide whether or not to compress the files in your volumes to create additional space. Once you enable file compression, you cannot turn it off without recreating the volumes.

▸ *Data shredding*: The Data Shredding feature overwrites purged disk blocks with random patterns of hexadecimal characters. This prevents unauthorized users from using a disk editor to access purged files. You can require that up to seven shred patterns be placed over deleted data.

▸ *User space restrictions*: From ConsoleOne, you can now limit the amount of space available to an individual user on a logical volume.

▸ *Directory space restrictions*: From ConsoleOne, you can now limit the space that can be assigned to a given directory or subdirectory.

▸ *Use CD-ROMs as read-only logical volumes*: NSS has full CD-ROM support for ISO9660 and HFS formats.

▸ *No memory required for mounting volumes*: NSS does not require large amounts of memory to mount volumes because it does not scan the entire file system during the mounting process. After the mounting is complete, NSS does not load files into memory until you access them. Therefore, no additional memory is required when you add files and mount volumes.

▸ *Hot Fix*: Over time, sections of your server hard disks may start to break down and lose their ability to reliably store data. NSS supports Hot Fix to prevent data from being written to unreliable blocks. Hot Fix redirects the original block of data to the Hot Fix redirection area, where the data can be stored correctly. To redirect a block of data, the operating system records the address of the defective block. Then the server no longer attempts to store data in that block. By default, 2 percent of a disk's space is set-aside as the Hot Fix redirection area. You can increase or decrease this amount. If Hot Fix is enabled, then it is always active unless the disk fails or the redirection area is full. You can view Hot Fix activity in NoRM by selecting the Disk/LAN Adapter link. Click on the disk adapter to which the drive is attached and click the appropriate drive link. The Redirection Blocks column will show you how many bocks have been redirected to the Hot Fix area.

IMPORTANT

You can disable the Hot Fix redirection area when you create disk partitions, which will save partition space. This may be useful if you are using a RAID system that provides its own fault tolerance. If you do not enable Hot Fix when the partition is created, you can add it later only by deleting the volumes from the partition, adding Hot Fix, and restoring the volumes from a backup.

► *Repair storage pools instead of individual volumes*: Use the repair utilities VERIFY and REBUILD to repair NSS systems. VERIFY and REBUILD function on the pool level rather than the individual volume level. Unlike VREPAIR for traditional NetWare volumes, these utilities should only be used as a last resort to recover the file system after data corruption.

  • VERIFY checks the file system integrity for an NSS pool by searching for inconsistent data blocks or other errors. This utility indicates if there are problems with the file system.

  • REBUILD verifies and uses the existing leaves of an object tree to rebuild all the other trees in the system. You need to deactivate pools (and all the volumes in the pools) before you run REBUILD so users cannot access the volumes you are rebuilding. When you deactivate a storage pool, all the volumes in the pool automatically deactivate.

► *Mirror partitions*: Mirroring protects your data by making exact duplicates of your partitions on different disk hardware. Both disks are updated simultaneously. You can setup mirroring on either NSS or traditional volumes with ConsoleOne.

► *Stripe data across storage devices (RAID)*: NSS lets you stripe data across multiple disk drives on your system, emulating an actual hardware RAID 0 system, as shown in Figure 8.2.

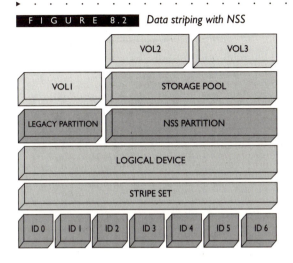

FIGURE 8.2 *Data striping with NSS*

Planning the File System

Now that you know a little about both traditional NetWare volumes and NSS volumes, you can plan your entire file system. This section offers tips for planning your file structure. Instructions for creating and managing both traditional and NSS volumes appear later in this chapter.

The following list includes some tips that may help you plan an accessible, easy-to-manage file system:

- ▶ You should probably reserve volume SYS for NetWare files and utilities. Avoid putting other types of files in SYS, such as applications or users' daily work files, particularly if those files are volatile (as they change a lot).

- ▶ Determine if there is any reason to create a traditional NetWare volume. Your best bet is to stick to NSS, if possible, to avoid incompatibilities down the road.

- ▶ To simplify backups, create a separate volume for applications and other non-NetWare utilities. That way, you can back up application volumes only occasionally since that data won't change very frequently. User data, on the other hand, can be backed up frequently without all the overhead of backing up their applications as well. For more information about backing up files, see the "Backing Up and Restoring Files" section later in this chapter.

▶ If different applications will be available to different groups of users, try to organize the applications' directory structures so you can assign comprehensive rights in a parent directory. This may help prevent you from having to create multiple individual rights assignments at lower-level subdirectories.

For more information about file system rights, see Chapter 6.

X-REF

▶ If you want to use file compression to compress less frequently used files, try to group those types of files into directories separate from other files that are used more often. That way you can turn on compression for the less-used directories and leave it turned off for the frequently used directories. For more information about file compression, see the "File Compression" section later in this chapter.

▶ Decide whether you want users' daily work files to reside in personal directories, in project-specific directories, or in some other type of directory structure. Encourage your users to store their files on the network so those files can be backed up regularly by the network backup process, and so the files can be protected by NetWare security.

▶ Decide if you want users to have their own individual home directories.

You can have home directories created automatically when you create a new user, as explained in Chapter 6.

TIP

These tips can help you effectively plan your file system. In addition, you should take into consideration the directories that NetWare creates automatically during installation, as well as plan for directories that will contain applications. These issues are described in the following sections.

Directories Created Automatically

When you first install NetWare 6 on the server, some directories are created automatically in the SYS volume. These directories contain the files needed to run and manage NetWare 6. You can create additional directories and subdirectories in volume SYS, or if you created additional volumes during installation, you can create directories for your users in the other volumes.

Following are a few of the directories that are created automatically on volume SYS:

▶ LOGIN contains utilities necessary to let users access Novell eDirectory and NetWare 6 servers so that they can log in. It also holds iPrint client and access pages, in HTML, since users don't necessarily have to authenticate to access network printers.

For more information on print security see Chapter 7.

X-REF

▶ SYSTEM contains NLMs and utilities that the network administrator can use to configure, manage, monitor, and add services on the NetWare server.

▶ PUBLIC and its subdirectories contain all of the NetWare utilities and related files that users and administrators may need to access. It also contains .PDF files (printer definition files) if you choose to install them on the server. You can add utilities or other software to this directory if you want users to have access to them. For example, you could create client subdirectories under PUBLIC. These client subdirectories could contain the files required for installing NetWare client software on workstations.

▶ APACHE holds the system files for the Apache Web server, which is used to support all NetWare 6 Web-based administrative tools such as Web Manager, NoRM, and iManage.

For more information on these tools see Chapter 3.

X-REF

▶ DELETED.SAV is used to store files that have been deleted, but have not yet been purged from the server. DELETED.SAV stores only deleted files whose directories have also been deleted; if the original directory still exists, the deleted file remains in that directory.

▶ ETC contains files used for managing protocols and routers, as well as some default log files, such as CONSOLE.LOG.

Because SYS volume contains many directories containing files required for running and managing your NetWare network, do not rename or delete any of them without making absolutely sure they're unnecessary in your particular network's situation. This is another good reason not to mix your business applications and data with the system files on SYS.

IMPORTANT

Application Directories

When planning your file system, decide where you want to put the directories that will contain applications and program files. It may be easier to assign file system trustee rights if you group all multiuser applications on the network under a single volume or parent directory. By installing, for example, your word-processing, spreadsheet, and other programs into their own subdirectories under a parent directory named APPS, you can assign all of your users the minimum necessary rights to APPS, and then the users will inherit those rights in each individual application's subdirectory.

X-REF

> For more information about file system rights, see Chapter 6.

If you install applications into subdirectories under a common parent directory, you can then usually designate that users' daily work files be stored in their own home directories elsewhere on the network.

When planning network subdirectories for your applications, follow any special instructions from the manufacturer for installing the application on a network. Some applications can be run either from a local hard disk on the workstation or from a network directory. Be sure to follow the instructions supplied by the manufacturer.

In some cases, the instructions may indicate that the application has to be installed at the root of a volume. If your application requires this, you can still install it in a subdirectory under the APPS directory if you want and then map a "fake root" to the application's subdirectory. A fake root mapping makes a subdirectory appear to be a volume so that the application runs correctly.

For example, suppose you want to install an application called ABC into a subdirectory under a directory called APPS on the volume called VOL1, but the application's instructions say that ABC must be installed at the root of the volume. Create a subdirectory called ABC under VOL1:APPS and install the application into ABC. Then, you can map a fake root to the ABC subdirectory and assign it to be a search drive at the same time by putting the following command into the appropriate login script:

```
MAP ROOT S16:=VOL1:APPS\ABC
```

Novell Client users can also create this mapping for the duration of their current session only, by right-clicking the red "N" in the System Tray in Windows and selecting Novell Map Network Drive.

For more information on mapping drives see Chapter 2.

X-REF

When you install an application, you may want to flag the application's executable files (usually files with the extension .COM or .EXE) with the Shareable and Read-Only file attributes. This will allow users to simultaneously use the applications, but will prevent users from deleting or modifying them. (This is more typically controlled by assigning restrictive trustee rights to users in those applications' directories.)

You can assign file attributes with ConsoleOne as described in Chapter 6.

X-REF

Working with Traditional NetWare Volumes

When you install the server, you will create at least one traditional volume that will be used to store network files. You can, however, create and modify traditional NetWare volumes after installation, if you choose. The following sections explain how to work with traditional volumes. Instructions for working with NSS volumes appear later in this chapter.

Creating and Mounting Traditional Volumes

Use ConsoleOne to create new traditional NetWare volumes after the initial server installation. You can create a new volume out of any free space on the disk. The free space may be space that was never assigned to a volume before, or it may be free space on a new hard disk that's just been added.

After you've created a volume, you must mount it before network users can access it.

To create a volume, complete the following steps:

1. If you're installing a new hard disk, install the hard disk according to the manufacturer's instructions.

2. Launch ConsoleOne and browse to the Server object on which you want to create the new volume.

3. Highlight the Server object and click Traditional Volume Disk Management, as shown in Figure 8.3.

NSS-related toolbar buttons in ConsoleOne

Partition disk management

Free space disk management   Pool disk management

RAID device disk management   Logical volume disk management

Device disk management   Traditional volume disk management

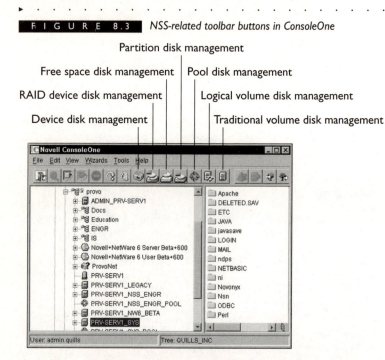

4. At the Traditional Volumes page, shown in Figure 8.4, click New to create the new volume.

5. At the Create a New Traditional Volume page, enter a name for the new volume and click Next.

6. At the Storage Information screen, check the box next to one or more of the unpartitioned storage areas and click Next. If you don't want to use all the available free space for this volume, you can double-click the Used column and specify the desired size of the new volume (in megabytes).

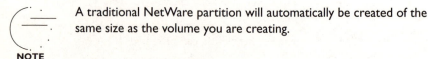

> **A traditional NetWare partition will automatically be created of the same size as the volume you are creating.**

NOTE

7. At the Attribute Information screen, specify the additional characteristics of this volume and click Finish.

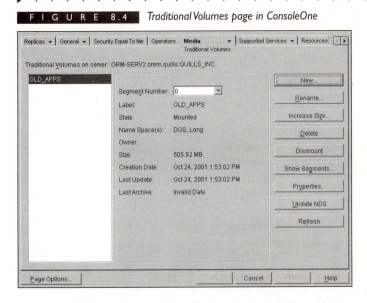

Traditional Volumes page in ConsoleOne

- *Block size*: Lets you specify the smallest addressable amount of space for this volume. If you know the type of data that will be stored on the volume, you can tailor the block size to best support the data. As a rule of thumb: small blocks for small files, big blocks for big files.

- *Compression*: Turns data compression on for this volume. Compression will use volume space much more efficiently at the cost of read performance. If volume data is not used constantly, then compression can be a good idea.

- *Migration*: Enables support for near-line storage such as optical subsystems. Migration creates a look-up key in the volume's File Allocation Table (FAT) that describes how to retrieve the data from the near-line storage system.

- *Suballocation*: Allows NetWare to divide regular blocks up into 512-byte chunks so multiple files can be stored in a single block.

- *Mount volume on creation*: Mounts the volume automatically when it is created. If left unchecked, you can manually mount the volume from the Traditional Volumes subpage in ConsoleOne. You can also use the MOUNT command from the server console.

8. Click Yes at the Warning screen to create the new volume.

NOTE

If you want to create a volume without Hot Fix or mirroring capabilities, you can create the partition manually from the Partitions subpage in ConsoleOne. After creating the partition, create the volume as described in the previous steps, selecting the partitioned space rather than the unpartitioned space in Step 6.

Dismounting and Deleting Traditional Volumes

Deleting a volume deletes all the files and directories on that volume as well, so be sure you delete a volume only if you don't need the files anymore, or if you have a reliable backup.

Before you delete a volume, you must dismount it so that its files are unavailable to users. You can dismount the volume you want to delete from the Traditional Volumes subpage in ConsoleOne. You can also use the DISMOUNT command from the server console.

To dismount and then delete a volume, complete the following steps:

1. Back up all files on the volume or move them to a different volume, if you want to keep them.

2. Launch ConsoleOne and browse to the Server object from which you want to remove a volume.

3. Highlight the Server object and click Traditional Volume Disk Management (refer to Figure 8.3).

4. At the Traditional Volumes page, highlight the volume you want to delete in the volume list and click Dismount. Click OK at the warning message.

5. Click Delete to remove the volume.

Increasing the Size of a Traditional Volume

To increase the size of a volume, you can add a volume segment to an existing volume. First, configure the free space as a NetWare partition, then add that segment to an existing volume. To increase the size of a traditional volume, complete the following steps:

1. Launch ConsoleOne and browse to the Server object from which you want to remove a volume.

2. Highlight the Server object and click Traditional Volume Disk Management (refer to Figure 8.3).

3. At the Traditional Volumes page, highlight the volume that you want to make bigger and click Increase Size.

4. At the Storage Information screen, check the box next to one or more of the unpartitioned storage areas and click Finish. If you don't want to use all the unpartitioned space for this volume, Double-click the Used column and specify the amount of space to add to the volume (in megabytes).

5. At the warning screen, click OK to add the specified space to your volume. The volume will dismount, the new segment will be added, and the volume will remount — all automatically.

Repairing Traditional Volumes with VREPAIR

Occasionally, a problem with a server hard disk may cause some type of problem that prevents the NetWare volume from mounting. This is often caused by some corruption in the primary File Allocation Table (FAT) or Directory Entry Table (DET). VREPAIR is designed to take care of these types of problems.

NetWare maintains two copies of the FAT and DET. VREPAIR compares the two tables for inconsistencies. If it finds an inconsistency between the two, it uses the most correct table entry to update the incorrect one. Then VREPAIR writes the corrected entry to both the primary and the secondary tables.

VREPAIR can also be used in the following circumstances:

▶ When a power failure corrupts the volume

▶ When a hardware problem causes a disk read error

▶ When bad blocks on the volume cause read or write errors, "data mirror" mismatch errors, multiple allocation errors, or fatal DIR errors

▶ When you want to remove a name space from a volume

If a volume doesn't mount when you boot the server, VREPAIR will run automatically and try to repair the volume. If the volume fails while the server is running, you can run VREPAIR manually. (Dismount the volume before running VREPAIR on it.)

TIP

Most volume problems that VREPAIR can fix are hardware related. Therefore, if you repeatedly have to repair the same volume, you should consider replacing the hard disk.

To use VREPAIR.NLM manually, load it at the server's console. VREPAIR.NLM is located on the server's DOS partition. If you are repairing a volume that has a non-DOS name space loaded (or if you're removing a name space from the volume), VREPAIR needs to load another NLM for that name space support. The VREPAIR name space modules are named V_namespace.NLM.

For example, for the MAC name space, VREPAIR looks for a module named V_MAC.NLM. If this module is located in the server's DOS partition (where it is installed by default), VREPAIR automatically loads it. If this module is in a different location, you'll have to load it manually before running VREPAIR.

Again, in many cases VREPAIR will run automatically. If you need to run VREPAIR manually, complete the following steps:

1. If it is not already, dismount the traditional volume you want to repair. You can do this from the Traditional Volume subpage in ConsoleOne. You can also use the DISMOUNT command from the server console.

2. At the server's console, load VREPAIR.NLM.

3. Choose 1 (Repair a Volume) to begin trying to fix the volume. If more than one volume is currently dismounted, you have to choose the volume you want to repair.

4. If you want to change how VREPAIR is displaying errors as it finds them, press F1. Then select option 1 if you don't want VREPAIR to pause after each error. Select 2 if you want the errors logged in a text file. Select 3 to stop the repair. Select 4 to resume the repair.

5. When the repair is finished, choose Yes when asked if you want to write repairs to the disk.

6. If VREPAIR found errors, run it again. Run VREPAIR repeatedly until it finds no errors on the volume.

7. When VREPAIR finds no more errors, remount the volume.

8. If the volume still won't mount, you are pretty much out of luck. Delete the volume, re-create it from ConsoleOne, and then restore all of its files from backups.

VREPAIR may have to delete some files during the repair operation. If it does, it stores those deleted files in new files named VR*nnnnnn*.FIL (where *n* is any number). These files are stored in the directories in which the original files were stored when they were found during VREPAIR's operation.

Files may be deleted if VREPAIR finds problems such as a file with a name that is invalid in DOS, or two files with the same filename.

Working with NSS Volumes

You created your first NSS volume when you installed NetWare 6, since the SYS volume now uses NSS. Given that, it is probably a good idea to understand the technology and storage concepts a little before you start doing a lot of storage management. As with traditional volumes, you can configure and manage NSS resources after installation with ConsoleOne. The following sections introduce you to some of the new NSS terminology and explain how to work with NSS volumes. Working with traditional NetWare volumes was covered in the previous section.

Creating NSS Storage Resources

With NSS, you use partitions, storage pools, and logical volumes. You create logical volumes in storage pools that are composed of free space from the various storage devices in your server.

NSS uses free space from multiple storage devices. NSS allows you to mount up to 255 volumes simultaneously and store up to 8 trillion files in a single volume — up to 8 terabytes in size.

You create and manage NSS resources from ConsoleOne, using a set of buttons on the toolbar (refer to Figure 8.3).

Partitions

A partition is a logical organization of space on a hard disk. Partitions are the lowest level of organization for disk storage and form the foundation for creating NSS storage pools. To create an NSS partition, complete the following steps:

1. Launch ConsoleOne and browse to the Server object on which you want to create a partition.

2. Highlight the Server object and click Partition Disk Management (refer to Figure 8.3).

3. At the Partitions page, as shown in Figure 8.5, click New. If you have more than one disk drive in your server, select the device on which you want to create the partition.

▶ · ◀

F I G U R E   8 . 5   *Partitions page in ConsoleOne*

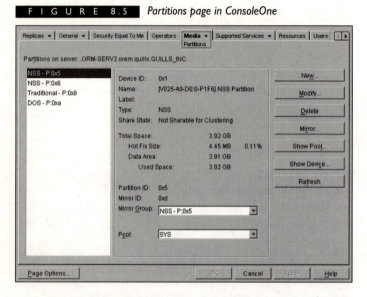

4. Specify the desired partition characteristics and click OK.

- *Type*: Specifies the type of partition to create. Select Traditional to add a segment to a traditional volume.

- *Size*: Specify the size of the partition. You can choose to specify the size in kilobytes, megabytes, or gigabytes.

- *Hot Fix*: Check to create a Hot Fix area for this partition. Specify the size of the Hot Fix area in kilobytes, megabytes, or gigabytes. You can also specify it as a percentage of the partition size.

- *Mirror*: Check if you want to be able to mirror the data stored in this partition. This option is linked with Hot Fix. You can't mirror without Hot Fix, and vice versa.

- *(Optional) Label*: Specify a name for the new partition. This can be useful for identification if you have several volumes on the server.

Storage pools

A storage pool is a specific amount of space you obtain from one or more storage devices in your server. You create storage pools after you create partitions on your storage devices, but before you create volumes. NSS storage pools provide the flexibility of NSS. They can be created to span either one or multiple partitions on the hardware side, and can be divided into one or multiple logical volumes on the User side.

After a pool is created, you can add storage devices to your server and add their free space to a new or existing storage pool, as needed. To create a new storage pool, complete the following steps:

I. Launch ConsoleOne and browse to the Server object on which you want to create a storage pool.

2. Highlight the Server object and click Pool Disk Management (refer to Figure 8.3).

3. At the NSS Pools page, as shown in Figure 8.6, click New. Specify a name for the storage pool and click Next.

F I G U R E   8.6   *NSS Pools page in ConsoleOne*

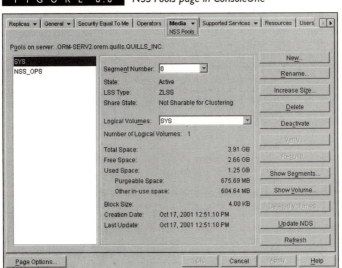

4. At the Storage Information screen, select the NSS partition(s) and/or free space from which you want to create the new storage pool and click Next.

NOTE

If you create a storage pool with free space, a partition for that free space will be created automatically, with Hot Fix and mirroring enabled. If you want to create the partition manually, complete the partition creation steps, described previously, before creating the storage pool.

5. At the Attribute Information screen, specify whether or not you want to activate the storage pool when it is created and click Finish. Activating a storage pool is analogous to mounting a volume in the traditional NetWare sense.

Logical volumes

A logical volume is an NSS volume that is analogous to a traditional volume used in previous versions of NetWare. Logical volumes can be set to a specific size or set to grow dynamically according to the amount of physical space you have. Because of this, you can add storage devices to your system without having to create new volumes.

After you've created the volume, you must mount it before network users can access it. To create and mount a new NSS volume, complete the following steps:

1. Launch ConsoleOne and browse to the Server object on which you want to create an NSS logical volume.

2. Highlight the Server object and click Logical Volume Disk Management (refer to Figure 8.3)

3. At the NSS Logical Volumes page, click New. At the New Logical Volume screen, specify a name for the new volume and click Next.

4. At the Storage Information screen, as shown in Figure 8.7, make your desired selections and click Next.

   • *Partition list*: Select the storage resource that you want to use to create the new volume. You can select from free space, existing NSS partitions, or existing NSS storage pools.

   • *Volume quota*: Specify a maximum size, in megabytes, for the volume. You must either set a quota or check the Allow volume quota to grow to the pool size box as described next.

   • *Allow volume quota to grow to the pool size*: Check this box to allow the new volume to fill the space in its storage pool. If this volume is sharing a pool with another volume, this may not be a good idea.

NOTE

If you select free space from which to create the NSS partition, you will be required to define an NSS partition and storage pool before creating the actual volume. Likewise, if you select an existing NSS partition you will be required to define a storage pool before creating the actual volume. Steps to complete both these operations are described in previous sections.

The Create Logical Volume Storage Information screen in ConsoleOne

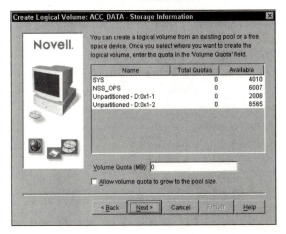

5. At the Attribute Information screen, select the desired characteristics for the new volume and click Finish.

- *Backup*: This option marks the volume data for backup, similar to setting the Archive bit on a file or directory.

- *Compression*: Turns data compression on for this volume. Compression will use volume space much more efficiently at the cost of read performance. If volume data is not used constantly, then compression can be a good idea.

- *Data shredding*: Instructs NetWare to overwrite deleted data with random characters to prevent recovery with disk reader software. Specify how many overwrite passes to make (1–7).

- *Directory quotas*: Sets a limit on the amount of space that any directory can occupy. This might be useful for restricting the size of application, log, or user directories you don't want to grow beyond a certain point.

- *Flush files immediately*: Instructs NetWare to write data to disk immediately upon file close, rather than waiting for the next write cycle.

- *Migration*: Enables support for near-line storage, such as optical subsystems. Migration creates a look-up key in the volume's File Allocation Table (FAT) that describes how to retrieve the data from the near-line storage system.

- *Modified file list*: Displays a list of files modified since the last backup cycle. Useful for archive utilities, so they don't have to scan the entire volume for changed files.

- *Salvage*: Instructs NetWare to keep deleted files until the space is needed for new data, so they can be recovered if necessary.

- *Snap shot-file level*: Instructs NetWare to keep a copy of the last closed version of each open file in this volume. That way, archive utilities can save the copy to provide some protection in the event of data loss.

- *User space restrictions*: Allows you to set usage limits for individual eDirectory users.

- *On creation*: Allows you to specify whether to activate and/or mount the new volume upon creation. Activating a volume is analogous to mounting a traditional NetWare volume in that it is prepared for use. Mounting a volume is a trivial exercise that sets a pointer in the Volume Mapping Table so that NetWare knows how to access it. If left unchecked, you can activate and mount a volume from the NSS Logical Volumes subpage in ConsoleOne. Once an NSS volume is activated, you can use the MOUNT command from the server console to mount the volume.

Once created, a new NSS logical volume will be listed in the available volumes list on the NSS Logical Volumes subpage in ConsoleOne. Volume data is also visible from the Volumes page in NoRM.

For more information on NoRM see Chapter 3.

X-REF

Mounting a DOS Partition as an NSS Volume

You can mount a server's DOS partition as a volume with NSS, so that you can access its files like any other network volume. To do this, you need to load DOSFAT.NSS on the NetWare 6 server. Type the following command at the server console:

```
DOSFAT.NSS
```

This command loads the necessary NLMs to support the DOS partition as a logical volume. It also mounts the DOS partition as a volume with the name DOSFAT_*x*, where *x* is the drive letter of the DOS partition — usually C.

Dismounting and Deleting NSS Volumes

Deleting a volume deletes all the files and directories on that volume as well, so be sure you delete a volume only if you don't need the files anymore, or if you have a reliable backup.

Before you delete a volume, you must dismount it so that its files are unavailable to users. To dismount and delete an NSS volume, complete the following steps.

1. Back up all files on the volume or move them to a different volume, if you want to keep them.

2. Launch ConsoleOne and browse to the Server object from which you want to remove a volume.

3. Highlight the Server object and click Logical Volume Disk Management.

4. At the NSS Logical Volumes page, highlight the volume you want to delete in the volume list and click Dismount, then click Deactivate. You may have to click through a warning message to complete each operation.

5. Click Delete to remove the volume.

TIP

You may also want to look at deleting storage pools and partitions if you are trying to free up disk space for something. This will depend on how you have your volumes, pools, and partitions configured.

Increasing the Size of an NSS Volume

Storage pools make it a painless process to add space to an existing volume. In fact, one nice thing about NSS volumes is that they can be self-regulating. When you create the volume, you can specify that it be allowed to grow to fill its pool size. If you did not make this selection when the volume was created and would like to make this change, complete the following steps:

1. Launch ConsoleOne and browse to the Server object for which you want to increase the volume quota.

2. Highlight the Server object and click Logical Volume Disk Management.

3. At the NSS Logical Volumes page, check Allow volume quota to grow to the pool size and click OK. Alternatively, you can increase the size of your current disk quota from the same page.

If you add new disk devices to your NetWare 6 server, complete the following steps to make the new space available:

I. Install the new hard disk according to the manufacturer's instructions.

> For more information on installing new hard disks see Chapter 4.

X-REF

2. Launch ConsoleOne and browse to the Server object for which you want to make new disk space available.

3. Highlight the Server object and click Device Disk Management, opening the Devices page shown in Figure 8.8.

F I G U R E 8 . 8   *Devices page in ConsoleOne*

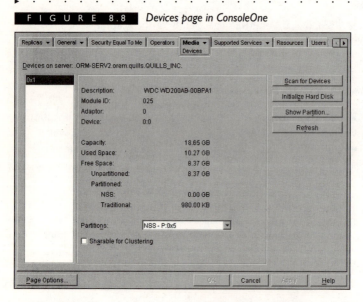

4. Highlight the device in the Devices list and click Show Partition. If you don't see the new device listed in the Devices list, click Scan for Devices to let NetWare search for the new device. From this point, creating the partition is exactly the same as outlined in the previous section on partitions.

5. Assign the new partition to a storage pool by going to the NSS Pools subpage and clicking Increase Size.

6. At the Storage Information screen, select the new partition and click Finish.

Once the new storage space is assigned to a pool, it is automatically available to the logical volumes assigned to that pool. You can increase quotas or let the volumes grow as needed to occupy the new space.

Repairing NSS Pools with REBUILD

Unlike traditional volumes, NSS does not allow you to make repairs at the volume level. Rather, you make repairs to the storage pool. There are two tool used to perform these repair operations:

▸ *VERIFY*: This utility checks the file system integrity for an NSS pool by searching for inconsistent data blocks or other errors. This utility indicates if there are problems with the file system.

▸ *REBUILD*: This utility actually makes repairs to the NSS storage pool should they prove necessary. You need to deactivate pools (and all the volumes in the pools) before you run REBUILD, so users do not attempt to access the volumes you are rebuilding. When you deactivate a storage pool, all the volumes in the pool automatically deactivate. REBUILD also copies errors and transactions into an error file called *volume_name*.RLF at the root of the DOS drive on your server. Every time you rebuild a particular NSS volume, the previous error file is overwritten. If you want to keep old error files, move them to another location. You can check the error file whenever an NSS volume does not come up in active mode after a rebuild.

NOTE

REBUILD should be a last resort and seldom necessary. The NSS file system is journaled, meaning that it keeps a log of disk activities while they are executing. When a disk crash or other problem occurs, NSS automatically rolls the file system state back to a known good state and then re-executes the operations in the journal to bring the system back up to date.

To run VERIFY, which is a read-only assessment of the storage pool, type the following command at the server console:

```
nss /poolverify
```

NSS provides a list of pools from which you can select. The VERIFY operation will return a summary screen of storage pool information, as shown in Figure 8.9.

► • ◄

| F I G U R E   8 . 9 | *VERIFY summary report* |

```
                          ZLSS Pool Verify
  Pool: NSS_ENGR          Total Size: 14928 Meg (3821824 blocks)
  ---------- Pool Scan Report ----------    ---------- Pool System Report ----------
  Crosslinked Blocks...............0         Total Blocks...............3821824
  Unaccounted Blocks...............0         Blocks in Use..................16522
  Free Tree Blocks..............(50)2        Purgeable Blocks...................0
  Object Tree Blocks...............2         Non-Purgeable blocks...............0
  Name Tree Blocks.................1         Pool Info Blocks...................2
  Journal Blocks...............16386         ------- Salvage System Report -------
  Purge Log Blocks.................2         Salvage Entries W/O IDs............0
  Super Blocks....................64         Salvage Entries W/O names..........0
  Pool Info Blocks.................2         Salvage Parents W/O IDs............0
  Other Tree Blocks................3         Salvage Parents W/O names..........0
  Used By Pool.................16522         Salvageable Objects................0
  Total In Use.................16522         Salvagable Blocks..................0
  Unused Blocks.................3805302
  Total Blocks.................3821824       Object Tree Levels.................1
  Highest LSN......0x00000001C00000FD        Name Tree Levels...................1
  Lowest LSN.......0x0000000000000000        Salvage Tree Levels................1
  Object Tree Entries..............3         User Rest. Tree Levels.............1
  Object Special Entries...........7         MFL Tree Levels....................0
  Salvage Tree Entries.............1         Logical Vols NOT Verified..........0
  <F1>Errs   <F2>Histograms   <F6>Conflicts      <Any Key>Next LU   <ESC>Exit
```

Should it become necessary, you can run REBUILD by typing the following command at the server console:

```
nss /poolrebuild
```

NSS provides a list of pools from which you can select. REBUILD verifies and accounts for all data blocks in the storage pool. If there are any errors, the errors appear on the screen; otherwise, it reverts to the active state. You must re-activate the pool and remount volume(s) before users will be able to access them again.

► • ◄

Saving Disk Space

NetWare 6 contains several features that will help you to conserve disk space:

▸ File compression, which compresses less frequently used files, typically can conserve up to 63 percent of your hard disk space. This feature is available only on traditional volumes.

▸ Block suballocation allows several files to share a single block to avoid wasting space unnecessarily. This feature is available only on traditional volumes.

▸ Restricting users' disk space enables you to decide how much disk space users can fill up on a volume.

▸ Purging files lets you free up disk space by removing files that have been deleted but were still retained in a salvageable state. (You can also salvage deleted files, instead of purging them, but of course that doesn't free up any disk space.)

File Compression

File compression typically can save up to 63 percent of the server's hard disk space by compressing unused files. Compressed files are automatically decompressed when a user accesses them, so the user doesn't necessarily know that the files were compressed.

Volumes are automatically enabled to support compression should you choose to use it. You can enable compression either during or after the creation of a traditional or logical volume. To enable compression on an existing volume, complete the following steps:

1. Launch ConsoleOne and browse to the Volume object for which you want to change the Compression settings.

2. Right-click the Volume object and select Properties.

3. Double-click the Attributes tab and select NSS Attributes.

4. Check Compression and click OK to save your changes.

You can also enable/disable volume compression for all volumes on a server by typing the following SET parameter from the server console:

```
SET Enable File Compression = ON|OFF
```

Disabling and re-enabling compression

Once compression is enabled on a volume it cannot be disabled except at the server level, using the SET parameter described in the previous section. This setting serves to suspend compression activities, but doesn't remove compression capabilities from the volume. The only way to remove compression from a volume is to delete and re-create it.

Managing compression

By default, once the volume is enabled and compression is turned on, files and directories are compressed automatically after they've been untouched for seven days.

You can change several aspects of file compression, however, such as how long the files wait before being compressed, the time of day the compression activity occurs, and which files never get compressed. To control file compression, you can use two file and directory attributes and several SET parameters.

To specify compression for specific files or directories, you can assign them the following file and directory attributes with ConsoleOne:

- ▶ *Immediate compress*: Instructs NetWare to compresses the file or directory immediately, without waiting the standard inactivity period.

► *Don't compress*: Instructs NetWare to never compress the file or directory, even if compression is turned on for a parent directory.

The SET parameters that affect file compression let you control compression characteristics for all enabled volumes on the server. You can set options such as when compression happens, how many files can be compressed at the same time, how many times a file must be accessed before it is decompressed, and so on. The easiest way to view and change these parameters is with NoRM, but you can also use MONITOR.NLM or the appropriate SET console command at the server console.

NOTE

Remember that if you change a SET parameter, the change affects all files and directories in all volumes on the server that have been enabled for compression.

To change the SET parameters complete the following steps:

1. Launch NoRM and click the SET Parameters link in the Navigation frame.

2. In the Set Parameter Categories window, click Common File System.

3. Modify any of the following compression-related SET parameters by clicking the value currently associated with that parameter.

- `Compression Daily Check Stop Hour=HOUR`: Specifies the hour when the file compressor stops searching volumes for files that need to be compressed. If this value is the same as the Compression Daily Check Starting Hour value, then the search starts at the specified starting hour and goes until all compressible files have been found. Default: 6 (6:00 a.m.). Values: 0 (midnight) to 23 (11:00 p.m.).

- `Compression Daily Check Starting Hour=HOUR`: Specifies the hour when the file compressor begins searching volumes for files that need to be compressed. Default: 0 (midnight). Values: 0 to 23 (11:00 p.m.).

- `Minimum Compression Percentage Gain=NUMBER`: Specifies the minimum percentage that a file must be able to be compressed in order to remain compressed. Default: 20. Values: 0 to 50.

- `Enable File Compression=ON|OFF`: When set to On, file compression is allowed to occur on volumes that are enabled for compression. If set to Off, file compression won't occur, even though the volume is still enabled for compression. Default: On.

- `Maximum Concurrent Compressions=NUMBER`: Specifies how many volumes can compress files at the same time. Increasing this value may slow down server performance during compression times. Default: 2. Values: 1 to 8.

- `Convert Compressed To Uncompressed Option=NUMBER`: Specifies how a compressed file is stored after it has been accessed. Default: 1. Values: 0 = always leave the file compressed; 1 = leave the file compressed after the first access within the time frame defined by the Days Untouched Before Compression parameter, then leave the file uncompressed after the second access; 2 = change the file to uncompressed after the first access.

- `Decompress Percent Disk Space Free To Allow Commit=NUMBER`: Specifies the percentage of free disk space that is required on a volume before committing an uncompressed file to disk. This helps you avoid running out of disk space by uncompressing files. Default: 10. Values: 0 to 75.

- `Decompress Free Space Warning Interval=TIME`: Specifies the interval between warnings when the volume doesn't have enough disk space for uncompressed files. Default: 30 min 57.2 sec. Values: 0 sec (which turns off warnings) to 29 days 15 hours, 50 min 3.8 sec.

- `Deleted Files Compression Option=NUMBER`: Specifies how the server handles deleted files. Default: 1. Values: 0 = don't compress deleted files; 1 = compress deleted files during the next day's search; 2 = compress deleted files immediately.

- `Days Untouched Before Compression=DAYS`: Specifies how many days a file or directory must remain untouched before being compressed. Default: 14. Values: 0 to 100000.

Block Suballocation

A block is a unit that is allocated to store a file. A file may take up more space on the disk than its actual size because NetWare allocates the disk into uniformly sized blocks that are used to store pieces of files. The default block size depends on the volume's size, as shown in Table 8.1. In general, larger block sizes are better for large database records, because they can help speed up access. Smaller block sizes require more server memory, but help prevent disk space from being wasted. Prior to NetWare 4.1x, there was nothing you could do to prevent the inefficient use of disk space if you wanted to use larger block sizes. For example, if your block size were 32K, a 35K file would take two 32K blocks, using a total of 64K of disk space.

TABLE 8.1	Default Block Sizes for Storing Files
VOLUME SIZE	BLOCK SIZE
0 to 31MB	4K
32 to 149MB	8K
150 to 499MB	16K
500MB to 1999MB	32K
2000MB or more	64K

However, NetWare now includes a feature for traditional volumes called block suballocation. Block suballocation lets the file system break a block into subunits as small as 512 bytes, so that several files (or pieces of files) can share a single block. With block suballocation turned on, a 35K file will use up one 32K block, plus enough suballocation blocks required, for a total of only 35K of disk space.

Block suballocation is available on traditional NetWare volumes only. It is enabled by default when NetWare 6 is installed. You do not need to do anything to use or manage block suballocation.

Restricting Users' Disk Space

You can restrict how much disk space a user can fill up on a particular volume. This can help prevent individual users from using an excessive amount of disk space. Both traditional and NSS logical volumes support user space restrictions by default. However, NSS logical volumes let you enable/disable this support through a special NSS attribute, User Space Restrictions.

To set space restrictions; use ConsoleOne to open the Volume properties page. From the Users with Space Restrictions tab you can see which users have restricted disk allowances on this volume, as shown in Figure 8.10. You can see what their restrictions are and how much space they still have available. To create a restriction, simply add a user to the list and define his or her space limit for that volume.

Users with Space Restrictions tab in ConsoleOne

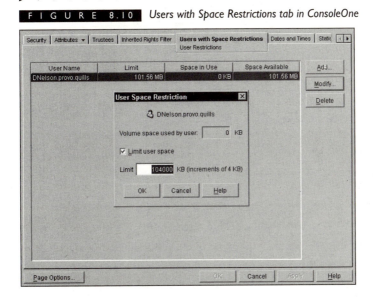

Purging and Salvaging Files

When files are deleted from a NetWare server, they are not actually removed from the server's hard disk. Instead, they are retained in a salvageable state.

Deleted files are usually stored in the same directory from which they were originally deleted. If, however, the directory itself was also deleted, the deleted files are stored in a special directory called DELETED.SAV at the volume's root.

Exceptions to the salvageable state

Deleted files are maintained in this salvageable state unless one of the following occurs:

▶ The file is salvaged, restoring it to its original form.

▶ The server runs out of free space on the disk and begins to overwrite files that have been deleted for a specified period of time. The oldest deleted files are overwritten first. A configurable SET parameter defines the amount of time a file must remain deleted before it can be overwritten.

▶ The administrator or user purges the file. (When purged, a file is completely removed from the disk and cannot be recovered.) You can purge files with ConsoleOne.

► The Immediate Purge attribute can be set at the file, directory, or volume level to prevent files from being salvaged. You can set this attribute with ConsoleOne.

► The administrator uses SET Immediate Purge of Deleted Files = ON. All volumes on that server will immediately purge deleted files. (The default for this parameter is Off.)

Purging and salvaging files with ConsoleOne

To use ConsoleOne to either purge or salvage a deleted file or directory, complete the following steps:

1. Launch ConsoleOne and browse to the directory containing the files or directories you want to salvage or purge.

2. From the View menu, select Deleted File View.

3. In the View window (right side), select a file or directory.

4. Click either the Salvage or Purge button on the ConsoleOne toolbar, as shown in Figure 8.11.

► . . . . ◄

F I G U R E   8.11   *Deleted File view in ConsoleOne*

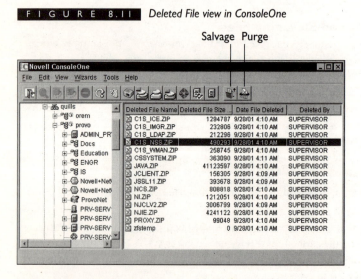

5. If you salvage files from an existing directory, the files are restored to that directory. If you salvage files from a deleted directory, the files are restored into the DELETED.SAV directory at the root of the volume.

NOTE

If you have data shredding enabled, it will happen upon file purge, not file delete. If you have very sensitive materials on which you want to use data shredding, it might be a good idea to enable the Immediate Purge attribute for the file or directory where such data is stored.

Adding a Name Space to a Volume

By default, NetWare 6 loads the DOS and LONG name spaces on traditional volumes when they are created. These name spaces would support the following operating system file formats: DOS, OS/2, Windows 95/98, and Windows NT/2000 file formats. If you want a volume to store other file formats — for example, Macintosh or UNIX (NFS) — you need to add name space support for those file formats to the volume. Name space support is a feature that extends the volume's storage characteristics, enabling the volume to store the longer filenames and additional information that different file formats may contain.

For example, Macintosh name space support enables the volume to store a Macintosh file's resource fork and long filename.

The following name spaces are available for NetWare 6:

- ▶ MAC.NAM: Macintosh file support
- ▶ LONG.NAM: OS/2, Windows NT/2000, and Windows 95/98 file support (installed by default).
- ▶ NFS.NAM: Network File System support for UNIX/Linux files.

Loading additional name spaces requires significant additional memory on a traditional NetWare volume, because it can double or triple the size of the Directory Entry Table (DET). Since traditional volumes cache the entire DET in memory, this could be a significant burden. For this reason, its best to load only those name spaces that you are actually going to use on a traditional volume.

To add name space support to a traditional volume, complete the following steps:

1. Load the name space loadable module on the server. For example, to load the Macintosh name space, type: **LOAD MAC**

2. Add the name space support to the desired volume by using the following console command:

   ```
   ADD NAME SPACE MAC TO <volume name>VOL1
   ```

Once you've added the name space support to a volume, the only ways you can remove the name space support are to run VREPAIR.NLM or delete and recreate the volume.

NSS logical volumes don't suffer from the limitations of traditional NetWare volumes, because they do not have to cache the entire DET in memory. Because of this, there is little pain associated with loading multiple name spaces. In fact, NSS logical volumes are created with all name spaces by default.

To see a list of all the volumes on a server and their name spaces, use the VOLUMES console command.

TIP

Backing Up and Restoring Files

Files can be lost or damaged in a variety of ways. They can be corrupted by viruses, accidentally deleted by users, overwritten by other applications, or destroyed when a hard disk fails. Despite all the best precautions, you can't always prevent files from being lost.

What you can do, however, is make sure that you always have current backup copies of your network data, so you can restore files. If you have a carefully planned and executed backup strategy, you can minimize the amount of work that will be lost if you have to restore a file from your archives.

Many different backup products are available on the market. NetWare 6 includes a backup utility called NWBACK32 that you can use as a stopgap until you find a more complete data backup solution. NWBACK32 can get the job done, but it lacks many of the conveniences, such as flexible scheduling options, that third-party products have. Backup products can back up data onto a variety of storage media, such as tapes and optical disks.

Backing up network files involves more than just making a copy of the files. It's important to use a backup product, such as NWBACK32, that backs up not just the files but also the NetWare information associated with those files, such as trustee rights, inherited rights filters, and file and directory attributes.

A solid backup strategy is critical to the well being of your network. The following section describes backup strategies that can be employed to protect your valuable data.

Planning a Backup Strategy

Planning an efficient backup strategy is one of the most beneficial tasks you can do as part of network management. With a good backup strategy, you can limit the time it takes to do backups, ensure that the least amount of working time is lost by your users, and avoid unnecessary headaches from searching for lost files.

Backup strategies can be different for every network. What works for someone else may not work well for you, and vice versa. When planning a backup strategy, you need to consider the following questions:

▶ What type of backup medium do you need to use?

▶ What backup schedule should you follow?

▶ How frequently should you rotate your backup medium?

▶ Where should the backups be stored?

▶ How often will you test the restore procedure?

The tips and suggestions in the next few sections can help you decide on your own backup strategy.

TIP Although it is possible to backup eDirectory database files, restoring them is a prescription for major grief. Rather than trying to restore eDirectory objects from tape, use partition replication to restore objects to a server. For more information on eDirectory design and replication see Chapter 5.

Choosing your backup medium

Before purchasing a backup device, you must decide what kind of backup medium you want to use, such as tapes or optical disks. Many manufacturers' backup products can back up data onto a variety of storage media, but it's a good idea to know what you want before you buy something that limits your choices. The medium you choose will probably depend on the following factors:

▶ How much you're willing to spend.

▶ How large your network is.

▶ How long you need to retain your backed-up data. (Some media deteriorate after a few years; other media may have a 100-year guarantee.)

Tape is probably the most common backup medium in use today, especially in small- to medium-sized businesses. Tapes are relatively easy to use, can be used in any size network, and are fairly inexpensive.

NOTE One of the downsides of tape is that backup manufacturers may use different, proprietary tape formats that aren't compatible with each other. Two tape standards have been established (one from Novell, and another from Microsoft), so some efforts have been made to

> standardize on one or the other, but there are still differences
> between manufacturers. Be sure any backup product you buy will be
> compatible with any other system with which you may need to
> share tapes.

You should study the pros and cons of the various tape formats to find the best balance between cost and performance before making a decision. Some of the tape formats currently in use include the following:

- ▶ DAT (Digital Audio Tape)
- ▶ QIC (Quarter-Inch Cartridge)
- ▶ Digital Linear Tape (DLT)
- ▶ 8mm

Tape, while easy to use and relatively affordable, is not necessarily suited to long-term storage of data. Like any magnetic medium, tape can oxidize or otherwise deteriorate over time; therefore, for long-term storage, you may want to consider some of the different types of optical disks. Some optical disks that are available currently include:

- ▶ CD-R (Compact Disk-Recordable)
- ▶ DVD
- ▶ Magneto-optical
- ▶ Floptical disks

Both tape and optical technologies have made advances in the last few years in terms of cost, performance, and ease of use. Talk to your reseller about your network's specific needs, and choose the medium that best suits your network.

Planning a backup schedule

A good way to determine how often to back up critical data is to calculate how long you can afford to spend recreating the information if it is lost. If you can't afford to lose more than a day's worth of work, you should perform daily backups of that information. If losing a week's worth of work is more of a nuisance than a devastating blow, perhaps you don't need to do daily backups and can rely on weekly backups instead.

Most backup products, including NWBACK32, let you determine not only when to back up your network, but also what types of information you back up each time. In many cases, you'll find that there's no point in backing up your entire network every night if only a few of the files change during the day.

With most products, you can choose between doing a full backup and an *incremental* backup. In an incremental backup, only the files that have been changed are detected and backed up. With a little careful planning, you can create a schedule that staggers complete backups with incremental backups, so you still get full coverage without spending more time and money than necessary.

For example, you can do a full backup of the network once a week. Then, once a day, do incremental backups of only those files that have changed. In the event of a total loss of files, you can restore all the files from the weekly backup, and then restore each of the daily tapes to update the files that changed during that week. In this way, you can cover all of your files while minimizing the time each backup session takes during the week.

TIP

Backup products will normally scan the file system to detect changed files when performing an incremental backup. It does this by looking for a special file attribute called the Archive Needed attribute (also called the Modify bit). When a file is changed, this attribute is assigned to it. NSS can speed this process up considerably with its Modified File List (MFL), in which it maintains a list of changed files. You might want to consider looking at backup products that support the MFL feature of NSS to make your life a little easier.

Another tip for minimizing backup time is to organize your directory (folder) structure so that often-changed files are separate from seldom-changed files. For example, there's no point in wasting your time by frequently backing up files such as applications and utilities, which seldom change. If you put applications in one directory and work files in another, you can skip the application directory completely during incremental backups, making the process go faster.

Finally, be sure to document your backup schedule and keep a backup log. A written record of all backups and your backup strategy can help someone else restore the files if you aren't there.

Planning the medium rotation

It's important to plan a rotation schedule for your backup medium. You should decide in advance how long you will retain old files, and how often you will reuse the same tapes or disks.

Assuming you're using tapes (although any re-writeable medium presents the same potential danger), if you have only one backup tape that you use every week, you could unknowingly back up corrupted files onto your single tape each time you replace the previous week's backup with the new one. In short, you're replacing your last good copy with a corrupted one.

To prevent this type of problem, plan to keep older backup tapes or disks on hand at all times. Many network administrators use four or more tapes or disks for the same set of files, cycling through them one at a time. Each week, the most outdated tape or disk is used for the new backup. This way, three or more versions of backups are available at any given time. How many tape or disk sets you'll need depends on your rotation schedule. If you want to keep four weeks' worth of daily and weekly backups, you'll need at least 20 sets of tapes or disks — five for each week.

Some backup products offer preset rotation schedules for you. They will automatically prompt you for the right set of media and keep track of the schedule.

Deciding where to store the backups

Another important aspect of your backup strategy is to plan where to store your backups. If you have backups of non-critical data, you may be comfortable keeping them on-site. However, when storing backups on-site, you should at least store them in a room separate from the server's room. If a fire breaks out in the server room, your backup tapes won't do you much good if they're lying melted beside the server.

For mission-critical data, you may need to keep backups in an off-site location. That way, if a physical disaster occurs (such as a fire, flood, or earthquake), they'll be safe. If the data is critical enough to store off-site, but you also want to have immediate access to it, consider making two backups and storing one off-site and the other on-site.

Testing the restore process

A backup is useful only if the data in it can be restored successfully. Too many people discover, too late, a problem with their backups when they're in the middle of an important restoration process. Practice restoring files before you need to do so. By practicing, you may identify problems you didn't realize you had. Don't wait until it's too late.

Preparing to Use NWBACK32

NWBACK32, the backup utility included in NetWare 6, can be used either from the server console or from a workstation. With this product, you can back up all the different types of files that can be stored on your server: DOS, Macintosh, OS/2, Windows NT/2000, Windows 95/98, and UNIX.

NWBACK32 enables you to select the type of backup you want to perform. There are three choices (all of which can be customized for your particular needs):

- *Full backup.* This option backs up all network files. It removes the Archive Needed file attribute — assigned to a file whenever the file is changed — from all files and directories. When the file is backed up, most backup products can remove the attribute so the next time the file is changed, the attribute is once again assigned.

- *Differential backup.* This option backs up only files that were modified since the last full backup. It does not remove the Archive Needed attribute from these files.

- *Incremental backup.* This option backs up only files that were modified since the last full or incremental backup. It removes the Archive Needed attribute from these files.

There are five major steps involved in configuring the NetWare 6 backup system for use:

1. Install the Storage Management Services (SMS) on a NetWare 6 server. SMS is the collection of files and utilities that comprise the NetWare backup solution. It also provides a foundation and common interface for third-party vendors that allow their backup applications to communicate with NetWare.

2. Install a backup device and load the device's drivers on a server. This server will be the host server (the backup server).

3. Load the necessary backup NLMs on the host server

4. Load the appropriate Target Service Agents (TSAs) on any servers or workstations whose files you want to back up. These servers and workstations are called *targets*.

5. Launch the NetWare backup utility on either the host server or a workstation. The server-based version of the backup utility is called SBCON.NLM. The workstation-based utility is called NWBACK32.EXE. Both utilities accomplish the same tasks, enabling you to back up and restore network files. It doesn't matter which utility you choose, so select the utility most convenient for you.

You will perform the first three steps in this process regardless of whether or not you choose to use NWBACK32 or SBCON as your preferred backup utility. NetWare 6 provides a common foundation and interface for backup processes known as Storage Management Services (SMS). Third-party vendors have designed their systems to integrate with the NetWare SMS interface so they don't have to recreate the low-level communications.

Installing Storage Management Services

SMS will normally be installed during the installation of NetWare 6, when it can be chosen as an optional Novell service. However, if necessary you can install SMS after the fact through Deployment Manager or the graphical server console. To install SMS through Deployment Manager, complete the following steps:

1. Insert the NetWare 6 Operating System CD into your workstation CD-ROM drive and launch NWDEPLOY.EXE from the root of the CD-ROM.

2. Double-click Post-Installation tasks and select Install NetWare 6 products.

3. At the Target Server screen, select the server to which you want to install SMS and click Next.

4. Authenticate as the admin user for your eDirectory tree and click OK. If you have trouble authenticating, click Details and check the Connect by Address box. Specify the IP address of the target server and try authenticating again.

5. At the components screen, click Clear All and select only Storage Management Services. Click Next.

6. At the Summary screen click Finish. After the SMS files are copied, click Close to complete the installation.

Setting up the host server and targets

Before you can run the NetWare Backup utility, you must first prepare the host server and any targets you want to back up, by completing the following steps:

1. Attach the backup device (tape or disk drive) to the host server, following the manufacturer's instructions.

2. Load the necessary backup device drivers on the host server, again following manufacturer's instructions.

3. Launch ConsoleOne and browse to the Server object on which the storage device is installed.

4. Highlight the Server object and click the Device Disk Management button on the ConsoleOne toolbar, as shown in Figure 8.12.

FIGURE 8.12 *The Device Disk Management button on the ConsoleOne toolbar*

Device disk management

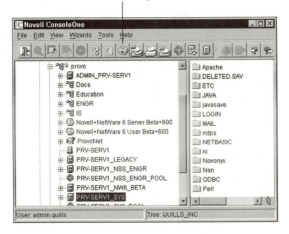

5. If you don't see your storage device listed in the Devices list, click Scan for Devices to have NetWare 6 register the new device. You could also use the following console command to register the device with NetWare:

SCAN FOR NEW DEVICES

TIP

Check the manufacturer's documentation to find out which drivers you need. Place the commands that load the backup device drivers in the server's STARTUP.NCF file if you want them to load automatically when the server is rebooted.

6. SMS includes a handy startup file called SMSSTART.NCF. It is stored in SYS:SYSTEM, and will automate the loading of all necessary SMS modules. You can put the SMSSTART command in your AUTOEXEC.NCF if you want to load SMS modules automatically when the server boots.

- *SMDR.NLM*: This is the SMS Data Requester. It automatically creates an SMS SMDR Group object in the server's context. The SMS SMDR Group object will contain each server and workstation to be backed up by this host server.

- *SMSDI.NLM*: This is the SMS Device Interface module, which will let the NWBACK32 program communicate with the backup device:
- *QMAN.NLM*: This is the SMS Queue Manager, which will create a job queue for the backup utility to use. The backup queue object is named "*Server* Backup Queue" (with the server's name substituted for *Server*).
- *SBSC.NLM*: This is the NWBACK32 communication module, which lets NWBACK32 communicate with the other SMS modules.

7. In addition to the SMS modules, SMSSTART will also load two Target Service Agent (TSA) modules. These modules are optional. If you aren't going to do the type of back up supported by the TSA, you may unload them.

- TSA600.NLM: This is the TSA for NetWare 6 servers. Load this module if you want to back up the network files that reside on this server.
- TSAPROXY: This module lets you back up Windows 95/98 and Windows NT/2000 workstations to the Host server.

8. (Optional) TSANDS.NLM: This TSA lets you back up the eDirectory database. It's usually best to load this on a server that contains a replica of the eDirectory tree's largest partition)

NOTE

You no longer need TSADOSP.NLM for backing up the server's DOS partition. Since NSS supports mounting the DOS partition as a logical volume, you can use the nss /DOSFAT command to make the DOS partition accessible through normal backup procedures.

9. (Optional) If you are going to back up any other target servers from this host server, you need to load the appropriate TSA(s) on the target server. The TSA modules that might be appropriate for a target server, which is not also functioning as a host, include the following:

- TSA600: Load on NetWare 6 target servers
- TSA500: Load on NetWare 5 target servers
- TSA410: Load on NetWare 4 target servers
- TSANDS: If you want to back up eDirectory, load TSANDS on a target server that holds a replica of the eDirectory tree's largest partition.
- TSADOSP: Load on a target server if you want to back up its DOS partition. This NLM is necessary only on older versions of NetWare. NetWare 6 no longer requires it.

When these steps are completed, the host server is prepared, and the target server is ready to be backed up. If you want to back up a Windows 95/98 or Windows NT/2000 workstation, you must take extra steps to configure TSAs on those workstations, as explained in the following sections. If you are ready to back up or restore files, skip to the "Backing up files" or "Restoring Files" sections later in this chapter.

Preparing to back up workstations

Although most people use NWBACK32 to back up files from network servers, you can also use it to back up files from the hard disks of Windows 95/98 or Windows NT/2000 workstations. To do this, you must load and configure TSA software on the workstations. The TSA software is provided as part of the Novell client.

The Client TSA is not installed by default, so you will need to perform a custom client installation and make sure that Novell Target Service Agent is selected as a client component to install. After the TSA software is installed, you must configure it, as described in the following sections.

X-REF

For more information on installing the Novell client and its optional components see Chapter 2.

Configuring the Windows 95/98 TSA   Before you back up files on a Windows 95/98 workstation for the first time, you must configure the client-side TSA. When the TSA is installed, you will see a round, shield-shaped icon in the Windows 95/98 system tray. When you put the cursor over this icon, the words "Novell TSA (Not Registered)" will appear.

To configure the TSA and register it with the host server, complete the following steps:

1. Double-click the shield icon in the workstation's system tray to open the Properties page for the Novell TSA for Windows 95/98.

2. Provide the appropriate information and click OK to save your changes.

   - *Username*: Specify a username that will be used to access your workstation while backing up its files.

   - *Password*: Specify a password for the user.

   - *Protocol*: Specify the protocol you want to use (IPX or TCP/IP).

   - *Servername*: Specify the name of the host server that will back up this workstation's files.

- *Resources available to TSA*: Specify the local drive(s) you want to back up.
- *Auto register at startup*: Check this option to automatically register this workstation with the host server when it boots up.
- *Show TSA icon on taskbar*: Check this box to be able to easily access the TSA configuration and check its status.

3. Reboot the workstation to make the changes take effect.

After the workstation is rebooted, the TSA icon in the system tray displays the words "Novell TSA (Listening)" when you run the mouse cursor over it. Now the workstation is ready to be backed up, and you can move on to the "Backing up files" section later in this chapter.

Configuring the Windows NT/2000 TSA   Before you try for the first time to back up files that reside on a Windows NT/2000 workstation, you must configure the TSA. Make sure you installed the TSA software during the client installation.

To configure the TSA and register it with the host server, complete the following steps:

1. Right-click My Network Places (Network Neighborhood on NT) and select Properties. Open Local Area Connections and click Properties.

2. Select Novell Target Service Agent and click Properties. This opens the TSA Preferences page, as shown in Figure 8.13.

3. Select the Preferences tab (It's the default page) and make your desired selections.
   - *Preferred server*: Specify the name of the host server that will back up this workstation's files. If you are using TCP/IP, use the IP address or DNS name of the host server.
   - *Protocol*: Specify the protocol you want to use (IPX or TCP/IP).
   - *Events to log*: Check the specific backup events that you want logged. These are viewable from the Events Log tab.
   - *Allow backup user*: Check this option to grant the backup user rights to the workstation files.
   - *Auto register*: Check this option to automatically register this workstation with the host server.

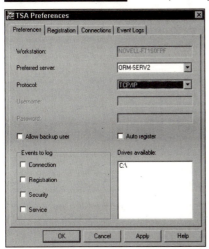

TSA Preferences page for Windows NT/2000

NOTE

The Username and Password fields are disabled on NT 4.0 and Windows 2000 workstations. You will use the workstation username and password, such as Administrator, to access the workstation during a backup or restore operation.

4. Select the Registration tab. Click Register to connect your client TSA to the TSAPROXY of the host server. The Withdraw button disconnects you from the host server.

5. Select the Connections tab. When you are actively performing a backup or restore operation, this page will show you the number of connections being used and the tasks being performed by each connection. Possible tasks include Idle, Scanning, Backing Up, and Restoring.

6. When you are finished configuring the TSA preferences, click OK to save your TSA settings.

Backing up files

After you've loaded the necessary NLMs on the host server and loaded a TSA on the target server or workstation, you are ready to back up the target's files. You can manage the backup process using either the server-based backup program (SBCON.NLM) or the workstation-based backup program (NWBACK32.EXE). Both programs accomplish the same tasks, so choose the program that is most convenient for you to use. The following sections explain how to use these programs.

Using the server-based utility

To use the server-based SBCON.NLM to back up files, complete the following steps:

1. Load SBCON.NLM from the server console.

2. From the main menu, choose Job Administration, and then choose Backup.

3. At the Backup Options screen, configure the backup session. When finished, press Esc to save your options

   - *Target service*: If you are backing up a server, select the target server to back up. If you're backing up a workstation, choose the workstation's host server, as defined in its TSA configuration. Enter the user name and password for the target. For other NetWare servers, specify the user's full name, with context and a leading dot. For Windows 95/98 workstations, specify the username and password that you defined in the TSA configuration. For Windows NT/2000 workstations, use the administrator account, or some other user account with administrator privileges.

   - *What to back up*: Press Enter to open the List Resources box. Press Ins and browse the list of volumes, directories, and files until you locate what you want to back up. Press Enter to select the item and Esc to move it to the List Resources box. When you have selected all the resources you want to back up, press Esc to return to the Backup Options menu.

   - *Description*: Enter a descriptive name for this backup session.

   - *Device/media name*: Choose the backup device and medium you will use. If only one device is available, the backup program will choose it for you. Specifying wildcard characters (*.*) will select the default device.

4. Open the Advanced Options menu to select specific session characteristics for the backup. Press Esc to save your choices.

   - *Backup type*: Specify Full, Differential, or Incremental backup.

   - *Subsets of what to back up*: Specify Include and Exclude options to customize what you want to back up. Use Exclude options when you want to back up most of the file system while omitting only a small part. Everything that you don't specifically exclude is backed up. Use Include options when you want to back up only a small portion of the file system. Everything you don't specifically include is excluded.

- *Scan options*: Specify what types of data to exclude from the back up process. Options include subdirectories, trustee rights, hidden files, and the like.

- *Execution time*: Specify the time you want the backup to occur. If you don't modify this, it will start immediately.

- *Scheduling*: Specify a schedule for the job you are creating, if you want it to run on a regular basis without having to reconfigure it each time.

5. Select Yes if your backup device allows you to put multiple sessions on a medium, and if one or more sessions are already on the medium you're using. Select No to overwrite any existing sessions.

6. When asked if you want to submit a job, select Yes to submit it to the SMS queue.

Using the workstation-based utility

To use the workstation-based NWBACK32.EXE from a Windows 95/98 or Windows NT/2000 workstation to back up files, complete the following steps:

1. From your workstation, log in to the host server.

2. Launch NWBACK32, which is located in SYS:PUBLIC.

3. From the Quick Access menu, shown in Figure 8.14, click Backup.

4. In the left pane, double-click What to Backup.

5. Double-click the item you want to back up. Options include NDS (eDirectory), NetWare servers, Workstations, NetWare Server DOS partition, or GroupWise Database. A list of servers that hold the type of resource you selected will appear beneath the item you double-click. If you selected Workstations, you will see a list of host servers from which to choose.

6. Double-click a server, and enter the appropriate user name and password to authenticate.

7. Click the information you want to back up so that an X appears in the box next to the item you want.

8. Double-click Where to Backup.

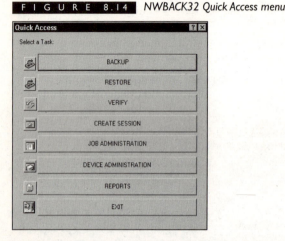

9. Double-click the context. (If you need to change contexts, click the Change to Context button on the toolbar.)

10. Double-click Queues to open a list of backup queues.

11. Right-click a queue and choose Submit the Job. Specify the characteristics of the back up session as you move through the various option screens:

    • *Backup type*: Specify Full, Differential, or Incremental backup.

    • *Subsets of what to back up*: Specify Include and Exclude options to customize what you want to back up. Use Exclude options when you want to back up most of the file system while omitting only a small part. Everything that you don't specifically exclude is backed up. Use Include options when you want to back up only a small portion of the file system. Everything you don't specifically include is excluded.

    • *Scan options*: Specify what types of data to exclude from the backup process. Options include subdirectories, trustee rights, hidden files, and the like.

    • *Execution time*: Specify the time you want the backup to occur. If you don't modify this, it will start immediately.

    • *Scheduling*: Specify a schedule for the job you are creating, if you want it to run on a regular basis without having to reconfigure it each time.

12. At the last screen, indicate whether you want to append this session to a tape that already contains previous sessions, then enter a description of this session and indicate whether you want to keep this job. Then press Finish.

13. When asked if you want to submit the job, answer Yes to begin the backup session.

Restoring Files

To restore files from a backup, you need to prepare the host server and targets the same way you did for the backup procedure. (See the section "Setting up the host server and targets" earlier in this chapter.)

After you've loaded the necessary NLMs on the host server and loaded a TSA on the target server or workstation, you can use either the server-based SBCON.NLM or the workstation-based NWBACK32.EXE to restore files. Both programs accomplish the same tasks, so choose the program that is most convenient for you to use. The following sections explain how to use these programs.

Using the server-based utility

To use the server-based SBCON.NLM to restore files, complete the following steps:

1. Load SBCON.NLM from the server console.

2. From the main menu, choose Job Administration, and then choose Restore.

3. At the Restore Options screen, configure the restore session. When finished, press Esc to save your options.

- *Target service*: If you are restoring to a server, select the target server. If you're restoring to a workstation, choose the workstation's host server, as defined in its TSA configuration. Enter the user name and password for the target. For other NetWare servers, specify the user's full name, with context and a leading dot. For Windows 95/98 workstations, specify the username and password that you defined in the TSA configuration. For Windows NT/2000 workstations, use the administrator account, or some other user account with administrator privileges.

- *Description*: Specify the name of the back up session that you want to restore.

- *Device/media name*: Choose the backup device and medium you will use for the restore session. If only one device is available, the backup program will choose it for you. Specifying wildcard characters (*.*) will select the default device.

4. Open the Advanced Options menu to select specific session characteristics for the restore operation. Press Esc to save your choices.

- *Rename data sets*: If you want to restore the data to a different location, specify the specific path here.

- *Subsets of what to restore*: Specify Include and Exclude options to customize what you want to restore. Use Exclude options when you want to restore most of the file system while omitting only a small part. Everything that you don't specifically exclude is restored. Use Include options when you want to restore only a small portion of the file system. Everything you don't specifically include will not be restored.

- *Open mode options*: Specify what types of data to exclude from the restore process. Options include data streams, trustee rights, space restrictions, and the like.

- *Overwrite parent*: Specify whether or not you want to overwrite existing data that might exist for Parent objects, which include servers, volumes, and directories.

- *Overwrite child*: Choose whether or not to overwrite files without regard for last backup time or date of existing file.

- *Execution time*: Specify the time you want the restore operation to occur. If you don't modify this, it will start immediately.

- *Scheduling*: Specify a schedule for the job you are creating if you want it to run on a regular basis without having to reconfigure it each time.

5. When asked if you want to submit a job, select Yes to submit the restore operation to the SMS queue.

Using the workstation-based utility

To use the workstation-based NWBACK32.EXE from a Windows 95/98 or Windows NT/2000 workstation to restore files, complete the following steps:

1. From your workstation, log in to the host server.

2. Launch NWBACK32, which is located in SYS:PUBLIC.

3. At the Quick Access menu, click Restore.

4. In the left pane, double-click What to Restore.

5. Double-click the context. (If you need to change contexts, click the Change to Context button on the toolbar.)

6. In succession, double-click Queues, and the Queue object; Servers, and the Server object; and Devices, and backup device from which you want to restore.

7. From the list of backup media, choose the one that has the files you want to restore.

8. In the right pane, double-click Where to Restore.

9. Double-click the item you want to restore. Options include: NDS (eDirectory), NetWare servers, Workstations, NetWare Server's DOS Partition, or GroupWise Database. A list of servers that hold the type of resource you selected will appear beneath the item you double-click. If you selected Workstations, you will see a list of host servers from which to choose.

10. Double-click a server, and then enter the appropriate username and password to authenticate to that server.

11. Right-click the server and choose Submit the Job. The screens that appear enable you to choose filtering options and scheduling options. Then press Finish.

12. When asked if you want to submit the job, answer Yes to begin the restore session.

Protecting Databases with TTS

Transaction Tracking System (TTS) is NetWare's feature for protecting database transactions. With TTS turned on, the transaction is completely backed out so the database isn't corrupted if a transaction is caught only half-completed when a problem such as a power outage occurs.

When a transaction is backed out, the database is restored to the original state it was in before the transaction began. TTS protects data by making a copy of the original data before it is overwritten by new data. Then, if a failure of some component occurs in the middle of the transaction, TTS restores the data to its original condition and discards the incomplete transaction.

TTS protects the eDirectory database and the queuing database files from corruption. In addition, you can use it to protect your own database files. If your database application doesn't offer its own form of transaction tracking,

NetWare's TTS can provide protection for it. If your database application does offer its own transaction tracking, NetWare's TTS may still benefit you by tracking the transactions in the server. Tracking the file writes in the server means less data is transferred across the network, and NetWare's disk caching system increases performance.

TTS can be used with any application that stores information in records and allocates record locks. It can't be used with applications such as word processors, which don't store data in discrete records.

Because TTS is used to protect the eDirectory database, TTS is enabled by default. You should not disable TTS. TTS may become disabled on its own if the SYS volume becomes full, because the SYS volume is the volume TTS uses for its back out data. In addition, TTS may become disabled if the server runs out of memory to run TTS. You can see if TTS has been disabled by using a text editor to read the TTS$LOG.ERR file at the root of the volume.

If TTS has been disabled, you can use the ENABLE TTS console utility to re-enable TTS after you correct the problem that caused it to become disabled.

Table 8.2 shows a few of the tasks you can use to manage how TTS works.

T A B L E   8.2   *TTS Tasks*

TASK	HOW TO DO IT
Make TTS track a file Transactional file attribute.	Use ConsoleOne to assign to the file the
Re-enable TTS	Use the console command ENABLE TTS.
Make the server automatically back out incomplete transactions without prompting you for input.	From NoRM, select Set Parameters ⇨ Traditional File System. Set Auto TTS Backout Flag ON (Default: On)
Keep an error log for TTS data	From NoRM, select Set Parameters ⇨ Traditional File System. Set TTS Abort Dump Flag ON. (Default: Off)

CHAPTER 9

NetWare 6 Web Servers

Instant Access

Installing the Enterprise Web server

- ▸ Install the NetWare Enterprise Web server as a standard NetWare 6 service using Deployment Manager or the graphical server console.

Managing the Enterprise Web server

- ▸ To manage the Enterprise Web server, use Web Manager.
- ▸ Use the pages in the Server Settings group to configure the behavior of the Web server itself.
- ▸ Use the pages in the Programs group to manage your Web applications.
- ▸ Use the pages in the Server Status group to monitor Web server activity. Both real-time monitoring and log files are available.
- ▸ Use the pages in the Styles group to easily apply logging options to the files or directories that you want monitor.
- ▸ Use the pages in the Content Management group to organize the Web content stored on your server.
- ▸ Enable WebDAV support to turn the Web into a collaborative document database.

Introduction to NetWare 6 Web Servers

There are three main components of the NetWare 6 Web server model:

▶ *NetWare Enterprise Web server*: The NetWare Enterprise Web server is an HTTP server used to serve up Web pages to the Internet, an intranet, or an extranet. It has been optimized to run in the NetWare environment and is based on the Netscape FastTrack server.

▶ *Apache Web server for NetWare*: The Apache Web server is an open source (read FREE) Web server that is responsible for serving more than 60 percent of all Web content. Apache is installed by default during your NetWare 6 installation and is largely invisible to users and administrators alike.

▶ *Tomcat servlet engine for NetWare*: Tomcat was developed by the same folks that gave us Apache and is used to serve up Web applications. It replaces the IBM WebSphere environment that shipped with NetWare 5.

This foundation of Web serving technologies is easy to install and configure and enables many of the new and exciting features in NetWare 6, such as:

▶ iFolder
▶ iPrint
▶ NetWare Web manager
▶ NetWare Web Search server
▶ NetWare Web access
▶ iManage

This chapter looks primarily at NetWare Enterprise Web server and the key features that let you use NetWare 6 as a Web server. However, it also looks briefly at the more elusive Apache Web server for NetWare and Tomcat servlet engine, which form the foundation for NetWare 6 administrative services.

NetWare Enterprise Web Server

The NetWare Enterprise Web server is a robust, high-performance Web server included with NetWare 6. The NetWare Enterprise Web server is based on the Netscape Enterprise Web server that originally shipped with NetWare 5.

The Enterprise Web server is based on open standards. It supports many leading Internet application development languages and enables NetWare 6 to be a powerful Web development platform. The Enterprise Web server is easy to install and use. Tight integration with Novell eDirectory and the use of LDAP make the Enterprise Web server excellent for use with intranets or the Internet.

The Enterprise Web server is managed through NetWare Web Manager, which runs on the Apache Web server for NetWare, so you have full browser-based management capabilities. Such an arrangement also ensures that if there is a problem with your Enterprise Web server, you can still get to the management interface.

Installing the Enterprise Web Server for NetWare

As with other NetWare 6 services, you can install the Enterprise Web server from either Deployment Manager or the graphical server console, as you prefer. To install Enterprise Web server through Deployment Manager, complete the following steps:

1. At your Windows 95/98 or Windows NT/2000 workstation, insert the NetWare 6 Operating System CD. Launch NWDEPLOY.EXE from the root of the CD-ROM.

2. From the Post-Installation Tasks folder, select Install NetWare 6 products.

3. At the Target Server screen, select the server to which you want to install Enterprise Web server and click Next.

4. Authenticate as a user with administrative rights to the server you have selected. If you get an error when authenticating, click Details and specify the IP address of your NetWare 6 server, then try authenticating again.

5. At the Components screen, click Clear All. Check only NetWare Enterprise Web server and click Next.

6. At the Configure IP-Based Services screen, specify how you want to resolve any port conflicts and click Next.

   • *Single IP address*: If you use this option you will have to specify unique ports for the Enterprise Web server if another service is using ports 80 and 443. Apache may likely be using these if you did not install Enterprise Web server when the NetWare 6 server was installed. Users will have to specify the port number as part of the URL in order to access the Web server.

- *Multiple IP addresses*: If users will access the Web server through a firewall, it is best to specify a secondary IP address so you can keep the default port numbers. That way you don't have to poke any more holes in the firewall. You can also specify a DNS name to assign to the new IP address.

7. At the Summary screen, click Finish to install the NetWare Enterprise Web server.

8. At the Installation Complete message, click Close. Exit Deployment Manager. The Enterprise Web server is now installed.

Once Enterprise Web server is installed, it inserts the following command in the server's AUTOEXEC.NCF to load the Web server automatically whenever the server starts:

```
NSWEB
```

With Enterprise Web server installed, you are ready to look at the typical configuration and management activities associated with it.

Enterprise Web Server Configuration

As with other NetWare 6 Web services, you configure and manage Enterprise Web server through NetWare Web Manager, as shown in Figure 9.1. You will see a new option once Enterprise Web server is active.

For more information on NetWare Web Manager see Chapter 3.

X-REF

Remember that Web Manager, like all other NetWare 6 management tools, runs on the Apache Web server, not the Enterprise Web server. When you are looking at Web Manager log files or stopping/starting the Web Manager service, you are not affecting the NetWare Enterprise Web server in any way.

NOTE

You must enable Java or JavaScript in your Web browser, because all the configuration forms in Web Manager and other management tools require one or both of these forms of Java to function. For information on enabling Java and JavaScript in your browser, see Chapter 3.

▶ • ◀

| F I G U R E   9 . I | *Enterprise Web servers management link from Web Manager* |

To open the Enterprise Web server management interface, select the server link under NetWare Enterprise Web servers. The management interface is shown in Figure 9.2. To access the management pages you will have to log in as a user with administrative privileges to the Web server.

Storing Web Content

Discussing the specifics of creating Web pages is beyond the scope of this book, but once you have your page(s) created, they need to be stored in such a way that they are accessible to your Web server's users. There are four features of Enterprise Web server that help you do this: Document Root, Additional Document Directories, Virtual Directories, and User Document Directories.

Document root

The home page associated with your Web server's IP address and/or DNS name is stored in the document root with the name INDEX.HTM (or .HTML). From the home page, you can create links to other pages, graphics, and applications as needed. Secondary resources can have any filename.

The document root, also called the *primary document directory*, is where the Web server will start looking for requested Web pages and resources. By default, the document root is set to the following location:

```
SYS:NOVONYX\SUITESPOT\DOCS
```

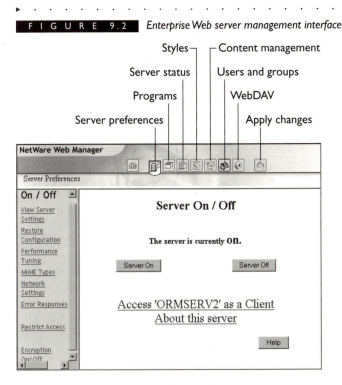

FIGURE 9.2 *Enterprise Web server management interface*

Since it's not necessarily a good idea to have your Web server using the SYS volume to store its data, you can reset the document root through Web Manager by completing the following steps:

1. From the Enterprise Web server management page (refer to Figure 9.2), click the Content Management button.

2. Select Primary Document Directory from the Navigation frame (on the left).

3. Specify the new directory in the Primary directory field and click OK. Enter the complete (absolute) path to the new primary document directory. Use the following syntax:

   ```
   volume:\directory\subdirectory
   ```

4. Click Save and Apply, after reviewing the proposed action, to define the new primary directory.

Additional document directories

You can also create additional document directories for those who want to publish their own content, but to whom you don't want to grant access to the primary document root. This also lets you easily distribute the responsibility for Web content to those responsible for it.

To set an additional document root, complete the following steps:

1. From the Enterprise Web server management page (refer to Figure 9.2), click the Content Management button.

2. Select Additional Document Directory from the Navigation frame (on the left).

3. At the Additional Document Directories page, specify the required information and click OK.

   • *URL prefix*: Specify the URL prefix or keyword you want to use to represent the path. This will be appended to your root domain name.

   • *Map to directory*: Specify the complete (absolute) path of the directory to which you want to map the URL prefix. Use the `volume:\directory\subdirectory` syntax.

   • *(Optional) Apply style*: Specify a configuration style to apply to this directory's configuration. Styles will be discussed in more detail later in this chapter.

NOTE

When you update information but don't save and apply changes, your information is retained so that you can access it later, even though the changes have not taken effect.

Virtual directories

This feature is a special case of additional document directory that lets Enterprise Web server pull Web content from directories that reside on different NetWare servers, as long as they are in the same eDirectory tree as the Web server.

Virtual directories are configured as additional document directories. To create a virtual directory, complete the following steps:

1. Use ConsoleOne to assign the Enterprise Web server as a trustee of the directory structure from which you will create virtual directories. The default read and filescan trustee rights are all that is needed. This ensures that the Web server will be able to access the Web content on the remote server(s).

2. From the Enterprise Web server management page (refer to Figure 9.2), click the Content Management button.

3. Select Additional Document Directory from the Navigation frame (on the left).

4. At the Additional Document Directories page, specify the required information and click OK.

- *URL prefix*: Specify the URL prefix or keyword you want to use to represent the path. This will be appended to your root domain name.

- *Map to directory*: Specify the complete (absolute) path of the directory to which you want to map the URL prefix. Use the `servername\volume:\directory\subdirectory` syntax.

- (*Optional*) *Apply style*: Specify a configuration style to apply to this directory's configuration. Styles will be discussed in more detail later in this chapter.

NOTE

If you are configuring a virtual directory on a NetWare 4.*x* server, you will need to load IPX support on the server running Enterprise Web server in order to support proper communication.

User document directories

This feature lets you to set up document directories for each user in your eDirectory tree. This lets users access their own files from a Web browser. Effectively, users can have their own personal Web sites. To create a document directory for a user, complete the following steps:

1. If you haven't already done so, use ConsoleOne to create a home directory for the User object.

2. In the User's home directory, create a PUBLIC_HTML directory. Copy an INDEX.HTM file to it. This can be any simple HTML template that the Web server can use to display the user's content. Users will typically modify the default file as they build their personal Web page.

3. Add the user's context to the Search Contexts list.

- From the Enterprise Web server management page, click the Users and Groups button.

- Click Insert Context and enter the fully distinguished name of the user's context, for example `OU=Mktg.OU=Provo.O=Quills`. Click OK.

- Click OK to save changes. Restart the Web server by selecting OK.

4. Reload Web Manager after the Enterprise Web server has restarted.

5. Activate User Document Directories in the Enterprise Web server. This step activates User directories so that users just enter the Web server's DNS name followed by /~username to access their home page.

- From the Enterprise Web server management page, click the Content Management button. Select User Document Directories in the Navigation frame.

- Click OK to activate the service.

NOTE

User objects that need access to User Document directories should be kept in the same container as the Web server, or the Web server should hold a read/write replica of any partition that has User objects that need access to User Document directories.

Hosting Multiple Web Sites

Enterprise Web server uses the idea of virtual Web servers to host multiple Web sites on a single physical server. This feature lets a single NetWare 6 server potentially host all your Web server needs. This is useful if you need to let different divisions or departments host their own Web resources, or if you are an ISP and need to host multiple Web sites for your clients without having a separate physical server for each one of them.

You can host two types of Web servers on your NetWare server:

▸ *Hardware virtual servers*: This option lets you define multiple IP addresses and assign each to a different document root. Hardware virtual servers require fewer system resources than multiple instances of the Web server, but all hardware virtual servers must share the same configuration. If you want to set up different servers for different purposes, this may not be the best solution.

▸ *Software virtual servers*: This option lets you map a single IP address to multiple server names. Each software virtual server can have its own home page, which allows you to host multiple Web sites from one IP address. However, to do this, your clients must support the HTTP host header in order to distinguish between one software virtual server and the next.

For more information on both of these virtual server options, see the Novell on-line documentation.

Hardware virtual servers

To set up hardware virtual servers, complete the following steps:

1. On your NetWare 6 server, create the secondary IP addresses that will be used for the hardware virtual servers by using the following console command:

```
add secondary IPaddress <IP address>
```

TIP

> **To make these assignments permanent, add the above command to the AUTOEXEC.NCF after the LOAD and BIND statements (or after the INITSYS.NCF statement, if INETCFG is being used).**

2. From the Enterprise Web Server Management page, click the Content Management button.

3. Select Hardware Virtual Servers from the Navigation frame.

4. At the Hardware Virtual Servers page, specify the required information and click OK.

   - *IP address*: Specify the secondary IP address that you want to use for this virtual server.

   - *Port number*: Specify the default port to use with this virtual server. Usually, the standard HTTP port of 80 is appropriate.

   - *Document root*: Specify the path to the document root for this virtual server, for example WEB_DATA:WEB_MKTG.

   - *Encryption*: Check this box to require encryption on this virtual server. More information on securing your Web server is provided later in this chapter.

5. Click Save and Apply to create the new hardware virtual server.

Software virtual servers

To create a software virtual server, complete the following steps:

1. Create a directory under your current document root directory. For example, if WEB_DATA:WEB_PAGES is your document root, you could create WEB_DATA:WEB_PAGES\CompanyB.

2. From the Enterprise Web Server Management page, click the Content Management button.

3. Select Software Virtual Servers from the Navigation frame.

4. At the Software Virtual Servers page, specify the required information and click OK.

- *URL host*: Specify the URL host name for which you are setting up the software virtual server, for example `www.companyB.com`.

- *Home page*: Specify the path to the home page you want to use for this virtual server, for example `CompanyB\INDEX.HTML`. If you enter a full path, the server uses that specific document. If you enter a partial path, the server interprets it as relative to your primary document directory.

5. Click Save and Apply to create the new software virtual server.

Adding Content to Your Web Site

Once Enterprise Web server has been installed and enabled, you can immediately access a sample Web page and some subpages that are included for demonstration. The default Web page is shown in Figure 9.3. This content is stored in the default document root at SYS:NOVONYX\SUITESPOT\DOCS.

To view the sample Web site, open a client Web browser on a workstation in your network and enter your NetWare server's IP address or DNS name. For example:

```
http://<server_IP_address>
```

or

```
http://<domain_name>
```

Once your Web server is running, you can start posting content for your Web server audience to access — whether that's your department, your company, or the whole world. Do this by placing files in the Web server's primary or additional document directories.

For example, suppose you created a new HTML file called MKTG_DOCS. HTM that includes links to the marketing collateral for your organization. You would probably copy that to the additional document directory assigned to the marketing organization, for example WEB_DATA:\WEB_PAGES\MARKETING.

Once the file is stored in the additional document directory, users can access the file by entering the Web servers DNS name together with the additional document directory identifier and the file name. For example:

```
HTTP://WWW.QUILLS.COM/MARKETING/MKTG_DOCS.HTM
```

The same general process governs the creation of any Web content, whether that content is an Internet site, a corporate intranet, a departmental page, or even a personal Web page. What differentiates one Web site from another is how it is available (internally versus externally) and what type of server it is running on. External sites and larger corporate sites are usually run on dedicated

Web servers or hardware virtual servers, while smaller departmental sites work well on software virtual servers, where users can easily create personalized pages, if necessary.

FIGURE 9.3 *Enterprise Web server default home page*

Publishing Content to a Web Site

When you are configuring an internal Web site, you will often have areas of a Web site that are available for contributors to publish their content. This makes it possible for users to communicate within a department, share information with other departments, and communicate items of general interest.

Web content contributors have three options for publishing content to your Web server:

- ► Mapping a network drive and creating or copying the content to the desired directory
- ► Using Internet Explorer 5.0 or higher
- ► Using Novell NetDrive to map a drive

Publishing content using a mapped drive

This is the simplest method if your contributors are using the Novell client. Use ConsoleOne to assign the appropriate rights to Web content contributors and provide users with the correct network path so they can map a drive to the content directory. You could also setup the drive mapping in a login script.

Publishing content using Internet Explorer

Web-Distributed Authoring and Versioning (WebDAV) is an industry standard protocol that enhances HTTP, turning the Web into a document database that enables collaborative creation, editing, and searching from remote locations.

WebDAV support is enabled by default, but you can enable/disable it from Web Manager by doing the following:

1. From the Enterprise Web Server Management page, click the WebDAV button.

2. Select Software Virtual servers from the Navigation frame.

3. At the WebDAV State screen, select On and click OK.

4. Click Save and Apply.

With WebDAV enabled, you can publish content directly from Internet Explorer by completing the following steps:

1. Launch Internet Explorer from a client workstation.

2. In the Address field, enter your Web server's domain name or IP address, followed by **My Network**, and press Enter. For example:

```
https://www.quills.com/My Network
https://137.65.192.249/My Network
```

3. Authenticate using your directory service username and password.

Publishing content with NetDrive

Novell NetDrive lets you map a drive to any server without using the traditional Novell client. This means that with NetDrive, you can access your files on any server and modify them through standard Windows utilities such as Windows Explorer. The NetDrive client can be installed from the NetWare 6 Client CD-ROM.

For more information on NetDrive see Chapter 10.

X-REF

Securing Web Content

Once you have content organized and published, you immediately start looking for ways to prevent unauthorized access and malicious tampering with your Web resources. There are three main areas that affect the security of Enterprise Web server: directory service, restricting access, and encryption.

Directory service

You have three options for selecting the directory with which Enterprise Web server will integrate. These options are available by clicking the Users and Groups button on the Enterprise Web Server Management page, as shown in Figure 9.4.

▶ *Local database*: This option stores all information in a local LDAP-based directory on your Web server. The local database is the simplest of the directory service choices. This option works well for a small number of users who do not need access to resources located anywhere else on the network. Keep in mind, though, that the local database information is available only to the Web servers running on that specific NetWare server. External Web resources will be unaffected by the settings in the local database.

▶ *LDAP directory server*: This option enables you to choose from any directory that supports LDAP access. The Web server will refer to the LDAP directory to determine access controls, authentication credentials, and so on.

▶ *Novell directory services*: This option integrates Enterprise Web server security with Novell eDirectory. If you select eDirectory, you will use ConsoleOne to manage access controls for the Enterprise Web server. All user, group, and ACL management features in the Enterprise Web server and the Admin server will be disabled. This allows you to use ConsoleOne utility to assign trustee rights through the NetWare file system. This gives users the same access to files, whether they are accessing a file through the browser or mapping a drive and opening a file through some other application. The advantage of this is that you have a single point of administration. Once access control has been set for the file system, it has been set for the Web server, too. A possible disadvantage is that you have given users the capability to access the file through both the Internet Web server and a workstation on the local network. If you use either of the LDAP options instead of the eDirectory option, you are only exposing files through the Web server.

Another limitation of native eDirectory is that you cannot limit access by IP address or hostname. If you need IP access control, use the LDAP option.

▶ · ◀

| F I G U R E   9 . 4 | *Users and Groups page in Web Manager* |

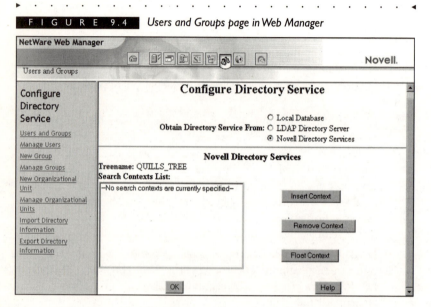

 TIP

> Regardless of the directory choice you make, you can perform several basic directory functions, such as adding, configuring, or removing User and Group objects from the Users and Groups page. Select the appropriate link from the Navigation frame to make changes.

If you choose to use the local database or Novell directory services, select the appropriate radio button and restart your Admin server. If you decide to use an LDAP Directory server, you will need to enter information about your server. For host name, you can enter the hostname or IP address. The standard LDAP port is 389; be sure to check your LDAP server and use the same port.

Restricting access

The Restrict Access page is all about configuring access controls for Enterprise Web server. Access control files have an .ACL extension. The default ACL file is GENERATED-HTTPS-*servername*.ACL, where *servername* is the name of your Enterprise Web server. A temporary working file is used when you are making changes. Its name is GENWORK-HTTPS-*servername*.ACL.

From forms on the Restrict Access page, you can modify these default ACL files to restrict access to servers, directories, and files, as necessary, to fit your specific needs. Complex ACL definitions restrictions are generally handled by modifying the ACL files directly, since more advanced features are available in this way. For more information on the syntax of ACL files, and the specifics of manual configuration, see the Novell on-line documentation.

The form available from the Restrict Access page varies, depending on the directory selection you have made. However, in any case, you can drill down to specific Web server resources and define the type of controls you want assigned to that resource.

LDAP access controls   Figure 9.5 shows the options available if you have selected LDAP or Local Database mode. This page allows you to define ACLs for specific LDAP resources. ACLs are stored in a text file on the Enterprise Web server. For more information on configuring and managing LDAP ACLs, see the Novell on-line documentation.

FIGURE 9.5   *Restrict Access page for LDAP in Web Manager*

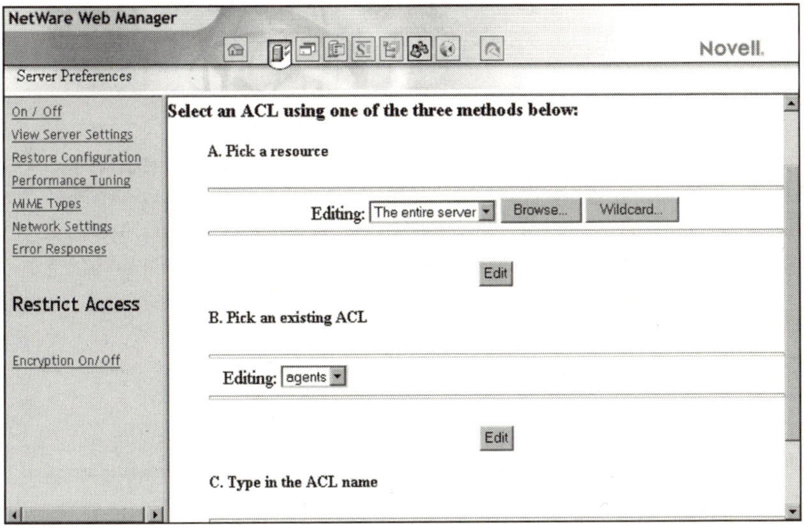

There are three different ways to access LDAP ACLs from the Restrict Access page:

► *Pick a resource*: This option lets you define a new ACL. In the Editing field you can specify the resource to which you want to apply the ACL.

You can apply the ACL to the entire server, or click-browse to drill down to a specific resource on the Web server. You can also use wildcards to help locate the correct resource.

▶ *Pick an existing ACL*: This option lets you modify an existing ACL. In the Editing field, you can select the ACL from the drop-down list.

▶ *Type in the ACL name*: This option lets you modify an existing ACL. Enter the name of the ACL to modify into the Editing field.

Once you have selected an ACL to modify, click the corresponding Edit button to open the LDAP ACL applet and define the specific ACL properties. Complete the following steps to modify an ACL:

1. Click the Access Control Is On checkbox. Without this checked, your rules do not function. Setting access control actions is the first thing you modify when creating a rule. Your options here are Allow or Deny. In most situations, you want to start with a rule that denies access to everyone. You then add new lines that create the access control model you are trying to achieve. Access control rules work from the top down. The server goes down the list and checks each rule until it finds a rule that doesn't match or that matches but is not set to continue. The last rule that matches is the one that is used to allow or deny access to a user.

2. Once you have defined the ACL as you want it, click Submit to continue.

3. Click Save and Apply Changes to make your new ACL active. When a JavaScript message appears, saying that the changes have been successfully saved and applied, click OK to continue.

4. Click the Users/Groups section of your rule. The following options are available for selecting user and setting rules:

• *Anyone*: Allows anyone to access your resource without logging in. This choice essentially removes all security.

• *Authenticated people only*: Must be selected if you are going to choose either of the following options: *All in the authentication database* allows any user who is located in the directory to access the resource. With this option selected, all users must supply a valid name and password for access. *Only the following people* allows you to grant access to specific users and groups. To grant access to a group of users, enter the LDAP name or click List to select the group from a list. To grant access to a user, enter the user ID. If you have more than one user, you can separate user IDs by commas.

Clicking the List button enables you to search through the user database. This is only a listing; you are still required to enter each user ID into the user field.

- *Prompt for authentication*: Allows you to enter a message that you would like to appear when a user is asked to authenticate. This text can be purely informational but can also serve a purpose. Netscape browsers cache a user's name and password as long as the login text is the same. If you would like a user to re-authenticate with each resource accessed, simply change the text for every prompt for authentication.

- *Authentication method*: Provides four methods from which to choose: *Default* uses the method specified in the obj.conf file. Default can be helpful if you have many ACLs, because it allows you to change the method for all ACLs by changing it one time in obj.conf. *Basic* is used if no settings have been made in obj.conf. (Basic uses HTTP authentication.) *SSL* uses client certificates to authenticate the user. Server SSL must be turned on to use this method. *Other* allows you to create a custom method by using the access control API.

- *Authentication database*: Allows you to select a database that the server uses to authenticate users.

5. Click Update to save your changes and return to the Access Control Rules page.

6. Click the From Host section of your rule. Now that you have specified which users to grant access to, you can specify the IP address a user must have to access your server. This feature gives you the capability to limit access only to people physically located on a specific network or location. This access is controlled regardless of what rights have been given to a specific user.

NOTE

Decide how you want to implement control. There are different ways to limit access based on IP information. The IP information you enter in this section determines the IP access control. You can enter specific IP addresses or groups of IP addresses. You can also use wildcards, such as 137.65.192.*. The * must be the right-most character. You can add multiple IP addresses or wildcard addresses by separating each entry with a comma. Entering hostnames is very similar to entering IP addresses; you can add specific hostnames or use wildcards. When using wildcards for hostnames, the * must be the left-most entry, as in *.QUILLS.COM or *.MKTG.QUILLS.COM.

7. Click Update to save your changes and return to the Access Control Rules page.

8. Click the Rights section of your rule.

9. Specify the file rights you want to grant. There are six different file attributes that you can control:

   - *Read access*: Allows users to view a file. It also allows GET, HEAD, POST, and INDEX.

   - *Write access*: Allows PUT, DELETE, MKDIR, RMDIR, and MOVE.

   - *Execute access*: Enables a user to execute an application, including CGI programs, Java applets, and Agents.

   - *Delete access*: Allows a user to delete a complete directory or individual files.

   - *List access*: Allows directory listings for all directories that do not contain an index.html file. List access is also used by the Web Publisher included in the Enterprise server.

   - *Info access*: Allows users to get file headers. (The HTTP header method is also used by the Web Publisher.)

10. Click Submit to save your access control rules. An information page appears, listing all of the changes the system is about to save and commit. Review the information. Click Back if you want to make changes, or click Save and Apply to commit the changes.

11. You will receive a JavaScript message saying that the changes have been successfully saved and applied. Click OK to continue.

eDirectory access controls   Figure 9.6 shows the options available if you have selected Novell eDirectory as your management directory for Enterprise Web server. The nice thing about eDirectory is that you don't have to create a secondary ACL structure; you just use the standard eDirectory file system rights to determine how access should be granted to Web users.

X-REF

For more information on file system rights in eDirectory, see Chapter 6.

FIGURE 9.6 *Restrict Access page for eDirectory in Web Manager*

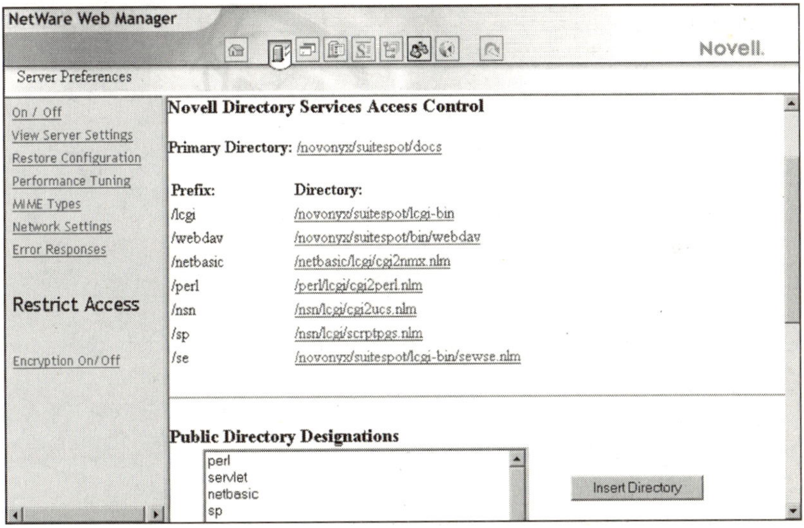

NetWare Web Manager

Novell.

Server Preferences

On / Off
View Server Settings
Restore Configuration
Performance Tuning
MIME Types
Network Settings
Error Responses

Restrict Access

Encryption On/Off

Novell Directory Services Access Control

Primary Directory: /novonyx/suitespot/docs

Prefix:	Directory:
/lcgi	/novonyx/suitespot/lcgi-bin
/webdav	/novonyx/suitespot/bin/webdav
/netbasic	/netbasic/lcgi/cgi2nmx.nlm
/perl	/perl/lcgi/cgi2perl.nlm
/nsn	/nsn/lcgi/cgi2ucs.nlm
/sp	/nsn/lcgi/scrptpgs.nlm
/se	/novonyx/suitespot/lcgi-bin/sewse.nlm

Public Directory Designations

perl
servlet
netbasic
sp

Insert Directory

To configure eDirectory access controls, complete the following steps:

1. From the Directory links, drill down to the specific resource for which you want to define an ACL.

2. At the Current eDirectory Object page, provide the necessary information and click Save.

   • *Contents link*: If your current object is a directory, the Contents link will show you the resources stored within.

   • *Access control list*: This is the default view. It lists the file attributes and inherited rights filter that applies to this object. Make the necessary changes by checking/unchecking the necessary rights and filters. You can also assign a new object trustee and assign specific object-level privileges from this page.

   • *Create directory*: Lets you create a new directory within the current directory. This is useful if you want to create a new location for storing a particular resource type on your Web server.

3. Use Public Directory Designation to specify those files and directories to which you want to allow public access. The Public Directory Designation box lists directories and files that are currently public with associated prefixes.

4. Password Expiration Redirection File lets you create a file that is displayed when a user's password has expired, informing them that they are using grace logins. When a password expires, this page will be displayed instead of INDEX.HTML.

5. Rights Checking Mode lets you define the granularity with which access rights are checked. Directory mode checks at the object level only. File mode reviews rights down to the individual file, at the cost of slower system performance.

Encryption

Encryption is the third aspect to a sound Web server security policy. Enterprise Web server leverages Novell Certificate server for its cryptographic keys and certificates. Certificate server lets you create server certificates, also called Key Material Objects (KMOs), that can be used to encrypt Web server communications with SSL. Once enabled, SSL requires that you use the HTTPS:// prefix rather than the standard HTTP:// prefix when specifying URLs.

X-REF

> For more information on Certificate server, see Chapter 6.

To enable Web server encryption, complete the following steps:

1. From the Enterprise Web Server Management page, select the Encryption On/Off link. This option is available only if you have created a KMO.

2. At the Encryption On/Off page, provide the necessary information and click OK.

   • *Encryption*: Check On to enable SSL encryption.

   • *Port number*: Displays the default port for SSL encryption, port 443. If you want to use a nonstandard port, make sure you specify it here.

   • *Server certificates*: From the drop-down list, select the certificate you want to use for Web server encryption.

3. Restart the Web server to enable encryption. You can do this by selecting the On/Off link in the Server Preferences page and clicking Server Off and then clicking Server On.

TIP

> Enterprise Web server creates a hardware virtual server by default that occupies port 443. Before enabling encryption for the entire server, you should delete this virtual server.

Enterprise Web Server Management

There are several pages of configuration options for the Enterprise Web server. They are organized into groups that correspond to the various buttons in the Header frame. In each group, the Navigation frame on the left provides links to specific configuration pages for Enterprise Web server. The following sections describe the features, not previously discussed, which are available in each group.

Server Preferences

This group of settings allows you to configure specific server-level settings that govern the behavior of the Web server itself. Server Preferences is the default group when the Enterprise Web server management interface is opened.

On/off

This page allows you to stop and restart the Web server remotely. It also has a link to access the Web page as a client.

View server settings

Enterprise Web server uses UNIX-style configuration files to store server-specific parameters. The main configuration files for the Enterprise Web server are MAGNUS.CONF and OBJ.CONF. They are stored in the SYS:NOVONYX\ SUITESPOT\HTTPS-*servername*\CONFIG directory, where *servername* is the name of your server.

The View Server Settings page displays an abbreviated look at MAGNUS. CONF, showing information about your server. Below the MAGNUS.CONF information is a section devoted to the OBJ.CONF settings. Clicking any of the links displays a page that allows you to edit the information in these files. Make any necessary changes, click OK, and then click Save to apply the changes.

WARNING

Because changes made to either of these files can have serious consequences, consult Novell on-line documentation before making changes.

Restore configuration

If you have made changes to your server that have caused unwanted results, the Restore Configuration page can help you get back on track. Down the left side of the page, you will see a list of dates and times. These are backups of every configuration that your server has had.

Enterprise Web server makes a backup copy of MAGNUS.CONF, OBJ.CONF, and all other configuration files each time you make a change. These previous versions of your configuration files are stored in the SYS:\NOVONYX\ SUITESPOT\HTTPS-*servername*\CONF_BK directory, where *servername* is the name of your Web server.

By clicking the button for a particular date and time, you can restore your server to the exact configuration it had at that specific time. Along with restoring a complete configuration, you can select specific configuration files you would like to restore. The View button enables you to look at a file before you restore it.

Performance tuning

The Performance Tuning page enables you to make some basic performance adjustments to the Web server. One such change recommended by Novell Technical Support is increasing maximum simultaneous requests to at least 96.

With this change, the default settings will be sufficient for most situations. However, the changes available through the Performance Tuning page are only the tip of the iceberg when compared to the performance enhancements that can be made by editing the OBJ.CONF by hand. In heavy-load environments, you can realize significant performance improvements through modifications to the OBJ.CONF. Consult the Novell on-line documentation and all related performance-tuning documents available from Novell or Netscape before attempting to do this on your own.

MIME types

MIME (Multipurpose Internet Mail Extension) types control what file types the Enterprise Web server recognizes and supports. The configuration file MIME.TYPES, located in the SYS:NOVONYX\SUITESPOT\HTTPS-*servername*\ CONF directory, also specifies which applications support different file extensions.

For example, if you want to put MP3 files on your server, you must add the MP3 extension to your MIME types. If this is not added, the server transfers the file to the user as text, instead of as a sound file. The Global MIME Types page makes it easy to add new types. From this page, you can also delete or modify existing types.

Complete the following steps to add new MIME types to your server:

I. Click the Type drop-down menu in the Category column. You can keep the default or choose enc or lang; enc is the encoding used for compression, and lang is used for language encoding.

2. In the Context_Type field, enter the context type that will be located in the HTTP header. This is the information the client uses to decide what to do with the requested file. You can look at the included MIME types as examples for adding an unsupported type or to use for adding types officially assigned and listed by the IANA (Internet Assigned Numbers Authority).

To see a list of the IANA's official context types, see the IANA Web site, at www.iana.org.

3. In the File Suffix field, enter the file extension.

4. Once you have entered the information, click New Type and your new MIME type will be added.

Network settings

The Network Settings page enables you to view or change configuration information contained in the MAGNUS.CONF file. You are automatically brought to this page when you click any of the MAGNUS.CONF change links on the View Server Settings page. Any changes you make to MAGNUS.CONF should be made with care.

Error responses

The error messages sent to a client are fairly generic and do not give much information, so you can use the Error Responses page to create custom error messages. When a server cannot complete a request, it can send one of the following four different error messages to the client:

▶ *Unauthorized*: Occurs when a user tries unsuccessfully to access a file in a secure area of the Web server.

▶ *Forbidden*: Occurs when the server does not have file system rights sufficient to read the requested data.

▶ *Not found*: Occurs when a user tries to access data that does not exist.

▶ *Server*: Occurs when the server is improperly configured or when a fatal error occurs (such as the system running out of memory).

There are many situations in which you may want to use custom messages. For example, if users are denied access, instead of receiving a message that simply says "Unauthorized," they could receive a custom error message that explains the reason they were denied access and points them to the help desk to have an account created.

To change the error response for your server, complete the following steps:

1. Select the error response you want to change (such as "Unauthorized").

2. Enter the path to the file that you would like to replace the default error message, such as SYS:\NOVONYX\CUSTOM\MESSAGES\ UNAUTHORIZED.CGI.

3. If this response is a CGI script, click the CGI checkbox.

4. Repeat this process for each error message you would like to change.

5. When finished, click OK to confirm the changes.

6. If you would like to return to the default error messages, simply delete the file path and click OK to save the changes.

Restrict access

Restrict access allows you to define ACLs for your Web server and/or your Web content. This page was discussed previously in the "Securing Web Content" section of the chapter.

Encryption on/off

Encryption On/Off allows you to enable/disable SSL encryption for your Web server. This page was discussed previously in the "Securing Web Content" section of the chapter.

Programs

Enterprise Web server offers many options for Web application development, such as PERL, Java, JavaScript, CGI, and Netbasic. The Programs pages help you manage the locations and configurations for your Web applications.

CGI directory

There are two ways to store Common Gateway Interface (CGI) programs on your Enterprise Web server. The first way is to select a directory that contains only CGI programs. (The second way is described in the next section.) The Web server will assume that every file located in this directory, regardless of extension, is a CGI program.

This option is useful if you want to restrict who can add CGI programs to the Web server. To specify a CGI directory in which to store CGI programs, provide the following information and click OK:

▶ *URL prefix:* Specify the URL prefix you want to use. This text is what you will enter as part of the page address to reach the new CGI directory.

▶ *CGI directory*: Specify a complete (absolute) path to your new CGI directory. This path doesn't need to be located in your document root. It can be located anywhere on your server.

Once created, the new directory will appear in the list of Current CGI directories. You can also modify or remove an existing CGI directory from this page.

CGI file type

This is the second way to store CGI files on Enterprise Web server. Instead of storing them all in a common directory, you can specify that the Web server assume that all executable files of type .CGI, .EXE, .NLM, and .BAT are CGI programs.

This option is useful if you want any user that creates HTML content to be able to add CGI programs to their pages. They can simply store their CGI files in the same directory as their HTML files. To use this CGI file option, complete the following steps:

1. In the Editing Field, specify the point in the file system at which you want the Web server to start looking for CGI applications. Click Browse to locate the specific point in the file structure, if desired.

2. Specify whether or not you want to activate CGI as a file type.

3. Click OK. Click Save and Apply to save the changes.

Query handler

The query handler specifies the CGI program you want to process text sent to it by the ISINDEX tag in an HTML file. ISINDEX is similar in function to a text field on a form document.

To set a query handler, do the following:

1. In the Editing field, specify the resource for which you want to set a default query handler. Click Browse to locate the specific resource, if desired. If you specify a directory rather than a file, the query handler you specify runs only when the server receives a URL for that directory or any file in that directory.

2. In the Default Query Handler field, enter the complete (absolute) path to the CGI program you want to use as the default query handler for the resource you specified.

3. Click OK. Click Save and Apply to save the changes.

Server-side JavaScript

JavaScript is one of the most widely used languages on the Internet today. Most JavaScript is client-based, meaning the JavaScript code is downloaded by the browser and executed on the workstation. Server-side JavaScript is different. Server-side JavaScript is code that has been compiled to form a Web file. This file is executed on a Web server. The information that is processed on the server is then passed to the client to be viewed.

A JavaScript compiler is included with Enterprise Web server. It is located in SYS:\NOVONYX\SUITESPOT\BIN\HTTPS. You need two files in this directory: JSAC.EXE and LIBESNSPR20.DLL.

The Enterprise Web server includes sample applications that are simple examples of what can be written with server-side JavaScript. However, since server-side JavaScript requires some server resources, it has been disabled by default. You should leave it disabled if it is not being used, so it doesn't use server resources unnecessarily.

To turn on server-side JavaScript, simply check Yes under Activate the server-side JavaScript application environment and click OK. Click Save and Apply to enable server-side JavaScript.

The JavaScript Application Manager

Now that you have activated server-side JavaScript, you will see a link to the Application Manager located on the Server-Side JavaScript page. When you click the link, it will launch a new browser window for the JavaScript Application Manager, as shown in Figure 9.7.

The Application Manager itself is a server-side JavaScript application that runs on Enterprise Web server. You use it to manage all of the server-side JavaScript applications running on your server.

On the Application Manager page, you will see a box listing all the applications currently running on the Enterprise Web server. When you click one of the applications, an information page appears, showing information about that JavaScript application.

Below the applications box, you will see several links:

- ► *Start*: Allows you to start an application that has been stopped. Note that when you enabled server-side JavaScript, all of the JavaScript applications on the server were started automatically.

- ► *Stop*: Unloads an individual application.

- ► *Restart*: Restarts an application. If an active application is not running correctly, you can click this button to stop and start the application automatically.

- ► *Run*: Brings up the application in a new browser window.
- ► *Debug*: Shows you what the application is doing. It can be displayed down the left side of the screen or in a separate window. (The debugging capabilities of this button are somewhat limited.)
- ► *Modify*: Allows you to change information located in the configuration fields.

FIGURE 9.7 *Server-side JavaScript Application Manager*

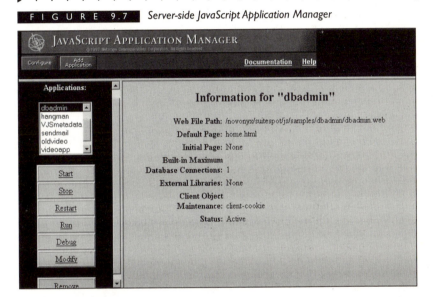

At the top of the Application Manager page, you will also see two other buttons: Configure and Add Application. Click the Add Application button at the top of the JavaScript Application Manager screen to see all the possible fields that are needed to add a new JavaScript application:

- ► *Name*: This is the name of your application. This name will also be the URL pointing to your application. If you name your application "account," the URL will be `http://server.com/account`. (Replace *server* with the name of your server.)
- ► *Web file path*: This is the location of your Web file (application). Web files can be located anywhere on the NetWare server.

IMPORTANT

> Be aware that all of the information for JavaScript applications is case sensitive.

▶ *Default page*: This is the HTML page that is accessed when you run the JavaScript application.

▶ *Initial page*: For database applications, this file contains information about the database objects you have used to create your application.

▶ *Built-in maximum database connections*: This number specifies the number of users who can be connected to a database application at any one time. (If the number of connections is specified in your JavaScript code, this number will be ignored.)

▶ *External libraries*: This is the location of any external libraries that may be used with your application.

▶ *Client object maintenance*: This allows you to select the client object maintenance mode. Your options are client-cookie, client-url, server-ip, server-cookie, and server-url.

Click the Configure button at the top of the JavaScript Application Manager screen to specify default values for the application information, except Name, that will be inserted each time you add a new application. This can be helpful if you are adding many applications that share the same files. There is also a list of preference changes you can make.

Server Status

Enterprise Web server gives you two ways to monitor your server's activity. The first method enables you to monitor the server's status in real time; showing what is happening at the current moment compared to past performance. The second method is to monitor your server by recording, archiving, and viewing log files.

View access log

This page lets you view the Admin server's log files, which are stored on your NetWare 6 server. The access log is named ACCESS and is stored in the SYS:\NOVONYX\SUITESPOT\HTTPS-*servername*\LOGS, where *servername* is the name of your Web server.

View error log

This option lets you view Enterprise Web server's error log file. The error log is named ERRORS and is stored in the SYS:\NOVONYX\SUITESPOT\ HTTPS-*servername*\LOGS, where *servername* is the name of your Web server.

Monitor current activity

This page lets you see real-time statistics for HTTP traffic on Enterprise Web server. You can specify the port from which to gather statistics.

Archive log

This page lets you configure how access and error logs will be archived. Click Archive to archive the logs immediately. You can also specify the days and time at which logs will be automatically archived.

Archived logs are saved using the same file name with a date and time appended so you can tell them apart. For example, ERRORS might become ERRORS.12NOV-02AM.

Log preferences

This page lets you configure the type of information that will be logged, including client accesses, domain names, or IP addresses, type of client data (for example, hostname, username, date, protocol), and those domain names or IP addresses to exclude from logging.

Generate report

This page offers a log analyzer that lets you generate statistical reports (such as a summary of activity), the most accessed URLs, highest utilization time frames, and which hosts are frequently accessing your server.

SNMP subagent configuration

This page lets you enable Enterprise Web server to gather statistical data for delivery to a Simple Network Management Protocol (SNMP) management console. The Enterprise Web server leverages the SNMP infrastructure that exists on the NetWare 6 platform. It reports the information to NetWare, and NetWare distributes it to the management console. For more information on SNMP management, see the Novell on-line documentation.

Styles

Configuration styles give you an easy way to apply logging options to specific files or directories that you want to monitor. Once configured, you assign the Style to each directory or file to which you want it to apply, thereby eliminating the need to configure logging for each file or directory individually.

The individual pages in the Styles group are pretty self-explanatory, they include:

- *New style*: Lets you specify the name for a new style.

- *Remove style*: Lets you delete an existing style.

- *Edit style*: Lets you change the configuration of an existing style, as shown in Figure 9.8. Styles can define the following parameters, all of which are discussed in other sections throughout this chapter:

  - CGI file type
  - Character set
  - Default query handler
  - Document footer
  - Error responses
  - Log preferences
  - Restrict access
  - Server-parsed HTML

FIGURE 9.8 *Edit Style page in the Styles group*

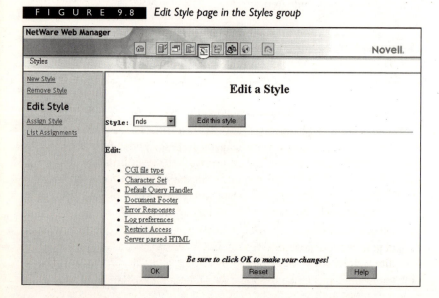

▶ *Assign style*: Assigns the specified style to a specific Web resource (directory or file), so that the specific style attributes will be applied to that Web resource.

▶ *List assignments*: Identifies the specific resources to which styles have been applied.

Content Management

Enterprise Web server supports a variety of methods for organizing the information on your server. This information is managed through the Content Management group.

Document directories are the most common way to manage your content. These directories enable you to keep all Web documents in a single location. This allows for easier management and provides a better structure for implementing access control. Document directories were previously discussed in the "Storing Web Content" section of this chapter.

The content management section of the Admin server also manages the use of virtual servers, both hardware and software, which were also discussed previously in the "Hosting Multiple Web Sites" section.

However, there are several other Content Management pages that have not yet been discussed. These options, along with those previously mentioned, provide the flexibility and structure to the organization of Web documents. They include the following:

Document preferences

The Document Preferences section of Content Management enables you to set default values for your Web site. Figure 9.9 shows the Document Preferences page.

You can configure the following document preferences from this screen:

▶ *Index filenames*: When a user connects to a URL and does not specify a document name, the server automatically displays the index file for that directory. By default, the Enterprise Web server first displays INDEX.HTML. If that file cannot be found, it then displays HOME.HTML. Through the Document Preferences link, you can change the default index files or add to the current list.

▶ *Directory indexing*: You will most likely have subdirectories off the root of your main document directory. You may want to access this directory structure through a browser interface. If you specify a URL without a specific file reference, the Web server first looks for your index files. If there is no index file present, the server then generates an index file that lists all files located in that directory. This listing is similar to looking at a directory in File Manager or Windows Explorer. It lists filenames, sizes, and other information. There are three options for displaying file information (and you can also specify the maximum number of files to return in an index):

- *Fancy*: Shows a graphic representation of the file including file type, the date the file was last modified, and the file size.

- *Simple*: Shows only the filename. The information is more limited but takes less time to load.

- *None*: Use this option if you want the contents of your directory to be hidden.

FIGURE 9.9 *Document Preferences page in the Content Management group*

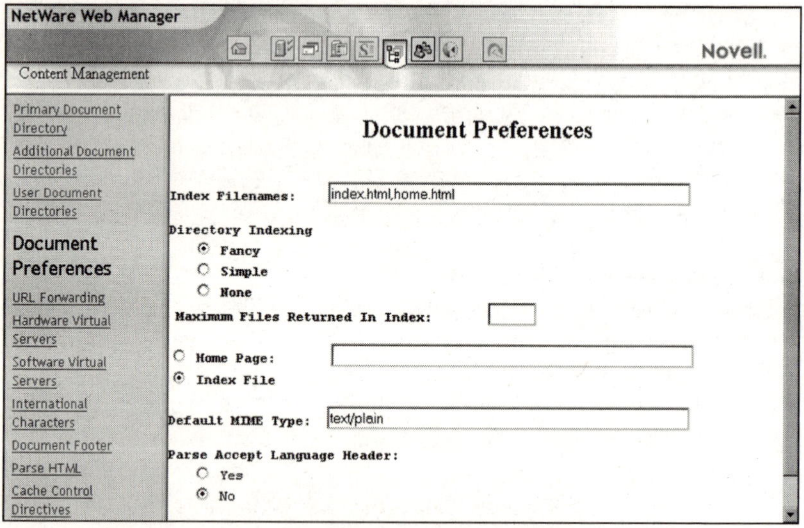

- ▶ *Home page*: To access your Web server, most users probably type www.server.com. By default, the server displays the index file (INDEX.HTM) for that directory. With the Server home page option, you can specify another file to be the server's home page.

- ▶ *Default MIME type*: MIME types give information to the client about each file that is requested. This information helps the client know in what format the file should be displayed. With file types that are not currently located in the MIME.TYPES file, the server does not know how the file should be displayed. By setting a default MIME type, any file that has not been defined is sent as the default type. In most situations, this is set to a text format, but any file type can be used.

▶ *Parse accepted language header*: HTTP v1.1 supports the ability of a client to specify the languages it supports as part of the HTTP packet header. This option enables Enterprise Web server to parse the language header information. Unless you host files in multiple languages, this option should be disabled.

URL forwarding

Forwarding URLs is a common task on the Internet, because Web sites move to new locations for various reasons. URL forwarding enables you to specify a forwarding address for any URL on your server. That way, if you move your Web site, a user can still type the old URL, but his or her browser automatically connects to the new location. To forward a URL, complete the following steps:

1. In the URL prefix field, type the URL prefix you want to forward.

2. Select whether you want to forward requests to a URL prefix, or to a fixed URL. If you want to forward requests to another location on the same server, select a URL prefix. To forward requests to another site on a different server, choose a fixed URL.

3. Click OK, and then click Save and Apply to commit your changes.

International characters

Enterprise Web server follows the character set specified in RFC 1700 (a document that defines Internet character set standards). You can override a browser's default character set setting for a document, a set of documents, or a directory by selecting a resource and entering a character set for that resource.

Document Footer

The document footer allows you to include the last-modified time in the footer of all the documents in a specific area on the server without using server-parsed HTML.

This footer works for all files except CGI scripts or parsed HTML files. To make a footer appear on CGI scripts or parsed HTML files, you must enter your footer text into a separate file and add the code to the script so that the file's contents are appended to the page's output. The default footer displays the modification date.

Parse HTML

When a client requests HTML data, the server normally reads the data and sends it "as is." However, with this option set, it is possible for the server to search the HTML files for special commands, modify the data (according to specific instructions), and then send it off to the requesting client. HTML parsing is disabled by default.

Cache-control directives

Cache-control directives are a way for Enterprise Web server to control what type of information proxy servers cache, and how it is cached. Cache-control directives allow you to override the default caching of the proxy to protect sensitive files or directories from being cached and retrieved.

Users and Groups

This group of configuration options defines the type of directory integration you are going to use and provides basic directory integration. If you are using Novell eDirectory integration, and you probably are, you will have very little to do with this group, since all your user, group, and organizational unit configuration will be done from ConsoleOne.

However, if you are using one of the LDAP directory options, you can use the User and Group pages to create objects in the LDAP directory. You can also import LDAP directory information using the standard LDIF (LDAP Data Interchange Format) files or create LDIF files based on your current LDAP directory structure, with which you can export your directory information.

For more information on directory options in Enterprise Web server, see the "Securing Web Content" section of this chapter.

WebDAV

Web-Distributed Authoring and Versioning (WebDAV) is an industry standard protocol that enhances HTTP, turning the Web into a document database that enables collaborative creation, editing, and searching from remote locations.

Microsoft Windows 98 and Windows 2000 both provide WebDAV support, letting users create Web folders without any need for special drive mappings or network clients. NetWare Enterprise Web server enables WebDAV support by default, so that users of these client operating systems, along with any other WebDAV-compliant operating system, can post files directly to the Web server through their Web folders.

For more information on WebDAV support on Enterprise Web server, see the "Publishing Content to a Web Site" section in this chapter.

Apache Web Server for NetWare

Apache Web server is an open-source Web server originally developed by the not-for-profit Apache Group. The Apache Web server is in use by more than 60 percent of all Web hosting companies.

As an integral part of Novell Web services, Apache is installed automatically during the NetWare 6 installation. It hides in the background, and it is unlikely that you will have to do any regular maintenance. Apache provides the foundation for the following NetWare 6 Web-based services:

- NetWare Web Manager
- NetWare Web Search Manager
- NetWare Web Search Print and Search services
- NetWare Web Access
- iFolder
- iManage

IMPORTANT Apache Web server is normally installed transparently during the NetWare 6 installation in order to support NetWare 6 Web services. However, if you install NetWare 6 as a pre-migration server in anticipation of using Migration Wizard, Apache does not get installed. Make sure you install the Web services manually after the migration is complete.

For additional information about Apache Web server for NetWare, be sure to review the Apache documentation that ships with NetWare 6. It is located in SYS:APACHE\HTDOCS\MANUAL. This documentation will acquaint you with the Apache configuration files that allow you configure Apache just as you can the Enterprise Web server.

SMART LINKS You can also visit http://www.apache.org for comprehensive information on the Apache Web server.

Default TCP Port Assignments

One of the most difficult parts of managing NetWare 6 may be keeping the IP addresses and TCP port assignments in mind as you add and configure services on your NetWare server.

Port numbers enable IP packets to be routed to the correct process on a computer. A total of 65,535 port numbers are available for use. Some port numbers are permanently assigned to a specific process; for example, email data under SMTP goes to port number 25. Other processes, such as Telnet sessions, receive a temporary port number during initialization. The Telnet port is reserved for use by the Telnet process only while the session is active. When the Telnet session terminates the port is released for potential use by another process.

Similarly, some port numbers in NetWare 6 can be reassigned, while others are permanent. The Port Resolver utility helps you identify and resolve conflicts as you install services, but won't prevent you from making changes after the fact. Table 9.1 shows the default port assignments for the NetWare 6 Web services as a starting point for planning the installation and configuration of your Web services.

T A B L E 9 . I	*Default Port Assignments*	
SERVICE	PORT NUMBER(S)	CONFIGURABLE?
Apache	80 or 443	Yes
Domain Name Service (DNS)	53	No
File Transfer Protocol (FTP)	20 and 21	No
iFolder	Uses LDAP and Apache ports	Indirectly
iMonitor	80	Yes
iPrint	631 and SSL port	Indirectly
Lightweight Directory Access Protocol (LDAP)	389 and 636	Yes
NetWare Core Protocol (NCP)	524	No
NetWare Enterprise Web server	80 and 443	Yes
NetWare File System	20, 111, and 2049	Only 2049 is configurable
NetWare Graphical User Interface	9000 and 9001	Yes
NetWare Remote Manager (NRM)	8008 and 8009	Yes
NetWare Web Access	Uses Apache port	Indirectly
Network Time Protocol (NTP)	123	No

SERVICE	PORT NUMBER(S)	CONFIGURABLE?
RConsoleJ	2034, 2036, and 2037	Yes
Compatibility Mode Driver (CMD)	2302	No
Service Location Protocol (SLP)	427	No
Simple Network Management Protocol (SNMP)	161	No
Telnet	23	No
Tomcat	8080	Yes
Web Manager	2200	Yes

Tomcat Servlet Engine for NetWare

Tomcat enables the NetWare Enterprise Web server to execute Java servlets. A servlet is an alternative to CGI and is similar to a server-side applet without a user interface.

In NetWare 5, IBM WebSphere Application server for NetWare provided this capability. Tomcat replaces WebSphere and provides a migration path so you don't have to recreate your Web applications. The WebSphere-to-Tomcat Migration utility is intended for use when upgrading a NetWare 5.1 server with WebSphere 3.02 or WebSphere 3.5.1 installed to NetWare 6.

For specific instructions on migrating WebSphere applications to Tomcat, see the Novell on-line documentation. Although similar to Apache Web server for NetWare, Tomcat documentation is not integrated with the rest of the NetWare 6 documentation. Tomcat documentation is stored in SYS:\TOMCAT\33\DOC\INDEX.HTML.

You can also get the latest Tomcat information and comprehensive documentation from http://jakarta.apache.org.

CHAPTER 10

NetWare File Access

Instant Access

Configuring and managing NetWare FTP server

- NetWare FTP server is a fully functional FTP server that adheres to File Transfer Protocol (FTP) RFC 959.
- FTP server configuration parameters are stored in SYS:ETC\ FTPSERV.CFG.
- Configure and manage FTP server through the FTP server management pages, which are accessible through Web Manager after FTP server is installed.
- FTP access requires that FTP server be installed and configured prior to use.

Using NetStorage

- NetStorage provides a WebDAV server interface for all NetWare 6 files and directories.
- Use any WebDAV-compliant application, such as Web browsers, Windows Explorer (My Network Places), or Office 2000 to access NetWare 6 files and folders.
- NetStorage can provide clientless access to iFolder files.
- NetStorage provides the WebDAV support for the NetDrive client.
- WebDAV access requires that NetStorage be installed and configured prior to use.

Working with NetDrive

- NetDrive client is available on the NetWare 6 Client CD-ROM.
- Supports access of NetWare 6 files and folders using standard protocols: FTP, WebDAV, or iFolder.

Synchronizing files with Novell iFolder

- Synchronizes files between remote clients and a centralized iFolder server, so that user data is available anytime, from anywhere.
- Configure and manage iFolder server through the iFolder management console, available through Web Manager once iFolder is installed.

- Use iFolder client to provide synchronization between the iFolder server and regularly used machines.
- If you are using a machine for one-time access, use NetStorage to access the iFolder server without having to synchronize all files.
- Use NetDrive to access the iFolder server without synchronizing the entire directory. Useful when the desktop application is not WebDAV-aware.
- iFolder access requires that the iFolder server be installed and configured prior to use.

Using NetWare WebAccess

- Uses preconfigured "gadgets" to make NetWare 6 files, and common services — such as iPrint, email, and eDirectory address book — available through a single portal Web site.
- Configure WebAccess through ConsoleOne by setting the properties of the WebAccess_Configuration_All_Users object.

Working with NetWare Web Search server

- Creates a Web search engine for use by internal users (indexes relevant Internet Web sites) or by external users (indexes your Web server information so it can be effectively searched).
- Configured and managed through the Web search management pages, which are accessible from Web Manager after Web Search server is installed.

Introduction to NetWare File Access

One of the major tenets of Novell's One Net philosophy is that users should have access to their files and data at anytime, from anywhere. To bring us closer to this ultimate goal, NetWare 6 includes a host of new methods for accessing network data.

These new access methods are built around the ideas of Internet standards and thin-clients, thereby eliminating, as much as possible, the need to modify workstations in order to support the new access options. Those access methods that do require a client of some sort make installation and configuration as easy as possible, so users can get on with their business.

This chapter takes a look at the new and the nontraditional forms of file access available in NetWare 6. These include:

- ► NetWare FTP server
- ► NetStorage
- ► Novell NetDrive
- ► Novell iFolder
- ► NetWare WebAccess
- ► NetWare Web Search server

NetWare FTP Server

NetWare FTP server is based on the standard ARPANET file transfer protocol that runs over TCP/IP and conforms to RFC 959. You can perform file transfers from any FTP client by using the FTP server to log into the Novell eDirectory tree.

FTP server is a fully functional FTP with many features, such as those in following list. This section provides basic installation and configuration information so you can use FTP file access with NetDrive. For detailed information on all FTP server features, see the NetWare 6 on-line documentation.

- ► *Run multiple copies of FTP server*: Multiple instances of NetWare FTP server software can be loaded on the same NetWare server, providing different FTP services to different sets of users.
- ► *FTP access restrictions*: FTP access can be restricted at various levels through comprehensive access rights controls.

▶ *Intruder detection*: Intruder hosts or users who try to log in using an invalid password can be detected and restricted.

▶ *Remote server access*: FTP users can navigate and access files from other NetWare servers in the same eDirectory tree, and even from remote IBM servers. Remote servers don't have to be running FTP server.

▶ *Anonymous user access*: Anonymous user accounts can be set up to provide users with basic access to public files.

▶ *Special quote site commands*: These are special, NetWare-specific commands used to change or view some NetWare-specific parameters.

▶ *Firewall support*: If the FTP client is behind a firewall, FTP server supports passive mode data transfer and the configuration of a range of passive data ports.

▶ *Active sessions display*: View details of all active FTP instances in real-time. This includes such information as a list of all instances, details of each instance, all sessions in an instance, and details of individual sessions within an instance.

▶ *Name space support*: FTP server supports both DOS and long name spaces. The FTP user can dynamically change the default name space by using one of the Quote Site commands.

▶ *SNMP error reporting*: Simple Network Management Protocol (SNMP) traps are issued when an FTP login request comes from an intruder host or from a node address restricted through Novell eDirectory. SNMP traps can be captured and viewed by any SNMP-compliant management console.

▶ *FTP logs*: The FTP service maintains a log of several activities, including FTP sessions, unsuccessful login attempts, active sessions details, and system error and FTP server-related messages.

▶ *Welcome banner and message file support*: FTP server displays a welcome banner when an FTP client establishes a connection as well as a message file when a user changes the directory in which the file exists. Both banners and message files are fully configurable.

▶ *NetWare Web Manager-based management*: Use Web Manager to start and stop FTP server, and configure server, security, user, and log settings.

For more information on Web Manager, see Chapter 3.

X-REF

- ► *Cluster services support*: NetWare FTP server can be configured with Novell Cluster Services (NCS) for high-availability.

- ► *Upgrade utility*: The Upgrade utility helps in upgrading the configuration of FTP server when upgrading from NetWare 5.1 to NetWare 6.

Installing FTP Server

FTP server can be installed as an optional component during the NetWare 6 installation or it can be installed later through Deployment Manager or the graphical server console. To install FTP server using Deployment Manager, complete the following steps:

1. Insert the NetWare 6 Operating System CD-ROM. Launch NWDEPLOY.EXE from the root of the CD.

2. Double-click Post-Installation Tasks and select Install NetWare 6 products.

3. At the Target Server screen, select the server to which you want to install FTP Server and click Next.

4. Login to the selected server. You may have to click details and specify the IP address of the target server if authentication does not work properly.

5. At the Components screen, click Clear All. Select NetWare FTP server and click Next.

6. At the Summary screen, click Finish to install FTP server. At the Installation Complete screen, click Close.

Configuring FTP Server

Before you start the NetWare FTP server software, you should configure it by setting the configuration parameters in the configuration file. The default configuration file is SYS:/ETC/FTPSERV.CFG. The parameters in this configuration file are commented with their default values.

When the NetWare FTP server is started, the IP address of the host (HOST_IP_ADDR) and the port number of the NetWare FTP server (FTP_PORT), as defined in the configuration file, are used to bind to and listen for FTP client connection requests. If these parameters are not defined in the configuration file, the FTP server binds to all configured network interfaces in the server and uses the standard FTP ports.

Multiple instances of the NetWare FTP server can run on a single machine with different IP addresses, or port numbers. The various parameters in the configuration file along with the default values are described in the tables presented later in this chapter.

You can use Web Manager as an access point for administering the NetWare 6 FTP service. To access the FTP management utility, point your browser to the Web Manager home page and click the server link under the NetWare FTP server heading. The FTP server utility is shown in Figure 10.1.

For more information on NetWare Web Manager, see Chapter 3.

X-REF

▶ · ◀

F I G U R E   1 0 . I   *FTP server configuration interface*

☒ FTP Server created by Novell®

🏠 ▯ ▤   **Novell.**

Server Preferences

On/Off

Server Settings
Security
User Settings
Log Settings

FTP Server On / Off

The server is currently On

[Server On]   [Server Off]

The FTP server configuration file can be edited manually with any text editor. However, it is often easier to configure and manage FTP server from its Web Manager interface. From the default On/Off page, you can start and stop the FTP server as necessary. This loads or unloads NWFTPD.NLM on the NetWare 6 server running FTP services.

The server reads the default configuration file SYS:/ETC/FTPSERV.CFG and configures itself accordingly. If there is any change in the FTP configuration file, you should stop and restart FTP server.

There are four other pages available in the FTP server management utility. Each provides access to specific types of configuration parameters and information, as described in the following sections.

Server settings

Click the Server Settings link to access general FTP server settings. When finished, click Save to record your settings or click Reset to revert to the previous settings. Table 10.1 lists the available server settings, with a brief description and the equivalent setting in the configuration file.

TABLE 10.1	Server Settings Parameters in Web Manager		
PARAMETER	CONFIG FILE	DEFAULT VALUE	DESCRIPTION
Welcome Banner file name	WELCOME_ BANNER	SYS:/ETC/ WELCOME.TXT	When the FTP client establishes a connection, the content of this file is displayed.
Message file name	MESSAGE_ FILE	MESSAGE.TXT	When the user changes the directory, the contents of this file are displayed. For this, the file with that name should exist in the directory.
Maximum number of FTP sessions	MAX_FTP_ SESSIONS	30	Maximum number of FTP sessions that can be active at any point of time. Minimum value is 1.
Sessions may remain idle for	IDLE_ SESSION_ TIMEOUT	600 (seconds)	Duration in seconds that any session can remain idle. The session will never time out if the value is set as negative.

PARAMETER	CONFIG FILE	DEFAULT VALUE	DESCRIPTION
Name Space	DEFAULT_NS	Long	The default name space. The valid values are DOS and LONG.
Minimum port number (passive)	PASSIVE_ PORT_MIN	I	Minimum port number used for establishing passive data connection. The port value range is I to 65534. The minimum value should always be less than or equal to the maximum value.
Maximum port number (passive)	PASSIVE_ PORT_MAX	65534	Maximum port number used for establishing passive data connection. The port value range = I to 65534. The maximum value should always be greater than or equal to the minimum value.

Security

Click the Security link to access intruder detection parameters for FTP server. When finished, click Save to record your settings or click Reset to revert to the previous settings. Table 10.2 lists the available security settings, with a brief description and the equivalent setting in the configuration file.

TABLE 10.2 *Security Settings in Web Manager*

PARAMETER	CONFIG FILE	DEFAULT VALUE	DESCRIPTION
Disable Host Intruder detection	See next parameter	No	Turns intruder detection On/Off for other FTP hosts that access FTP server.
Invalid login attempts for detection (Host)	INTRUDER_HOST_ ATTEMPTS	20	The number of unsuccessful login attempts for intruder host detection. When set to 0, intruder host login detection is disabled.
Intruder host is not allowed to login	HOST_RESET_TIME	10	Time interval in minutes during which the intruder host is not allowed to log in.
Disable User Intruder detection	See next parameter	No	Turns intruder detection for FTP clients that access FTP server.
Invalid login attempts for detection (User)	INTRUDER_USER_ ATTEMPTS	5	The number of unsuccessful login attempts for intruder host detection. When set to 0, intruder host login detection is disabled.
Intruder user is not allowed to login	USER_RESET_TIME	5	Time interval in minutes during which the intruder user is not allowed to log in.

User settings

Click the User Settings link to access parameters that control file access and user authentication for FTP server. When finished, click Save to record your settings or click Reset to revert to the previous settings. Table 10.3 lists the available user settings, with a brief description and the equivalent setting in the configuration file.

T A B L E 1 0 . 3	User Settings in Web Manager		
PARAMETER	**CONFIG FILE**	**DEFAULT VALUE**	**DESCRIPTION**
Use FTP for	NA	No	Sets home directory to Web publishing SYS:/NOVONYX/SUIT ESPOT/DOCS/ FTPWEBS. Lets content publishers copy files to a Web server via FTP.
Default user home server	DEFAULT_USER_ HOME-SERVER	Server where FTP is running	Specifies the name of the server that the default home directory is on.
Default home directory	DEFAULT_USER_ HOME	SYS:\PUBLIC	The default home directory of the user.
Ignore NDS user home directory and stay in default FTP server directory	IGNORE_ REMOTE_ HOME	No	Specifies whether to ignore the home directory and go to the default directory.
Ignore NDS user home directory if it's on a remote NetWare server	IGNORE_ HOME_DIR	No	Specifies whether to ignore the home directory, if it is on a remote server, and go to the default directory.
FTP user restrictions file	RESTRICT_FILE	SYS:/ETC/ FTPREST.TXT	FTP server can define access restrictions to various levels of users, hosts, and so on. These restrictions are defined in a file, which can be specified here.

(continued)

T A B L E 1 0 . 3	User Settings in Web Manager (continued)		
PARAMETER	**CONFIG FILE**	**DEFAULT VALUE**	**DESCRIPTION**
Search List	SEARCH_LIST	None	A list of fully distinguished names of containers in which FTP users will be looked for, separated by commas. The length of this string including the commas should not exceed 2048 bytes. You can specify a maximum of 25 containers.
Allow anonymous access	ANONYMOUS_ ACCESS	No	Specifies whether anonymous user access is allowed.
Anonymous user's home directory	ANONYMOUS_ HOME	SYS:/PUBLIC	The Anonymous user's home directory.
Require email address for password	ANONYMOUS_ PASSWORD_ REQUIRED	Yes	Specifies whether to ask for an Email ID as the password for Anonymous user to log in.

Log settings

Click the Log Settings link to access log file parameters for FTP server. All FTP logs are created automatically. You control only the types of messages that are logged and how large the log files will grow. When finished, click Save to record your settings or click Reset to revert to the previous settings. Table 10.4 lists the available log settings, with a brief description and the equivalent setting in the configuration file.

TABLE 10.4 *Log Settings in Web Manager*

PARAMETER	CONFIG FILE	DEFAULT VALUE	DESCRIPTION
Log messages of type	LOG_LEVEL	Errors, Warnings, and Information	Indicates the types of messages that are logged.
Number of log messages	NUM_LOG_MSG	32000	Maximum number of messages that will be logged in each log file.

This information will give you an FTP server suitable for use with NetDrive, which is described later in this section. For more information on using FTP server in more general situations, see the NetWare 6 on-line documentation.

NetStorage

NetStorage provides a transparent WebDAV interface to NetWare 6 files. This is probably one of the most exciting NetWare 6 features that you've never heard of. Effectively, NetStorage lets you access files on a NetWare 6 server without a NetWare client. NetStorage is integrated with iFolder, NetDrive, and WebAccess to make accessing your network files as easy and seamless as possible — all without using the traditional Novell Client.

Installing NetStorage

NetStorage can be installed during the installation of the NetWare 6 server, or after the fact through Deployment Manager or the graphical server console. Typically, you will need to install NetStorage only on one NetWare 6 server in your eDirectory tree, or on one server at each geographical site, although very heavy usage might require more than one per site.

NOTE During the NetStorage installation, you are prompted for certain configuration parameters. If you want to change NetStorage configuration parameters, you must re-install NetStorage with the new configuration parameters.

To install NetStorage through Deployment Manager, complete the following steps:

1. Insert the NetWare 6 Operating System CD-ROM. Launch NWDEPLOY.EXE from the root of the CD.

2. Double-click Post-Installation Tasks and select Install NetWare 6 products.

3. At the Target Server screen, select the server to which you want to install NetStorage and click Next.

4. Login to the selected server. You may have to click details and specify the IP address of the target server if authentication is not working properly.

5. At the Components screen, click Clear All. Select Novell NetStorage and click Next.

6. At the NetStorage Install screen, specify the required information and click Next.

- *Primary eDirectory server*: Specify the DNS name or IP address of a server in your eDirectory tree that hosts a master or a read/write replica of eDirectory. This does not have to be the server where NetStorage is being installed. NetStorage will use this server to authenticate users when they attempt to log into NetStorage.

TIP

If you want NetStorage to search a specific eDirectory context for user information, you can add that context to the end of the DNS name or IP address, separated by a colon (:). If no context is specified, NetStorage searches the entire eDirectory partition stored on the specified eDirectory server for user information.

- *(Optional) Alternate eDirectory server*: Specify up to two other eDirectory servers to use for user authentication. These can be different servers entirely, or the same server but a different associated context.

- *(Optional) iFolder server*: Specify the DNS name or IP address of your iFolder server, as well as the port number used by the iFolder service. This will make iFolder contents available via NetStorage (WebDAV). More information on iFolder is available later in this chapter.

7. At the Summary screen, click Finish to install NetStorage. At the Installation Complete screen, click Close.

IMPORTANT

If you install NetStorage after the NetWare 6 installation, you must restart your NetWare 6 server after completing the NetStorage installation.

Configuring NetStorage

Once you install NetStorage, it will start automatically when you start your NetWare 6 server. Novell recommends that the date and time on the NetStorage server and the WebDAV client be reasonably close, within a few hours of each other, to avoid potential confusion over file versions.

You can access NetStorage from any WebDAV client. Two of the most obvious are Web browsers and Microsoft Windows "Web Folders." However, there are WebDAV clients for Macintosh and UNIX/Linux systems as well. The following process is equally applicable to those environments.

I. From your WebDAV client, enter the magic NetStorage URL, which is the DNS name or IP address of your NetStorage server with `/oneNet/NetStorage` appended to the end. Remember to include the `http://` prefix and remember that URLs are case sensitive. For example:

`http://ormserv2.quills.com/oneNet/NetStorage`

NOTE

To use Web folders in Windows 2000, open My Network Places (the Windows WebDAV client) and double-click Add Network Place. This opens a wizard for creating a new folder in My Network Places.

2. At the authentication screen, specify your eDirectory username and password. This User object must be accessible from the eDirectory server(s) you specified during the NetStorage installation.

Once authenticated, your WebDAV client displays the network files and folders currently accessible to you. To do this, NetStorage reads the user's NetWare login script to determine drive mappings, reads eDirectory User object properties to determine the path to the user's home directory, and then displays a list of files and folders based on mapped drives and home directories. Figure 10.2 shows NetStorage views from both a Web browser and Windows Web folders.

▶ . . . . ◀

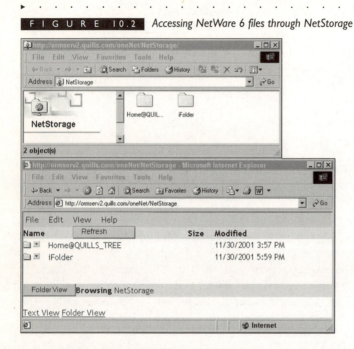

F I G U R E 10.2   *Accessing NetWare 6 files through NetStorage*

TIP   If you specified eDirectory servers from different eDirectory trees during the NetStorage installation, NetStorage will read only the user login script from the primary eDirectory server when calculating mapped drives to display. However, NetStorage will read User object properties from all trees and display multiple home directories — as long as the User object has the same name in each tree. This is useful if a user normally logs in to more than one eDirectory tree.

If you have an iFolder account, you will see an iFolder folder in addition to your mapped drives and home directory, as shown in Figure 10.2. The first time you open the iFolder folder, all you will see is a file called PASSPHRASE.HTM. To access the contents of your iFolder directory, open PASSPHRASE.HTM, as shown in Figure 10.3, and specify the passphrase of your iFolder account.

F I G U R E   1 0 . 3 *Specifying your passphrase to access iFolder from NetStorage*

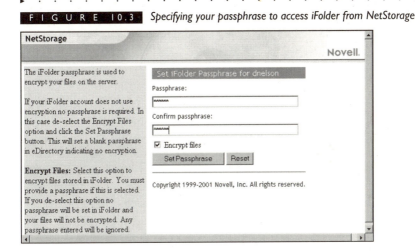

This lets NetStorage decrypt your iFolder files so it can interpret them properly. The passphrase for NetStorage is stored as an encrypted attribute on your User object, so it is not at risk of discovery.

Using NetStorage

Once connected to your NetWare files through WebDAV, you have full access to them. You can browse, open, and close folders; copy files to your local drive; and open files with WebDAV-compliant applications such as Web browsers, Microsoft Office 2000, and so on.

In addition, if you use Microsoft Windows Web folders, you can use all the normal Windows mechanisms for copying, cutting, pasting, and renaming files. To perform similar actions from a browser interface, click the Down arrow next to the file or folder with which you want to work.

If you need to use a file with a non-WebDAV application, you will need to copy the file to your local drive so the application can use normal operating system mechanisms for working with the file. This is the only real drawback to NetStorage: It does not provide low-level integration with the operating system, such as creating a drive letter that lets applications access the files as if they were local.

Novell resolves this issue for Windows workstations with NetDrive, which is described in the next section. The trade-off is having full access to network files as if they were local versus having a clientless solution for accessing your network files.

Novell NetDrive

Novell NetDrive lets you to map a network drive to any NetWare 6 server without using Novell Client software. This means that with NetDrive, you can access and modify your files from any workstation using just an Internet connection. Once a network drive is mapped, the drive letter that you assigned during the mapping appears in Windows Explorer and functions just like those that are mapped through Novell client.

NetDrive Prerequisites

NetDrive runs on any Windows workstation, including Windows 95/98/Me and Windows NT/2000. You need only 2MB of available space on your hard drive to install and run the NetDrive client.

 If you are installing the NetDrive client on a Windows 95 workstation, make sure you install the Winsock 2 update from Microsoft. It is available on the Microsoft Web site.
IMPORTANT

NetDrive supports three different protocols for accessing network files:

- ► *WebDAV*: NetDrive integrates with NetStorage to provide a comprehensive file access solution with very little client overhead. NetStorage must be installed and configured prior to using NetDrive with WebDAV.

- ► *FTP*: NetDrive can access network files using the standard File Transfer Protocol (FTP). An FTP server must be installed and configured on your network before using NetDrive with FTP. You can use the NetWare FTP server, described earlier in this chapter, to provide this type of access.

- ► *iFolder*: NetDrive can access files from your directory on the iFolder server. iFolder must be installed, and your iFolder account configured, prior to using NetDrive with iFolder.

Installing NetDrive

The NetDrive client is available on the NetWare 6 Client CD-ROM. To install the NetDrive client, complete the following steps:

1. Insert the NetWare 6 Client CD-ROM. The CD-ROM will autoplay and present you with the Novell Client Installation menu. If the CD-ROM does not autoplay, run WINSETUP.EXE from the root of the Client CD-ROM.

2. At the Client Installation screen, select Novell NetDrive Client 4.0.

3. At the Welcome screen, click Next.

4. At the License Agreement screen, click Yes.

5. At the Destination Location screen, specify the location where the NetDrive client should be installed and click Next.

6. At the Install Complete screen, select Yes, I want to restart my computer now and click Finish.

After your workstation reboots you are ready to use NetDrive to access your files over the network.

Using NetDrive

With the NetDrive client installed, you can access files on your NetWare 6 servers using standard Internet protocols. However, not every protocol is supported on every version of Windows.

- *iFolder*: Windows NT and 2000
- *FTP*: Windows 95, 98, Me, NT, and 2000
- *WebDAV (HTTP)*: Windows 95, 98, Me, NT, and 2000
- *Secure WebDAV (SSL)*: Windows NT and 2000

The NetDrive installation inserts an icon in the Windows system tray (lower-right corner of the Explorer window). To configure NetDrive and begin using it to access your network files, complete the following steps:

1. Click the NetDrive icon in the system tray.

2. From the main NetDrive window, as shown in Figure 10.4, you can create new sites, map network drives, and configure and manage the Web sites to which you have mapped drives.

F I G U R E   10.4   *Main NetDrive configuration window*

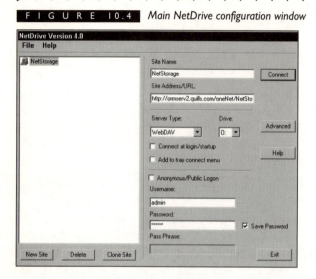

Adding a Site to NetDrive

This makes a NetWare 6 site available to NetDrive so that drive mapping can take place. To add a site to NetDrive, complete the following steps:

1. In the main NetDrive window, click New Site.

2. At the Add New Site screen, enter the requested information and click Finish.

- *Name for your new site*: Enter a descriptive name for the new NetDrive site.

- *Address/URL*: For an FTP connection, specify the DNS name or IP address of your FTP server (`ftp://ftp.quills.com/files`). For a WebDAV connection, specify the DNS name or IP address of the server where NetStorage is installed, along with the NetStorage access path (`http://ormserv2.quills.com/oneNet/NetStorage`). For iFolder, specify the DNS name or IP address of your iFolder service (`http://ifolder.quills.com`). If you omit the FTP or HTTP prefix, NetDrive defaults to FTP. If you want to use a non-standard HTTP port, make sure you append it to the end of the URL.

If you want to connect with WebDAV and SSL encryption, remember to specify the HTTPS prefix as part of the URL.

Once you have created a site, the name of the new site, along with the URL of the NetWare 6 server, is listed in the main NetDrive window. The rest of the page defaults to common connection options for the file protocol you have chosen (refer to Figure 10.4). However, you can change any of this information after the fact:

▶ *Server type*: Specify the protocol that you will use to access this site.

▶ *Drive*: Specify the drive letter that you want to use for the mapped drive.

▶ *Connect at login/startup*: Check this box to have NetDrive map its drive automatically when your workstation starts.

▶ *Add tray connect menu*: If you right-click the NetDrive icon in the system tray, you will see a Connect to option. Check this box to add the site to those listed in the Connect to menu.

▶ *Anonymous/public logon*: Check this box to bypass user authentication for an FTP connection. Both WebDAV and iFolder access require specific user authentication. Leave this box unchecked if you want to require authentication in order to access the site. If you do this, you will have to enter a valid username and password.

▶ *(Conditional) Passphrase*: If you are connecting to an iFolder server, enter a passphrase. This is used to encrypt your files as they are transferred over the Internet. iFolder is discussed later in this chapter.

▶ *Save password*: Check this box if you want NetDrive to remember your authentication password.

Click the Advanced button to set optional download, caching, and file locking parameters for the NetDrive site. You won't normally have to do anything in the Advanced area.

When you are finished configuring site properties, click Connect to actually map the drive. When NetDrive maps the drive, Windows opens a new window corresponding to the drive letter that you have just mapped.

Once NetDrive has successfully mapped a drive to the site, the Monitor window appears. It provides you with connection status, file transfer statistics, and a connection log. With the newly mapped drive, you can copy, cut, and paste files as you would in any other Windows drive.

If you have problems viewing the mapped directory, or connecting to a server using FTP, specify the server IP address instead of the URL. You may also need to enable passive mode if the problem does not go away. Click Advanced and select PASV–Passive Mode. Then try connecting to the Web server again.

Novell iFolder

Novell iFolder gives you automatic, secure, and transparent synchronization of files between your hard drive and the iFolder server, which results in easy access to personal files anywhere, anytime.

Being able to access your files from any computer, any location, eliminates the mistakes and updating that is frequently necessary when your local files are not accessible over the network.

There are three components to Novell iFolder:

▶ *iFolder server software*: Once you have installed the iFolder server software on your server, users can install the iFolder client in order to access their iFolder files. Administrators use the Server Management console and the iFolder Web site to manage iFolder user accounts.

The Server Management console lets you perform administrative tasks for all iFolder user accounts. From the iFolder Web site, iFolder users download the iFolder client. It is also where you can access the Java applet and view your iFolder files from a browser. The iFolder Web site can, and should, be customized to fit the look and feel of your organization.

▶ *iFolder client software*: Novell iFolder client is compatible with Windows 95/98/Me and Windows 2000/NT workstations. The iFolder client must be installed on every workstation that you will use to access your iFolder files. When the iFolder client is installed, it does three things:

• It creates a shortcut to your iFolder directory on your desktop. The iFolder directory, which by default is located in My_Documents\ iFolder\userid\Home, is where you will keep the files you want to synchronize with the iFolder server. When a file is placed in the iFolder directory, it is synchronized out to the iFolder server, from which it can be accessed by all workstations that are logged into your iFolder account.

- An iFolder icon is placed in the workstation system tray. Right-clicking the system tray icon gives users access to their user-configurable preferences and the iFolder status screen, which displays a history of the transactions that have occurred between the iFolder server and the client.

- A user account is created on the iFolder server. iFolder user accounts are created automatically when a user downloads and installs the iFolder client. When you log in, iFolder asks you for a username and a password. Next, iFolder prompts you for a passphrase. This passphrase is used to encrypt files that are uploaded to the server.

NOTE

Uninstalling the iFolder client does not delete the associated user account on the iFolder server. This can be done only from the Server Management console.

▶ *iFolder Java applet*: Use the iFolder Java applet to access iFolder files from a workstation on which the iFolder client is not installed.

iFolder Prerequisites

Remember the following prerequisites when you are installing iFolder:

▶ iFolder requires Internet Explorer 5.0 or 5.5 to be installed on every workstation where you are installing the iFolder client.

▶ You need 10MB of free space on the SYS: volume where you plan to install iFolder.

▶ Novell iFolder is compatible with Windows 95, 98, 2000, NT, and Me workstations. The iFolder client requires about 2MB of free space on your workstation.

NOTE

If you are installing the iFolder client on a Windows 95 workstation, make sure you install the Winsock 2 update from Microsoft. It is available on Microsoft's Web site.

Installing iFolder

Novell iFolder can be installed as part of the NetWare 6 server installation, or it can be installed after the fact through either Deployment Manager or the graphical server console. To install iFolder with Deployment Manager, complete the following steps:

I. Insert the NetWare 6 Operating System CD-ROM. Launch NWDEPLOY. EXE from the root of the CD.

2. Double-click Post-Installation Tasks and select Install NetWare 6 products.

3. At the Target Server screen, select the server to which you want to install iFolder and click Next.

4. Log in to the selected server. You may have to click details and specify the IP address of the target server if authentication is not working properly.

5. At the Components screen, click Clear All. Select Novell iFolder Storage Services and click Next.

6. (Conditional) If other Web services such as the Enterprise Web server, or the Apache Web server, are already installed, the Port Resolver screen allows you to specify how you want to resolve any IP port conflicts. Click Next when finished.

7. At the iFolder Server Options screen, as shown in Figure 10.5, provide the required information and click Next.

FIGURE 10.5 *iFolder server configuration during installation*

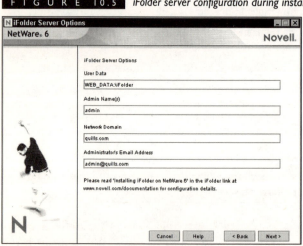

- *User data*: Enter the path to the directory where you want the iFolder user data to be stored on the iFolder server.

- *Admin name(s)*: Enter the names of all the administrators who need rights to modify iFolder user account information via the Server

Management console. Separate multiple names with semicolons, not spaces.

- *Network domain*: Enter the DNS domain of your network, for example `quills.com`.

- *Administrator's email address*: Enter an email address for each of the iFolder admin users. Separate multiple addresses with semicolons, not spaces.

8. At the Summary screen, click Finish to install iFolder. However, if you need to configure LDAP settings for iFolder, click Customize. Open NetWare 6 Services, highlight Novell iFolder Storage Services, and click configure. Select the iFolder Primary LDAP Settings tab, as shown in Figure 10.6. Provide the required information and click OK when finished.

▶ · ◀

F I G U R E   10.6   *iFolder LDAP configuration screen*

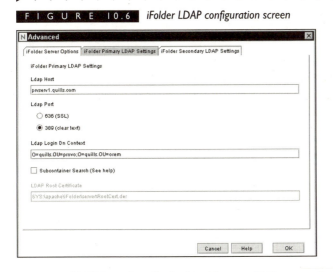

- *LDAP host*: Specify the IP address or DNS name of your LDAP server.
- *LDAP port*: Enter the LDAP port you want to use. Use the default LDAP port (389) for unencrypted communications or port 636 for SSL-encrypted communications. If you use port 389, make sure your LDAP Group object in eDirectory is marked to allow clear text passwords. Similarly, if you use port 636, make sure your LDAP server is configured to support SSL. If you want to use SSL

with iFolder, and your LDAP service and iFolder are not on the same server, you need to export your LDAP server's trusted root certificate and copy it to the iFolder server. This Root certificate (ROOTCERT.DER) is typically located in the SYS:PUBLIC directory of the LDAP server. It should be copied to the SYS:Apache\ iFolder\Server directory on the iFolder server.

TIP

If you plan on using unencrypted LDAP communications, port 389 is a good choice. This is particularly true if iFolder and LDAP are running on the same server, and no LDAP communications have to cross the network. For more information on LDAP configuration, see Chapter 5.

- *LDAP login Dn context*: This is the context of the container where your User objects are located. Use a semicolon to separate multiple context entries, not spaces.

- *Subcontainer search*: Check this box to have iFolder search all containers below the specified LDAP login context. To do this, you must either assign the CN property to the Public object in eDirectory or create an LDAP proxy user. iFolder will not work properly until this is done.

For more information on either of these tasks, see Chapter 5.

X-REF

- (Conditional) If you have a secondary LDAP server, select the iFolder Secondary LDAP Settings tab and provide the same information provided for the primary LDAP server. You should need to do this only if you have users in more than one LDAP directory that need iFolder access.

- (Conditional) If you have a DNS name configured for your iFolder server, verify that the DNS name and its corresponding IP address are in the SYS:ETC\HOSTS file of your iFolder server.

9. When the iFolder installation is complete, click OK at the Installation Complete screen.

Managing Novell iFolder

The first time the iFolder client is installed, a user account is automatically created on your iFolder server. In addition to the default iFolder Web site, another Web site is available for performing server management. The iFolder Server Management console is shown in Figure 10.7.

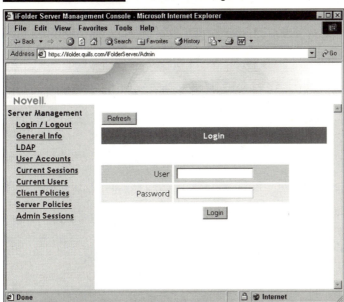

FIGURE 10.7 *iFolder Server Management console*

When iFolder is installed, Web Manager automatically creates a link to the Server Management console, but it is available directly through the following URL: `https://<iFolder server DNS or IP address>/iFolderServer/Admin`. For example:

`https://ifolder.quills.com/iFolderServer/Admin`

The iFolder Server Management console lets you perform administrative tasks and manage the activity between the server and the iFolder clients. Before you can administer anything, you have to log in via LDAP. Use an administrative user account you specified during the iFolder installation. Once logged in, you can perform the following general administrative tasks on the iFolder environment:

- ▶ View iFolder status and usage
- ▶ Configure server settings
- ▶ Configure User policies
- ▶ iFolder Account Management

iFolder status and usage

The General Information link, which is the default home page for the Server Management console, gives you basic information about the iFolder server, including software revisions, currently logged in sessions, and the total number of user accounts created in iFolder.

You can also get real-time usage information from the User Accounts, Current Sessions, Current Users, and Admin Sessions links. The combination of this information will give you a pretty good view of how iFolder is performing and how it is being used.

Server settings

To configure the iFolder server environment, you will use two different links: LDAP and Server Policies.

The LDAP link allows you to review and modify the LDAP settings that you defined during the iFolder installation. You can configure both primary and secondary LDAP information, just as you did during the installation. LDAP settings are stored in a configuration file: SYS:Apache\iFolder\Server\ HTTPD_NW_ADDITIONS.CONF. You can also modify this file by hand, if desired.

The Server Policies link lets you configure server parameters that affect the operation of iFolder user accounts:

- ► *Initial client quota*: This parameter defines how much disk space will be allotted for each client account. The default is 200MB. You should calculate this based on the expected number of iFolder users and the server resources available.

- ► *Session timeout*: Defines the time, in minutes, that an iFolder session will remain open with no user activity. The default is 60 minutes.

- ► *Debug output*: This option is used to capture debug information while iFolder is running. It should be used only when working with Novell support to try and solve a problem with your iFolder environment.

Client policies

The Client Policies link allows you to configure several default user parameters that govern how iFolder accounts will behave. The Client Policies page is shown in Figure 10.8.

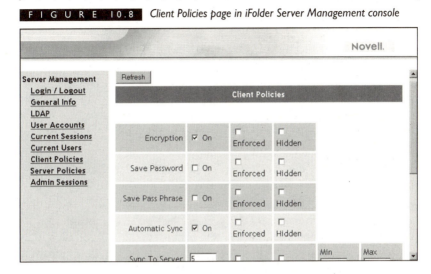

FIGURE 10.8 *Client Policies page in iFolder Server Management console*

The first column lets you set the default value for the given parameter. The Enforced checkbox prevents users from modifying that parameter from its default value. The Hidden checkbox removes the parameter from iFolder client dialogs so they don't even know the parameter exists.

- ▶ *Encryption*: Default: On. Defines whether files will be encrypted while stored on the iFolder server.

- ▶ *Save password*: Default: Off. Defines whether the iFolder client will remember a user's password so they don't have to type it every time the login to iFolder.

- ▶ *Save passphrase*: Default: Off. Defines whether the iFolder client will remember a user's passphrase so they don't have to type it every time the login to iFolder.

- ▶ *Automatic sync*: Default: On. Defines whether iFolder will synchronize files automatically while a user is logged in.

- ▶ *Sync to server*: Default: 5 sec. Min: 3 sec. Max: 86400 sec. Defines how quickly a client will synchronize changed files with the iFolder server.

▶ *Sync from server*: Default: 20 sec. Min: 10 sec. Max: 86400 sec. Defines how often a client will contact the iFolder server to look for changed files.

▶ *Conflict bin space*: Default: 25MB. Min: 0MB. Max: 100MB. Defines the size of the conflict bin, which stores copies of files that are changed or deleted during synchronization in order to prevent potential data loss.

iFolder account management

There are several account management tasks that you can perform as an iFolder administrator.

▶ *Change a user's disk quota*: Select the User Accounts link and click the username with which you want to work. Change the Disk Quota value and click Change.

▶ *Change an individual user's policy*: Select the User Accounts link and click the username with which you want to work. Click the Set button next to Policy. This opens a page identical to the Client Policies page, but changes are applied to the current user only.

▶ *Remove a user account*: Select the User Accounts link and click the username with which you want to work. At the bottom of the page, click Remove User.

Using iFolder

Once iFolder is installed and configured on the server, users can begin to take advantage of iFolder's file synchronization capabilities. The first thing iFolder users need to do is install the iFolder client. The iFolder client is available from the default iFolder server Web site, shown in Figure 10.9. To access the default iFolder Web site, users can point their browsers to the iFolder server, for example `https://ifolder.quills.com`.

To install the iFolder client, complete the following steps:

1. From the default iFolder client page, click Download.

2. At the File Download screen, choose to either save the client file to disk or run it directly from the server, and then click OK. If you are accessing the server from a remote location, it will probably be faster to download the file prior to installing the iFolder client. If you do this, specify a location for the file. Once the download is complete, execute the file you downloaded.

3. If you get a Security Warning screen from Windows, click Yes.

4. At the Welcome screen, click Next.

5. At the License Agreement Language screen, select the language in which to view the license agreement and click Next. This will open a browser window with the iFolder license agreement. To continue the installation, close the browser window.

6. At the License Agreement screen, click Yes to accept the agreement.

7. At the Installation Complete screen, select Yes, I want to restart my computer now and click Finish.

FIGURE 10.9   *Default iFolder Web site*

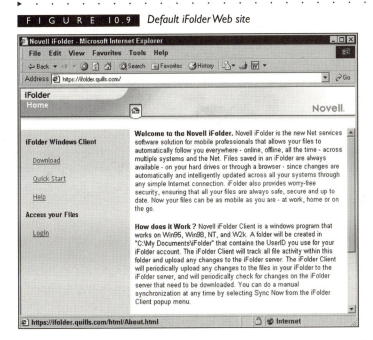

After your workstation reboots, the iFolder Login screen will be displayed, as shown in Figure 10.10. Specify a user name (typically your NetWare username), a password, and the DNS name or IP address of your iFolder server.

The first time you log in, iFolder will go through the process of creating an account for you on the iFolder server. If you use encryption, you will be prompted for a passphrase, which is used as a key to encrypt your files.

Do not forget your passphrase. Files cannot be recovered from an iFolder server without the passphrase.

WARNING

F I G U R E 10.10   *iFolder Login screen*

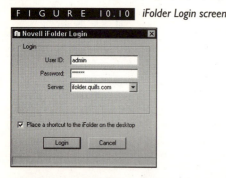

Once you log in, you will see new iFolder icons on your desktop and in the Windows system tray (lower-right corner of the desktop). The desktop icon is a shortcut to your iFolder files. The system tray icon gives you access to iFolder user account information and configuration parameters. To do this, right-click the iFolder icon that appears on the system tray of your workstation. The following major menu options are available:

▶ *Logout/login*: If currently logged in, the Logout option is displayed, which will log you off of the iFolder server and stop all iFolder synchronization. If currently logged out, the Login option is displayed, which allows you to login to the iFolder and initiate synchronization activities.

▶ *Sync now*: Forces a synchronization between the workstation and the iFolder server to begin immediately.

▶ *Account information*: This option lets you view account settings and synchronization activity, as well as letting you set account synchronization preferences. The Account Information screen is shown in Figure 10.11. From the Account Information screen you can do the following:

• *Account Information tab*: Displays basic account information, including username, iFolder directory location, iFolder servername, account space statistics, and to-be-synchronized statistics.

• *View Activity tab*: Lets you view, save, and clear your iFolder account activity log. The log is automatically cleared each time you log into iFolder.

• *Preferences tab*: Lets you enable/disable automatic synchronization and define how often files will be synchronized to/from the iFolder server. You can also choose to have the iFolder client remember your iFolder password and passphrase so you don't have to type them each time you log in.

F I G U R E   I 0 . I I   *iFolder Account Information screen*

- ▶ *Open iFolder*: Opens the iFolder directory associated with your iFolder client account. This is equivalent to double-clicking the iFolder icon that is created, by default, on the Windows desktop.

- ▶ *View conflict bin*: The conflict bin exists to save files that were deleted or changed during an iFolder synchronization. You can manually review the files in the conflict bin to make sure that the correct version of the file has been synchronized.

- ▶ *iFolder Web site*: Selecting this option opens the iFolder Web site associated with your iFolder server. From this page you can download the iFolder client, view iFolder product information and instructions, and access your iFolder account via a Web browser.

- ▶ *Exit*: This option closes the iFolder client interface, and effectively logs you out of the iFolder server. You can restart the iFolder client by clicking Start ➪ Programs ➪ Novell iFolder ➪ iFolder Client.

Accessing iFolder through a browser

iFolder has a browser-based option that eliminates the need for the iFolder client in order to access files in your account on the iFolder server. With iFolder Web access, you can download only the files that you need, as opposed to synchronizing the entire directory. With the iFolder Web access, all you need is Internet access to get to your iFolder account.

To access your iFolder account through a Web browser, complete the following steps:

1. From the default iFolder Web site, click Login.

2. Enter your iFolder username, password, and passphrase, and click Connect.

Once logged in, you will see your iFolder files, listed in a directory structure in the browser window, as shown in Figure 10.12. Expand folders by double-clicking them.

▶ . . . . ◀

FIGURE 10.12 *Browser-based interface to iFolder*

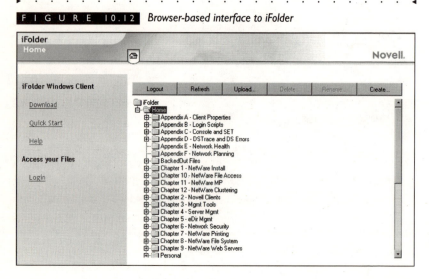

From the browser interface, you can download, upload, delete, create, and rename files. However, changes to downloaded files are not synchronized automatically. Make sure you upload files after making changes, so they can be synchronized to all other workstations where you have installed the iFolder client.

Accessing iFolder from NetStorage or NetDrive

Accessing an iFolder server from either NetStorage or NetDrive was described earlier in this chapter in the sections for each of those products. However, the important thing to remember is that you are accessing files on the server only. You don't get the effects of synchronization between client and server as you do with the iFolder client.

The advantage of this scenario is that you can access files from any workstation without fear of accidentally leaving data on a foreign machine. This might lead some to consider using iFolder without installing the iFolder client at all. This is a possible solution, but remember that files are not replicated to multiple locations. If the server experienced a problem, or you forget your passphrase, files on the iFolder server could be lost or unrecoverable.

TIP

The best solution is one that uses each technology where it makes sense, without relying too heavily on only one type of file access solution.

NetWare Web Access

NetWare WebAccess allows network administrators to quickly and easily provide browser-based access to network resources. Effectively, WebAccess allows you to create personalized user portals through which users can access their data and applications from a single Web site.

Perhaps most important to you as a network administrator, WebAccess doesn't require any complicated Web development or programming. It's pretty much ready to go right out of the box.

WebAccess relies on the concept of *gadgets*, which are little Java-based servlets or applications that provide access to specific types of network resources. NetWare 6 includes several gadgets for accessing network resources and performing common network tasks:

▶ *NetStorage*: Provides access to the Novell NetStorage service. NetStorage provides Internet-based access to file storage on a NetWare 6 server.

▶ *Novell iPrint*: Provides access to Internet printing via iPrint.

▶ *Email and calendaring*: Provides support for popular email applications and protocols, including Novell GroupWise, Microsoft Exchange, Lotus Notes, Novell Internet Messaging System (NIMS), POP3, and IMAP.

▶ *Address book*: Provides a simplified screen to access phone numbers and other user information stored in eDirectory.

▶ *Password*: Links to a page where a user can change their password in eDirectory.

Installing WebAccess

NetWare WebAccess can be installed as an optional component during the NetWare 6 installation or it can be installed later through Deployment Manager or the graphical server console.

NOTE

For most networks, you will need to install WebAccess on only one server in each eDirectory tree.

The only requirement for WebAccess, beyond the minimum requirements for a NetWare 6 server, is a browser (Netscape v4.7 or later, or Internet Explorer v5.0 or later). To install WebAccess using Deployment Manager, complete the following steps:

1. Insert the NetWare 6 Operating System CD-ROM. Launch NWDEPLOY.EXE from the root of the CD.

2. Double-click Post-Installation Tasks and select Install NetWare 6 products.

3. At the Target Server screen, select the server to which you want to install WebAccess and click Next.

4. Log in to the selected server. You may have to click Details and specify the IP address of the target server if authentication does not work properly.

5. At the Components screen, click Clear All. Select NetWare WebAccess and click Next.

6. At the WebAccess Objects screen, specify a container into which WebAccess objects should be installed and click Next.

7. At the Gadget screen, select those gadgets that you want to be installed into your eDirectory tree. Objects will be created for each gadget so they can be managed through ConsoleOne.

8. At the Summary screen, click Finish to install WebAccess. When the Installation Complete screen appears, click Close.

9. Once the installation is complete, you need to restart the Tomcat servlet engine to load WebAccess. In order to avoid problems with other Web services, the easiest way to do this is to restart the server.

Once loaded, you can access a default WebAccess page by pointing your browser to the following page: `http://<server DNS name or IP address>/webaccess`. For example:

```
http://ormserv2.quills.com/webaccess
```

This page will include links to all the gadgets you selected during the WebAccess installation.

Using WebAccess

Once installed, WebAccess starts automatically when the NetWare 6 server starts. If you are having trouble accessing WebAccess, the first thing you should probably do is try to restart the server, since the reboot typically allows all services to start properly.

To use WebAccess, complete the following steps:

1. Open the WebAccess URL in your browser, for example:

   `http://ormserv2.quills.com/webaccess`

2. At the Login screen, specify your eDirectory username and password.

3. You will see the default WebAccess page, as shown in Figure 10.13. From here, you can click on any of the gadgets listed in the navigation frame on the left to access that service or application from your browser.

FIGURE 10.13 *Default WebAccess Web page*

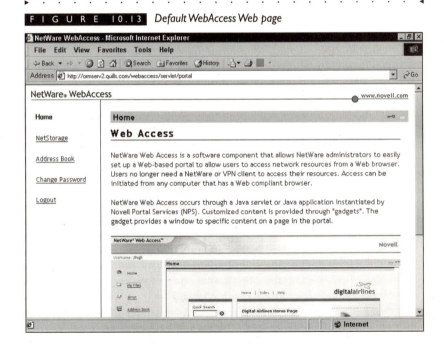

Configuring WebAccess

You can make only minor changes to the gadgets that ship with NetWare 6, since they are already configured to perform very specific tasks. Basically, you can edit the service or application URL, and add/remove gadgets from the WebAccess Web page. If you are interested in doing more advanced customization, or in creating your own gadgets, you can purchase Novell Portal Services, which includes all the information and tools necessary for doing this.

Gadgets are represented as objects in eDirectory, and can be modified through ConsoleOne. To configure the WebAccess home page, complete the following steps:

1. Launch ConsoleOne and browse to the container where you installed the WebAccess objects.

2. In the right pane, double-click the WebAccess_Configuration_All_Users object.

3. At the General NetWare WebAccess page, click Configure to start the WebAccess Configuration Wizard. At the Welcome screen, click Next.

4. At the Available Services screen, select those gadgets (services) that you want to make available from your WebAccess home page, and click Next.

5. Continue through the next pages of the wizard, providing the necessary configuration information for each gadget you selected in Step 4.

- *Home Page gadget*: Provide the URL to the home page that will be displayed when users go to WebAccess. This page will be displayed along with the gadgets you have chosen to use.

- *NetStorage gadget*: You must have NetStorage installed and configured before configuring this gadget.

NOTE

Provide the URL (DNS name or IP address) of the server where NetStorage is installed. If Apache Web services are running on a port other than 80, make sure you specify the port as part of the URL. The NetStorage path is oneNet/NetStorage. The path cannot be changed, and is automatically added to the NetStorage URL by NetWare WebAccess. The Default Username field controls the login dialog. You can enter %cn% to have Web Access get the user's eDirectory username and automatically add it to the username field on the NetStorage login screen, so the user only has to enter their password. If you leave the field blank, the user will be required to enter both a username and a password. For more information on NetStorage, see Chapter 8.

- *Email gadget*: The configuration for this gadget will vary, depending on the email system you are using. For specific information on configuring the Email gadget, see the Novell on-line documentation.

- *iPrint gadget*: You must have NDPS and Novell iPrint installed and configured before configuring this gadget.

NOTE

Provide the URL to the Novell iPrint access page. By default, this is `http://<print service DNS name or IP address>:631/ipp`, for example, `http://printing.quills.com:631/ipp`. For information on Novell iPrint, see Chapter 7.

- *Address Book gadget*: No configuration required
- *Change Password gadget*: No configuration required

6. At the Summary screen, click Finish to save the gadget configuration.

NetWare Web Search Server

While Web Search server isn't necessarily a way to access NetWare files, it is all about making Internet and intranet data available to employees and customers as quickly and accurately as possible. Supporting everything from simple internal search solutions, to complex search services that you can offer to organizations for a fee, Web Search server is one of the fastest and most accurate search engines currently available.

Web Search server offers a powerful, full-text search engine you can use to add search capabilities to your Internet or intranet Web sites. Compatible with the NetWare Enterprise Web server, you can create custom search forms and search result pages either from scratch or by using the included templates.

This section introduces you to Web Search server and its basic installation and configuration. However, for comprehensive information, see the NetWare 6 on-line documentation.

Web Search Server Capabilities

With NetWare Web Search server, you can:

- ▶ Support searching multiple language indexes from a single interface
- ▶ Host search services for multiple organizations

- ▶ Organize collections of related files from diverse sources as a single document

- ▶ Create custom search and print results and error and response messages and apply them to individual language searches or across all supported languages

Originally released with NetWare 5.1, NetWare Web Search server has been greatly enhanced for NetWare 6 with new features and improved usability. The following list highlights several of the new features and enhancements to NetWare Web Search server:

- ▶ Multiprocessor enabled

- ▶ Faster indexing and searching, particularly on multiword searches and the ability to search multiple indexes simultaneously

- ▶ Creating and managing multiple search sites simultaneously

- ▶ Ability to display search and print template pages in user-specified language, as defined in their Web browser's language preferences

- ▶ Cluster-enabled for high-availability

- ▶ More efficient indexing control, including the ability to exclude repetitive portions of a document — such as headers, footers, and navigation bars — from the indexing process

- ▶ Expanded support for document formats such as QuattroPro, PowerPoint, RTF, XML, HTML, TXT, and Word

- ▶ XML support improving search results by allowing Web Search server to search only document titles, document meta tags, and so on.

- ▶ Template debugging feature displaying all errors related to information sent or received by a template

- ▶ Date-based search and sorting of results

- ▶ Ability to search for a specific filename, path, URL, or file extension (for example, filtering searches or restricting searches when a document location is known)

- ▶ Expanded types of search operators and parameters for generating more accurate search results

Installing Web Search Server

NetWare Web Search server can be installed as an optional component during the NetWare 6 installation, or it can be installed after the NetWare 6 through Deployment Manager or the graphical server console.

To install Web Search server using Deployment Manager, complete the following steps:

1. Insert the NetWare 6 Operating System CD-ROM. Launch NWDEPLOY.EXE from the root of the CD.

2. Double-click Post-Installation Tasks and select Install NetWare 6 products.

3. At the Target Server screen, select the server to which you want to install Web Search server and click Next.

4. Log in to the selected server. You may have to click details and specify the IP address of the target server if authentication does not work properly.

5. At the Components screen, click Clear All. Select NetWare Web Search and click Next.

6. At the Summary screen, click Finish to install NetWare Web Search server. At the Installation Complete screen, click Close.

7. Once the installation is complete, start the NetWare 6 server where Web Search server is installed.

Understanding Web Search Basics

Before you get started creating and managing search sites, you should understand the basics of Web Search. The version of Web Search server that is included with NetWare 6 supports the creation of up to three different search sites.

TIP

If you need more than this, you can purchase the Enterprise version of Web Search server as an add-on product for NetWare 6. For more information, visit the Novell Web Search server home page at http://www.novell.com/products/websearch/.

Components of a search site

By definition, a search site is a collection of one or more indexes and their related configuration files. A typical Web Search site consists of the following:

▶ *Indexes*: Indexes are at the heart of a search site. An index is an optimized binary file that contains keywords found in documents hosted on a Web or file server. Indexes are used by Web Search to return search results to users.

NOTE

When you install NetWare Web Search server, some of your server's content is automatically indexed and appears on the default search form as the "NetWare Web Search" and "Doc Root" indexes.

▶ *Log files*: A log file keeps record of search statistics and performance of the search site.

▶ *Search and print templates*: These are templates that become populated with the results of a search and then are displayed to the user. Depending on which templates are used, the level of detail displayed in search and print results varies.

▶ *Scheduled events*: Index management, such as updating or regenerating, can be automated to occur at specific intervals using the Scheduling feature.

▶ *Themes*: A theme instantly adds a common look and feel to your search page, search and print results pages, and response and error message pages.

Testing Web Search

Once you start the Enterprise Web server, you can open the search page using your Web browser and perform a search against the content that has been automatically indexed. To test NetWare Web Search using the default search page, do the following:

1. Point your browser to the default search page at `http://<server DNS name of IP address>/novellsearch`. Remember that the URL is case sensitive. For example:

```
http://ormserv2.quills.com/novellsearch
```

2. In the Search field, type **NetWare** and press Enter.

Working with Web Search Server

Once installed, Web Search server automatically adds a link for NetWare Web Search Manager to the Web Manager home page. That way, Web Search Manager can be accessed in the same way as all other Web services in NetWare 6.

To open Web Search Manager, click the Web Search Configuration link under NetWare Web Search server in Web Manager. The Web Search server Manager interface is shown in Figure 10.14.

F I G U R E   10.14 *Web Search server Manager interface*

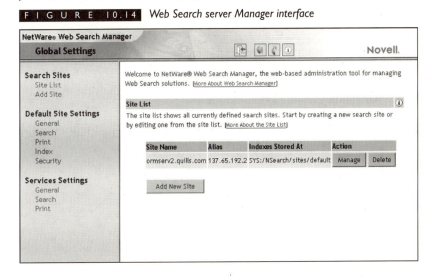

There are four primary tasks associated with configuring and managing Web Search server. Each is described in the following sections.

▶ Creating a search site

▶ Creating and managing indexes

▶ Generating indexes

▶ Scheduling index events

Creating a search site

Using Web Search Manager, you can create and configure search sites, and then begin adding indexes to them. To create a new search site, click the Add Site link in the Navigation frame, or click the Add New Site button on the Site List page. The Add Site page is shown in Figure 10.15. Provide the following information:

▶ *Site name:* Specify a name for the new search site. This is typically the DNS or domain name of your server. When Web Search server receives a query, it must determine which of the available search sites it should use to handle the request. There are two ways to do this:

   • Matching the domain name in the search query with a search site name in Web Search

- Using the `SITE=searchsitename` query parameter to find matching search site names

▶ *Site alias*: Specify a secondary name for the search site. This is typically the IP address of your server. An alias name typically follows one of two conventions:

- An IP address could be used either in the domain name portion of a URL or be included in a search query using the `&site` query parameter. Using an IP address in place of a domain name to select a search site works only in a hardware virtual server configuration where each search site has its own unique IP address.

- Any other numeric or textual value that can be passed as the value of the `&site` query parameter

For more information on virtual Web servers, see Chapter 9.

X-REF

▶ *Store site files at*: Specify the path to where you want the index and configuration files to be stored. If this field is left blank, Web Search will store the search site files in the */searchroot*/sites/*sitename* directory. You can store the files on any volume on the server where Web Search is installed, but not on other servers.

FIGURE 10.15 *The Add Site page in Web Search Manager*

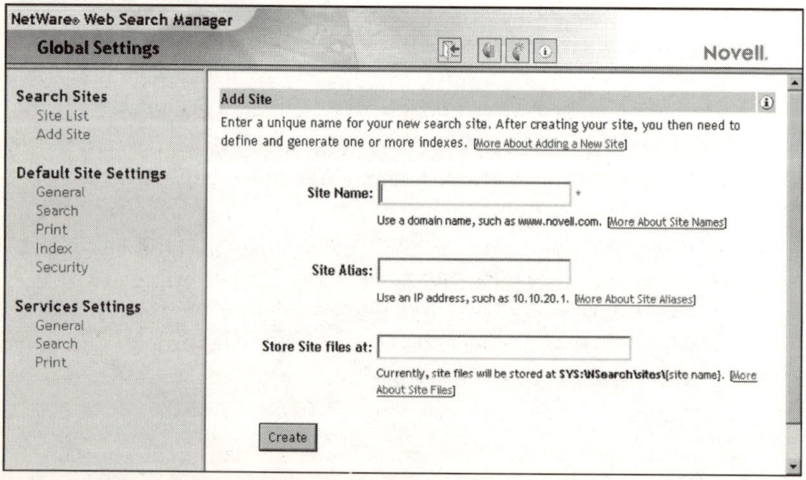

NetWare® Web Search Manager	
Global Settings	Novell.

Search Sites
Site List
Add Site

Default Site Settings
General
Search
Print
Index
Security

Services Settings
General
Search
Print

Add Site

Enter a unique name for your new search site. After creating your site, you then need to define and generate one or more indexes. [More About Adding a New Site]

Site Name: [   ] *

Use a domain name, such as www.novell.com. [More About Site Names]

Site Alias: [   ]

Use an IP address, such as 10.10.20.1. [More About Site Aliases]

Store Site files at: [   ]

Currently, site files will be stored at SYS:\WSearch\sites\[site name]. [More About Site Files]

[Create]

Creating and managing indexes

Web Search server supports two types of indexes:

▶ *Crawled*: Follows hypertext links until it reaches a dead end. Web Search server can crawl one or more Web sites, specific areas of a Web site, or specific URLs, all the way down to specific file names.

▶ *File system*: Indexes content on a file server. Web Search can index one or more paths on multiple volumes, including Storage Area Network (SAN) systems.

There are two forms you can use to create each type of index: the standard form and the advanced form. The standard form is discussed here. For information on the advanced form, see the NetWare 6 on-line documentation.

Web Search server can search across multiple indexes within a single search site, but cannot search across multiple search sites.

Searching a single index is generally faster than searching across multiple indexes.

TIP

To create a new crawled index, complete the following steps:

1. From Web Search Manager, click Site List. Click the Manage button next to the site for which you want to create an Index.

2. In the Define a New Index box, select New Crawled Index and click Define Index.

3. In the Define Crawled Index screen, provide the required information and click Apply Settings.

- *Index name*: Specify a name for the new index. The name can be a word, phrase, or a numeric value. If you are going to have a large number of indexes, you should use a naming scheme so you can effectively manage your indexes. Keep in mind that the index name will be visible to users, so you might want to choose a name that will mean something to them.

- *URL of Web site*: Specify the URL of the Web site you want to index You can enter a URL by itself or include a path down to a specific file level. The Standard index form includes two URL fields. Click Add more URLs to specify more than two URLs to be indexed.

To create a new file system index, complete the following steps:

1. From Web Search Manager, click Site List. Click the Manage button next to the site for which you want to create an index.

2. In the Define a New Index box, select New File System Index and click Define Index.

3. In the Define Crawled Index screen, provide the required information and click Apply Settings. You can specify multiple paths for a single index by clicking Add more paths.

   - *Index name*: Specify a name for the new index. The name can be a word, phrase, or a numeric value. If you are going to have a large number of indexes, you should use a naming scheme so you can effectively manage your indexes. Keep in mind that the index name will be visible to users, so you might want to choose a name that will mean something to them.

   - *Server path to be indexed*: Specify the absolute path to the folder containing the information that you want indexed, for example SYS:\MARKETING\COLLATERAL.

   - *Corresponding URL prefix*: Specify the URL that should be used by the search results page to access the individual files. This corresponds to a Document Directory (Document Root) that has been defined on the Web server.

For more information on document directories, see Chapter 9.

X-REF

Generating indexes

Once you define an index, you must generate it before it can be used for searching. This is the actual process of examining Web site content or Web server files to gather keywords, titles, and descriptions and to place them in the index file.

To generate a newly defined index, complete the following steps:

1. From Web Search Manager, click Site List. Click the Generate button next to the site for which you want to generate an index.

2. At the Active Jobs screen you will see the status of the current indexing jobs. If there is no current index job, the status page will read No indexing jobs are currently running or defined. To cancel the current indexing jobs, click the Cancel link in the Status column.

Scheduling index events

Web Search server can automatically update your indexes on specific dates and times by scheduling events. To configure an automatic generation event, complete the following steps:

1. From the Site List page, click Manage next to the site with which you want to work.

2. Click the Scheduling link in the Navigation frame.

3. Click Add Event.

4. At the Schedule New Event screen, provide the required information and click Apply Settings.

   - *Date, days of week, and time*: Specify the month, days, days of the week, or time (in hours and minutes) when you want Web Search server to run the event. You can use the Ctrl and Shift keys to select multiple dates and times.

   - *Operation*: Select the type of operation you want performed on your indexes. Update will add any new content from the Web site or file system to the index file. Optimize will remove unnecessary content and make the index file smaller and faster. Regenerate replaces the existing index with a new one.

   - *Perform operations on*: Determine whether you want the chosen operation performed on all indexes in the search site, or only on specified indexes. If you have large indexes, it may be best to create multiple events to update indexes at different times.

Managing Web Search Server

Services settings give the Web Search server administrator global control over the search services provided by NetWare Web Search server, including the ability to completely disable searching. These pages also control overall performance of the Web Search server.

Services settings are organized under the Services Settings heading in the Navigation frame. The three categories of settings are covered in the following sections.

General

General services settings define error log and site list settings for all search sites. The General Services Settings page is shown in Figure 10.16.

► . . . . ◄

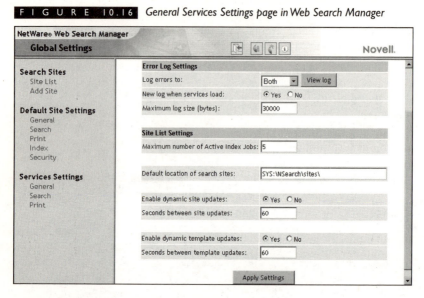

F I G U R E   10.16   *General Services Settings page in Web Search Manager*

You can set the following parameters from the General Services Settings page. Click Apply Settings when you are done making changes.

- ► *Log errors to*: Select where you want log results displayed:

  - • *File*: This option lets you view log files from a Web browser by clicking the View log button.

  - • *Console*: This option lets you view log results in a dedicated Tomcat servlet engine console screen. Use Ctrl+Esc to change to this page on the server console.

  - • *Both*: This option lets you view log results from either a browser or the system console.

- ► *New log when services load*: When set to Yes, this option starts a new log file each time you restart the Web Search server.

- ► *Maximum log size (bytes)*: Limit the size of the log file to the size you specify (in bytes).

- ► *Maximum number of active index jobs*: Limits the number of indexing jobs that can run at the same time. Default is 5.

- ► *Default location of search sites*: Specifies the path to where you want all search site files to be stored, including index and configuration files.

Changing this setting won't move existing sites to a new location, but all new search sites will be placed here.

▶ *Enable dynamic site updates*: When set to Yes, this option directs Web Search server to reload configuration files that are modified manually, instead of using Web Search Manager.

▶ *Seconds between site updates*: Specifies how often Web Search server will look for manually modified configuration files, in seconds.

▶ *Enable dynamic template updates*: When set to Yes, this option directs Web Search server to templates that have been modified.

▶ *Seconds between template updates*: Specifies how often Web Search server should reload search, print, results, and error templates, in seconds. Any changes to templates will be recognized within the time period specified here.

Search

Search services settings let you turn search capabilities on or off and manage debugging and statistics settings. The Search Services Settings page is shown in Figure 10.17.

F I G U R E 1 0 . 1 7   *Search Settings page in Web Search Manager*

You can set the following parameters from the Search Services Settings page. Click Apply Settings when you are done making changes.

▶ *Enable search service*: Enables search services for all search sites on the Web Search server.

▶ *Enable search debugging*: When set to Yes, this option keeps a log of all searches and query results going to all search sites. This option should be enabled only during troubleshooting because the log file can grow very quickly.

▶ *Log debug messages to*: Specifies where you want debug log results displayed:

  • *File*: This option lets you view log files from a Web browser by clicking the View log button.

  • *Console*: This option lets you view log results in a dedicated Tomcat servlet engine console screen. Use Ctrl+Esc to change to this page on the server console.

  • *Both*: This option lets you view log results from either a browser or the system console. To start a new log file each time you restart the Web Search server, click Yes next to New Log When Services Load.

▶ *New log when servlet loads*: When set to Yes, this option starts a new debug log each time you restart the Web Search server.

▶ *Maximum log size (bytes)*: Limit the size of the debug log file, to the size you specify (in bytes).

▶ *Enable search statistics logging*: When set to Yes, generates an updated log file containing statistics about searches performed against all search sites on your Web Search server.

▶ *Seconds between statistics updates*: Specifies the time, in seconds, between updates of the statistics log file.

▶ *Log statistics to*: Specifies where you want statistics displayed:

  • *File*: This option lets you view statistics from a Web browser by clicking the View log button.

  • *Console*: This option lets you view statistics in a dedicated Tomcat servlet engine console screen. Use Ctrl+Esc to change to this page on the server console.

  • *Both*: This option lets you view statistics from either a browser or the system console. To start a new log file each time you restart the Web Search server, click Yes next to New Log When Services Load.

▶ *Maximum log file size*: Limits the size of the statistics log file to the size you specify (in bytes).

▶ *New log when servlet loads*: When set to Yes, this option starts a new debug log each time you restart the Web Search server.

▶ *Log error if search time exceeds (seconds)*: Specifies the timeout, in seconds, before Web Search server should record the current search as exceeding the specified time limit on the statistics display.

Print

This page manages Print services debug and statistics and has the same type of options and parameters described in the Search section above. Click Apply Settings to save any changes you make to this page.

Managing Search Sites

The default site settings define characteristics for search sites that are created on Web Search server. Changes to the parameters defined on these pages will be automatically applied to any new search sites that are created, unless overridden through the use of the Advanced Index definition form.

In this way, you can manage your search sites by exception, rather than by having to define every setting for every site manually when it is created. There are five categories of default site settings, which are detailed in the following sections.

General

General settings let you manage query, response, and error log settings for all newly created search sites. The General Default Site Settings page is shown in Figure 10.18.

You can set the following parameters from the General Default Site Settings page. Click Apply Settings when you are done making changes.

▶ *Default query encoding*: Specifies an encoding that represents the character set encoding that most of your user queries will use. Default is UTF-8.

▶ *Maximum query duration (seconds)*: Specifies the maximum duration of any query, in seconds. Any query that reaches this limit will terminate, whether or not the query has actually finished. Default is 30 seconds. This option helps you protect server resources from malicious rogue searches, which are intended to slow site performance by consuming server resources.

▶ *Default encoding for response pages*: Specifies the encoding Web Search server will use when responding to user queries with Search and Print Results templates, and Error and Response Messages templates.

▶ *Refuse queries if potential hits exceed*: Specifies the maximum effective size of a search for Web Search server. Use this field to cancel the processing of search results that might take a long time to complete because of the number of hits that are being returned.

▶ *Maximum log size (bytes)*: Specifies the maximum size, in bytes, to which Web Search server will allow the log file to grow. This protects your server hard drive resources, particularly on a busy search server.

FIGURE 10.18 *General Default Site Settings page in Web Search Manager*

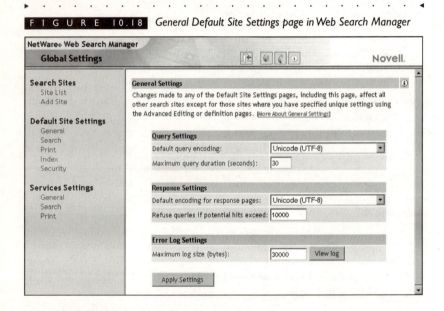

Search

Search default site settings let you turn search capabilities on or off and manage debugging and statistics settings. The Search Default Site Settings page is shown in Figure 10.19.

You can set the following parameters from the Default Search Site Settings page. Click Apply Settings when you are done making changes.

▶ *Default number of results to display*: Specifies the number of search results that will be displayed on each search results page.

▶ *Maximum number of results per page*: Sets a limit on the number of results allowed on any results page.

▶ *Highest allowed result number*: Specifies the maximum number of results that will be returned for any query.

▶ *Templates directory*: Specifies the location of the Web Search server templates files. The default path is *volume:\searchroot\Templates.*

▶ *Default encoding for templates*: Specifies the character set that your templates are written in. This is a default value that will be used with templates that do not specify a specific encoding.

▶ *Default search page template*: Specifies the name of the search page template file you want to use.

▶ *Default search results template*: Specifies the name of the search results template file you want to use.

▶ *Template to use if no results returned*: Specifies the name of the template file to be used if no results are found.

▶ *Template to use if error occurs*: Specifies the name of the template file to be used if there are errors while processing a query.

FIGURE 10.19 *Search Default Site Settings page for Web Search Manager*

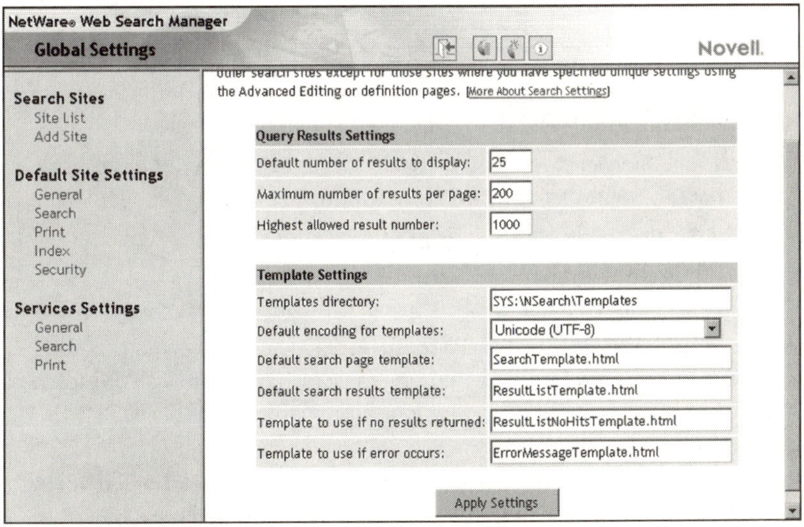

Print

Print default site settings let you manage print results templates and parameters that affect result printing. The Print Default Site Settings page is shown in Figure 10.20.

FIGURE 10.20 *Print Default Site Settings page in Web Search Manager*

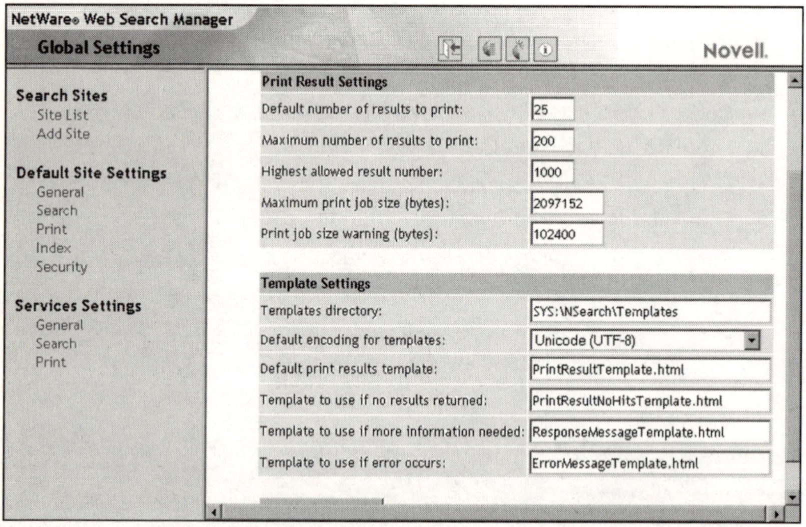

You can set the following parameters from the Default Print Site Settings page. Click Apply Settings when you are done making changes.

- *Default number of results to print*: Specifies the number of print results that you want displayed on each print results page.

- *Maximum number of results to print*: Sets a limit on the number of results allowed on any results page.

- *Highest allowed result number*: Specifies the maximum number of results that will be returned for any query.

- *Maximum print job size (bytes)*: Specifies the largest allowable print job size, in bytes. Any request for a print job larger than this value will receive an error message.

- *Print job size warning (bytes)*: When a print job exceeds the specified size, in bytes, Web Search server will send a warning message to the user via the ResponseMessageTemplate.html file. It then prompts the user to confirm the print job before continuing.

- *Templates directory*: Specifies the location of the Web Search server templates files. The default path is *volume:\searchroot\Templates*.

- *Default encoding for templates*: Specifies the character set that your templates are written in. This is a default value that will be used with templates that do not specify a specific encoding.

- *Default print results template*: Specifies the name of the print results page template file you want to use.

- *Template to use if no results returned*: Specifies the name of the template file to be used if no results are found.

- *Template to use if more information is needed*: Specifies the name of the template file to be sent back to users whose print jobs exceed the size specified in the Print Job Size field.

- *Template to use if error occurs*: Specifies the name of the template file to be used if there are errors while processing a query.

Index

The index default site settings make the process of creating indexes easier by letting you configure common default settings. The Index Default Site Settings page is shown in Figure 10.21.

FIGURE 10.21 *Index Default Site Settings page in Web Search Manager*

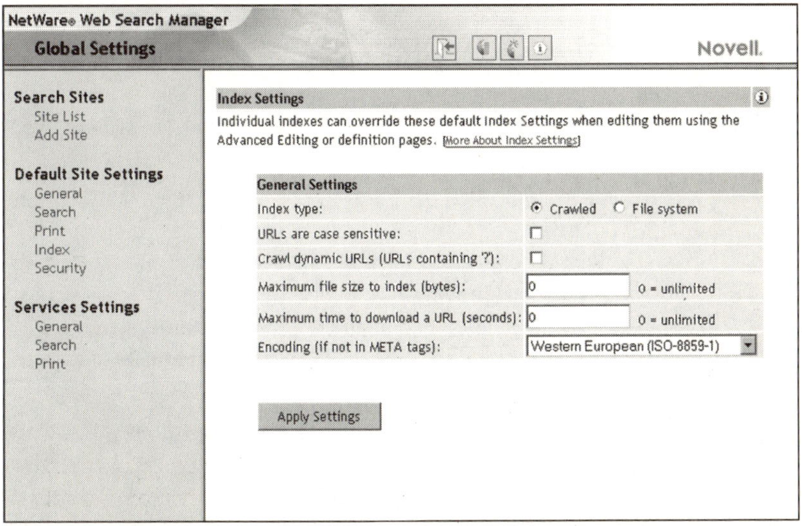

You can set the following parameters from the Default Index Site Settings page. Click Apply Settings when you are done making changes.

- ▶ *Index type*: Specifies the default index as either Crawled or File System.

- ▶ *URLs are case sensitive*: Check this box if you want Web Search server to distinguish between URLs that are different only in character case. Leaving this unchecked can help indexing duplicate information that comes from URLs that use different cases but point to the same information.

- ▶ *Crawl dynamic URLs (URLs containing '?')*: Check this box if you want both dynamic and static content indexed.

- ▶ *Maximum file size to index (bytes)*: Specifies the largest file, in bytes, that Web Search server will index.

- ▶ *Maximum time to download a URL (seconds)*: Specifies the maximum time, in seconds, that Web Search server will attempt to download a URL before it bypasses indexing of that URL.

- ▶ *Encoding (if not in META tags)*: Specifies the encoding to be used when indexing files that do not contain an encoding specification. Usually, HTML files will specify their encoding with a Content-Type META tag.

Security

Default security settings manage access to indexed content by requiring users to authenticate to a server before seeing rights-protected search results. The Security Default Site Settings page is shown in Figure 10.22.

You can set the following parameters from the Security Default Site Settings page. Click Apply Settings when you are done making changes.

- ▶ *Basis for authorization*: Specifies the level of authorization that you want applied to the file system indexes created on Web Search server:

  - • *Allow all*: Although the Login button appears on the default search page, no authentication will be required to view information. All results, whether contained in public or private directories, are returned. Web Search will not ask who the user is. This doesn't mean that if information is contained in an eDirectory protected folder that the user will be able to click the link in the results page and be given access.

  - • *Allow public*: Private content will not be returned in the search results.

- *User login*: Based on what you select for Unauthorized hits filtered by, described below, unauthorized search results will be filtered out either by a results template or by the NetWare Web search engine.

▶ *Unauthorized hits filtered by*: Specifies how unauthorized hits are filtered out of the search results, by the search engine itself or by the search results template.

▶ *Require https*: Select Yes if you want to protect usernames and passwords via SSL as they are sent across the network or Internet.

▶ *Auto-logout time (minutes)*: Specifies the amount of time, in minutes, that a user can be idle before they are logged out of Web Search server.

▶ *Authentication realm string*: Defines the responsible authentication system accepted by Web Search server. By default, Web Search server will perform authentication itself, but you can set the Enterprise server authentication realm string in this field, so users who authenticate to NetWare Enterprise Web server won't have to authenticate again when using Web Search server to search and access protected information.

F I G U R E   10.22   *Security Default Site Settings page in Web Search Manager*

NetWare® Web Search Manager

Global Settings   **Novell.**

Search Sites
Site List
Add Site

Default Site Settings
General
Search
Print
Index
Security

Services Settings
General
Search
Print

Security Settings

Changes made to any of the Default Site Settings pages, including this page, affect all other search sites except for those sites where you have specified unique settings using the Advanced Editing or definition pages. [More About Security Settings]

Search Results Settings
Basis for authorization: Allow all ▼
Unauthorized hits filtered by: ⦿ Search engine   ○ Template

Connection Settings
Require https: ⦿ Yes   ○ No
Auto-logout time (minutes):   30   ☐ Disable auto-logout

Authentication Settings
Authentication realm string: NetWare Web Search Server

[Apply Settings]

PART IV

Enabling Constant
Availability

In This Part

Today it seems like it's all about the network. The Internet has created an environment in which the network really is the computing platform of the twenty-first century. With this emphasis on the network, you had better keep yours up all the time. Many organizations that rely on their networks for customer interaction now measure network outages in thousands, or even millions, of dollars per hour. Obviously, these types of mission-critical environments require network components that are always available.

NetWare 6 offers powerful, high-availability solutions to help you keep your network ready for high profile attention. Chapter 11 discusses the multiprocessing technology available in NetWare 6. Multiprocessing, while not specifically a high-availability solution, lets you do a lot more with the hardware space you have. It removes one of the major bottle-necks to efficient server operation and generally makes life much easier for users of busy networks.

Chapter 12 introduces the latest iteration of Novell clustering services. Clustering lets you link multiple physical servers into a single virtual server for seamless recovery from the loss of any of its members. When used in conjunction with Network Attached Storage (NAS) or Storage Area Network (SAN) technologies, you can create a network-computing infrastructure that is virtually indestructible from the client perspective. Services and data are always available; servers are always up. Business processes, therefore, run more efficiently—ensuring the network infra-structure is helping, rather than hindering, an organization's money-making operations.

CHAPTER 11

NetWare Multiprocessor Support

Instant Access

Introducing multiprocessor-enabled services

- The integrated NetWare 6 Multiprocessing Kernel (MPK) is responsible for providing all multiprocessing capabilities in the NetWare 6 environment.

- For the first time, all NetWare core services are multiprocessor-enabled, including the TCP/IP protocol stack, Novell eDirectory, and the NetWare Core Protocol (NCP) engine.

- NetWare 6 easily accommodates both multiprocessor-aware and non-multiprocessor applications. Non-multiprocessor applications are simply funneled to processor 0, where they execute as if they are on a uniprocessor system.

Understanding multiprocessor concepts

- Threads are the basis for multiprocessing. A *thread* is a single flow of execution within a server, responsible for completing one very specific task.

- NetWare 6 uses a scheduler process and multiple local thread queues to distribute threads to processors for execution.

- NetWare 6 uses a load-balancing algorithm to make sure that no processor gets overloaded.

Multiprocessor hardware support

- Platform Support Modules (PSM) provide a "driver" for multiple processors that adds a layer of abstraction between the NetWare 6 operating system and the complexity of the hardware itself.

- NetWare 6 provides a PSM compatible with the Intel Multiprocessor Specification (MPS), which will support any hardware designed using this specification.

History of NetWare Multiprocessing

NetWare 6 significantly extends the multiprocessor support that has been available in the NetWare operating system since the time of NetWare 4. This chapter presents an overview of the NetWare 6 multiprocessor environment and how some common multiprocessor issues have been resolved.

Novell first introduced multiprocessor functionality, in a limited fashion, with NetWare 4. Although NetWare 4 provided multiprocessor capabilities, all its own core operating system processes were not multiprocessor-enabled. External multiprocessor applications could leverage secondary processors, but all operating systems processes, such as disk access, network I/O, and so on had to be funneled through the primary processor, also known as processor 0.

With the release of NetWare 5, multiprocessor functionality was rewritten and integrated with the NetWare operating system kernel to create the Multiprocessor Kernel (MPK). This effort made all but a few of the native NetWare 5 processes multiprocessor compatible. Unfortunately, two of the most important processes, namely LAN drivers and disk drivers, remained tied to processor 0.

Finally, with the release of NetWare 6, all core operating system processes are multiprocessor compliant. This means that the entire path between network wire and server storage is now multi-processor aware and can take advantage of multiple processors in the server hardware.

NetWare 6 Multiprocessing Improvements

The core of the NetWare operating system is the integrated Multiprocessing Kernel (MPK). The MPK manages threads, schedules processor resources, handles interrupts and exceptions, and manages access to memory and the I/O subsystems.

The NetWare 6 MPK is similar to that in NetWare 5, but with quite a few improvements. Besides incorporating all the bug fixes to the NetWare 5 version, the biggest difference is the fact that all NetWare 6 software subsystems are now multiprocessor-enabled. For the first time, NetWare 6 can itself take full advantage of the power of a multiprocessing system. Table 11.1 lists the NetWare 6 services that are multiprocessor-enabled.

Although all of these services are very important, probably the most advantageous from the perspective of improving overall server performance is the TCP/IP stack. With the popularity of the Internet, many companies are networking with TCP/IP only. As a result, all network traffic processed on a NetWare 6 server goes through the TCP/IP protocol stack. Prior to NetWare 6, this meant processing every packet that enters and leaves the server with processor 0, along with all the other threads from non-multiprocessor-enabled applications and services. Now this potential bottleneck has been removed. Multiple instances of the TCP/IP stack can exist simultaneously and concurrently process multiple TCP/IP packets. The only limitation is the number of processors in your server.

T A B L E I I . I	Multiprocessor-Enabled Services in NetWare 6
SERVICE TYPE	**SERVICE COMPONENTS**
Protocol stacks	NetWare Core Protocols (NCP)
	Service Location Protocols (SLP)
	IP stack
	HTTP
	Ethernet connectivity
	Token Ring connectivity
	Web Distributed Authoring and Versioning (WebDAV)
	Lightweight Directory Access Protocol (LDAP)
Storage services	Novell Storage Services (NSS)
	Distributed File Service (DSS)
	Protocol services
	Request dispatcher
	Transport service
	Fiber channel disk support
Security services	Novell International Cryptographic Infrastructure (NICI)
	Authentication
	ConsoleOne authentication snap-ins
Miscellaneous services	Novell eDirectory
	Novell Java Virtual Machine (JVM)
	Web engines
	Additional Web features

In addition to improved performance and greater scalability, NetWare 6 multiprocessing offers these benefits:

- ► Complete backward compatibility with applications written for the older SMP.NLM (written for NetWare 4.11), as well as any legacy CLIB application that does not support multiprocessing (they are just funneled to processor 0).

- ► An integrated Multiprocessing Kernel (MPK) that supports both uniprocessing and multiprocessing platforms.

- ► Kernel-level support for preemption. The NetWare 6 kernel now supports applications written for a preemptive multitasking environment natively.

▸ A single Platform Support Module (PSM) provides full integration between the multiprocessing hardware and the NetWare MPK.

Running Programs on NetWare 6

After you have installed NetWare 6 on your multiprocessing hardware, the NetWare 6 MPK determines how many processors are in the system. Next, the kernel scheduler determines the processor on which to run the waiting threads. This decision is based on information about the threads themselves and on the availability of processors.

Three types of programs can run on NetWare 6:

▸ *Multiprocessor safe*: Multiprocessing Safe programs are typically NLMs that are not multiprocessing-enabled, but are safe to run in a multiprocessing environment. These programs run on processor 0, which is home to all multiprocessing safe programs. NetWare 6 is very accommodating to programs that were written prior to the introduction of the NetWare MPK. These non-multiprocessing-aware applications are automatically scheduled to run on processor 0 upon execution.

▸ *Multiprocessor compliant*: Multiprocessing complaint programs are specifically written to run in a multiprocessing environment. When one of these programs loads, the NetWare 6 scheduler automatically assigns the different threads to available processors. The Intel MPS specification allows programs to indicate if their specific threads want to run on a specific processor. In this case, the NetWare scheduler will assign that thread to run on the requested processor. Although this functionality is available in NetWare 6 for those multiprocessing utilities and other programs that require the ability to run on a specific processor, Novell engineering discourages developers from writing programs this way.

NOTE

When a multiprocessing compliant program is loaded, the NetWare scheduler checks for an available processor on which to run the thread (provided its threads don't request a specific processor). If the first available processor is processor 3, the thread is scheduled to run there. The next thread would go to processor 4, and so on. This assumes that the processors make themselves available in consecutive order. If the system only has one processor, all the applications' threads will be queued up to run on processor 0, which is always the first processor regardless of whether it is an MP or non-MP environment.

▸ *NetWare OS*: Lastly, the NetWare OS is completely MP compliant, allowing its multitude of threads to run on available processors as needed.

Multiprocessing Concepts

This chapter offers a brief look at a core NetWare 6 technology in hopes that this information will be useful should you ever need to troubleshoot a multiprocessing issue in your network environment. In order to understand multiprocessing in general, and the NetWare 6 multiprocessing architecture in particular, you should be familiar with the multiprocessing concepts described in the following sections.

IMPORTANT

Before discussing the specifics of multiprocessing, it is important to clear up a common misperception about multiprocessing systems. Many people assume that a multiprocessor server with two processors will be twice as powerful as the same server with a single processor. While this may be the theoretical goal of multiprocessor hardware engineers, you won't see this linear increase in performance in our imperfect world. Generally, as the number of processors in a server increases, the processing power of the system also increases, although to a lesser degree. Practically, this means that a two-processor system gives you about 1.8 times the processing power as the same system with a single processor. A four-processor system delivers roughly 3.5 times as much processing power, and a six-processor system offers about 5.2 times the processing power.

NetWare 6 supports up to 32 processors in a single server, which works out to a whole lot of processing horsepower!

Threads

A thread is not some bit of code that the processor is executing. Rather, a thread represents an independent stream of control within the processing environment. Since NetWare was first released, it has been using threads to allow operating system processes to function efficiently. Here's how they work:

▸ Processes and threads are not equivalent, but they are similar. The main difference between the two is that a process may typically be swapped out of memory to make room for another process (preemptive), while a thread is normally allowed to run to completion once it starts (non-preemptive).

▸ NetWare 6 keeps track of all the threads that run in the server environment with a scheduler and thread queues. The scheduler is multiprocessor-enabled itself, and an integral part of the NetWare 6 MPK. As a result, each processor maintains its own scheduler for managing its thread execution.

▶ Each processor also maintains three different thread queues for organizing thread execution. The three queues are the Run queue, the Work To Do queue, and the Miscellaneous queue.

▶ The threads in the Run queue have priority over threads in the other two queues. Run queue threads are non-blocking, meaning that they do not relinquish control of the processor until they are done. The Run queue is typically reserved for critical systems such as protocol stacks and many of the other NetWare kernel processes.

▶ When a Run queue thread completes, the processor checks for additional threads in the Run queue. If no threads are currently in the Run queue, the processor looks in the Work To Do queue. Unlike the Run queue, Work To Do threads may relinquish control of the processor if they rely on less-important functions that can be blocked by the scheduler. The Work To Do queue is usually used by non-critical NetWare services and NLMs.

▶ Finally, the Miscellaneous queue is checked after the Work To Do queue. The Miscellaneous queue holds most application threads that are running in the NetWare environment.

NOTE

NetWare Loadable Modules (NLMs) often establish multiple threads, each representing a distinct path of execution. Make sure you don't equate a thread with NLM execution.

In a multiprocessing environment, should you use a single Global Run queue to service all available processors, or create multiple Local Run queues, each associated with a single processor?

▶ *Global queues*: This approach to distributing threads has the advantage of automatic load balancing. Waiting threads are automatically doled out to the processor that becomes available first. Unfortunately, the Global queue itself becomes the bottleneck as the number of processors and the number of executing threads increases in a system.

▶ *Local queues*: This approach does not have the bottleneck problem associated with the Global queue because a Run queue is created for each processor in the system. It also makes it possible to preferentially schedule threads on the processor on which they last ran, which can increase the efficiency of the system as a whole. The downside to Local queues, however, is it becomes necessary to manually spread the load on the processors as evenly as possible. Without a load balancing mechanism, threads might pile up at one processor while another processor remains idle.

Novell chose to use Local queues with NetWare 6 because of the scalability advantages that were offered over a Global queue solution. Then they implemented a sophisticated load-balancing algorithm to prevent processor imbalances from occurring.

Load Balancing

When Novell engineers began considering the details of their load-balancing algorithm they identified two primary requirements:

- *Stability*: Load balancing would do little good for the system if it reacted to small changes in thread balance, moving threads back and forth between processors pell mell.

- *Quick distribution*: When the scheduler identifies a situation that requires load balancing, the algorithm better be able to make the necessary changes very quickly so as not to affect the overall performance of the system.

NetWare 6 addresses the issue of stability by using a threshold. The threshold determines how far out of balance the thread distribution must get before the system takes action to fix the situation. The next question was where to set the threshold.

A low threshold would keep processors in closer balance at the risk of causing excessive thread movement due to frequent load balancing. A high threshold would greatly reduce the risk of excessive thread movement at the risk of having some processors with a significantly higher load than others, reducing the overall performance of the system. To resolve this problem, NetWare 6 defines its threshold as a range, within which a processor load is deemed acceptable.

To determine where in the load spectrum the threshold should be placed, the scheduler calculates system-wide load and from that the average processor load, on a regular basis. The average processor load becomes the mid-point of the threshold range, as shown in Figure 11.1.

The upper and lower bounds of the threshold become high/low trigger points for the load balancing system. A processor is overloaded when its load exceeds the high trigger. A processor is underloaded when it is below the low trigger.

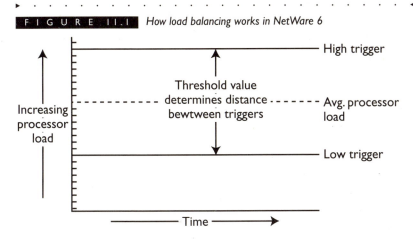

FIGURE 11.1 *How load balancing works in NetWare 6*

When this happens, the scheduler moves threads from the overloaded processor to the under loaded processor to bring the system back into balance. You can actually configure the load-balancing threshold in NoRM by completing the following steps:

1. From NoRM, select the Set Parameters page and click Multiprocessor.

2. Click the value currently listed for the System Threshold parameter.

3. Specify a new value and click OK.

IMPORTANT

Novell strongly recommends using the default value, unless you have carefully considered your reasons for changing it and tested the new setting in a lab environment before committing it to your production server(s).

Preemptive Thread Execution

As mentioned previously, when discussing the NetWare MPK queues, NetWare 6 does allow certain non-critical threads to be preempted, or blocked, in order to make operation of the system as a whole more efficient.

Earlier versions of NetWare did not support process preemption. Rather, they implemented a round-robin (first-in, first-out) scheduling policy where threads were scheduled to run in the order they entered the Run queue. This makes for a simple and very fast operating environment at the expense of overall flexibility.

To support a preemptive environment, applications must be explicitly written to identify those critical sections that cannot be blocked. These sections are identified to the scheduler so the thread cannot be preempted while in a critical section.

NetWare will only preempt an application thread under the following conditions:

▶ The code where the thread is running must be preemptable. This is indicated by a flag set in the module's NLM file format. When the code is loaded into memory, the memory pages are flagged as preemptable.

▶ The thread cannot be in a critical section of the code.

▶ The thread has run long enough to qualify for preemption. The scheduler checks the elapsed time with every tick.

Support for preemption provides

▶ An execution environment that allows simplified application development. Developers can rely on the Scheduler to handle preemption.

▶ A way to forcibly manage modules that are monopolizing the processor.

The NetWare kernel itself cannot be preempted.

NOTE

Multiprocessing Memory Issues

In a uniprocessing environment there is no problem with memory management, since a single processor controls all interaction with system memory. Unfortunately, in a multiprocessing environment, things get a lot more complicated, with multiple processors competing for the use of system memory and the I/O channel. NetWare has to have control logic to manage processor interaction with other subsystems to prevent memory corruption (process crashes) and, basically, to keep the whole thing from melting down.

For example, it is possible for a single application to have multiple threads running on multiple processors simultaneously. In this situation, it is possible that multiple threads could have a need to update the same memory location at the same time. This is known as a *race condition*. Without the proper thread management, you could easily end up with bad data being written to memory.

To avoid this type of dangerous condition, NetWare 6 requires that threads emanating from the same connection run on the same processor. By doing this, NetWare ensures that application threads are queued up and run sequentially to eliminate the possibility of memory corruption.

Beyond this, NetWare 6 also has to manage requests for server subsystems between all the different application threads that might be executing at any given time. To do this, NetWare 6 uses what are known as *synchronization primitives*, which are processes that manage access to shared resources, so everything stays in sync. Synchronization primitives include the following:

▶ *Mutually exclusive lock (mutex)*: This mechanism ensures that only one thread can access a shared resource at a time, such as system memory or the I/O channel.

▶ *Semaphores*: These are somewhat similar to mutexes, but semaphores use counters to control access to RAM memory or other protected resources.

▶ *Read-write locks*: Similar to mutexes, read-write locks work with mutexes to ensure that only one thread at a time has access to a protected resource.

▶ *Condition variables*: These are based on an external station. In so doing, they can be used to synchronize threads. Since they are external to the thread synchronization code, they can be used to ensure that only one thread accesses a protected resource at a time.

NetWare 6 also uses two other synchronization primitives that are restricted to the kernel address space (ring 0): spin locks and barriers. These primitives are not accessible to applications that run in a protected address space.

Platform Support Modules

Besides NetWare, all that is necessary to enable multiprocessing on a multi-processor computer is the Platform Support Module (PSM) for your specific hardware platform and NetWare. No other modules are required.

The PSM is a kind of device driver for the processors in your multiprocessing server. It provides an abstraction layer between the multiprocessor hardware and the NetWare 6 operating system that shields NetWare from the details and intricacies of the vendor-specific multiprocessing implementation. It also enables secondary processors to be brought online and taken offline without having to shut down the server.

During installation, NetWare detects multiple processors by reading the multiprocessor configuration table in the server's BIOS, and from that information determines which of the available NetWare PSM drivers matches the particular multiprocessing hardware platform.

Once installation is complete, you can choose not to load the PSM, which results in NetWare running only on processor 0. By default, the NetWare 6 installation routine will add the PSM load line to the STARTUP.NCF so that it will load whenever the server is started.

Novell provides MPS14.PSM, which supports any hardware platform that complies with the Intel Multiprocessor Specification (MPS) v1.1 and v1.4. Compaq also provides a PSM for its specific multiprocessing system requirements.

Intel MPS v1.4 defines an environment in which all of the processors in the system work and function together similarly. All the processors in the system share a common I/O subsystem and use the same memory pool. MPS-compatible operating systems, such as NetWare 6, can run on systems that comply with this specification without any special modifications.

Since NetWare 6 complies with Intel's specification, it will automatically take advantage of all the processors in your MPS-compliant hardware. At this time, most major computer manufacturers already offer multiprocessing systems compatible with the Intel specification.

More information on the Intel MPS v1.4 specification is available from Intel at: `http://developer.intel.com/design/intarch/MANUALS/242016.htm`.

CHAPTER 12

NetWare Cluster Services

Instant Access

Installing NetWare cluster services

► You can install NetWare Cluster Services (NCS) from Deployment Manager. NetWare 6 ships with a license for a 2-node cluster. Clusters of a larger size require additional licenses, which are purchased separately.

► If you are upgrading an existing NetWare 5 cluster, make sure you perform the pre-upgrade routine in Deployment Manager prior to upgrading the cluster.

Configuring clusters

► Configuration can be done from both ConsoleOne and NoRM.

► Configure general cluster parameters from the Cluster object properties pages.

► Cluster-enable a volume or application through the File drop-down menu by selecting New ⇨ Cluster and selecting the type of resource you would like to cluster-enable.

► Configuration parameters for individual cluster resources are available through the property pages of the Cluster Resource object.

Monitoring clusters

► Monitoring can be done from both ConsoleOne and NoRM.

► Use the Cluster State view to see the status of the cluster.

NetWare Clustering Services

In order to remain competitive, your organization needs to provide customers and employees uninterrupted access to data, applications, Web sites, and other services 24 hours a day, 7 days a week, 365 days a year.

This makes high availability of your organization's services more than a technical issue. It's a business issue that requires a reliable solution.

Novell Clustering Services (NCS) is a multi-node clustering system for NetWare 6 that is integrated with Novell eDirectory. NCS ensures high availability and manageability of critical network resources including data (server volumes), applications, and NetWare 6 services. NCS supports failover, failback, and migration (load balancing) of individually managed cluster resources.

 A license for a 2-node NCS cluster is included with NetWare 6 package. Licenses for additional cluster nodes can be purchased separately from Novell.

NOTE

Clustering Benefits

NCS allows you to configure up to 32 NetWare servers into a high-availability cluster, where resources can be dynamically switched or moved to any server in the cluster. Resources can be configured to automatically switch or move to another node in the event of a server failure. They can also be moved manually, if necessary, to troubleshoot hardware or balance server workload.

One of the best things about NCS is that it lets you create a high-availability environment from "off-the-shelf" components. You don't have to spend millions when you create a cluster, and you can add servers to the cluster as your needs change and grow over time.

Equally important is the ability to greatly reduce unplanned service outages that result from server failures of some sort. You can even reduce the frequency of planned outages for software and hardware maintenance and upgrades, since individual nodes can be removed from the cluster without affecting service availability to network users.

NCS provides the following advantages over a non-clustered environment:

- ► Increased availability
- ► Improved performance
- ► Low cost of operation
- ► Scalability
- ► Disaster recovery

▸ Data protection

▸ Shared resources

Clustering Fundamentals

Suppose you have configured a two-node cluster, with a Web server installed on each of the nodes. Each of the servers in the cluster hosts two Web sites. All of the content for all four Web sites are stored on a shared disk subsystem connected to each of the servers in the cluster. Figure 12.1 shows how such an environment might look.

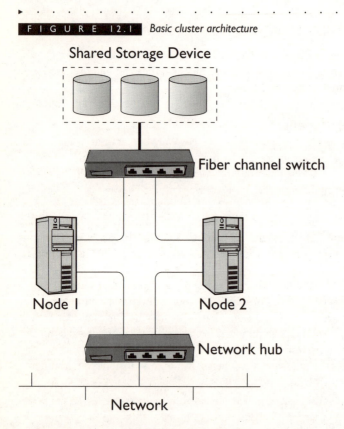

FIGURE 12.1 *Basic cluster architecture*

Shared Storage Device

Fiber channel switch

Node 1   Node 2

Network hub

Network

During normal operation, each clustered node is in constant communication with the other nodes in the cluster through periodic polling. In this way, a node can quickly detect if something happens to another node in the cluster.

If node 2 fails due to some hardware or software problems, users currently attached to the Web server will lose their connections. The IP address associated with node 2, and all its services, are migrated to node 1. Users would likely have to re-load their Web pages, which would be available from the new node within a few seconds.

Once the problem in node 2 is located and repaired, it is restarted and automatically re-inserts itself back into the cluster. Node 1 detects the return of node 2 and seamlessly passes back all the addresses and services originally assigned to node 2. The cluster returns to its normal configuration without any administrator intervention at all.

Clustering Terminology

We all know that clustering provides a high-availability platform for your network infrastructure. High-availability is becoming increasingly important for two different purposes: file access and network services. The following sections discuss NCS configuration for both of these situations. However, before you start working with an NCS cluster, you should be familiar with the terms described in the following sections.

Master node

The first server that comes up in an NCS cluster is assigned the cluster IP address and becomes the master node. (Other nodes in the cluster are often referred to as *slave* nodes.) The master node updates information transmitted between the cluster and eDirectory, and monitors the health of the cluster nodes. If the master node fails, NCS migrates the cluster IP address to another server in the cluster, and that server becomes the master node.

Cluster-enabled volume

A cluster-enabled volume is an NSS volume configured to provide location-transparent access to NetWare file services. The volume is associated with an eDirectory virtual server object that provides a unique secondary IP address for locating the volume on the cluster's shared storage device. The volume provides read/write file access to users.

NOTE

While NetWare 5 clusters failover volumes, NetWare 6 clusters fail-over storage pools. This means you can migrate more than one volume at a time to another node if they are part of the same storage pool. For more information on NetWare 6 storage services, see Chapter 8.

Cluster resource

A cluster resource is an object in eDirectory that represents an application or other type of service (such as DHCP or the master IP address) that you can migrate or failover from one node to another in an NCS cluster. The cluster resource object includes scripts for unloading the service from one node and loading it on another node. In most cases, make sure the service is installed on all nodes in the cluster that will host the service.

Heartbeats and the split-brain detector

NCS uses heartbeats on the LAN and a Split-Brain Detector (SBD) on the shared storage device to keeps all services highly available on the cluster when a node fails. NCS determines when a node fails over the LAN and casts off the failed node through the following process:

▶ Every second (by default), each node in an NCS cluster sends out a heartbeat message over the network.

▶ The master node monitors the heartbeats of all other nodes in the cluster to determine if they are still functioning.

▶ If a heartbeat is not received from a node during a predefined timeout (8 seconds by default), that node is removed (cast off) from the cluster, and migration of services begins.

NOTE

If the master node fails to send a heartbeat within the predefined timeout, it is cast off, and another node takes over as the master node.

NCS also uses the SBD to determine when a node fails through the following process:

▶ Each node writes an epoch number to a special SBD partition on the shared storage device. An epoch occurs each time a node leaves or joins the cluster. The epoch number is written at half the predefined timeout value (4 seconds by default).

▶ Each node reads all epoch numbers for all other nodes in the SBD partition.

▶ When the master node sees an epoch number for a specific node that is lower than the others, it knows that the node has failed, and the node is cast off.

Fan-out failover

When a node fails in an NCS cluster, the cluster-enabled volumes and resources assigned to that node are migrated to other nodes in the cluster. Although this migration happens automatically, you must design and configure where each volume and resource migrates during failover.

TIP

You will probably want to distribute, or *fan out*, the volumes and resources to several nodes based on factors such server load and the availability of installed applications. NCS relies on you to define where clustered resources will be assigned should a failure occur.

Installing Clustering Services

The following list specifies the minimum hardware requirements for installing NCS:

- ▶ A minimum of two NetWare 6 servers.

- ▶ At least 256MB of memory on all servers in the cluster. Novell recommends 512MB of memory for failing multiple applications to the same server node.

- ▶ At least one local disk device, not shared, on which to place the SYS: volume of each node.

- ▶ A shared disk system, either Storage Area Network (SAN) or shared SCSI, is required for each cluster in order for all cluster data to be available to each node. This is how data high-availability is achieved.

NOTE

NCS will create a special cluster partition using one cylinder of one drive of the shared disk system. This will require roughly 15MB of free disk space on the shared disk system for creating the cluster partition.

- ▶ Make sure the disk system is installed and configured properly. You can verify that all servers in the cluster recognize the drives in the shared disk system by using the LIST DEVICES console command.

- ▶ Make sure that the disks in the shared disk system are configured in some type of fault tolerant configuration, such as mirroring or RAID 5. If this is not done, a single disk error could potentially cause a volume failure across the entire cluster.

Preparing an Existing Cluster

If you have an existing NCS cluster and want to upgrade it to NCS 1.6, you need to prepare the existing cluster for the upgrade procedure. The preparation process performs the following tasks:

▶ Saves all trustee assignments, so they will not be lost during the upgrade.

▶ Identifies shared partitions, so the new NetWare 6 safety features can be installed.

▶ Deactivates the cluster in preparation for the upgrade.

This process also assumes that you have already made the upgrade to the latest version of Novell eDirectory.

For more information on upgrading to eDirectory with Deployment Manager, see Chapter 1.

X-REF

1. Insert the NetWare 6 Operating System CD in your workstation CD-ROM drive and launch Deployment Manager by executing NWDEPLOY.EXE from the root of the CD-ROM.

2. From Deployment Manager, open the Network Preparation folder and click Prepare a Novell Cluster for Upgrade.

3. At the Welcome screen select Next.

4. At the NCS Cluster Selection screen, specify the required information and click Next.

- *Cluster object name*: Specify the name of the existing Cluster object in your eDirectory tree.

- *Directory services tree*: Specify the name of your eDirectory tree.

- *Directory services context*: Specify the context of the Cluster object.

5. At the Down Servers screen, Choose whether or not you want the clustered servers you are working with to go down after the pre-upgrade procedure and click Next. Bringing down all cluster servers before an upgrade ensures NSS volumes on shared storage devices are deactivated prior to the NCS upgrade.

If you choose to not to take down all clustered servers after the pre-upgrade, you must do it manually before upgrading cluster servers to NetWare 6.

TIP

Installing a Cluster

NetWare 6 includes an NCS installation program that you use to do the following:

▶ Create a cluster

▶ Add nodes to an existing cluster

▶ Upgrade NCS software in an existing cluster

To install Novell Cluster Services, complete the following steps:

1. Insert the NetWare 6 Operating System CD in your workstation CD-ROM drive and launch Deployment Manager by executing NWDEPLOY.EXE from the root of the CD-ROM.

2. From Deployment Manager, open the Post-Installation Tasks folder and click Install or Upgrade a NetWare Cluster.

3. At the Welcome screen, click Next.

4. At the NCS Action screen, select the installation option you would like to use and click Next.

- *Create new cluster*: Choose this option to create a new cluster in your network.

- *Add new nodes to existing cluster*: Check this option to add another node to an existing cluster.

- *Upgrade software in existing cluster*: Choose this option to upgrade an existing cluster to NCS 1.6. Make sure that you have performed the pre-upgrade.

NOTE

Checking Skip File Copy prevents NCS files from being copied during the installation. Since NCS files are copied to a NetWare 6 server during its original installation, you normally don't have to copy the files again. However, if you want to refresh the NCS files on cluster servers, you can uncheck this box.

5. At the NCS Cluster Selection screen, specify the required information and click Next.

- *If this is a new cluster*: Specify a name for the Cluster object, the name of your eDirectory tree, and the context for the Cluster object.

- *If you are adding nodes*: Specify the name of the Cluster object to which you want to add nodes, your eDirectory Tree, and the context of the Cluster object.

- *If you are upgrading software*: Specify the name of the Cluster object to be upgraded, your eDirectory Tree, and the context of the Cluster object. Skip to Step 9.

6. At the NCS Cluster Node Modification screen, click the Browse button to open a secondary window from which you can select all the server objects you want to add to the cluster. Click OK to exit the secondary window and Next to continue with the installation.

NOTE

You can remove a node from the cluster by selecting it from the NetWare Servers in Cluster list and clicking Remove. NCS automatically detects the IP address of a server that is added to a cluster. If a specified server has more than one IP address, you will be prompted to select the IP address you want Novell Cluster Services to use.

7. At the Cluster IP Address Selection screen, specify a unique IP address for the Cluster object and click Next. The cluster IP address is separate from the server IP address. ConsoleOne and NoRM use it for cluster management functions. The cluster IP address will be bound to the master node and will remain with the master node, even as it moves from server to server during failover events.

8. (Conditional) If you are creating a new cluster, specify the requested information and click Next.

   - Specify whether or not the cluster will be using a shared storage device such as a SAN or shared SCSI system. If you do have shared media, select the shared device from the drop-down list.

   - Choose whether or not you want to mirror the cluster partition. If you do want to mirror the cluster partition, select a location for the mirror partition from the drop-down list.

IMPORTANT

As previously mentioned, you must have roughly 15MB of free (unpartitioned) space on one of the shared disk drives to create the cluster partition. If no free space is available, Novell Cluster Services can't use the shared disk drives.

9. At the Start Clustering screen, choose whether or not you want the servers you are upgrading or adding to your cluster to start NCS software after the installation, and then click Next. If you choose not to start NCS, you will need to manually start it after the installation. You can do this by typing **LDNCS** from the server console of each cluster server.

10. (Conditional) If you are creating a cluster with more than 2 nodes, browse to and select the Cluster Server License files and click Add. NCS licenses are available separately from Novell. If you do not install NCS licenses during installation, you can add them later with iManage. However, NCS will not function until proper licenses are installed.

11. At the Summary screen, click Finish to install NCS. At the Installation Complete message, click Close.

Once NCS is installed and running, you will have access to a new Cluster State view in ConsoleOne, which is shown in Figure 12.2. You can open the Cluster State view by browsing to the Cluster object in ConsoleOne and, with the Cluster object highlighted, select View ➪ Cluster State View.

FIGURE 12.2 *Cluster State view in ConsoleOne*

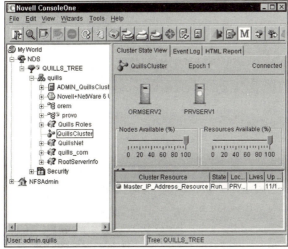

You can see a similar page from NoRM by selecting the Cluster Management link from the Navigation frame.

TIP

Configuring Cluster Services

Depending on your needs and cluster setup, some general configuration of the clustering environment may be required. This is done through the property pages of the Cluster object and the Cluster Node objects. You can view and edit the Cluster object properties through ConsoleOne. Browse to the Cluster object, right-click it and select Properties. There are five unique property pages in the Cluster object, in addition to cluster node properties, which are described in the following sections.

Quorum

The Quorum page is used to define two trigger values that are used during the startup of the cluster:

▶ *Timeout*: Timeout specifies the amount of time to wait for the number of servers defined in the Membership field to be up and running. If the timeout period elapses before the quorum membership reaches its specified number, resources will automatically start loading on the servers that are currently up and running in the cluster.

▶ *Membership*: The quorum membership is the number of nodes that must be running in the cluster before resources will start to load. When you first bring up servers in your cluster, NCS reads the number specified in the Membership field and waits until that number of servers is up and running in the cluster before it starts loading resources. Set the membership value to a number greater than 1 so that all resources don't automatically load on the first server that is brought up in the cluster.

Protocol

You can use the Protocol pages to view or edit the transmit frequency and tolerance settings for all nodes in the cluster, including the master node. The master node is generally the first node brought online in the cluster, but if that node fails, any of the other nodes in the cluster can become the master.

Cluster protocol settings

The Cluster Protocol Settings page lets you make changes to the communications-related properties of the cluster.

▶ *Heartbeat*: Heartbeat specifies the amount of time between transmits for all nodes in the cluster except the master. For example, if you set this value to 1, non-master nodes in the cluster will send a signal that they are alive to the master node every second.

▶ *Tolerance*: Tolerance specifies the amount of time the master node gives all other nodes in the cluster to signal that they are alive. For example, setting this value to 4 means that if the master node does not receive an "I'm alive" signal from a node in the cluster within four seconds, that node will be removed from the cluster.

▶ *Master watchdog*: Master watchdog specifies the amount of time between transmits for the master node in the cluster. For example, if you set this value to 1, the master node in the cluster will transmit an "I'm alive" signal to all the other nodes in the cluster every second.

▶ *Slave watchdog*: Slave watchdog specifies the amount of time the master node has to signal that it is alive. For example, setting this value to 5 means that if the non-master nodes in the cluster do not receive an "I'm alive" signal from the master within five seconds, the master node will be removed from the cluster and one of the other nodes will become the master node.

▶ *Max retransmits*: This option is not currently used with Novell Cluster Services but will be used for future versions.

Cluster protocol internals

The Internals page lets you view the script used to configure the cluster protocol settings, but you cannot change it. The script is created based on the settings you make in the Cluster Protocol Settings page.

Management

The Management page lets you view and change the IP address and port assigned to the Cluster object when you installed NCS. The Cluster IP address normally does need to be changed, but can be if needed.

The default cluster port number is 7023, and is automatically assigned when the cluster is created. The cluster port number should not be changed unless there is a TCP port conflict with another resource using the same port. If there is a conflict, you can change the port number to any other value that doesn't cause a conflict.

Resource Priority

The Resource Priority page allows you to control the order in which multiple resources start on a given node when the cluster is brought up, or during a failover or failback. For example, if a node fails and two resources failover to another node, the resource priority will determine which resource loads first. This is useful for ensuring that the most critical resources load first and are available to users before less critical resources.

- ► *Priority*: To change the priority for a resource, select the resource in the list and then click the Increase or Decrease button to move the resource up or down in the list. This changes the load order of the resource relative to other resources on the same node.

- ► *Reset*: Select a resource and then click the Selected button to reset the resource back to its default load order.

Notification

NCS can automatically send out email messages for certain cluster events like cluster and resource state changes or nodes joining or leaving the cluster.

- ► *Notification email addresses*: If you enable email notification, add the desired email address in the field provided and click the button next to the field to add the address to the list. Repeat this process for each address you want on the Notification list. You can specify up to eight email addresses in the Notification list.

- ► *Enable cluster notification events*: Check this box to enable email notifications. If you enable email notification, specify the type of cluster events for which you want administrators to receive messages.

- ► *Receive only critical events*: Check this box if you only want administrators to receive notification of critical events like a node failure or a resource going comatose.

- ► *Verbose messages*: Check this box if you want administrators to receive notification of all cluster state changes, including critical events, resource state changes, and nodes joining and leaving the cluster.

- ► *XML messages*: Check this box if you want administrators to receive notifications in XML format. XML messages can be interpreted and formatted in a way that lets you customize the message information for your specific needs.

Cluster Node Properties

You can view or edit the cluster node number or IP address of the selected node or view the context for the NetWare Server object. You access cluster node properties in ConsoleOne by browsing to and selecting the Cluster object, right-clicking the desired node in the right pane, and selecting Properties.

The Node tab is the only unique page for cluster node properties. It allows you to view and/or set the following parameters:

▶ *Number+IP address*: Specifies the cluster node number and IP address for the selected node. If the cluster node number or IP address changes for the selected node, the new information is not automatically updated in eDirectory. Edit the information and click Apply to update it.

▶ *NCP server*: The NCP Server field is used to view the name and context for the NetWare Server object.

Always Available File Access

The whole point in creating a cluster is to provide constant access to network resources. One of the principal resources on a network is data. To make network data constantly available through your newly-created cluster, you need to create and configure shared cluster volumes.

When configuring NCS for making data and files highly available to users, you perform the following tasks:

▶ Create a shared disk partition

▶ Create an NSS volume and pool on a shared storage device

▶ Cluster-enable the volume and pool

NOTE

ConsoleOne is the preferred management utility for all cluster-related activities. However, several tasks associated with clustering can also be performed through NoRM.

Create a Shared Disk Partition

Before creating disk partitions on shared storage devices, NCS must be installed. You should carefully plan how you want to configure your shared storage prior to installing NCS.

X-REF

If you are not familiar with NetWare 6 storage concepts, see Chapter 8 before continuing.

To create a shared disk partition on a storage area network, complete the following steps:

1. Launch ConsoleOne and browse to the Cluster object, as shown in Figure 12.3.

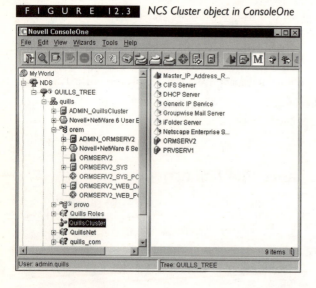

FIGURE 12.3   *NCS Cluster object in ConsoleOne*

2. Select the Server object of one of the nodes in the cluster; and click Device Disk Management on the ConsoleOne toolbar.

3. Select the device where you want to create the shared partition.

4. Make sure that Sharable for Clustering is checked for the selected device. Normally, NetWare 6 will detect that the device makes this selection automatically.

5. Click the Media tab and select Partitions. Click New.

6. In the Device list on the left, select the shareable device you chose in Step 4.

7. In the Create a new partition screen, provide the necessary information and click OK.

   • Specify the desired size of the partition

   • Check NSS as the partition type

   • Check both Hot Fix and Mirror

   • Select Create New Mirror Group

Now that you have the partition defined properly, you can create the NSS storage pool and logical volume at the same time. To create an NSS volume on your shared storage device, complete the following steps:

1. Launch ConsoleOne and browse to the Server object for a node in the cluster.

2. Select the Server object and click Logical Volume Disk Management on the ConsoleOne toolbar.

3. On the Logical Volumes page, click New.

4. At the Create a New Logical Volume screen, enter a name for the new volume and click Next.

5. At the Storage Information screen, specify the volume information and click Next. Select the NSS partition that you just created on the shared storage device. Enter a quota for the volume, or select Allow volume quota to grow to the pool size.

6. At the Create a New Pool screen, specify a name for the storage pool and click OK.

7. At the Attribute Information screen, select the desired attributes for your shared volume and click Finish.

For more information on volume attributes, see Chapter 8.

X-REF

Cluster-Enabling a Volume

Even though the volume you just created is on the shared storage device, it is currently assigned as a local volume for the Server object that you selected before creating the new volume. Because of this, if the server ever goes down, the server IP address is no longer broadcast and the volume becomes inaccessible and cannot be migrated to a new server for high availability.

To cluster-enable an NSS volume and pool, you associate the volume and pool with a Virtual Server object that has its own IP address. By doing this, the volume remains accessible even if a given physical server fails.

During the cluster-enabling process, the existing Volume object is replaced with a new Volume object that is associated with the storage pool. The Pool object is then replaced with a new Pool object, which has been associated with a Virtual Server object. After the volume is cluster-enabled, a Volume Resource object is created for the cluster-enabled resource. The Resource object dictates what happens to the volume when a failure occurs.

The following rules apply for cluster-enabled pools or volumes with NCS 1.6:

▶ When you cluster-enable a volume it automatically cluster-enables the storage in which the volume is located.

▶ Even though a storage pool is cluster-enabled, you must still cluster-enable each volume in the pool individually, if you want them to be able to failover to another node.

▶ When a node fails, any cluster-enabled pools being accessed by that node are migrated to other nodes in the cluster.

▶ All volumes in the pool are migrated with the pool, but only the volumes that have been cluster-enabled are mounted. Any volumes in the pool that are not cluster-enabled must be mounted manually.

▶ If you want each cluster-enabled volume to be its own cluster resource, so each can be managed separately, then each volume must have its own storage pool.

▶ Pools should be deactivated and volumes dismounted before being cluster-enabled.

To cluster-enable a volume (and pool) using ConsoleOne, do the following:

1. Launch ConsoleOne and browse to the Cluster object in your tree.

2. Select the Cluster object and click the File drop-down menu. Select New ➪ Cluster ➪ Cluster Volume.

3. At the New Cluster Volume screen, provide the required information and click Create. Make sure you select Define Additional Properties so you can define how the cluster-enabled volume responds to a failure.

   • *Volume*: Browse to the volume on the shared disk system that you want to cluster-enable.

   • *IP address*: Specify an IP address for the volume. This IP address is actually assigned to the storage pool and not the volume, so you only have to do this for the first volume to be cluster-enabled in a given pool.

   • *(Optional) Virtual server name*: Change the name of the default Virtual Server object. When you cluster-enable a pool, the Virtual Server object is named by combining the Cluster object name and the Pool object name. For example: QuillsCluster_SharePool_Server.

NOTE

If you are cluster-enabling a volume in a pool that is already cluster-enabled, the Virtual Server object has already been created, and cannot be renamed.

- *(Optional) Cluster volume name*: Specify the name of the new cluster-enabled Volume object. Combining the Cluster object name and the Volume object name creates the default name. For example: `QuillsCluster_VolA`.

- *Online resource after create*: Check this box to mount the cluster-enabled volume immediately after it is created.

- *Verify IP address*: Check this box to have NCS verify there are no conflicts with the IP address you have chosen.

Assign nodes to the cluster-enabled volume

When you cluster-enable a storage pool, all nodes in the cluster are automatically assigned to the pool. The order of assignment is the order the nodes appear in the list. To assign or un-assign nodes, or to change the failover order, complete the following steps:

1. Launch ConsoleOne and browse to the Cluster object.

2. With the Cluster object selected, right-click the new Virtual Server object in the right pane and select Properties.

3. Select the Nodes tab. Configure the nodes for the cluster-enabled volume as needed and click OK. Use the right- and left-arrow buttons to move nodes on and off the Assigned Nodes list, as desired. Use the up- and down-arrow buttons to re-order the failover sequence. The first server in the Assigned Nodes list will be the preferred node for the cluster-enabled volume. Failover will occur sequentially down the list.

NOTE You can also modify node assignments from NoRM. Select the Clustering link and click Cluster Config. From the list of resources, select the desired resource. On the Resource Information screen, click Nodes.

Configure volume policies

Once a volume has been cluster-enabled, you can configure the start, failover, and failback parameters. To set resource Start, Failover, and Failback modes, complete the following steps:

1. Launch ConsoleOne and browse to the Cluster object.

2. With the Cluster object selected, right-click the new Virtual Server object in the right pane and select Properties.

3. Select the Policies tab. Configure the Virtual Server policies as you would like them and click OK.

- *Ignore quorum*: Check this box if you don't want the cluster-wide timeout period and node number limit enforced. This makes sure the resource is launched immediately as soon as any server in the Assigned Nodes list is brought on-line. You can modify the default quorum values from the Cluster Object properties page.

- *Start mode*: When set to Auto, the resource will start automatically whenever the cluster is brought on-line. When set to Manual, you must start the device after the cluster comes on-line. The default is Auto.

- *Failover mode*: When set to Auto, the resource will automatically move to the next server in the Assigned Nodes list if the node it is currently running on fails. When set to Manual, you will intervene after a failure and re-assign the resource to a functioning node. The default is Auto.

- *Master only*: Select this option if you want the resource to run only on the master node in the cluster. If the master node fails, the resource will failover to the node that becomes the new master node in the cluster.

- *Failback mode*: When this is set to Auto, the cluster resource will migrate back to its preferred node when it comes back on-line. The preferred node is the first node listed in its Assigned Nodes table. When set to Manual, the cluster resource will not failback until you allow it to happen. When set to Disable, the cluster resource will not failback to its most preferred node when the most preferred node rejoins the cluster. The default is Disable.

NOTE

You can also set these parameters from NoRM. Select the Clustering link and click Cluster Config. From the list of resources, select the desired resource. On the Resource Information screen, click Policies.

Migrating a cluster-enabled volume

A node doesn't have to fail in order to migrate a volume from one node to another. You might want to do this in order to perform some type of maintenance on one of the nodes or just to balance out the node workload, if one is getting too busy.

To migrate a cluster-enabled volume, complete the following steps:

1. Launch ConsoleOne and browse to the Cluster object that contains the volume you want to migrate.

2. Open the Cluster State view by selecting View ⇨ Cluster State View from the drop-down menus.

3. In the Cluster Resource list, select the resource you want to migrate.

4. At the Cluster Resource Manager screen, select the server (node) to which you want to move the resource, and then click Migrate.

Understanding resource states

When running or testing an NCS cluster, you can view valuable information about cluster resource states from the Cluster State view in ConsoleOne or from the Cluster Status view in NetWare Remote Manager.

Table 12.1 describes different resource states you might see in the Cluster State view of ConsoleOne and provides some possible actions for each state:

TABLE 12.1 *Cluster Resource States*

RESOURCE STATE	DESCRIPTION	ACTION
Alert	One of the resource policies has been set to Manual. The resource is waiting for admin instructions.	Click the Alert Status indicator and you will be prompted to Start, Failover, or Failback the resource.
Comatose	The resource is not running and requires administrator intervention.	Select the Comatose Status indicator and take the resource off-line. After resource problems are resolved, the resource can be put back on-line.
Unloading	The resource is unloading from the server it was running on.	None.

(continued)

TABLE 12.1	*Cluster Resource States (continued)*	
RESOURCE STATE	**DESCRIPTION**	**ACTION**
Running	The resource is in a normal running state.	Select the Running Status indicator, and you can choose to either migrate the resource to a different node; or take the resource off-line.
Loading	The resource is loading on a server.	None.
Unassigned	None of the nodes in the Assigned Node list are currently online.	Select the Unassigned Status indicator and you can take the resource off-line. This will prevent the resource from running on any of its preferred nodes should one or more of them re-join the cluster.
NDS_Sync	The properties of the resource have changed and the changes are still being synchronized in eDirectory.	None.
Offline	The resource is shut down or is in a dormant or inactive state.	Select the Offline Status indicator and if desired, click the Online button to load the resource. NCS will choose the best node possible, given the current state of the cluster and the resource's Assigned Nodes list.
Quorum wait	The resource is waiting for a quorum to be established so it can begin loading.	None.

Always Available Network Services

When you are ready to start loading applications and services in a clustered environment, there are some extra steps you have to take beyond the standard installation and configuration provided by the application or service. As with a cluster volume, you will most likely need to cluster-enable the application or service. You may also have to make some changes to the Cluster object and the cluster nodes so they can properly support the new application or service.

Cluster Resource Applications

When creating a resource for an NCS cluster, you need to be familiar with the following types of applications:

- *Cluster aware*: Cluster-aware applications are specifically designed to take advantage of a clustered environment. These applications and services recognize when they are running on a cluster. They will automatically tweak their internal settings to be more tolerant of communication lapses that may occur in a clustered system.

- *Cluster naive*: Although you can cluster-enable any application, if it is not designed to recognize that it is running on a cluster, the application is referred to as cluster-naive. For a cluster-naive application or service, NCS does all the work to ensure that the resource is reloaded on another node if the assigned cluster node fails.

There are many NetWare 6 services, and some third-party applications as well, that are designed to take advantage of Novell Clustering Services when it is detected:

- Apache Web server
- AppleTalk Filing Protocol (AFP)
- BorderManager (proxy and VPN)
- DHCP server
- Enterprise Web server (LDAP and NDS)
- GroupWise v5.5 and v6 (MTA, POA, GWIA, WebAccess)
- iFolder
- iManage
- iPrint
- NetWare FTP server

- ► NFAP Common Internet File System (CIFS)
- ► NFS 3.0
- ► NDPS
- ► Novell clients (Windows 98 and Windows 2000)
- ► Oracle DB
- ► Pervasive Btrieve
- ► Symantec Norton AntiVirus
- ► WebDAV
- ► ZENworks for Servers
- ► ZENworks for Desktops 2 and 3

Cluster-Enabling an Application

You cluster-enable a service or application by creating a Cluster Resource object for it in eDirectory. The cluster resource includes a unique IP address, which lets it be migrated from node to node within the cluster, as necessary. Cluster resources are created for both cluster-aware and cluster-naive applications.

To create a cluster resource for an application, complete the following steps:

1. Launch ConsoleOne and browse to the Cluster object for which you want to create a new cluster resource.

2. Select File from the drop-down menu in ConsoleOne and click New ➪ Cluster ➪ Cluster Resource.

3. At the New Cluster Resource screen, shown in Figure 12.4, supply the necessary information and click Create.

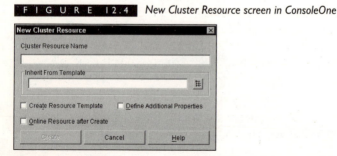

F I G U R E 12.4 *New Cluster Resource screen in ConsoleOne*

- *Cluster resource name*: Specify a name for the new cluster resource.

- *Inherit from template*: If a resource template exists for the resource you are creating, browse to and select the appropriate Template object.

- *Create resource template*: Similar to templates for other eDirectory objects, Cluster Resource templates simplify the process of creating similar or identical cluster resources. If you want to create multiple instances of the same resource on different servers, you can create a template that will automatically assign all the necessary properties when the resource object is created, rather than having to set each one up manually.

NOTE

NCS provides resource templates for DHCP, GroupWise, NetWare Enterprise Web server, and generic IP services. The generic IP Service template can be used when configuring certain server applications to run on your cluster. You can edit and customize any of the templates for your specific needs.

- *Define additional properties*: If a resource template does not exist, check this box so you can set the Cluster Resource object properties after it is created.

- *(Optional) Online resource after create*: Check this box if you want the resource to start on the master node as soon as it is created and configured.

NOTE

You can also create Cluster Resource objects from NoRM. Select the Cluster Config link and click New Cluster Resource.

Assign nodes to the cluster-enabled resource

When you create a cluster-enabled resource, all nodes in the cluster are automatically assigned to the resource. The order of assignment is determined by the order the nodes appear in the Assigned Nodes list. To assign or un-assign nodes, or to change the failover order for the resource, complete the following steps:

1. Launch ConsoleOne and browse to the Cluster object.

2. With the Cluster object selected, right-click the new Virtual Server object in the right pane, and then select Properties.

3. Select the Nodes tab. Configure the nodes for the cluster-enabled volume as needed and click OK. Use the right- and left-arrow buttons to move nodes on and off the Assigned Nodes list, as desired. Use the up- and down-arrow buttons to re-order the failover sequence. The first server in the Assigned Nodes list will be the preferred node for the clustered resource. Failover will occur sequentially down the list.

NOTE

You can also modify node assignments from NoRM. Select the Clustering link and click Cluster Config. From the list of resources, select the desired resource. On the Resource Information screen, click Nodes.

Configure clustered resource policies

Once a resource has been cluster-enabled, you can configure the start, failover, and failback parameters. To do this, complete the following steps:

1. Launch ConsoleOne and browse to the Cluster object.

2. With the Cluster object selected, right-click the new Virtual Server object in the right pane and select Properties.

3. Select the Policies tab. Configure the Virtual Server policies as you would like them and click OK.

- *Ignore quorum*: Check this box if you don't want the cluster-wide timeout period and node number limit enforced. This makes sure the resource is launched immediately as soon as any server in the Assigned Nodes list is brought on-line. You can modify the default quorum values from the Cluster Object properties page.

- *Start mode*: When set to Auto, the resource will start automatically whenever the cluster is brought on-line. When set to Manual, you must start the device after the cluster comes on-line. The default is Auto.

- *Failover mode*: When set to Auto, the resource will automatically move to the next server in the Assigned Nodes list if the node it is currently running on fails. When set to Manual, you will intervene after a failure and re-assign the resource to a functioning node. The default is Auto.

- *Master only*: Select this option if you want the resource to run only on the master node in the cluster. If the master node fails, the resource will failover to the node that becomes the new master node in the cluster.

- *Failback mode*: When this is set to Auto, the cluster resource will migrate back to its preferred node when it comes back on-line. The preferred node is the first node listed in its Assigned Nodes table. When set to Manual, the cluster resource will not failback until you allow it to happen. When set to Disable, the cluster resource will not failback to its most preferred node when the most preferred node rejoins the cluster. The default is Disable.

NOTE

You can also set these parameters from NoRM. Select the Clustering link and click Cluster Config. From the list of resources, select the desired resource. On the Resource Information screen, click Policies.

Configuring load and unload scripts

Load scripts are required for each resource or volume in your cluster. The load script specifies the commands to start the resource or mount the volume on a node. Unload scripts are used to ensure that when a resource is removed from a node that all modules and resources are properly cleaned up in the process.

You use the same commands in a load script that you would use to create any other NetWare configuration file (such as AUTOEXEC.NCF) that runs from the server console. Applications and services will often include pre-built NCF files for loading and unloading application modules. You can use these as a template for creating load and unload scripts. Consult the application or service documentation for information on necessary load and unload commands.

TIP

Load and unload scripts are created automatically for disk pools when they are cluster-enabled. Because of this, you shouldn't have to mess with scripts for cluster-enabled volumes and pools.

To view or edit a script, complete the following steps:

1. Launch ConsoleOne and browse to the appropriate Cluster Resource object.

2. Right-click the Cluster Resource object and select Properties.

3. Double-click the Scripts tab. Select either Cluster Resource Load Script or Cluster Resource Unload Script.

4. Edit or add the necessary commands to the script to load or unload the resource on a node. Some commands might require command line input. You can add << to a command to indicate command-line input. For example: LOAD SLPDA <<Y. This means that when the module SLPDA is loaded, it will receive a "Y" response to its command-line

prompt, presumably to a question that needs a yes answer. You can string multiple inputs together by specifying them on subsequent lines, as follows (a string up to 32 characters in length):

```
LOAD SLPDA <<Y
<<Y
<<N
```

5. Specify a timeout value. The timeout value determines how much time the script is given to complete. If the script does not complete within the specified time, the resource becomes comatose. The default is 600 seconds (10 minutes).

NOTE

You can also configure scripts from NoRM. Select the Clustering link and click Cluster Config. From the list of resources, select the desired resource. On the Resource Information screen, click Loading or Unloading.

eDirectory Reference Materials

As you probably know by now, eDirectory is an extremely complex environment. Fortunately, it is largely self-sufficient. Most of the day-to-day tasks of maintaining and protecting directory data are handled automatically and transparently. Not only does eDirectory have many built-in integrity features, but it also employs several background processes that keep the directory environment stable and healthy.

eDirectory Background Processes

This section provides a look at the main background processes that do all the heavy lifting associated with eDirectory operations. They are:

- Database initialization
- Flat cleaner
- Janitor
- Replica sync
- Replica purger
- Limber
- Backlinker
- Schema sync
- Time sync

When you use the various eDirectory monitoring and repair tools, of which some were discussed in Chapter 5 and more are discussed later in this appendix, these background processes and their effects are what you monitor and repair. For this reason it's a good idea to know a little bit about what you are looking at.

Database Initialization

The Database Initialization (DB Init) background process is automatically initiated whenever the file system is mounted on the eDirectory server. It also executes anytime the eDirectory database is opened or if eDirectory is reloaded. DB Init is responsible for:

- Verifying the usability of the eDirectory database files on this server
- Scheduling the running of other eDirectory background processes
- Initializing the various global variables and data structures used by eDirectory

▶ Opening the eDirectory database files for use by the version of eDirectory running on this server

DSTrace provides the ability to monitor the DB Init process directly.

Flat Cleaner

The Flat Cleaner background process is used to eliminate eDirectory variables and attributes that are no longer needed by the database. Flat Cleaner is responsible for:

▶ Eliminating unused Bindery and External Reference (X-ref) objects and/or attributes.

▶ Making sure that the objects in a partition replica maintained on this server each have a valid Public Key attribute.

▶ Eliminating X-ref obituaries that have been set as purgeable.

▶ Making sure that the server objects in partition replicas hosted on this server have maintained accurate Status and Version attributes. The server object maintains an attribute that specifies server status (up, down, initializing, etc. It also keeps a record of the version of eDirectory running on that server.

Flat Cleaner can be indirectly monitored through the use of Check External References in DSRepair. DSTrace also provides the ability to monitor the Janitor process directly.

Janitor

As its name implies, the Janitor process is responsible for routine cleanup of eDirectory environment. Janitor is responsible for:

▶ Monitoring the value of the NCP status attribute maintained in the eDirectory Server object for this server.

▶ Keeping track of the [Root]-most partition replica on the server and the overall replica depth of the server. The [Root]-most partition is the Partition Root object highest in the tree (closest to [Root]). Replica depth describes how many levels down from [Root] the highest partition replica hosted by that server is.

▶ Executing the Flat Cleaner process at regular intervals.

▶ Optimizing the eDirectory database at regular intervals.

▶ Reporting synthetic time use by a partition replica on the server. Synthetic time occurs when a server clock set to a future time is reset to the correct time. Any eDirectory changes made while the clock was set at the future time will bear incorrect time stamps. This problem will self-correct as long as the gap between current and synthetic time is not too large.

▸ Making sure the inherited rights for each partition root object on this server are properly maintained.

Like Flat Cleaner, Janitor can be monitored indirectly by examining the Replica Ring repair options, Time Synchronization status and Replica Synchronization status operations with DSRepair. DSTrace also provides the ability to monitor the Janitor process directly.

Replica Sync

The Replica Synchronization background process is responsible for two primary tasks:

▸ Distributing modifications to eDirectory objects contained within partition replicas maintained by the eDirectory server

▸ Receiving and processing partition operations involving partition replicas hosted by the eDirectory server

DSRepair can report the status of the replica synchronization process from a number of different perspectives:

▸ Report synchronization status

▸ Report synchronization status of all servers

▸ Report synchronization status on the selected server

DSTrace also provides the ability to monitor the Replica Synchronization process directly.

Replica Purger

Replica Sync schedules the execution of the Replica Purger background process. It is responsible for:

▸ Purging any unused objects and/or attributes that exist in eDirectory partition replicas hosted on this server

▸ Processing obituaries for objects maintained within partition replicas hosted on this server.

DSTrace also provides the ability to monitor the Replica Purger process directly, commonly referred to as Skulker.

Limber

After questioning several different sources, it is still unclear why this process is named "Limber", so that will remain a mystery for now. However, naming issues aside, Limber is responsible for:

- ▶ Making sure that the eDirectory referral information for this server is properly maintained in each partition hosted on this server.

- ▶ Making sure that the server hosting the Master replica of the partition in which the Server object for this server resides has the correct Relative Distinguished Name (RDN) for this server. The RDN identifies a target eDirectory object's context in relation to the context of the source eDirectory object. For example, the admin object in O = Quills would receive the following RDN for CN = jharris.OU = Education.OU = Provo.O = Quills: jharris.Education.Provo. The O = Quills is assumed from the location of the admin object itself.

- ▶ Making sure the server object in eDirectory correctly reflects the operating system version and network address in use on this server.

- ▶ Making sure the name of the eDirectory tree in which this server resides is correctly reported.

- ▶ Monitoring the external reference/DRL links between this server and the partition replica that holds this server's eDirectory Server object. This is done to make sure that the eDirectory server can be properly accessed via its eDirectory object.

- ▶ Making sure this server's identification information is correct.

Limber can be monitored indirectly through Check External Reference, Report Synchronization Status and Replica Ring repair options in DSRepair. DSTrace also provides the ability to monitor Limber directly.

Backlinker

The Backlinker background process helps maintain referential integrity within the eDirectory environment. Backlinker is responsible for:

- ▶ Making sure that all external references (X-Ref) maintained by this server are still required.

- ▶ Making sure that each X-Ref is properly backlinked to a server that hosts a partition replica that holds the eDirectory object specified in the X-ref.

- ▶ Eliminating X-refs that are no longer necessary. As part of doing this the server hosting the partition replica that holds the referenced eDirectory object is notified of the elimination of the X-ref.

Backlinker can be monitored indirectly through Check External References in DSRepair. DSTrace also provides the ability to monitor Backlinker directly.

Schema Sync

The Schema Sync background process is responsible for synchronizing the schema updates received by this server with other eDirectory servers. DSTrace also provides the ability to monitor Schema Synchronization directly.

Time Sync

While time sync is not an eDirectory process, it is necessary in order to perform some partition operations such as moves or merges. The underlying time sync mechanism is not important as long as the eDirectory servers are, in fact, synchronized. Time Sync can be monitored directly through the Time Synchronization option in DSRepair.

► . . . . ◄

DSRepair

Every database needs a tool for repairing inconsistencies when they occur. DSRepair has been serving in this capacity as long as eDirectory has existed. Even though Novell is shifting its focus toward Web-based tools, DSRepair is still essential for working on your eDirectory on a day-to-day basis. DSRepair offers three main groups of features:

- ► Unattended full repair
- ► eDirectory monitor operations
- ► eDirectory repair operations

To load DSRepair on your NetWare 6 server, load DSREPAIR.NLM at the server console. Throughout this section, when describing steps for performing a DSRepair operation it is assumed that you have already loaded the utility. Figure A.1 shows the main menu of DSRepair.

All DSRepair operations and results can be logged to file for review. The default log file SYS:SYSTEM\DSREPAIR.LOG. DSRepair on NetWare has a menu for configuring the log file. To access this menu select Advanced Options Menu, then Log File And Login Configuration.

This following three sections will describe the features available in each of the three main categories of DSRepair operations: Unattended Full Repair, eDirectory Monitor Operations, and eDirectory Repair Operations.

Main menu of DSRepair

Unattended Full Repair

The Unattended Full Repair (UFR) is probably the most-used feature in DSRepair (although the huge database sizes now being supported by eDirectory may change that). UFR checks for and repairs most non-critical eDirectory errors in the eDirectory database files of a given server. UFR is activated by selecting Unattended Full Repair from the main DSREPAIR menu.

The UFR performs eight primary operations each time it is run, none of which require any intervention by the administrator. These operations are described in Table A.1. During some of these operations the local database is locked. UFR builds a temporary set of local database files and runs the repair operations against those files. That way, if a serious problem develops the original files are still in tact.

TIP

Rebuilding the operational indexes used by eDirectory is only possible when the local database is locked. Given this, it is good to schedule a locked database repair on a regular basis, even in large eDirectory environments.

Operations Performed by Unattended Full Repair

OPERATION	LOCKED?	DESCRIPTION
Database structure and index check	Yes	Reviews the structure and format of database records and indexes. This ensures that no structural corruption has been introduced into the eDirectory environment at the database level.

(continued)

T A B L E A.1		Operations Performed by Unattended Full Repair (continued)
OPERATION	**LOCKED?**	**DESCRIPTION**
Rebuild the entire database	Yes	This operation is used to resolve errors found during structure and index checks. It restores proper data structures and recreates the eDirectory database and index files.
Perform tree structure check	Yes	Examines the links between database records to make sure that each child record has a valid parent. This helps ensure database consistency. Invalid records are marked so they can be restored from another partition replica during the eDirectory replica synchronization process.
Repair all local replicas	Yes	This operation resolves eDirectory database inconsistencies by checking each object and attribute against schema definitions. It also checks the format of all internal data structures.

Repair all local replicas can also resolve inconsistencies found during the tree structure check by removing invalid records from the database. As a result, all child records linked through the invalid record will be marked as orphans. These orphan records are not lost but this process could potentially generate a large number of errors while the database is being rebuilt. Do not be overly alarmed. This is normal and the orphan objects will be reorganized automatically over the course of replica synchronization. |

OPERATION	LOCKED?	DESCRIPTION
Check local references	Yes	Local References are pointers to other objects maintained in the eDirectory database on this server. Check Local References will evaluate the internal database pointers to make sure they are pointing to the correct eDirectory objects. If invalid references are found an error will be reported in DSREPAIR.LOG.
Repair network addresses	No	This operation checks server network addresses stored in eDirectory against the values maintained in local SAP or SLP tables to make sure eDirectory still has accurate information. If a discrepancy is found, eDirectory will be updated with the correct information.
Validate stream syntax files	Yes	Stream Syntax Files such as login scripts are stored in a special area of the eDirectory database. Validate Stream Syntax Files checks to make sure that each stream syntax file is associated with a valid eDirectory object. If not, the stream syntax file is deleted.

(continued)

TABLE A.1	Operations Performed by Unattended Full Repair (continued)	
OPERATION	LOCKED?	DESCRIPTION
Check volume objects and trustees	No	Check Volume Objects and Trustees first makes sure that each volume on the NetWare server is associated with a Volume object in eDirectory. If not, it will search the context in which the server resides to see if a Volume object exists. If no Volume object exists one will be created.
		After validating the volume information, the list of trustee IDs will be validated. Each object in eDirectory has a unique trustee ID. This ID is used to grant rights to other objects, including NetWare volumes, in the eDirectory tree. This task makes sure that each trustee ID in the volume list is a valid eDirectory object. If not, the trustee ID is removed from the volume list.

WARNING

When the local database is locked, no changes will be permitted while the operations execute. Some of these operations, when performed on very large eDirectory databases, will take an extended period of time to complete. When working with a large eDirectory database it is best to schedule these types of operations carefully so as not to disrupt network operations.

DSRepair Monitor Operations

DSRepair offers several partition, replica, and server operations that are available to monitor the health of the eDirectory environment. These operations can be performed individually or as groups to help keep eDirectory stable and healthy.

Some of the DSRepair operations described in this section are available only when DSRepair is loaded in "advanced" mode. This is done by typing the following at the server console:

DSREPAIR -a

The first category of operations can be loosely grouped into Monitor operations that are designed to report eDirectory status and health. You will likely perform most of these tasks from iMonitor with NetWare 6, but they are still available from DSRepair. Table A.2 describes the monitor operations available with DSRepair.

TABLE A.2 *DSRepair Monitor Operations on NetWare*

OPERATION	HOW TO ACCESS	DESCRIPTION
Report sync status	Select Report Synchronization Status	Reports the sync status for every partition that hosts a replica on this server.
Report sync status of all servers	Select Advanced Options Menu. Select Replica And Partition Operations, then select a partition. Select Report Synchronization Status Of All Servers.	Queries each server hosting a replica of the selected partition and reports the sync status of each replica.
Report sync status on selected server	Select Advanced Options Menu. Select Replica And Partition Operations and then select a partition. Select View Replica Ring and choose a server. Select Report Synchronization Status On Selected Server.	Reports the sync status of the replica hosted by this server for the selected partition.

(continued)

	TABLE A.2	*DSRepair Monitor Operations on NetWare (continued)*
OPERATION	**HOW TO ACCESS**	**DESCRIPTION**
Time sync	Load DSRepair at the NetWare console and select Time Synchronization.	Reports status of Time Synchronization.
Perform database structure and index check	Select Advanced Options Menu, then Repair local DS database.	Reviews the structure and format of database records and indexes. This ensures that no structural corruption has been introduced into the eDirectory environment at the database level.
Perform tree structure check	Select Advanced Options Menu, then Repair local DS database.	Examines the links between database records to make sure that each child record has a valid parent. This helps ensure database consistency. Invalid records are marked so they can be restored from another partition replica during the eDirectory replica synchronization process.
Servers known to this database	Select Advanced options menu, then select Servers Known To This Database.	Queries the local database and compiles a list of servers known to this partition.
View entire server name	Select Advanced options menu, then select Servers Known To This Database. Select a server, then select View Entire Server's Name.	Displays the distinguished eDirectory name for this server.

OPERATION	HOW TO ACCESS	DESCRIPTION
View replica ring	Select Advanced Options, then select Replica And Partition Operations. Select a partition and then select View Replica Ring.	Displays a list of all servers that host a replica of the selected partition.
View entire partition name	Select Advanced options menu, then select Replica and Partition Operations. Select a partition, then select View Entire Partition Name.	Displays the distinguished eDirectory name for this partition root object.

DSRepair Repair Operations

While monitoring the condition of the eDirectory database is important, it does little good if there are no tools for repairing inconsistencies when they occur. DSREPAIR offers several eDirectory repair operations. These repair operations can be organized into three categories:

- ▶ Database Repair Operations
- ▶ Partition and Replica Repair Operations
- ▶ Other Repair Operations

Database repair

All Database Repair options are accessible from the same menu in DSRepair, as shown in Figure A.2. Access these operations by selecting Advanced Options Menu and then Repair Local DS Database.

▶ · · · · · · · · · · · · · · · · · ◀

FIGURE A.2   *Database repair options available from DSRepair*

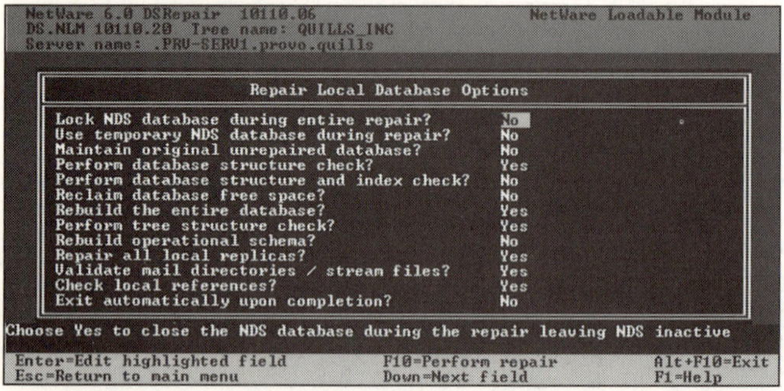

```
NetWare 6.0 DSRepair  10110.06              NetWare Loadable Module
DS.NLM 10110.20  Tree name: QUILLS_INC
Server name: .PRV-SERV1.provo.quills

┌──────────────────────────────────────────────────────────────────┐
│                  Repair Local Database Options                     │
│                                                                    │
│  Lock NDS database during entire repair?         No                │
│  Use temporary NDS database during repair?       No                │
│  Maintain original unrepaired database?          No                │
│  Perform database structure check?               Yes               │
│  Perform database structure and index check?     No                │
│  Reclaim database free space?                    No                │
│  Rebuild the entire database?                    Yes               │
│  Perform tree structure check?                   Yes               │
│  Rebuild operational schema?                     No                │
│  Repair all local replicas?                      Yes               │
│  Validate mail directories / stream files?       Yes               │
│  Check local references?                         Yes               │
│  Exit automatically upon completion?             No                │
└──────────────────────────────────────────────────────────────────┘
Choose Yes to close the NDS database during the repair leaving NDS inactive

 Enter=Edit highlighted field       F10=Perform repair        Alt+F10=Exit
 Esc=Return to main menu            Down=Next field            F1=Help
```

Table A.3 describes the repair operations available from this menu.

TABLE A.3   *DSREPAIR Database Operations on NetWare*

OPERATION	DESCRIPTION
Rebuild entire database	This operation is used to resolve errors found during structure and index checks. It restores proper data structures and recreates the eDirectory database and index files.
Repair all local replicas	This operation resolves eDirectory database inconsistencies by checking each object and attribute against schema definitions. It also checks the format of all internal data structures.
	Repair all local replicas can also resolve inconsistencies found during the tree structure check by removing invalid records from the database. As a result, all child records linked through the invalid record will be marked as orphans. These orphan records are not lost but this process could potentially generate a large number of errors while the database is being rebuilt. Do not be overly alarmed. This is normal and the orphan objects will be reorganized automatically over the course of replica synchronization.

OPERATION	DESCRIPTION
Validate mail directoriesAnd stream syntax files	Both of these operations are only used with NetWare. By default, eDirectory creates mail directories in the SYS:Mail directory of NetWare servers in order to support legacy bindery users. Login scripts for bindery users are stored in their mail directory. Validate Mail Directories checks to make sure each mail directory is associated with a valid eDirectory user object. If not, the mail directory is deleted. Stream Syntax Files such as login scripts are stored in a special area of the eDirectory database. Validate Stream Syntax Files checks to make sure that each stream syntax file is associated with a valid eDirectory object. If not, the stream syntax file is deleted.
Check local references	Local References are pointers to other objects maintained in the eDirectory database on this file server. Check Local References will evaluate the internal database pointers to make sure they are pointing to the correct eDirectory objects. If invalid references are found an error will be reported in DSREPAIR.LOG.
Reclaim database free space	This operation searches for unused database records and deletes them to free up disk space.
Rebuild operational schema	This operation rebuilds the base schema classes and attributes needed by eDirectory for basic functionality.

Partition and replica repair

In addition to these database repair options, DSRepair offers a menu of partition and replica operations designed to keep the distributed eDirectory environment functioning properly. This changes our focus from the local database to the partition and all the replicas of that partition stored on servers across the network. Access these operations by selecting Advanced Options Menu and then Replica and Partition Options, as shown in Figure A.3

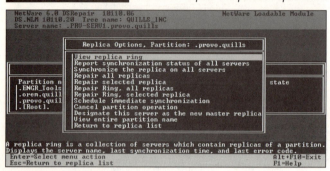

F I G U R E A.3   *DSREPAIR Replica and partition options in DSRepair*

Table A.4 describes the various partition and replica operations that are available.

T A B L E A.4   *DSRepair Partition and Replica Operations*

OPERATION	DESCRIPTION
Sync replica on all servers	Each server holding a replica of the selected partition is contacted and then a synchronization cycle is initiated.
Repair all replicas	This operation resolves eDirectory database inconsistencies by checking each object and attribute against schema definitions. It also checks the format of all internal data structures.
Repair selected replica	Performs a replica repair on the selected replica only.
Repair ring – selected replicas	Performs a replica repair operation on each server that hosts a replica of the selected partition.
Repair ring – all replicas	Performs the replica ring repair operation for each replica ring in which this server participates.
Schedule immediate sync	Initiates a replica synchronization cycle for each partition with a replica hosted on this server. This is useful for forcing the recognition of recent database changes.

OPERATION	DESCRIPTION
Designate this server as new master replica	If the Master replica of a given partition is lost due to hardware failure, this operation can be used to designate a new Master in order for partition operations to function normally.

Three other replica operations are available by doing the following:

1. Select Advanced Options Menu, then select Replica And Partition Operations.
2. Select a replica and then choose View Replica Ring.
3. Select a server from the list.

These three operations are described in Table A.5.

TABLE A.5 *DSRepair Replica Ring Operations on NetWare*

OPERATION	DESCRIPTION
Synchronize the replica on the selected server	Reports the synchronization status of the selected partition's replica that is hosted on this server.
Send all objects to every replica in the ring	The operation will rebuild every replica in the ring according to the objects found in this server's replica. Warning: Any changes made to other replicas that have not yet updated to this server will be lost.
Receive all objects from master to this replica	This operation will rebuild the local replica from object information received from the Master replica. Warning: Any changes made to this replica that have not yet updated to the Master replica will be lost.

Finally, there are four miscellaneous repair operations that are accessible from other areas of the DSREPAIR utility. Table A.6 describes these operations.

T A B L E A . 6	Other DSRepair Operations	
OPERATION	**HOW TO ACCESS**	**DESCRIPTION**
Repair all network addresses	Select Advanced Options Menu, then Servers Known To This Database. Select a server from the list.	This operation checks server network addresses stored in all Root Partition objects in the tree against the values maintained in local SAP or SLP tables. If a discrepancy is found, eDirectory will be updated with the correct information. If no corresponding SAP or SLP entry is found, DSRepair will report an error.
Repair selected server's network addresses	Select Advanced Options Menu, then Servers Known To This Database. Select a server, then select Repair Selected Server's Network Addresses.	Same as above, but only the Root Partition objects on the local server are checked.

OPERATION	HOW TO ACCESS	DESCRIPTION
Check volume objects and trustees	Select Advanced Options Menu, then Check Volume Objects and Trustees.	Check Volume Objects and Trustees first makes sure that each volume on the NetWare server is associated with a Volume object in eDirectory. If not, it will search the context in which the server resides to see if a Volume object exists. If no Volume object exists one will be created. After validating the volume information, the list of trustee IDs will be validated. Each object in eDirectory has a unique trustee ID. This ID is used to grant rights to other objects, including NetWare volumes, in the eDirectory tree. This task makes sure that each trustee ID in the volume list is a valid eDirectory object. If not, the trustee ID is removed from the volume list.

(continued)

TABLE A.6	*Other DSRepair Operations (continued)*	
OPERATION	HOW TO ACCESS	DESCRIPTION
Check external references	Select Advanced Options Menu, then Check External References.	External References are pointers to eDirectory objects not stored in partition replicas on this server. Check External References evaluates each reference to an external object to make sure it is pointing to a valid eDirectory object. The external reference check also verifies the need for all obituaries maintained in the local database. An obituary is used to maintain database consistency while eDirectory is replicating changes such as object moves, deletes or name changes. If a replica attempts to reference the changed object using old information because it has not received the replica sync yet, the obituary entry permits it to do so without generating an error. Once all replicas have synchronized the new information, the Janitor process eliminates the obituary.

By using the operations described in this section you will be able to manage most non-catastrophic problems in your eDirectory environment.

DSREPAIR Command Line Switches

Novell recommends that some DSRepair operations be performed on a regular basis in order to keep the eDirectory tree healthy. To facilitate this, Novell has also made DSRepair functionality available through command line switches. These switches make it possible to use batch schedulers to perform regular eDirectory tree maintenance automatically without any input from the administrator. Table A.7 describes the various command line switches that are provided for automating basic DSRepair tasks.

TABLE A.7 *Command Line DSRepair Switches*

SWITCH	PARAMETER	DESCRIPTION
-D	None	Performs a database repair on the DIB with the filename extension specified as an argument. Default extension is .eDirectory.
-L	Filename (with path)	Specify location for DSRepair log file. Appends to existing log file if it exists. Default is SYS:SYSTEM\DSREPAIR.LOG.
-U	None	Performs Unattended Full Repair and automatically unloads when complete.
-RC	None	Create an eDirectory Dump File. This file is a snapshot of the local eDirectory database that can be used for troubleshooting. The dump file is stored as SYS:SYSTEM\DSR_DIB.
-RD	None	Repair Local Database. Executes using default database repair options, which includes: Structure and Index check, Rebuild database, Tree Structure check, Repair all local replicas, Validate Mail/Stream files and Check local references.
-RN	None	Repair Network Addresses.
-RV	None	Perform Volume Object Repair.
-RVT	Volume Name	Perform Volume Object Repair and Trustee Check.

Advanced DSRepair switches

In addition to the numerous functions described above, DSRepair also has some advanced features that are hidden from normal use. These advanced features are enabled through switches when loading the DSRepair utility. Table A.8 provides an overview of the advanced functionality available on each platform.

WARNING

The features described in this section can (and will (cause irreversible damage to your eDirectory tree if used improperly. We recommend that these features only be used under the guidance of eDirectory professionals, such as the Novell Technical Services team in order to resolve serious database issues. Always make a full backup of the eDirectory tree before using any of these features on a production tree. If you are going to use these features be **sure** you understand **all** the consequences before proceeding.

TABLE A.8	Advanced DSRepair Features
SWITCH	**DESCRIPTION**
-M	Reports "move inhibit" obituaries. This will tell you if a partition Move operation has completed. If it hasn't, move inhibit obituaries may still be processing or be broken.
-MR	Removes all "move inhibit" obituaries.
-N	Limits the number of days a user object can be connected to a given server to the number specified as a command line argument. When this number is reached a user connection will be terminated. The default value is 60 days.
-OR	Deletes all obituaries.
-P	Marks all eDirectory objects of type "Unknown" as referenced. Referenced objects do not participate in the eDirectory replica synchronization process.
-RS	Removes the server identified by the Partition Root ID provided as a command line argument from the replica ring for that partition. This might be necessary if a Read/Write replica becomes corrupt and needs to be eliminated.

SWITCH	DESCRIPTION
-A	Load DSRepair with advanced options available. This uncovers additional menu options that are not normally visible. Select Advanced Options Menu, then select Replica And Partition Operations and choose the partition with which you want to work. You will see the following additional menu items: – Repair time stamps and declare a new epoch – Destroy the selected replica on this server – Delete unknown leaf objects This switch also allows the Designate this server as the new master replica option to assign a Subordinate Reference as the new Master replica. Be Careful!! If you select the View Replica Ring option and select a replica you will see an additional option on that menu as well: – Remove this server from the replica ring
-XK2	Kill all eDirectory objects in this server's eDirectory database. This operation is used only to destroy a corrupt replica that cannot be removed in any other way.
-XK3	Kill all external references in this server's eDirectory database. This operation is used to destroy all external references in a non-functioning replica. If the references are the source of the problem, eDirectory can then recreate the references in order to get the replica functioning again.

These advanced options are seldom used because they are only needed for the most serious of cases. However, it is nice to know they exist when you get into a jam.

It is highly recommended that you work with these switches in a test environment and study carefully the ramifications of these radical operations. Sometimes the cure may be worse than the problem.

DSTrace

DSTrace is a monitor tool that allows you to view the real time flow of eDirectory communications between partition replicas. It also allows you to perform certain operations that are very useful in understanding what is happening within the eDirectory environment. DSTrace is available from the server console or through a page in iMonitor. When DSTrace is loaded, it provides the ability to open a configurable monitor window and/or a log file that displays messages from the various eDirectory processes that are running on the network. You can monitor the execution of background processes, note any errors, and use DSTrace to isolate the cause of any problems (see Figure A.4).

FIGURE A.4 *Typical DSTrace screen*

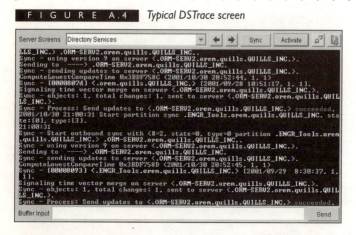

DSTrace was originally designed to help Engineering and Support locate problems in the eDirectory environment. It is not a highly refined tool, but it provides invaluable information about the state of your eDirectory environment. There are two main tasks performed by the DSTrace utility:

▶ Monitor eDirectory background processes

▶ Activate and tune eDirectory background processes

DSTrace functionality is actually available in two different ways. The "traditional" method is through a trace screen that is built into DS.NLM itself. The second method, which was first released with NetWare 5, is DSTRACE.NLM. Both methods provide similar information and both make use of the same tools for activating and tuning eDirectory background processes. The only significant difference lies in the monitor interface for eDirectory background processes. To distinguish between the two trace tools, I will refer to the version integrated into DS.NLM as DSTrace and the other by its filename DSTRACE.NLM.

With either trace utility, you use an extensive set of command line parameters to start, configure and use DSTrace features. Command line parameters are not case sensitive. However, there are a few differences between the parameters used with either trace utility, which will be pointed out. Actual DSTrace operators, which force some action to take place, are similar between the two utilities. DSTrace operators are described in Table A.9.

T A B L E A . 9	Valid Operators for DSTrace Flags
OPERATOR	**DESCRIPTION**
+	Enables a DSTrace flag. If a flag is specified with no operator the "+" is assumed. For example, either of the following command enables the replica synchronization flag: `SET DSTRACE= +SYNC` or `SET DSTRACE= SYNC`
-	Disables a DSTrace flag. For example, the following command disables the replica synchronization flag: `SET DSTRACE= -SYNC`
( )	This operator is valid with DSTrace only. Enclosing a flag within parenthesis enables that flag while simultaneously disabling all other flags that are currently enabled. For example, the following command enables the replica synchronization flag while disabling all other flags: `SET DSTRACE= (SYNC)`
*	The "star" operator is used to activate eDirectory background processes. For example, the following command executes the Janitor process immediately: `SET DSTRACE= *J`
!	The "bang" operator is used to configure the tunable parameters for eDirectory background processes. For example, the following command configures the Backlink process to occur every 8 minutes: `SET DSTRACE= !B8`

Besides sharing most operators, both DSTrace and DSTRACE.NLM also share all commands related to the activation and tuning of eDirectory background processes. These commands make use of the "*" and "!" operators and take the form:

```
SET DSTRACE= <operator> <parameter> [optional argument]
```

Arguments are not required in every case. Table A.10 describes the valid Star and Bang commands available for DSTrace and DSTRACE.NLM.

T A B L E A . I 0	*Star and Bang Commands*	
COMMAND	**ARGUMENT(S)**	**DESCRIPTION**
*.	None	Unloads and reloads eDirectory executable. Allows you to update the version of eDirectory without having to restart the server.
*B	None	Forces the backlink process to run. This can be a traffic-intensive operation. Schedule during times of off-peak network usage.
!B	Interval in minutes Min: 2 Max: 10080 Default: 1500	Sets the interval for the Backlink process
*C	None	Checks all Dynamic Reference Links (DRL).
*CD	None	Display the source server's connection table (comma delimited).
*CT	None	Display the source server's connection table (space delimited).
*D	None	Aborts the Send All Updates process (*I). This process can loop endlessly if one of the servers in the replica ring is unreachable.
*F	None	Forces the Flat Cleaner process to run.
!F	Interval in minutes Min: 2 Max: N/A Default: 240	Sets the interval for the Flat Cleaner process.
*G	None	Sets the server status to "Down" in eDirectory. Used when a server has become overloaded with pending eDirectory requests.
*H	None	Forces the eDirectory replica synchronization and schema synchronization processes to run. This is also known as the eDirectory "Heartbeat".

COMMAND	ARGUMENT(S)	DESCRIPTION
!H	Interval in minutes Min: 1 Max: 1440 Default: 30	Sets the interval for the eDirectory Replica Synchronization process.
*I	Partition Root ID	Forces the replica specified to send a copy of all its objects to all other servers hosting replicas of the same partition. Same as "Send All Objects" operation in DSRepair.
!I	Interval in minutes Min: 2 Max: 1440 Default: 30	Sets the interval for schema synchronization.
*J	None	Forces the Janitor process to run.
!J	Interval in minutes Min: 1 Max: 10080 Default: 2	Sets the interval for the Janitor process.
*L	None	Forces the Limber process to run.
*M	File size in bytes Min: 10,000 Max: 100 MB Default: 500,000	Used with DSTrace only. Sets the maximize size of the DSTrace debug file. If the maximum file size is reached the debug file will "wrap around" and start writing at the beginning again.
*P	None	Displays the tunable parameters and their default settings.
*R	Filename	Resets the DSTrace debug file. All previously saved information will be lost. If no filename is specified this command will specify the default SYS:SYSTEM\DSTRACE.DBG.
*S	None	Forces the replica synchronization process to run. Any replicas scheduled for synchronization will be synchronized. Will not synchronize replicas not already scheduled for synchronization.

(continued)

TABLE A.10   *Star and Bang Commands (continued)*

COMMAND	ARGUMENT(S)	DESCRIPTION
*SS	None	Forces schema synchronization process to run. This only targets servers with which the background schema sync process has not synchronized in the last 24 hours.
*SSA	None	Forces schema synchronization process to run. All servers should be synchronized.
*SSD	None	Resets the server's target schema sync list. This list identifies the servers to which this server should sync during a schema synchronization cycle.
*SSL	None	Displays the schema sync list. Also identifies other servers that are holding this server open for a schema operation.
*ST	None	Display server's background process status. Includes information on External Reference, Schema, Obituary and Limber.
*STL	None	Displays the server's Backlink background process status.
!T	Interval in minutes Min: 1 Max: 720 Default: 30	Sets the interval for checking the server state (UP, DOWN, etc.).
*U	Server ID (optional)	Forces the server state of all servers in a replica list to UP. This allows certain partition operations to complete successfully.
*UD	Server ID (optional)	Forces the server state of all servers in a replica list to DOWN.
!V	List of eDirectory versions	Defines those versions of eDirectory with which this server should not interact. This is useful in case older versions of NDS are running in the same tree with eDirectory.

COMMAND	ARGUMENT(S)	DESCRIPTION
!W	Interval in ticks Min: I Max: 2000 Default: I5	Changes the length of time to wait after getting a transport protocol time-out before resending the packet.
!X	Number of retries Min: I Max: 50 Default: 3	Changes the number of transport protocol retries for the DS (server-to-server) client. Exceeding this retry count causes an eDirectory error - 625 to be displayed.
!Y	Integer Min: 0 Max: 530 Default: 2	The integer input is used to calculate estimated trip delay using the equation: Time-out = (T *Y) + Z. This is where T is equal to the ticks required to get to the destination server.
!Z	Integer Min: 0 Max: 500 Default: 4	Specifies the additional delay for the transport protocol time-out. When increasing the time-out it is best to change this parameter first. It is used in the equation IPX Time-out = (T *Y) + Z, where T is equal to the ticks required to get to the destination server.

So, what you do and how you do it is similar across both utilities. However, what you see and how you see it is significantly different. The following two sections describe how to monitor eDirectory background processes using these two distinct utilities.

DSTrace Monitor

eDirectory administrators and Novell Support personnel have used the DSTrace Monitor for years. DSTrace functions most consistently when a single parameter is specified per command line. For this reason it is useful to create .NCF files for the DSTrace configuration you use most. That way you just have to execute the .NCF file to execute all the commands you want. Every DSTrace command takes the form:

```
SET DSTRACE=<operator><parameter>[optional argument]
```

The following are some sample DSTrace commands:

- ▶ SET DSTRACE = ON
- ▶ SET DSTRACE = +SYNC
- ▶ SET DSTRACE = *H
- ▶ SET DSTRACE = !J20

DSTrace is started and configured using the parameters described in Table A.11.

TABLE A.11	Directory Service Trace Configuration Parameters
PARAMETER	**DESCRIPTION**
ON	Starts the eDirectory trace screen. If this is the first time that DSTrace has been used since DS.NLM was last loaded, the "Minimum" flag is activated. Otherwise, DSTrace will start using the same configuration used previously.
OFF	Disables the DSTrace monitor. The current configuration will be retained as long as DS.NLM itself is not unloaded.
ALL	Starts the DSTrace monitor with all flags enabled. When a flag is enabled, information of that type will be displayed on screen and/or log file.
AGENT	Starts the eDirectory trace screen with the following flags enabled: BACKLINK, DSAGENT, JANITOR, RESNAME, VCLIENT. This parameter also activates a global variable used by the Flat Cleaner background process. This variable causes the local entry IDs of the records being examined by Flat Cleaner to be displayed.
DEBUG	Turns on DSTrace with the following flags enabled: BACKLINK, ERRORS, EMU, FRAGGER, INIT, INSPECTOR, JANITOR, LIMBER, MISC, PART, RECMAN, REPAIR, SCHEMA, SKULKER, STREAMS, VCLIENT. Warning: This action instructs the server to automatically open the NetWare debugger in the event of certain error conditions. This option should only be used for brief periods of time when tracking a specific issue.
NODEBUG	This parameter leaves the Directory Service Trace screen ON, but disabled all previously enabled flags. This is useful when you want to reconfigure DSTrace.

Once DSTrace is initially configured, it can be fine-tuned to monitor only the information necessary to support your current needs. This is done through the enabling and/or disabling of trace flags. Flags are enabled or disabled from the command line by using the "+" and "-" operators from Table A.9.

The actual flags supported by DSTrace are enumerated in Table A.12. Some flags can be enabled using multiple names. These alternative names have been listed as well.

TABLE A.12 *Flags Supported by DSTrace*

FLAG	DESCRIPTION
AUDIT	Trace messages related to eDirectory audit.
AUTHEN	Trace messages related to eDirectory authentication events.
BACKLINK BLINK	Trace messages related to the Backlink process.
BUFFERS	Trace messages related to allocation of inbound and outbound packet buffers related to eDirectory requests.
COLLISION COLL	Trace messages related to the receipt of duplicate update packets. These duplicate packets usually occur on very busy networks.
DSAGENT	Trace messages related to incoming eDirectory requests.
EMU	Trace messages related to Bindery Emulation.
ERRET	Displays debug errors. This option is only of use to eDirectory engineers.
ERRORS ERR E	Displays error messages in DSTrace. Identifies what the error was and where it came from.
FRAGGER FRAG	Trace messages related to the packet fragmenter that breaks up eDirectory messages for transmission in multiple packets.
IN	Trace messages related to incoming eDirectory requests and processes.
INIT	Trace messages related to the opening of the local eDirectory database.
INSPECTOR I	Messages related to the Inspector process. Inspector is part of the Janitor that verifies the structural integrity of the eDirectory database.

(continued)

T A B L E A.12	Flags Supported by DSTrace (continued)
FLAG	**DESCRIPTION**
JANITOR J	Trace Janitor messages. The Janitor cleans up eDirectory by removing objects that are no longer needed.
LIMBER	Trace Limber messages. The Limber monitors connectivity between all replicas.
LOCKING LOCKS	Trace messages related to manipulation of the local eDirectory database locks.
MIN	Minimum functionality. Trace generic messages and error reports from various sources in eDirectory. By default, SET DSTRACE = ON enables this flag only.
MISC	Trace all miscellaneous messages.
PART	Trace partition operations and messages.
RECMAN	Trace messages related to low level database operations.
RESNAME RN	Trace messages related to eDirectory name resolution.
SAP	Trace messages related to the SAP protocol.
SCHEMA	Trace schema modification and synchronization messages.
SKULKER SYNC S	Trace messages related to the Skulker process, which manages replica and schema synchronization.
STREAMS	Trace messages related to Stream attributes in eDirectory.
TIMEVECTOR TV	Trace messages related to transitive vectors, which describe how "caught up" the replica is in the synchronization process.
VCLIENT VC	Trace messages related to server-to-server Virtual Client connections.
WANMAN	Trace messages related to WAN Traffic Manager.

This DSTrace monitor information will do you little good when it is whizzing by faster than you can read it. In a large network environment this is often the case.

IMPORTANT The DSTrace log file does not impose any maximum size so it will continue to grow in size as long as logging is enabled. Don't use the DSTrace log file option continuously. Enable the log file as needed to capture information and then shut it down.

To resolve this problem DSTrace monitor information can be logged to a file. This file holds any messages displayed on the DSTrace monitor. It also includes event-timing information that can be used to identify which messages should be grouped together. The DSTrace debug file is stored in the SYS:SYSTEM sub-directory by default. The default filename is DSTRACE.DBG. To enable the DSTrace debug file you must execute the following console command:

```
SET TTF=ON
```

The *M and *R commands can be used to configure the DSTrace debug file. These two commands are described in Table A.10.

The information in the DSTrace debug file includes timing information that allow you to identify event sequence; group related messages together; and determine how long ago a problem occurred. This can be critical when analyzing DSTrace data off-line.

Figure A.5 shows the additional timing information appended to DSTrace messages in the DSTrace log file:

FIGURE A.5   *Sample DSTrace log file*

```
3BDF778D:88861396:d0b25620:047 Sync - Start outbound sync with (#=2, state=0, type=1 partition .
3BDF778D:88861403:d0b25620:047 Sync - using version 9 on server <.ORM-SERV2.orem.quills.QUILLS_I
3BDF778D:88861403:d0b25620:047 Sending to  ----> .ORM-SERV2.orem.quills.QUILLS_INC.
3BDF778D:88861403:d0b25620:047 Sync - sending updates to server <.ORM-SERV2.orem.quills.QUILLS_I
3BDF778D:88861403:d0b25620:047 ComputeLowestCompareTime 0x3BDF775F (2001/10/30 21:00:31, 1, 1)
3BDF778D:88861404:d0b25620:047 Sync - [0000802d] <.provo.quills.QUILLS_INC.> [2001/09/28  9:33:1
3BDF778D:88861455:d0b25620:047 Signaling time vector merge on server <.ORM-SERV2.orem.quills.QUI
3BDF778D:88861455:d0b25620:047 Sync - objects: 1, total changes: 3, sent to server <.ORM-SERV2.o
3BDF778D:88861455:d0b25620:047 Sync - Process: Send updates to <.ORM-SERV2.orem.quills.QUILLS_IN
3BDF7790:88864334:d0b25620:047 2001/10/30 21:01:20 Start partition sync .orem.quills.QUILLS_INC.
3BDF7790:88864348:d0b25620:047 Sync - Start outbound sync with (#=2, state=0, type=0 partition .
3BDF7790:88864356:d0b25620:047 Sending to  ----> .ORM-SERV2.orem.quills.QUILLS_INC.
3BDF7790:88864356:d0b25620:047 Sync - sending updates to server <.ORM-SERV2.orem.quills.QUILLS_I
3BDF7790:88864356:d0b25620:047 ComputeLowestCompareTime 0x3BDF775F (2001/10/30 21:00:31, 1, 1)
3BDF7790:88864356:d0b25620:047 Sync - [0000807d] <.orem.quills.QUILLS_INC.> [2001/09/28 10:51:17
3BDF7790:88864396:d0b25620:047 Sync - objects: 1, total changes: 1, sent to server <.ORM-SERV2.o
3BDF7790:88864396:d0b25620:047 Sync - Process: Send updates to <.ORM-SERV2.orem.quills.QUILLS_IN
3BDF7791:88865332:d0b25620:047 2001/10/30 21:01:21 Start partition sync .ENGR_Tools.orem.quills.
3BDF7791:88865346:d0b25620:047 Sync - Start outbound sync with (#=2, state=0, type=0 partition .
3BDF7791:88865355:d0b25620:047 Sync - using version 9 on server <.ORM-SERV2.orem.quills.QUILLS_I
3BDF7791:88865355:d0b25620:047 Sending to  ----> .ORM-SERV2.orem.quills.QUILLS_INC.
3BDF7791:88865355:d0b25620:047 Sync - sending updates to server <.ORM-SERV2.orem.quills.QUILLS_I
3BDF7791:88865356:d0b25620:047 ComputeLowestCompareTime 0x3BDF775F (2001/10/30 21:00:31, 1, 1)
3BDF7791:88865356:d0b25620:047 Sync - [00008093] <.ENGR_Tools.orem.quills.QUILLS_INC.> [2001/09/
3BDF7791:88865390:d0b25620:047 Signaling time vector merge on server <.ORM-SERV2.orem.quills.QUI
3BDF7791:88865390:d0b25620:047 Sync - objects: 1, total changes: 1, sent to server <.ORM-SERV2.o
```

The DSTrace debug message appends four sets of numbers, separated by colons, to the front of the message. These values are described in Table A.13.

TABLE A.13	*DSTrace Debug Timing Information*
TIMING ELEMENT	**DESCRIPTION**
Date and time	The date and time when this DSTrace message was displayed. This hex value is the number of seconds that have elapsed since 00:00:00, January 1, 1970.
Number of events	The number of events that have occurred during this second, reported as a decimal value. A 0 is returned if more than 999 events occur during any given second.
Operating system thread	This hex value identifies the operating system thread assigned to the eDirectory background process or function that generated this DSTrace message. Since DSTrace messages can become intermixed, this value can be used to identify those messages generated by the same eDirectory background process or operation.

Thread numbers are reusable values, so it is not a good idea to rely solely on this value when identifying messages generated by a given process. If a great deal of time has passed (as noted by the date and time value) then it is likely that these messages are from two different processes using the same thread number. |
| Connection ID | This is the numeric identifier assigned to the eDirectory process when it began to execute. |

The rest of the message is identical to what is found on the DSTrace monitor screen itself.

DSTRACE.NLM Monitoring

DSTRACE.NLM is a newer way of accessing eDirectory performance data. To use it, load DSTRACE.NLM at the server console. Once loaded, DSTRACE.NLM can be configured through the use of the configuration options outlined in Table A.14.

TABLE A.14   *DSTRACE Configuration Options*

CONFIGURATION OPTION	DESCRIPTION
DSTRACE ON	Enables DSTrace. Default options are Journal, Print to Screen, Print to File DSTRACE.LOG. The following flags are set for capture: BASE, MISC, PART, VCLN, AREQ, BEMU, FRAG, JNTR, MOVE, SAPM, SKLK, BLNK, INIT, LMBR, SCMA, STRM, TVEC. DSTRACE flags are described in the next section of this chapter.
DSTRACE OFF	Disables DSTrace.
DSTRACE FILE	Specifies that DSTRACE.NLM should write its data to a log file.
DSTRACE FMAX =	Specifies maximum log file size in bytes.
DSTRACE FNAME =	Specifies name of log file. Default is DSTRACE.LOG.
DSTRACE SCREEN	Specifies that DSTrace should write to the server console.
DSTRACE INLINE	Have eDirectory handle the actual "display to screen" function that sends DSTrace data to the console screen. This is a faster method of displaying the data but places increased overhead on the eDirectory processing thread.
DSTRACE JOURNAL	Pass DSTRACE.NLM data to the standard display queue processing thread for the "print to screen" function. This relieves eDirectory of some overhead but can also delay the display of DSTrace messages since they will have to wait their turn in the queue.

DSTRACE.NLM allows administrators to specify the type(s) of information that will be displayed and logged in DSTRACE.LOG, as shown in Figure A.6.

DSTRACE.NLM Configuration screen

In large eDirectory tree environments there can be a great number of things happening. In order to use DSTRACE.NLM effectively you need to know what you are looking for and how to best view that information. DSTRACE.NLM flags, which are listed in Table A.15, take the following form:

```
DSTRACE <operator><flag>
```

The "+" and "-" operators are used to enable and disable DSTRACE.NLM flags, respectively. For example:

- ▶ DSTRACE +SYNC
- ▶ DSTRACE –JNTR

T A B L E A.15 *DSTRACE.NLM Flags*

DSTRACE FLAG	DESCRIPTION
ABUF	Trace messages related to allocation of inbound and outbound packet buffers related to eDirectory requests.
ALOC	Trace messages related to allocation of memory for eDirectory processes.
AREQ	Trace messages related to incoming eDirectory requests.
AUMN	Trace messages related to the eDirectory audit process.
AUNC	Trace Audit NCP (NetWare Core Protocol) events.
AUSK	Trace audit messages related to the replica sync process.

DSTRACE FLAG	DESCRIPTION
AUTH	Trace messages related to eDirectory authentication events.
BASE	Trace a base set of eDirectory messages.
BEMU	Trace messages related to Bindery Emulation.
BLNK	Trace messages related to the Backlink process.
CBUF	Events related to memory buffers maintained for client connections.
CHNG	Trace messages related to the changing of the eDirectory memory cache.
COLL	Trace messages related to the receipt of duplicate update packets. These duplicate packets usually occur on very busy networks.
DRLK	Trace messages related to Distributed Reference Link operations.
FRAG	Trace messages related to the packet fragmenter that breaks up eDirectory messages for transmission in multiple packets.
INIT	Trace messages related to the opening of the local eDirectory database.
INSP	Messages related to the Inspector process. Inspector is part of the Janitor that verifies the structural integrity of the eDirectory database.
JNTR	Trace Janitor messages. The Janitor cleans up eDirectory by removing objects that are no longer needed.
LMBR	Trace Limber messages. The Limber monitors connectivity between all replicas.
LDAP	Trace messages related to LDAP communications.
LOCK	Trace messages related to manipulation of the local eDirectory database locks.
LOST	Trace messages related to obituaries, eDirectory attributes and stream files.
MISC	Trace all miscellaneous messages.

(continued)

T A B L E A . 15	DSTRACE.NLM Flags (continued)
DSTRACE FLAG	**DESCRIPTION**
MOVE	Trace messages related to eDirectory Object move operations.
NCPE	Trace messages related to the NCP engine.
PART	Trace partition operations and messages.
PURG	Trace replica purger messages.
RECM	Trace messages related to low level database operations.
RSLV	Trace messages related to eDirectory name resolution when traversing the eDirectory tree.
SAPM	Trace messages related to the SAP protocol.
SCMA	Trace schema modification and synchronization messages.
SPKT	Trace messages related to server packets.
SKLK	Trace messages related to the Skulker process, which manages replica and schema synchronization.
STRM	Trace messages related to Stream attributes in eDirectory.
SYNC	Trace messages related to background replica sync.
TAGS	Show event tags as part of the DSTRACE messages.
THRD	Trace messages related to the management of processor threads used with eDirectory.
TIME	Show event times as part of DSTRACE output.
TVEC	Trace messages related to transitive vectors, which describe how "caught up" the replica is in the synchronization process.
VCLN	Trace messages related to server-to-server Virtual Client connections.
WANM	Trace messages related to WAN Traffic Manager.

DSTRACE.NLM uses the exact same SET commands to configure and activate eDirectory background processes as are used with DSTrace, as outlined in Table A.10.

As with DSTrace, DSTRACE.NLM log traces information to a file for review off-line. The default filename is SYS:SYSTEM\DSTRACE.LOG. However, unlike DSTrace, DSTRACE.NLM allows you to configure the log file using the commands described in Table A.15. The log file contains information identical to the DSTRACE.NLM monitor screen. However, it is organized slightly differently, as shown in Figure A.7.

F I G U R E A.7 *Sample DSTRACE.LOG*

```
AREQ: [2001/10/30 20:36:14] Calling DSAGetServerAddress conn:6 for client
.PRV-SERV1.provo.quills.QUILLS_INC.
AREQ: [2001/10/30 20:36:14] Calling DSAResolveName conn:21 for client
.PRV-SERV1.provo.quills.QUILLS_INC.
AREQ: [2001/10/30 20:36:14] DSAResolveName failed, no such entry (-601).
AREQ: [2001/10/30 20:36:14] Calling DSAGetServerAddress conn:21 for client
.PRV-SERV1.provo.quills.QUILLS_INC.
AREQ: [2001/10/30 20:36:14] Calling DSAReadEntryInfo conn:15 for client .[Public].
SKLK: [2001/10/30 20:36:15] 2001/10/30 20:36:15 Start partition sync
.provo.quills.QUILLS_INC. state:[0], type:[0].
PART: [2001/10/30 20:36:15] Start state transitions for .provo.quills.QUILLS_INC.,
current state 0
PART: [2001/10/30 20:36:15] all replicas of .provo.quills.QUILLS_INC. have seen this
ring state
PART: [2001/10/30 20:36:15] Finish state transitions for .provo.quills.QUILLS_INC.
SKLK: [2001/10/30 20:36:15] Sync - Start outbound sync with (#=2, state=0, type=1
partition .provo.quills.QUILLS_INC.) .ORM-SERV2.orem.quills.QUILLS_INC..
MISC: [2001/10/30 20:36:15] LocalSetServerVersion succeeded, for server
.ORM-SERV2.orem.quills.QUILLS_INC..
SKLK: [2001/10/30 20:36:15] Sync - using version 9 on server
<.ORM-SERV2.orem.quills.QUILLS_INC.>.
SKLK: [2001/10/30 20:36:15] Sending to  ----> .ORM-SERV2.orem.quills.QUILLS_INC.
SKLK: [2001/10/30 20:36:15] Sync - sending updates to server
<.ORM-SERV2.orem.quills.QUILLS_INC.>.
SKLK: [2001/10/30 20:36:15] ComputeLowestCompareTime 0x3BDF71A7 (2001/10/30
20:36:07, 1, 1)
SKLK: [2001/10/30 20:36:15] Sync - [0000802d] <.provo.quills.QUILLS_INC.>
[2001/09/28  9:33:18, 1, 37].
```

The first column identifies the eDirectory process that generated this message. The second column, enclosed in angle brackets [], provides timestamp information so that the timing of the message can be determined. Thankfully, it is much less cryptic than DSTrace timing information.

The rest of the message is identical in format to the message as it appears on the DSTRACE.NLM monitor screen.

eDirectory Errors

There are a wide variety of error codes and conditions that can be reported in your Novell eDirectory environment. Specific information on each error is available in the Novell On-line documentation. You can also link to error code information from iMonitor by clicking on an error from the Trace screen. eDirectory error codes are usually displayed in decimal numbers.

NOTE

Because the eDirectory is designed as a loosely consistent database, temporary errors are normal. Don't be alarmed if temporary error conditions come and go as part of normal eDirectory operation. However, if errors persist for a significant period of time you may need to take some action to resolve the problem.

eDirectory error codes can be categorized as follows:

eDirectory Agent Errors

These are the error codes with which you will typically work when tackling some eDirectory problem. They come in two ranges:

- ► -601 to -799
- ► –6001 or higher

The 6001 range is new to recent versions of eDirectory. These error codes identify errors originating in the eDirectory Agent running on your NetWare 6 server.

Operating System Errors

Certain eDirectory background processes or operations, such as network communications or time synchronization, require the use or functionality provided by the operating system on which eDirectory is running. These functions can return operating system-specific error codes to eDirectory. These error codes are passed on to the eDirectory process or operation that initiated a request.

Generally, negative numbers identify all eDirectory-generated operating system errors, while positive numbers identify all other operating system errors:

- ► *-1 to -256*: eDirectory-generated operating system errors
- ► *1 - 255*: Operating system-generated errors

This is an esoteric distinction for your information only. During troubleshooting you should treat occurrences of operating system errors with the same number, whether negative or positive, as relating to the same event.

Client Errors

In some cases, an eDirectory server will function as a directory client in order to perform certain background processes or operations. This can result in client-specific error codes being returned to eDirectory background processes and operations. These error codes are generated by the eDirectory client that is built into DS.NLM. Client error codes fall in the range of -301 through -399.

Other eDirectory Errors

Some eDirectory background processes and operations require interaction with other NLMs running on the NetWare 6 server. Examples of this include TIMESYNC.NLM and UNICODE.NLM. If any of these external NLMs encounter an error, it can be passed on to DS.NLM. Errors in this category utilize codes ranging between -400 and -599.

NetWare Basics and Planning Worksheets

This appendix contains introductory information about NetWare networks, for those of you who are new to Novell networking, or have had some of the stuff you learned a long time ago pushed out of your head by other material. It also includes network-planning worksheets to help you organize and plan network tasks, so you don't forget anything important.

Components of a NetWare 6 Network

To understand a NetWare 6 network, it helps to begin with the components that make up the network. This appendix explores the three fundamental aspects of any network:

- The network's hardware, including the cabling, the connectors, and the network architectures those hardware elements create

- The network's software, including the software that must run on the server and the workstations to enable those machines to communicate, as well as the software that provides the network services users need to use (such as printing services, mail services, file services, and so on)

- The communication protocols that regulate how all of the network's components communicate with each other

First, let's look at the network's hardware, and how that hardware works inside the most common network topologies and network architectures.

Network Topologies and Architectures

The format in which a network's servers, workstations, printers, and other equipment are laid out is called the network's *topology*. For example, a network can be laid out in a bus format (see Figure B.1), a ring format (see Figure B.2), or a star format (see Figure B.3). Variations or combinations of these topologies are also commonly used.

The cabling scheme that connects the servers, workstations, and other devices together into these topologies can be called the *network cabling architecture*, or just network architecture. The most common network architectures currently are Ethernet, Token Ring, and AppleTalk. Ethernet architectures include the newer high-speed Ethernet specifications such as Fast Ethernet, which operates at 100Mbps and Gigabit Ethernet, which operates at, you guessed it, 1 Gbps (1000Mbps).

Because each of these network architectures handles data in a different way, each requires a unique type of network hardware.

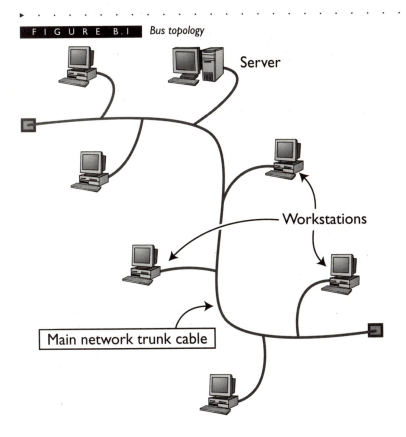

FIGURE B.1   *Bus topology*

Server

Workstations

Main network trunk cable

FIGURE B.2   *Ring topology*

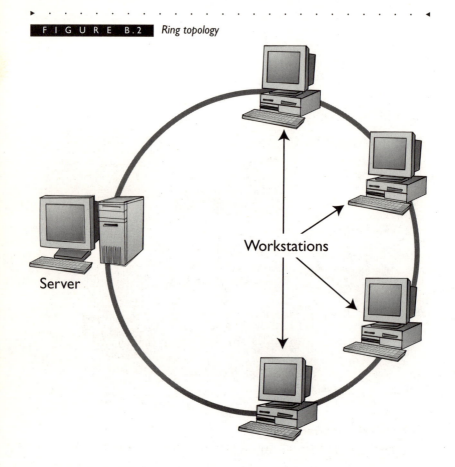

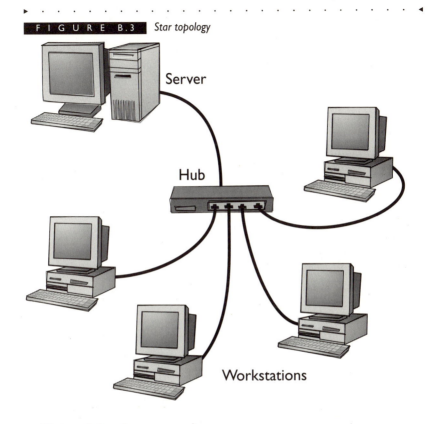

FIGURE B.3 *Star topology*

Server

Hub

Workstations

Network hardware overview

Networking hardware consists of the following components:

▶ *Network boards*: These special circuit boards, installed in each workstation or server, connect the computer to the network cables. (Some computers come with the network boards integrated into the rest of the computer system hardware. These boards are sometimes called built-in adapters.)

▶ *Cables*: Network cables connect each workstation and server to the network. These cables can be coaxial (also called coax), unshielded twisted-pair, shielded twisted-pair, or fiber-optic. The type of cable you use depends on the requirements of the topology you install.

► *Connectors and terminators*: Each type of cable requires different types of connectors to join cables together or connect them to other pieces of hardware (such as network boards). Some types of cable also require special connectors known as terminators to be attached to the open ends of any cables. Terminators keep electrical signals from reflecting back across the network, causing bad packets on the network.

► *Hubs*: Some network architectures require that the cables attached to workstations all feed into a separate piece of hardware before being connected to the main network cable. *Passive hubs* simply gather the signals and relay them. *Active hubs* actually boost the signals before sending them on their way. (The terms active hub and concentrator are often used interchangeably.)

► *Routers, switches, and gateways*: These devices are used to link distinct networks together so that data can move seamlessly between them. These are discussed in more detail in the Other Network Components section.

Ethernet network architecture

Ethernet is currently the most commonly used network architecture. It is relatively easy to install at a moderate cost. Because Ethernet has been so widely used for many years, its technology has been well tested. Ethernet networks can use either bus or star topologies.

There are several variants of Ethernet, each of which package *data packets* (units of information packaged into a sort of electronic envelope and sent across the network) in different ways. These different types of Ethernet packet formats are called *frame types*. In some cases, a given network will support only one Ethernet frame type. However, NetWare allows a single network board to support more than one frame type by configuring the LAN driver for the server's network board to recognize two or more types.

Ethernet frame types   The four Ethernet frame types are shown in Table B.1.

TABLE B.1	Ethernet Frame Types
FRAME TYPE	**DESCRIPTION**
Ethernet II	This is the original "official" Ethernet frame type. It is used on networks that use AppleTalk Phase 1 addressing or TCP/IP.

FRAME TYPE	DESCRIPTION
Ethernet 802.3	This is the default frame type for old versions of NetWare (3.11 and earlier). This frame type can support either a bus or star topology. It is also called the *raw frame type*, because it uses only the defined 802.3 header and doesn't include the standard header extensions defined by the 802.2 and SNAP variants of Ethernet. Ethernet 802.3 is not a standard and was used primarily by Novell. Don't use this frame type on networks that use protocols other than IPX.
Ethernet 802.2	This frame type is used with the IPX protocol, and can support either a bus or star topology. Because it is an IEEE standard, NetWare 6 uses this frame type by default. Ethernet 802.2 packet frames have both the 802.3 header and the 802.2 header extension.
Ethernet SNAP	This is a variant of the 802.2 packet format. It is used on networks that have workstations using protocols such as AppleTalk Phase 2 addressing. Ethernet SNAP packet frames have both the 802.3 header and the SNAP header extension. SNAP stands for Sub-Network Access Protocol.

Ethernet cable options   In an Ethernet topology, the cables that connect the machines together are laid out in a specific fashion. The cables you use fall into three general types of functions. These are described in Table B.2.

TABLE B.2	*Categories of Cable Functions in an Ethernet Network*
CABLE'S FUNCTION	**DESCRIPTION**
Trunk cable	The trunk cable is the backbone of the network. All other nodes (workstations, servers, and so on) are connected to this trunk.
Drop cable	The drop cable can be used to connect a node to the trunk cable in a thick Ethernet network.
Patch cable	The patch cable can be used to connect two hubs, or connect a node to a hub.

How these types of cables are laid out depends on the cabling hardware (physical wiring) you select. Ethernet networks can be wired using any of the following types of physical cables:

- ▶ Thin coaxial cable (also called Thin Ethernet cable)
- ▶ Thick coaxial cable (also called Thick Ethernet cable)
- ▶ Twisted-pair cable

These types of cables are explained in the following sections.

Thin Ethernet cable   Thin Ethernet cable is RG-58 (50-ohm) coaxial cable. It is 3/16 inch in size. It is also called ThinNet, and 10Base2. Thin Ethernet cabling is more popular than Thick Ethernet cable because it is less bulky, more flexible, and relatively easy to handle.

Thin Ethernet, like most coaxial cable, is covered with PVC so it can be run through air-conditioning and heating ducts. However, PVC-covered cable cannot be used in the space between a false ceiling and the next floor (called the *plenum space*) because PVC is quite toxic if it burns. Another type of cable, called *plenum cable,* must be used in those areas. If you use thin Ethernet, you will need the following types of hardware components:

- ▶ Ethernet network boards are necessary for each workstation and server.
- ▶ BNC barrel connectors are used to connect lengths of the trunk cable together into one trunk segment.
- ▶ BNC T-connectors are used to connect each node to the network cable.
- ▶ BNC terminators are used to terminate one end of each trunk segment.
- ▶ BNC grounded terminators are used to terminate and ground the other end of each trunk segment.
- ▶ Repeaters, if needed, regenerate the signal and pass it on to another trunk segment, thereby extending the normal limits of the network. (Be sure to follow cabling guidelines, however.)

Thin Ethernet cable, like all cable, has limits and restrictions (described in Table B.3) that will affect how you can set up the network.

TABLE B.3	*Limits and Restrictions of Thin Ethernet Cable*
NETWORK ITEM	**LIMITS AND RESTRICTIONS**
Trunk segments	Maximum segment length (segments can consist of several shorter cables linked with BNC barrel connectors) is 607 feet (185 meters). Maximum number of segments per network (linked by repeaters) is five, for a total of 3,035 feet (925 meters). Only three of the segments can be populated with nodes, however. All trunk segments must be terminated at one end and terminated and grounded at the other end.
Nodes	Maximum number of nodes per trunk segment (including repeaters, which count as nodes) is 30. Maximum number of nodes (including repeaters) on the entire network is 90. Minimum cable distance between nodes is 1.6 feet (0.5 meters).

Thick Ethernet cable   Thick Ethernet cable is RG-8 (50-ohm) coaxial cable. It is 3/8 inch in size. It is also called ThickNet, Standard Ethernet, or 10Base5. Thick Ethernet is seldom used today, but may still be relatively common in buildings with older network build-outs.

Thick Ethernet, like most coaxial cable, is covered with PVC so it can be run through air-conditioning and heating ducts. As previously mentioned, however, PVC-covered cable cannot be used in the space between a false ceiling and the next floor because PVC is toxic if it burns. Another type of cable, called plenum cable, must be used in those areas.

If you use thick Ethernet, you will need the following types of hardware components:

- ► Ethernet network boards are necessary for each workstation and server.

- ► N-series barrel connectors are used to connect lengths of the trunk cable together into one trunk segment.

- ► Transceivers (one for every node) connect the nodes' drop cables to the trunk segment.

- ► N-series T-connectors or vampire taps attach the transceivers to the trunk cable.

▸ Drop cables (also called transceiver cables) connect the network board in the node to the transceiver. The drop cable must have DIX connectors on each end.

▸ N-series terminators are used to terminate one end of each trunk segment.

▸ N-series grounded terminators are used to terminate and ground the other end of each trunk segment.

▸ Repeaters, if needed, regenerate the signal and pass it on to another trunk segment, thereby extending the normal limits of the network.

Thick Ethernet cable, like all cable, has limits and restrictions (described in Table B.4) that will affect how you can set up the network.

T A B L E B.4	*Limits and Restrictions of Thick Ethernet Cable*
NETWORK ITEM	**LIMITS AND RESTRICTIONS**
Trunk segments	Maximum segment length (segments can consist of several shorter cables linked with N-series barrel connectors) is 1,640 feet (500 meters). Maximum number of segments per network (linked by repeaters) is five, for a total of 8,200 feet (2,500 meters). Only three of the segments can be populated with nodes, however. All trunk segments must be terminated at one end and terminated and grounded at the other end.
Nodes	Maximum number of nodes per trunk segment (including repeaters, which count as nodes) is 100. Maximum number of nodes (including repeaters) on the entire network is 300. Every node must have its own drop cable connected to its own transceiver to connect to the trunk. Minimum cable distance between transceivers is 8 feet (2.5 meters). Maximum drop cable length between node and transceiver is 165 feet (50 meters).

Twisted-pair cable   Unshielded twisted-pair cable is commonly used as telephone wire and as network cabling, because it is found in abundance in buildings. Because it does not have a foil shielding, it is more susceptible to electromagnetic interference from sources such as fluorescent lights, mechanical equipment such as elevators, and telephone ring signals. Unshielded Twisted Pair is also called UTP Ethernet or 10BaseT.

If you use twisted-pair cabling, you will need the following types of hardware components:

▶ Ethernet network boards are necessary for each workstation and server.

▶ Wiring hubs can be used to connect nodes to the network. *Standalone hubs* are devices with their own power supply. *Peer hubs* are boards that can be installed in one of the computers on the network and physically connected to that computer's network board.

▶ Twisted-pair cables connect the nodes to wiring hubs.

▶ An external concentrator, if needed, connects nodes that use coaxial or fiber-optic cable to the network.

▶ Punch-down blocks, if desired, make cable termination easier to change.

▶ RJ-45 connectors are used to connect the cables to wall plates, network boards, and wiring hubs.

Twisted-pair cable, like all cable, has limits and restrictions (described in Table B.5) that will affect how you can set up the network.

TABLE B.5	*Limits and Restrictions of Twisted-Pair Cable*
NETWORK ITEM	**LIMITS AND RESTRICTIONS**
Hubs	The maximum distance between a node and a wiring hub is 330 feet (100 meters). A twisted-pair network can have up to four linked wiring hubs.
Nodes	All nodes must be connected to a wiring hub, either directly (through a cable) or through a wall plate or concentrator.

Token Ring network architecture

A Token Ring network is cabled like a star, but it acts like a ring. Data flows from workstation to workstation around the ring. Because the network is cabled like a star, however, the data ends up going through the central point between each workstation on the trip around the ring.

Token Ring networks can run on twisted-pair (either shielded or unshielded) or fiber-optic cables. They generally work well in situations that involve heavy data traffic because Token Ring is reliable. It is also fairly easy to install, but it is more expensive than Ethernet networks.

Unshielded twisted-pair cabling is a poorer choice for network cabling because it can be very susceptible to electromagnetic interference from sources such as fluorescent lights, elevators, and telephone ring signals.

Shielded twisted-pair is a better choice for networks because of its extra insulation and foil shielding.

There are two different versions of Token Ring — one that supports a 4Mbps transmission speed and one that supports 16Mbps. A single network can run only one or the other, but networks of differing speeds can be connected through a bridge or router.

If you use Token Ring, you will need the following types of hardware components:

- ▶ Token Ring network boards are necessary for each workstation and server.

- ▶ Multistation Access Units (MAUs) are wiring concentrators. Nodes connect to these MAUs, which in turn are connected to other MAUs to form the ring. The wiring inside a MAU forms a ring of the attached nodes.

- ▶ Cabling is necessary to connect the MAUs in the main ring.

- ▶ Patch cables are used to connect the nodes to the MAUs.

- ▶ Repeaters, if needed, regenerate the signal and pass it on, thereby extending the normal limits of the network.

IBM defined different types of cabling for use in Token Ring networks. These cabling types are as follows:

- ▶ Type 1 cable is shielded twisted-pair cable. It has two pairs of 22-gauge solid wire and can supply data-quality transmission. It can be used for the main ring (similar to a trunk cable in an Ethernet network) or to connect nodes to MAUs.

- ▶ Type 2 cable is a hybrid cable, containing four pairs of unshielded 22-gauge solid wire for voice transmission, and two pairs of shielded 22-gauge solid wire for data transmission.

- ▶ Type 3 cable is unshielded twisted-pair cable, which is only required to support voice-quality transmission. It can have two, three, or four pairs of 22-gauge or 24-gauge solid wire, with each pair having at least two twists per foot. This cable is not recommended for Token Ring networks.

- ▶ Type 4 cable is undefined.

- ▶ Type 5 cable is fiber-optic cable, with two glass fiber cores. Type 5 cables are used to cable the main ring in a Token Ring network and can also be used to extend the distance between MAUs or to connect network segments between buildings.

▶ Type 6 cable is shielded twisted-pair cable, with two pairs of 26-gauge stranded wire. Type 6 cable is commonly used as an adapter cable to connect a node to an MAU.

▶ Type 7 cable is undefined.

▶ Type 8 cable is shielded twisted-pair cable, with two pairs of flat, 26-gauge solid wire. It is designed to run underneath carpeting.

▶ Type 9 cable is shielded twisted-pair cable, with two pairs of 26-gauge solid or stranded wire. It is covered with a plenum jacket and is used to go between floors.

Token Ring cable, like all cable, has limits and restrictions (described in Table B.6) that will affect how you can set up the network.

TABLE B.6 *Limits and Restrictions of Token Ring Cable*

NETWORK ITEM	LIMITS AND RESTRICTIONS
MAUs	Maximum number of MAUs on a network that uses Type 1 or 2 cabling is 33. Maximum number of MAUs on a network that uses Type 6 or 9 cabling is 12.
Cabling	Maximum distance between a node and an MAU is as follows: —Type 1 and 2 cable: 330 feet (100 meters) —Type 6 and 9 cable: 220 feet (66 meters) — UTP: 150 feet (45 meters) Maximum distance between MAUs is as follows: —Type 1 and 2 cable: 660 feet (200 meters) —Type 6 cable: 140 feet (45 meters) — UTP: 400 feet (120 meters) — Fiber: 0.6 miles (1 km) Maximum number of cable segments (separated by repeaters) in a series is three. All cable segments must be terminated at one end and terminated and grounded at the other.
Nodes	Maximum number of nodes is as follows: Networks using Type 1 and 2 cable: 255 Networks using Type 6 and 9 cable: 96 Networks using UTP: 72 Minimum cable distance between a node and an MAU is 8 feet (2.5 meters).

AppleTalk network architectures

AppleTalk is the networking protocol suite developed by Apple Computers. It provides peer-to-peer networking capabilities between all Macintoshes and Apple hardware. AppleTalk capability is automatically built into every Macintosh.

AppleTalk can run with several types of architectures:

► LocalTalk was Apple's built-in architecture in older Macintoshes. A Macintosh doesn't need a separate network board to communicate over LocalTalk cables, but it does need a separate network board to use other topologies.

► EtherTalk is Apple's implementation of Ethernet. EtherTalk Phase 1 was based on the Ethernet II version of Ethernet. EtherTalk Phase 2 is based on the Ethernet 802.3 version. EtherTalk Phase 2 has replaced LocalTalk as the built-in networking architecture in most newer Macintoshes.

► TokenTalk is Apple's Token Ring implementation.

► FDDITalk is Apple's implementation of the 100Mbps FDDI architecture.

For more information about using AppleTalk with NetWare 6, see NetWare 6 on-line documentation.

High-speed network architectures

Several new types of high-speed network architectures currently are being developed. Fast Ethernet has become the standard of choice for most local networks, transmitting at 100Mbps over unshielded twisted-pair cable.

Now Gigabit Ethernet is making strong inroads in the WAN market, using fiber-optic cabling to achieve speeds of—you guessed it—1Gbps (1000Mbps). Because cutting-edge technologies and standards are evolving, sometimes rapidly, your best bet is to work with a qualified, experienced vendor to design and implement your high-speed network. Most communications providers provide a group devoted to the needs of high-speed networks.

Optical networks

In its most basic configuration, an optical network is one that uses light pulses to transmit data rather than an electrical current. The attraction of optical networks, when compared to an electrical network, is the vast amount of information that can be transmitted.

On one end, a laser sends pulses of high-intensity light through a piece of glass fiber. The laser pulses on and off in order to encode data for transmission, kind of like Morse code. The speed with which the laser can pulse (turn on and off) determines how fast data can be sent. Modern networks can transmit 10Gbps from a single laser. That's 10 billion flashes per second!

At the other end of the optical fiber, a light detector senses the on-off flashes of light and converts them back into the original data type, whether that's a voice, a Web page, or a feature length motion picture.

Connecting the laser and the light detector is a length of optical fiber. Optical fiber is created from extremely pure strands of silica glass, surrounded by a second layer of glass cladding, which serves to keep light waves pointed down the fiber, instead of exiting it through the sides. Surrounding the cladding is a polymer sheath that protects the glass strand.

Most optical networks use what is known as *Single mode* fiber. This fiber has an extremely small glass core, about 10 micrometers, with a cladding layer about 125 micrometers. A micrometer is .00001 meters, by the way. Including the polymer sheath, a single mode fiber is only about .25 millimeters in diameter. The small size of single mode fiber allows only a single light wave from each optical signal to travel down the fiber at a time.

Optical fiber doesn't have any joints or junctions. It runs in a single strand that can be many hundreds or even thousands of miles long. Many fibers are usually bundled together into a single cable and the cable is then laid underground or even underwater to connect the cities and countries that are part of the optical network. Organizations then link into this vast network backbone to transmit data between their sites around the world.

Other Network Components

There are a few other common network components with which you should be familiar if you are going to work on a NetWare 6 network.

Drivers

Drivers are small software programs associated with a piece of hardware. A driver enables the hardware device to communicate with the computer in which it's installed.

On a network, you will install a LAN driver on each server and workstation. A LAN driver enables a network board to communicate with the computer in which it's installed, as well as with other devices on the network. Most network boards require their own matched brand of driver.

Disk drivers are another important type of driver. They make it possible for the computer to communicate with its hard disk (actually, with the hard disk's controller board). CD-ROM drives and tape drives also have their own corresponding drivers. The term *device drivers* is sometimes used as a generic name for all the hardware-related drivers your computer may require.

When you install NetWare, the installation program looks at your hardware and attempts to find a matching LAN driver and disk driver. It then attempts to install them automatically from the set of drivers shipped on the NetWare CD-ROM. If it can't find a driver it needs, the installation program will ask you to insert a diskette with the necessary driver on it. (When you buy a network board, the package usually includes a diskette with the board's associated LAN driver on it.)

NOTE

Novell's NetWare includes a large selection of the most common types of LAN drivers. However, board manufacturers frequently update their drivers; so if you're installing a network board, check the manufacturer's Web site for the latest driver.

Routers

Routers are devices that enable network communication to travel across networks of mixed topologies, architectures, or protocols. Routers take packets of data from one network and reformat them (if necessary) to conform to the next network's requirements. The routers then send the packets along to their destination. Routers can also track routes between servers or networks. They keep track of which servers are up and running, which route between two servers is shortest, and so on. This ensures that network communication isn't interrupted or slowed down unnecessarily.

Routing software is built into the server in NetWare. The server forms the physical connection between two networks. You accomplish this by placing more than one network adapter into the server and connecting one to each network. For example, the server may have both an Ethernet network board and a Token Ring network board installed in it. The router software in NetWare 6 then manages the flow of data packets between the two networks via their respective network boards.

Switches

A switch is a more intelligent version of a router. Router technology does not distinguish between one network connection and another. Data comes in and is "broadcast" out to all other networks to which the router is connected.

Switches reduce this unnecessary network traffic by targeting communications to the network that actually needs it. This results in faster network performance and fewer errors. Packets could be sent directly from one computer to another without wasting the bandwidth of the entire network attached to that switch.

The switch accomplishes its task by using a little bit of intelligence. Switches typically buffer an entire packet, examine it to find the destination address, and then route the packet directly to the destination. This way, only the necessary network receives the packet, instead of all of them.

Switches can also reduce network collisions. The switch examines the network lines and holds any packets that would result in a collision until the lines are clear. The switch can also detect packets with errors and direct the computer to resend them.

Gateways

Gateways are used to translate one form of communication into another, and back again. The difference between routers and gateways is a little confusing, and with advancements in technology, the line between them is getting somewhat blurred.

One way to look at the difference, although it's not necessarily a precise definition, is that a router links multiple networks so they appear to be one seamless network. If your company has hundreds of servers scattered all over the globe, you're using a large number of routers every time you communicate with someone. The routers work together to scatter information across a spider web of connections to get the data to its destination. A piece of data, traveling across the network, may go through a variety of paths. If one router is down, the data can travel through another router on a different path, but still wind up at the same destination.

A gateway generally connects your network to a different type of network or computer system through a single point. It functions as a protocol translator. For example, Gateways are often used to connect a network of PCs to a mainframe so that network users can access data on the mainframe. The gateway takes your data and translates it to a form understandable by the mainframe, and vice versa. It is important to recognize that if the gateway is down; you won't be able to communicate with the mainframe.

Network Protocols

A protocol is a standardized set of rules that controls how some task or process is accomplished. In the network world, protocols control pretty much everything, from how electrical impulses are transmitted and interpreted to how an application takes advantage of encryption to protect data in transit.

The International Standardization Organization, or ISO, developed the most famous network-oriented protocol model in the 1960s. It is cleverly known as the OSI model, and consists of seven layers. Each layer corresponds to a different type of network activity.

The advantage of this model is that it eliminated the need for a single vendor to create a comprehensive network environment, from wire to application, in order to participate in the networking market. Vendors started to specialize in specific areas of the network communications process, confident that if they adhered to the communications standards that their technology would be able to communicate with products from other vendors.

Network protocols control how data is transferred over a network. When data is sent across the network, it (the data) is organized into discrete packages for transmission. These packages of data include some amount of data, coupled with addressing and handling information that makes sure the data gets to the right destination. Protocols at each layer of the OSI model dictate exactly how these data packages should be formed and interpreted within their sphere of control. This way, every device on the network knows how to interpret and respond to the data packages it receives. Each protocol uses a unique packaging standard to distinguish itself from other protocols that might also be in use on the network.

In order for network communications to occur, control is passed from one layer to the next, starting at the application layer in one station, proceeding to the bottom layer, over the channel to the next station and back up the hierarchy.

▶ *Application (Layer 7)*: This layer supports application and end-user processes such as quality of service, user authentication, user privacy. All services and communications at this layer are application-specific. For example: file transfer, email, and other network services.

▶ *Presentation (Layer 6)*: This layer transforms data into the form that the application layer can accept. It also supports formatting and encryption of data to be sent across a network.

▶ *Session (Layer 5)*: This layer establishes, manages and terminates connections between applications. It deals with coordination between sessions for lower layers and connection for upper layers.

▶ *Transport (Layer 4)*: This layer is responsible for transparent and reliable end-to-end communication between systems, including error recovery and flow control. Transfer Control Protocol (TCP) is the most significant Transport layer protocol.

▸ *Network (Layer 3)*: This layer provides switching and routing for the network by creating logical paths for data transfer known as virtual circuits. Packet forwarding, addressing, sequencing, and error handling are typical Network layer functions. Internet Protocol (IP) is the most significant Network layer protocol.

▸ *Data Link (Layer 2)*: This layer converts data packets into bits, and vice versa. It handles physical transmission errors, flow control and frame synchronization. The data link layer is divided into two sublayers: Media Access Control (MAC) layer and Logical Link Control (LLC) layer. MAC controls how a computer on the network gains access to the data and permission to transmit it. LLC controls frame synchronization, flow control and error checking.

▸ *Physical (Layer 1)*: This layer converts bits into the actual transmission medium, such as electrical impulse or light wave. It controls the means of sending and receiving data on a carrier, including the definition of cables and other physical connections.

When you configure a NetWare network, you will primarily deal with protocols in the bottom four layers. Applications will often provide the functionality of the upper three layers, although they may be separate processes under the covers.

▸ *Transport*: TCP, SPX

▸ *Network*: IP, IPX, AppleTalk

▸ *Datalink*: Ethernet, Token Ring, FDDI

▸ *Physical*: 802.2, Ethernet_II, RS232

Network Planning Worksheets

Keeping accurate and up-to-date documentation about the various aspects of your network can save you a tremendous amount of time and energy if something goes wrong. You can photocopy and use the worksheets in this section to begin documenting your network. If you prefer, you can design your own forms or databases for tracking important information such as hardware and software inventory, eDirectory information, and backup schedules.

Worksheet A: Server Installation and Configuration

Server name: _____

Make and model: _____

Current location: _____

Serial number: _____

CPU speed: _____

Number of processors: _____

Memory: _____

Storage adapter name: _____

   Attached storage device: _____

   Attached storage device: _____

Storage adapter name: _____

   Attached storage device: _____

   Attached storage device: _____

Hard disk size: _____

DOS partition size: _____

Disks mirrored?   Yes: __ No: __

Disks duplexed?   Yes: __ No: __

Network board name: _____

   LAN driver: _____

   Protocol bound: _____ Frame type: _____

   Protocol bound: _____ Frame type: _____

   Settings: _____

   Node address: _____

   IP address (TCP/IP): _____

   Subnet mask (TCP/IP): _____

Network board name: _____

   LAN driver: _____

   Protocol bound: _____ Frame type: _____

   Protocol bound: _____ Frame type: _____

   Settings: _____

   Node address: _____

IP address (TCP/IP): _____

Subnet mask (TCP/IP): _____

Protocols loaded on server:

　　IPX:　　　　Yes:__　No:__

　　　　　Internal Net number: _____

　　IP:　　　　Yes:__　No:__

　　　　　Compatibility Mode On?　　Yes: __　No: __

　　　　　Migration Agent installed?　　Yes: __　No: __

　　　　　Server's IP address: _____

　　　　　Server's subnet mask: _____

　　　　　Router (gateway) address: _____

　　　　　DNS domain name: _____

　　AppleTalk:　　Yes:__　No:__

NDPS Broker installed?_____

Server's time zone:_____

Directory tree name: _____

Server's name context in the Directory tree: _____

Admin's name and context: _____

Type of TimeSync server: _____

Other boards or devices installed in server:

　　Name: _____

　　Settings: _____

　　Name: _____

　　Settings: _____

　　Name: _____

　　Settings: _____

　　Name: _____

　　Settings: _____

Comments: _____

_____

_____

_____

_____

Worksheet B: Volumes

Server name: _____

SYS Volume:

    Size: _____

    Name spaces: _____

    File compression on?   Yes: __   No: __

    Block suballocation on?   Yes: __   No: __

Other volume (name): _____

    Size: _____

    Name spaces: _____

    NSS or Traditional? _____

    File compression on?   Yes: __   No: __

    Block suballocation on?   Yes: __   No: __

Other volume (name): _____

    Size: _____

    Name spaces: _____

    NSS or Traditional? _____

    File compression on?   Yes: __   No: __

    Block suballocation on?   Yes: __   No: __

Other volume (name): _____

    Size: _____

    Name spaces: _____

    NSS or Traditional? _____

    File compression on?   Yes: __   No: __

    Block suballocation on?   Yes: __   No: __

Comments: _____

_____

_____

_____

_____

_____

Worksheet C: Hardware and Software Purchases

Product: _____

Serial number: _____

Version number: _____

Vendor name: _____

    Address: _____

    _____

    Phone: _____

    Fax: _____

    E-mail or Web site: _____

Manufacturer name: _____

    Address: _____

    _____

    Phone: _____

    Fax: _____

    Email or Web site: _____

Purchase date: _____

Purchase order number: _____

Purchase price: _____

Product Registered?   Yes: __   No: __   Not applicable: __

Length of warranty _____

Current location of product: _____

Comments: _____

_____

_____

_____

_____

_____

Worksheet D: Hardware Maintenance

Product: _____

Serial number: _____

Repair date: _____

Purchase order number: _____

Repair vendor name:_____

    Address: _____

    _____

    Phone:_____

    Fax: _____

    Email or Web site: _____

Repair cost: _____

    Repaired under warranty?   Yes: __   No: __

    New warranty granted?   Yes: __   No: __

    Warranty expiration date: _____

Comments: _____

_____

_____

_____

_____

_____

Worksheet E: Time Synchronization Servers

eDirectory tree: _____

Single Reference server: _____

Reference server: _____

Primary servers: _____

_____

_____

_____

Comments: _____

_____

_____

_____

Worksheet F: Hot Fix Bad Block Tracking

Server: _____

Disk: _____

Total redirection area: _____

Date: _____ Hot Fix blocks used: _____

Date: _____ Hot Fix blocks used: _____

Date: _____ Hot Fix blocks used: _____

Date: _____ Hot Fix blocks used: _____

Date: _____ Hot Fix blocks used: _____

Date: _____ Hot Fix blocks used: _____

Date: _____ Hot Fix blocks used: _____

Date: _____ Hot Fix blocks used: _____

Date: _____ Hot Fix blocks used: _____

Date: _____ Hot Fix blocks used: _____

Date: _____ Hot Fix blocks used: _____

Date: _____ Hot Fix blocks used: _____

Comments: _____

_____

_____

_____

Worksheet G: Workstation Installation and Configuration

Workstation's user and/or location: _____

Make and model: _____

Serial number: _____

OS and version number: _____

Memory: _____

Size of hard disk: C:_____   D:_____

CD-ROM drive?   Yes:__   No:__

Novell client software version: _____

Protocols installed: _____

Network Board:_____

    Type: _____   Node address: _____

    LAN driver: _____   Frame type: _____

    Settings: _____

Network Board:_____

    Type: _____   Node address: _____

    LAN driver: _____   Frame type: _____

    Settings: _____

Other Boards:

    Name: _____

    Settings: _____

    Name: _____

    Settings: _____

    Name: _____

    Settings: _____

    Name: _____

    Settings: _____

Comments: _____

_____

_____

_____

Worksheet H: Backup Schedule

Server name (of server backed up): _____

Server location: _____

Backup system used (hardware and software): _____

_____

_____

Type of backup media used: _____

Location of backup media: _____

_____

_____

Backup schedule: _____

    Full backup: _____

    Incremental backup: _____

    Differential backup: _____

If custom backups are done, describe: _____

_____

_____

_____

Media rotation schedule: _____

_____

_____

Media labeling instructions: _____

_____

_____

Location of session and error log files: _____

_____

Primary backup administrator name: _____

    Phone numbers: _____

_____

Secondary backup administrator name: _____

    Phone numbers: _____

_____

Comments: _____

_____

_____

_____

Worksheet I: Printer Installation and Configuration

Printer object's full name: _____

Make and model: _____

Current location: _____

Serial number: _____

Directory tree name: _____

How is the printer attached: To server: __ To workstation: __ Direct: __

Printer type (parallel, serial, AppleTalk, etc.): _____

Interrupt mode (polled or specific IRQ): _____

Parallel printer configuration: _____

    Port (LPT1, LPT2, or LPT3): _____

    Poll: _____

    Interrupt (LPT1=7, LPT2=8): _____

Queue-Based:

    Printer number: _____

    Print queues assigned: _____

    _____

    Print server assigned: _____

    Print queue operators: _____

    Print server operators:_____

NDPS/iPrint:

    Printer agent _____

    Gateway used:_____

    NDPS Manager object: _____

    Public access or controlled access?_____

    Printer Managers: _____

    Printer Operators: _____

Comments: _____

    _____

    _____

Disaster Planning and More Information

This appendix provides you with some tips for preparing for the worst, and gives you some ideas on where to look when a problem crops up for which you are not ready.

Why Plan for Disasters?

Disasters come in many guises. A disaster that affects your network could be anything from a crashed hard disk on your server, to a security breach, to a fire that destroys your building. When it comes to computers, a malfunctioning water sprinkler system can cause as much damage as a hurricane.

The best way to recover from a disaster, regardless of its type, is to have planned for one ahead of time. Armed with a disaster plan, good backups, and accurate records of your network, the task of reestablishing your network will not seem nearly as daunting.

Planning Ahead

If you haven't already created a disaster plan, do it today. It doesn't need to be a difficult task, and it could save a tremendous amount of wasted time, frustrated users, lost revenue, and sleepless nights. An earthquake or electrical fire isn't going to wait for a convenient time in your schedule to occur, so the sooner you plan for it, the better.

Be sure to document the plan. Write it down, get it approved by your organization's upper management, and then make copies and store them in several locations so you'll be able to find at least one copy if disaster strikes.

It's important to have a documented plan, because having the plan in your head only works if you happen to be around, of course. More important, if you've gotten the CEO to approve your plan to restore the production department's network before the administration department's, you won't have to deal with politics and egos while you're trying to restring cables.

What should be included in a disaster plan? Everyone's disaster plan will be different, but there are a few key points to consider when planning yours:

▶ Decide where you will store your emergency plan. It needs to be in a location where you or others can get to it easily. Ideally, there should be multiple copies of the plan, perhaps assigned to different individuals. Just storing the emergency plan in your office will not be adequate if the building burns down, so you may consider storing a copy off-site, such as in a safety deposit box or even at your home.

▶ List people to call in case of an emergency and include their names, home phone numbers, pager numbers, and cellular phone numbers in your emergency plan. Include key network personnel, such as any network administrators for various branches of the eDirectory tree, personnel who perform the weekly and daily backups, and so on. You may want to include names of security personnel who should be notified in case of a potential security breach.

▶ Plan the order in which you will restore service to your company. Who needs to be back online first? Is there a critical department that should be restored before any other? Are there key individuals who need to be reconnected first?

▶ Once you've identified the key people who need to be reconnected, determine whether there is an order to the files or services they'll need. Which servers need to be restored first? Which applications must those users have immediately? Which files will they need to access?

▶ Document the location of your network records. Where do you keep your hardware inventory, purchase requisitions, backup logs, and so forth?

▶ Document the location of your network backup tapes or disks. Don't forget to document instructions for restoring files (or indicate the location of the backup system's documentation), in case the backup operator is unavailable. Record your backup rotation schedule so other people can figure out how to restore files efficiently.

▶ Include a drawing of the network layout, showing the exact location of cables, servers, workstations, and other computers. Highlight the critical components, so anyone else reading your plan will know at a glance where to find the priority servers.

In addition to writing a disaster plan, there are other ways you can plan ahead to avert — or at least diminish — disaster. Some of these preparatory measures include:

▶ Keeping a faithful schedule of backups, and practice restores so that files can be restored quickly.

▶ Implementing disk mirroring (or duplexing), so that a simple hard disk failure in the server won't cause users to lose working time and files because the server is down and they can't do their work. Alternatively, look at using a shared network storage device to make sure that data is always available.

▶ Using NetWare's TTS (Transaction Tracking System) if you use database applications. TTS ensures that any transactions that are in progress when the server dies or the power goes out are backed out completely, so the database isn't corrupted.

▶ Implementing a high-availability solution using NetWare Clustering Services (NCS), for those absolutely, gotta-have-it environments.

▶ Periodically reviewing your network's security, so you can make sure there are no potential security leaks. Investigate security measures such as NCP Packet Signature, access rights, and password security to make sure that your network is as secure as you need it to be.

Keeping Good Records of Your Network

Another line in your defense against disaster is to maintain up-to-date records about your network. When something goes wrong with your network, it is much easier to spot the problem if you have accurate documentation.

Good network documentation isn't just helpful in an emergency. Doing paperwork is always a distasteful task, but you'll be thankful you did it the next time you have to add new hardware to the network, resolve an interrupt conflict, justify your hardware budget to management, get a workstation repaired under warranty, call for technical support, or train a new assistant.

How you track your network information is up to you. You may want to keep a three-ring binder with printed information about the network, or you may prefer to keep the information online in databases or spreadsheets.

However you document your network, be sure you keep the information in more than one location. If a disaster occurs, you don't want to lose your only copy of the information that can help you restore the network quickly. Try to keep copies of your network information in separate buildings, if possible, so you won't lose everything if you can't access one building.

What types of network information should you record? Again, networks vary, so your documentation needs will vary, too.

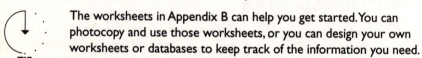

The worksheets in Appendix B can help you get started. You can photocopy and use those worksheets, or you can design your own worksheets or databases to keep track of the information you need.

TIP

Although you may need additional types of network documentation depending on your situation, most experts recommend that you maintain at least the following types of information:

▶ An inventory of hardware and software purchases. Record the product's version number, serial number, vendor, purchase date, length of warranty, and so on. This can help you when management asks for current capital assets or budget-planning information. It can also help you with insurance reports and replacements if a loss occurs.

▶ A record of configuration settings for servers, workstations, printers, and other hardware. This information can save you hours that you would otherwise spend locating and resolving interrupt conflicts.

▶ A history of hardware repairs. You may want to file all paperwork associated with repairs along with the worksheet that documents your original purchase of the item.

▶ A drawing of the network layout. If you store this with your disaster plan, you (and others) will be able to locate critical components quickly. On the drawing, show how all the workstations, servers, printers, and other equipment are connected. The drawing doesn't have to be to scale, but it should show each machine in its approximate location. Label each workstation with its make and model, its location, and its user. Show the cables that connect the hardware, and indicate what types of cable they are.

▶ Batch files and workstation boot files. Use a text editor or other program to print out these files and keep them with the worksheets that document the workstation. You may also want to store copies of the files on diskette. If you need to reinstall the workstation, you can re-create the user's environment quickly if you have archived these files.

▶ Backup information. It is very important to record your backup rotation schedule, the location of backup tapes or disks, the names of any backup operators, the labeling system you use on your backup tapes or disks, and any other information someone may need if you're not around to restore the system.

Troubleshooting Tips

Unfortunately, despite the best possible planning, something may still go wrong with your network. The majority of network problems are related to hardware issues — interrupt conflicts, faulty components, incompatible hardware, and so on. However, software creates its own set of problems, such as application incompatibility, OS bugs and incompatibility, and installation errors.

There are endless combinations of servers, workstations, cabling, networking hardware, operating systems, and applications. This makes it impossible to predict and document every possible problem. The best anyone can do is use a methodical system for isolating the problem, and then fixing it.

The following troubleshooting guidelines can help you isolate the problem and find solutions.

Narrow Down the List of Suspects

First, of course, you need to try to narrow your search to suspicious areas by answering the following types of questions:

- ► Were there any error messages? If so, look up their explanations in the NetWare 6 on-line documentation.

- ► How many machines did the problem affect? If multiple machines were affected, the problem is affecting the network and could be related to the network cabling or network software. If the problem is isolated to one workstation, then the problem is most likely contained within the workstation's own hardware or software configuration.

- ► Can you identify a particular cabling segment that has the problem? If so, it could be a problem with the cable connections, the cabling itself, a hub or concentrator, a network address conflict, or the like.

- ► Is the problem isolated to a particular branch of the eDirectory tree?

- ► Does the problem occur only when a user accesses a particular application, or does it occur only when the user executes applications in a particular order? This could indicate an application problem that has nothing to do with the network. It could be related to the workstation's memory, to a conflict between two applications or devices that both expect to use the same port or address, or the like.

- ► If the problem occurred when you installed new workstations or servers on the network, have you checked their network addresses, IP addresses (if used), and hardware settings for conflicts with other boards or with machines that already exist on the network? Also, double-check the installation documentation to make sure you didn't misspell a command or accidentally skip a step.

- ► Are the servers and workstations using the same frame type to communicate? If a server is using Ethernet 802.2 and a workstation is using Ethernet 802.3, for example, they won't see each other.

▶ Are the servers and workstations using compatible NCP Packet Signature levels to communicate?

See Chapter 6 for more information about NCP Packet Signatures and about file security.

X-REF

▶ If a user is having trouble working with files or applications, have you checked the security features? Does the user have appropriate rights in the necessary directories? Are the files already opened by someone else? Have the files or directories been assigned attributes that restrict the user from some actions?

▶ Is there a problem with a user's path commands? Look in the login scripts for search drive mappings that were mapped without using the INS keyword (which inserts the mapping into the path instead of overwriting existing paths).

▶ If a user can't see an NDPS printer, did you configure the printer so that its drivers will be installed automatically on users' workstations?

▶ If NDPS printers aren't available, make sure NDPSM.NLM is loaded on the server.

See Chapter 7 for more information about NDPS printing.

X-REF

▶ Do you have a volume that won't mount? If it is an NSS volume, you may need to run the REBUILD utility to fix it, although this is a last resort. If it is a traditional NetWare volume, you may need to run VREPAIR.NLM to fix it. (However, VREPAIR will usually run automatically if NetWare detects a problem with a traditional volume.)

REBUILD and VREPAIR are explained in Chapter 8.

X-REF

▶ Are all of the servers in the eDirectory tree running the same version of DS.NLM? If all servers are not running the same version, some conflicts could occur.

See Chapter 5 for more information about eDirectory.

X-REF

Check the Hardware

Hardware problems can be relatively common in networks. Network cables are notorious for developing problems, partly because of the abuse they get from being coiled up, walked on, bent around corners, and so on. A network analyzer, such as NetWare LANalyzer, can be a useful tool for diagnosing cable problems. As you diagnose hardware problems, keep the following tips in mind:

▶ Cables have an annoying tendency to work loose from their connectors, so check all connections between cables and boards first.

▶ Test suspicious cables by replacing them with cables you know are working, and then see if the problem persists.

▶ Make sure cables are terminated correctly and that they don't exceed length limits. In addition, ensure that the cables are not connected into endless loops (unless you're using a topology that permits loops).

▶ If the problem is with a computer or printer, try disconnecting the problematic machine from the network and running it in standalone mode. If the problem still shows up in standalone mode, it's probably not a problem with the network connection. You can then eliminate the network components and concentrate on the configuration of the machine itself.

▶ Isolate sections of the network segment until the problem disappears. Add each section back to the network until you have identified the problem cable, board, connector, terminator, or other component.

▶ If the problem occurred when you installed a new workstation or server, or added a board to an existing computer, check hardware settings for conflicts with other boards or with machines that already exist on the network.

Refer to the Documentation

Forget the jokes about only reading the manual as a last resort. The NetWare 6 on-line documentation contains a mountain of information about services, and explanations of error messages that may occur.

Be sure to check the manufacturer's documentation for any network hardware or applications you're using. Some applications have special instructions for installing on a network.

Look for Patches, Updates, or Workarounds

When Novell engineers find a problem with NetWare, they usually solve the problem with a patch (a piece of software that loads as an NLM on your server and repairs the problem), an updated version of a file, or a recommended workaround.

Novell distributes these patches, updates, and workarounds on its support Web site and in the "Support Connection Library," a set of update CD-ROMs available by subscription. Other sources of information are discussed later in this appendix.

 Novell patches, updates, and workarounds can be found on its support Web site: support.novell.com.

Try Each Solution by Itself

After you've isolated the problem, try implementing the solutions you've found one at a time. Start with the easiest, cheapest solution, and work up from there.

Most of us give in to the tendency to try several possible fixes simultaneously to save time. However, trying solutions simultaneously may save time in the short run, but it could cost you extra money for unnecessary repairs or replacements. For example, if you change the cable, the network board, and reinstall the NetWare client software all at the same time, you will have no way of knowing which one was the real solution. You may have just wasted money unnecessarily on a new network board.

In addition, you won't know for sure what fixed the problem, so you'll have to start from scratch again if the problem reappears on another machine or at another time.

Call for Technical Support

A wide variety of places exist where you can get help, advice, tips, and fixes for your NetWare problems or issues. The latter portion of this appendix lists several of the resources you should know about. These resources range from Internet user groups, to classes, to publications that deal with NetWare support issues. If you're looking for more formal technical support, try these ideas:

- You can often find the technical help you need online, through the Internet user groups and mailing lists that focus on NetWare or through Novell's Internet Web site.

You can access Novell's Internet Web site at www.novell.com.

► Try calling your reseller or consultant for help.

► Novell's technical support is available by calling 1-800-NETWARE — but it is not free. You will be charged a fee for each incident, so have your credit card handy. (An incident may involve more than one phone call in order to gather, analyze, and develop a solution, if necessary.)

► Before you call technical support, be sure you've tried your other resources first — especially the documentation. It's embarrassing and expensive to have technical support tell you that the answer to your question is on page 25 of the manual.

Document the Solution

When you find a solution, write it down and store it with your network documentation. This may prevent you or someone else from going through the same troubleshooting process to fix a similar problem later.

Sources of More Information

Whenever a product becomes as popular and as widely used as NetWare, an entire support industry develops around it. If you are looking for more information about NetWare, you're in luck. You can go to a variety of places for help.

NetWare information is as local as your bookstore or local user group, and as international as the Internet forums that focus on NetWare. It can be as informal as an article in a magazine, or as structured as a college course. This appendix describes the ways you can get more information or technical support for NetWare:

► General Novell product information

► Novell on the Internet

► Novell technical support

► Novell consulting services

► DeveloperNet, Novell's developer support

► Novell AppNotes

► Novell Education classes and CNE certification

► NetWare Users International (NUI)

► Network Professional Association (NPA)

General Novell Product Information

The main Novell information number, 1-800-NETWARE, is your inroad to all types of pre-sales information about Novell or its products.

By calling this number, you can obtain information about Novell products, the locations of your nearest resellers, pricing information, and phone numbers for other Novell programs.

For information on Novell's upgrade programs, call 1-800-304-7533.

To order the printed manuals for NetWare 6, you can use the order form that came in the Red Box, or call 800-336-3892 (in the United States) or 510-780-1250 (International).

Novell on the Internet

There is a tremendous amount of information about Novell and NetWare products, both official and unofficial, on the Internet. Officially, you can obtain the latest information about Novell from Novell's Web site. Novell also helps support several user forums that deal specifically with NetWare or generally with networking and computers.

 Novell's Web site is at www.novell.com and the Novell user forums can be found at support.novell.com/forums/.

These user forums are not managed directly by Novell employees, but offer users access to a wide variety of information and files dealing with NetWare and other Novell products, such as GroupWise. You can receive information such as technical advice from sysops (system operators) and other users, updated files and drivers, and the latest patches and workarounds for known problems in Novell products.

The Novell sites also provide a database of technical information from the Novell Technical Support division, as well as information about programs such as Novell Education classes and NetWare Users International (NUI). You can also find marketing and sales information about the various products that Novell produces.

Novell Technical Support

If you encounter a problem with your network that you can't solve on your own, there are several places you can go for help:

- ▶ Try calling your reseller or consultant.
- ▶ Go online, and see if anyone in the online forums or Usenet forums knows about the problem or can offer a solution. The knowledge of

the people in those forums is broad and deep. Don't hesitate to take advantage of it, and don't forget to return the favor if you know some tidbit that might help others.

▶ Call Novell technical support. You may want to reserve this as a last resort, simply because Novell technical support charges a fee for each incident (an incident may involve more than one phone call, if necessary). The fee depends on the product for which you're requesting support.

When you call technical support, make sure you have all the necessary information ready, such as the versions of NetWare and any utility or application you're using, the type of hardware you're using, network or node addresses and hardware settings for any workstations or other machines being affected, and so on. You'll also need a major credit card.

Novell's technical support department also offers online information, technical bulletins, downloadable patches and drivers, and so on. In addition, they offer a subscription to the "Support Connection Library," a collection of CD-ROMs that is updated regularly. The Novell Support Connection CD-ROMs contain technical information such as:

▶ Novell technical information documents

▶ Novell labs hardware and software test bulletins

▶ Online product documentation

▶ Novell AppNotes

▶ All available NetWare patches, updates, fixes, and drivers

 To get in touch with Novell's technical support, or to find out more about Novell's technical support options, visit support.novell.com. To open a technical support incident call, call 1-800-858-4000.

Novell Consulting Services

Novell offers comprehensive, fee-based consulting services for customers needing system planning and design services, custom development, or any other type of customized assistance for their network environment.

 For more information about Novell consulting services, see the Novell Web site at www.novell.com/consulting/.

DeveloperNet: Novell's Developer Support

Developers who create applications designed to run on NetWare may qualify to join Novell's program for professional developers, called DeveloperNet. Subscription fees for joining DeveloperNet vary, depending on the subscription level and options you choose. If you are a developer, some of the benefits you can receive by joining DeveloperNet are:

- ▶ Novell development CD-ROMs, which contain development tools you can use to create and test your applications in NetWare environments

- ▶ Special pre-releases and early access releases of upcoming Novell products

- ▶ Special technical support geared specifically toward developers

- ▶ Discounts on various events, products, and Novell Press books

For more information, visit Novell's developer Web site at developer.novell.com. You can also apply for membership or to order an SDK by calling 800-REDWORD.

Novell AppNotes

Novell's Research Department produces a monthly publication called Novell AppNotes. Each issue of AppNotes contains research reports and articles on a wide range of topics. The articles delve into topics such as network design, implementation, administration, and integration.

AppNotes are available on-line at developer.novell.com/ research. You can also purchase a hard copy subscription by calling 800-377-4136.

Novell Education Classes and CNE Certification

Are you looking for a way to learn about NetWare in a classroom setting, with hands-on labs and knowledgeable instructors? Novell offers a variety of classes on various aspects of running NetWare networks.

NetWare classes are taught at over 1,000 Novell Authorized Education Centers (NAECs) throughout the world. They are also taught at more than 100 NEAPs (Novell Education Authorized Partners), which are universities and colleges that teach these courses.

These classes often offer the best way to get some direct, hands-on training in just a few days. Some of the classes are also available in Computer-Based Training (CBT) form, in case you'd rather work through the material at your own pace, on your own workstation, than attend a class.

These classes also help prepare you if you want to become certified as a CNE, signifying that you are a Novell NetWare professional.

The Novell CNE program provides a way to ensure that networking professionals meet the necessary criteria to adequately install and manage NetWare networks. To achieve CNE status, you take a series of exams on different aspects of NetWare. In many cases, you may want to take the classes Novell offers through its NAECs to prepare for the exams, but the classes aren't required.

The classes and exams you take depend somewhat on the level of certification you want to achieve. Although certain core exams are required for all levels, you may also take additional "electives" to achieve the certification and specialization you want.

The following levels of certification are available:

- ▶ *CNA (Certified Novell Administrator)*: This certification is the most basic level. It prepares you to manage your own NetWare network. It does not delve into the more complex and technical aspects of NetWare. If you are relatively new to NetWare, the class offered for this certification is highly recommended.

- ▶ *CNE (Certified Novell Engineer)*: This certification level ensures that you can adequately install, manage, and support NetWare networks. While pursuing your CNE certification, you "declare a major," meaning that you choose to specialize in a particular Novell product family. For example, you may become a NetWare 6 CNE or a GroupWise CNE. There are several exams (and corresponding classes) involved in achieving this level of certification.

- ▶ *Master CNE*: This certification level allows you to go beyond CNE certification. To get a Master CNE, you declare a "graduate major." You will delve deeper into the integration- and solution-oriented aspects of running a network than does the CNE level.

- ▶ *CNI (Certified Novell Instructor)*: CNIs are authorized to teach NetWare classes through NAECs. The tests and classes specific to this level ensure that the individual taking them will be able to adequately teach others how to install and manage NetWare.

- ▶ *Certified Directory Engineer*: A Novell Certification Elite training and certification for IT experts using directory-enabled solutions.

- ▶ *Specialist Certificates*: These one-course, one-test certificates provide you with the solution-focused training you need to implement Novell products and solutions.

CNEs and Master CNEs qualify for membership in the Network Professional Association (NPA), which is explained later in this Appendix.

 For more information about Novell Education certifications, classes and programs, visit their Web site at www.novell.com/education/.

Numerous organizations also provide classes and seminars on NetWare products. Some of these unauthorized classes are quite good. Others are probably of lower quality, because Novell does not have any control over their course content or instructor qualifications. If you choose an unauthorized provider for your NetWare classes, try to talk to others who have taken a class from the provider before, so you'll have a better idea of how good the class is.

NetWare Users International

NetWare Users International (NUI) is a nonprofit association for networking professionals. With more than 250 affiliated groups worldwide, NUI provides a forum for networking professionals to meet face to face, to learn from each other, to trade recommendations, or just to share war stories.

By joining the NetWare user group in your area, you can take advantage of the following benefits:

▸ Local user groups that hold regularly scheduled meetings

▸ A discount on Novell Press books through *NetWare Connection* magazine and also at NUI meetings and conferences

▸ *NetWare Connection*, a monthly magazine that provides feature articles on new technologies, network management tips, product reviews, NUI news, and other helpful information

▸ Regional NUI conferences, held in different major cities throughout the year (with a discount for members)

The best news is, there's usually no fee or only a very low fee for joining an NUI user group.

 For more information or to join an NUI user group, visit the NUI Web site at www.nuinet.com, or call 800-228-4NUI. For more information about NetWare Connection magazine, or to order a free subscription, visit the NetWare Connection Web site at www.nwconnection.com.

Network Professional Association

If you've achieved, or are working toward, your CNE certification, you may want to join the Network Professional Association (NPA). The NPA is an organization for network computing professionals, including those who have certified as networking professionals in Novell, Microsoft, Banyan, and other manufacturers' products as well. Its goal is to keep its members current with the latest technology and information in the industry.

If you're a certified CNE, you can join the NPA as a full member. If you've started the certification process, but aren't finished yet, or if you are a CNA, you can join as an associate member (which gives you all the benefits of a full member except for the right to vote in the NPA's elections).

When you join the NPA, you can enjoy the following benefits:

- ▶ Local NPA chapters (more than 100 worldwide) that hold regularly scheduled meetings that include presentations and hands-on demonstrations of the latest technology

- ▶ A subscription to *Network Professional Journal*

- ▶ Access to NPA Labs that contain up-to-date technology and software for hands-on experience

- ▶ Job postings

- ▶ NPA's own professional certification programs

- ▶ Discounts or free admission to major trade shows and conferences, including NPA's own conferences

For more information or to join NPA, see their Web site at www.npa.org, or call 630-369-2488.

Index

Continued

Q

R

Continued

Continued